THE CORRESPONDENCE OF
KING GEORGE THE THIRD

FROM 1760 TO DECEMBER 1783

THE CORRESPONDENCE OF
KING GEORGE THE THIRD

From 1760 to December 1783

PRINTED FROM THE ORIGINAL PAPERS
IN THE ROYAL ARCHIVES AT WINDSOR CASTLE

ARRANGED AND EDITED

BY

SIR JOHN FORTESCUE

IN SIX VOLUMES

VOLUME VI

May 1782 to December 1783

Routledge
Taylor & Francis Group

LONDON AND NEW YORK

Published by
Routledge
2 Park Square, Milton Park, Abingdon, Oxfordshire OX14 4RN
711 Third Avenue, New York, NY 10017
by arrangement with Curtis Brown Ltd.

First issued in paperback 2014

Routledge is an imprint of the Taylor and Francis Group, an informa business

| First edition | 1927-28 |
| New impression | 1967 |

ISBN 13: 978-0-714-61108-2 (hbk)
ISBN 13: 978-0-415-76032-4 (pbk)

INTRODUCTION

THE earliest important papers in this volume relate to
Lord North's Civil Service accounts (3714, 3715, 3753),
the story of which does not end until later than the
period embraced in these pages, but may still be completed in some future volume. Current political business
is resumed when Lord Shelburne sends the King a copy
of the bill for excluding contractors from the House of
Commons (3718); and the King in his answer takes
occasion to lament the precipitancy of Fox as a negotiator
and his eagerness to yield American Independence un-
conditionally (3719). It should certainly seem to be
wise as a general principle, when a treaty is in question,
to be ready indeed to make concessions, but to withhold
the grant of them until concessions can be asked in
return, for a treaty is after all no more than the record
of a bargain, and the essence of a bargain is to take as
well as to give. Fox, however, seems to have been
equally hasty in all affairs, as may be seen from the
rather irritable tone of his letter to the King about the
prosecution of Sir Thomas Rumbold and East Indian
matters generally (3725), concerning which Shelburne
took a more temperate view (3739). Meanwhile, as
several documents remind us, the war was still going on,
and there were high hopes of a great engagement with
the Dutch at sea (3721, 3731-3734, 3740); but at the same
time a lucrative place fell vacant, and there was much

correspondence as to who should fill it (3736-3738), Shelburne and Rockingham being apparently at variance (3738, 3743, 3745-3747) over what the King rather contemptuously styled "the competition in the Spencer family" (3744).

Welcome news arrived in the second week of May of successful attacks in the Dutch settlements in the East Indies (3749), which it was hoped would make both France and Holland more tractable (3750, 3752) ; and almost immediately afterwards came the intelligence of Rodney's great victory at the battle of the Saints, which encouraged Ministers to give a new turn to the negotiations for peace (3757-3758). The King did not expect much from it (3760), and meanwhile there was copious discussion as to the reward that should be conferred on Rodney (3759, 3761, 3762, 3765). Keppel wished to institute a Naval Order of Merit, which was frowned upon by the King ; and it is somewhat curious that when the Order of Merit was instituted by King Edward VII. in 1902, the first naval officer to receive it was another Keppel, Lord Keppel's great-great-nephew. An English barony being proposed for Rodney, the King at once suspected that Lord Keppel wished to create a vacancy for the City of Westminster in the Commons ; to which Shelburne rejoined that the vacancy would probably be filled by Mr. Pitt, and that an opportunity might offer for gaining Mr. Pitt. "I own ", he wrote, "I should desire very much that Mr. Pitt should feel himself somewhat obliged to your Majesty, and I think it material to your service " (3765), and the King fully appreciated the point (3768).

The negotiations for peace now became more active. The documents concerned with them begin to fill the greater portion of the pages for a time, Fox having ascertained that America was prepared to make a separate peace with England, irrespective of France, Spain and Holland (3771). The King, deeply distrustful of Franklin, was sceptical of such a prospect, and openly answered that he would hear what Shelburne had to say before committing himself to any opinion (3772). Shelburne presently reassured the King by telling him that the independence of America would not be granted except as the price of peace—" a dreadful price " as the King mournfully commented (3777, 3778). Then came a little interlude. Influenza was raging at this time; Shelburne fell victim to it; and before he could recover, he was involved in wrangles with his colleagues over two matters of patronage—the appointments of Governor of Portsmouth and Governor-General of India (3782, 3783, 3789-3793). Poor Rockingham was a dying man, but a question of patronage could always infuse temporary life into him. In the midst of these comparative trifles the King pressed for the relief of Gibraltar, which the Admiralty, represented by Keppel, either could not or would not attend to (3797). Franklin, it seems, was dabbling with Gibraltar as part of a scheme for a general peace, which he thought should embody all separate peaces, if such were made ; a project which was steadily discouraged by the King (3808). At the same time, the reported departure of two French princes of the blood to the siege of Gibraltar pointed to the probability of a serious attack (3807)—the great attack, in fact, which was actually delivered on the 13th of September. Indeed the intentions of France at the end of June seemed to be by no means pacific (3819). The King stirred up Keppel to prepare to meet the combined fleets of France and Spain (3819), and Fox grasped eagerly at the hope of making a treaty with Russia (3821). On the 30th of June Rockingham was known to be dying, and Shelburne wrote to the King to warn him of the two issues which his death would certainly raise : (1) whether the independence of America should be a condition of peace or not; (2) what should be the position of Fox in a new Ministry (3824).

Rockingham died on the 1st of July, and the King complained that the knowledge of his desperate state had been concealed both from Shelburne and himself (3825). He then appointed Shelburne First Lord of the Treasury, with instructions to consult Grafton and Thurlow as to the formation of a new Government (3828). Fox alone showed any ill-humour over the new arrangement (3830), and resigned, carrying Lord John Cavendish, the Duke of Portland, and some minor officials with him. The course of Shelburne's proceedings may be followed in his letters, and those of others (3831-3834, 3837-3843, 3846, 3847), which close with two rather mysterious references to Fox (3853, 3854) ; and then we come upon the first minute of the new Cabinet, with Mr. Pitt as Chancellor of the Exchequer, and Thomas Townshend and Lord Grantham as Secretaries of State (3855). As Lord Temple had been appointed Lord-Lieutenant of Ireland, and had taken his brother William as Chief Secretary, the clique of Pitt and Grenville was strong in the new Government, though Thomas Grenville had been recalled from his mission in Paris to avert a breach in the precious family (3842).

The negotiations were now forwarded by summoning Alleyne Fitzherbert from Brussels to Paris in place of Thomas Grenville (3856), and giving Richard Oswald a definite commission to treat with the American delegates (3859). Arrangements for the withdrawal of the English garrison from America show that American independence, though it was to be conditional, was to be not the less real (3864) ; and meanwhile Shelburne did not forget Gibraltar (3862, 3863). The King then approached

North in order to gain his support in the Commons in the contest which was to decide whether " the sole direction of my kingdoms shall be trusted in the hands of Mr. Fox " (3872, *and see* 3847). North's reply was cautious (3873), with good reason, as the sequel showed. The negotiations with America now took a bad turn, for which both Shelburne and the King rightly or wrongly held Fox responsible ; and Shelburne sought counsel with Rodney's prisoner, Comte de Grasse, as to the intentions of France. He also took Keppel seriously to task for the Admiralty's neglect of Gibraltar (3877, 3878). Then for some time the papers are practically occupied wholly with the progress of the negotiations and the orders to the fleet. The letter in which the King denounces the wiles of Franklin is characteristic (3894). Shelburne hated both peace and American independence as heartily as the King, but was fain to bow to fate in accepting them (p. 128). The course of the proceedings in Paris and London, and the vicissitudes of the negotiations, can be traced almost from day to day ; and the reader will find examples (*e.g.* 3954, 3977) of the old constitutional practice that the Cabinet should not meet without the King's leave. The King from time to time could not refrain from a lament over the humiliation that was thrust upon him (3962, 3987), particularly as it seemed to him, even at the end of November, that France was not sincere in her desire for peace (3987). But Shelburne soon convinced him to the contrary (3988, 3989). He had already assured the King on " the certainty of an honourable and lasting peace, America out of the question," and he had testified that " any evils which may result to Great Britain . . . do not lie at your Majesty's door but at that of others ". After all, the grand attack on Gibraltar had been repulsed with disaster to the assailants ; and the English fleet, never before so powerful and efficient, defied the fleets of France, Spain and Holland.

A separate peace with the American Colonies was signed on the 30th of November, and, when Parliament met, young Mr. Pitt made a slip of speech which gave a verbal triumph to Fox (4014, 4015). The long discussion of the terms of the treaty continued, the King, curiously enough, constantly asserting his willingness, and even eagerness, to give up Gibraltar in return for one or more West Indian Islands (3987, 4020, 4021, 4034), reserving Minorca as a means of capturing the Mediterranean trade (4021). The idea was not so extravagant then as it seems now. The wealth of the Antilles was prodigious; and English possession of Gibraltar was always a burning grievance to Spain. The period of suspense was long, and was chequered by many anxious moments (4025, 4026). It would seem that the hasty negotiation opened by Thomas Grenville, under the direction of Fox, was a continual obstacle to Fitzherbert (4037). A secret expedition, under the command of Sir John Jervis, was ready to start in case the French and Spaniards should not come to terms (4042, 4043), for at the end of the year peace still seemed to be uncertain; but with the new year prospects improved (4055), though the Duke of Richmond and Keppel were both of them sore at being kept in the dark as to what was going forward (4055, 4056). At last, on the 17th of January, 1783, the preliminaries were signed with France and Spain (4078), to the immense relief and thankfulness of the King (4081).

Then as usual there was trouble over troops which claimed their discharge, the British soldier being unable to distinguish between such refinements as armistice, preliminary articles and definitive treaties (4089-4092, 4095-4101); and there was a mutiny which was not judiciously handled by General Conway (4101). This made a little diversion from the coming political troubles. Any Government which concludes a treaty after an unsuccessful war is sure of bitter attacks in Parliament; and Shelburne, in order to be ready for them, made overtures to Fox through Pitt, which were instantly rejected by Fox (4109, 4110). The King, by no means surprised, authorised Shelburne to seek support in other quarters. North at the beginning of November had promised to support the Government (3972); but, when Fox and his followers fell violently upon the treaties in February, North joined them, and Shelburne, defeated in the Commons by a majority of seventeen (4124), was fain to resign (4130). The King's comments on the proceeding are sufficiently forcible (4125, 4127, 4131); but the immediate result was that the Government instantly arrested all preparations for disarmament, evidently expecting that France and Spain might take advantage of Fox's accession to power (4128, 4129). Rightly or wrongly, they considered that the predominance of Fox was to the advantage of his country's enemies.

The ensuing pages are filled with the details of the long struggle whereby the King sought to escape from the domination of Fox and North. The reader may be referred to the careful summary which the King wrote at the time (4268), and may learn the facts from him at first hand. It is significant that at this time George III. prepared two draft messages of abdication (4259, 4260); and it seems that he was turned from this purpose by the advice of Thomas Pitt, who adjured him to give Fox and North rope enough to hang themselves (4261). On the 1st of April he gave way, writing a bitter account of the whole affair to Lord Temple (4272); and on the following day the reign of the "unprincipled coalition" began. Shelburne's last act was to send the King the accounts of Secret Service money (4287), a matter which must have reminded the King of Lord North's neglect of that particular department of business.

It now fell to Fox to look to the conclusion of the Definitive Treaties, which proved to be more troublesome than he probably expected. He did not receive any great encouragement from the King (4316, 4322, 4339), who was careful to point out that, if a country openly avows that it will fight rebellious subjects no more, her enemies will naturally presume upon her weakness (4422, 4488). The King did not spare North either for slovenly conduct of business (4426). But it was upon the Duke of Portland, who had made clumsy proposals for the discharge of the Prince of Wales's debts (4380), that the King opened all the vials of his wrath. His answer to the Duke is the strongest in language that I have encountered among the whole of his papers (4384) ; and, as the rest of the correspondence on the subject will show, he would not abate a word of it (4385, 4386, 4388, 4390-4393). Amid such amenities, the Coalition began its short reign. It accomplished the conclusion of peace, in which the King declined to rejoice, since " it compleats the downfall of the lustre of the Empire " (4470). " After Britain has so much lowered herself, can one be surprised that Courts treat her accordingly ? " (4468). He wrote thus bitterly because he knew that it was the faction headed by Fox in Parliament which had brought about the loss of America. Whether this faction did well or ill herein men will dispute to the end of time ; whether its motives were lofty or mean will likewise be a matter of controversy. But the fact that, whether for good or for evil, whether with justification or without, it had worked steadily with its country's enemies, cannot, I think, be denied.

We catch a piteous glimpse of the impotent helplessness of the Prince of Orange and the distracted state of

Holland (4487, 4496), with a hint that James Harris would proceed shortly to The Hague to set matters right (4497)—as in due time he did. And then the new session of Parliament opens, and presently we hear of the introduction of Fox's East India Bill into the Lords (4540), and of its rejection eight days later (4543). On the morrow the King requires Fox and North to return their seals (4546); and the reign of the unprincipled Coalition is over.

For the rest the King's conscientiousness in ecclesiastical matters appears in No. 3718. There is a reference to an addition to his art collection in No. 4320, and an account of a meteor seen at Windsor (which is pictured in an aquatint by one of the brothers Sandby) in No. 4320. There is an extremely interesting and instructive table of sinecure offices in No. 4016; and, if it be thought scandalous, as well it may be, let it be remembered that the governing class always provides for itself out of the public purse, that it is doing so at this moment, and that the cost under the new governing class is about a thousand times as great as under the old.

J. W. F.

No. 3704—*Lord Shelburne to the King.*

SIR—The Message passed the Cabinet without further alteration. No mention was made of Sir Hugh Palliser.

It has occurr'd to me since to submit to Your Majesty, as a safe and unexceptional step for Your Majesty to direct very explicitly Lord Rockingham and Lord John Cavendish, who are both to attend you, for the Messages to the respective Houses, that any Bill or Bills which shall be to be brought in for perfecting what Your Majesty has been pleas'd to do, shall be prepared by Your Majesty's Attorney and Solicitor General, and communicated by them to the three Law Lords now in Your Majesty's Cabinet, and distinctly approved by them before they are brought in.

I saw the Duke of Marlborough on Monday evening, and he went from me perfectly well disposed. Lord Rockingham is quite reconciled to Lord Weymouth's appointment by his sensible manner, but I find he has offered the Steward's Staff to Lord Carlisle, who is to give him his answer this day. I told Lord Rockingham my desire of its being offered to the Duke of Marlborough, especially if Lord Charles Spencer is not provided for to his satisfaction—and the whole is deferr'd to Your Majesty. I confide in Your Majesty's great goodness, that the Staff may not be disposed of till the Duke of Marlborough is somehow satisfied. My happiness in Your Majesty's service depends upon it, on account of old obligations I owe the Duke of Marlborough, for whom in all situations I have preserved infinite managements. In the meantime I shall call upon the Duke of Marlborough in my way to Court and tell him with simplicity what has passed since Monday.

I have the honour to be, with the highest respect, Your Majesty's most dutyfull subject and faithfull servant,

May 1st, 1782. 10 m. past 11 A.M.　　　　　　　　SHELBURNE.

Endorsed by the King.

B

No. 3705—*The King to Lord Shelburne.*

QUEEN'S HOUSE, *May 1st,* 1782
m. 50 *past* 11 A.M.

The idea of directing the Ms. of Rockingham and the Chancellor of the Exchequer that any Bill or Bills for perfecting the reductions now fixed in the Civil List Establishments shall be drawn up by the Attorney General and the Solicitor, and by them be communicated to the three Law Lords, is highly material.

The Ms. of Rockingham wrote to Me yesterday in favour of Ld Carlisle, but I took care not to toutch on the Steward's Staff in my answer, on purpose to keep that consideration open, till I knew exactly how matters stood between the Duke of Marlborough and Lord Shelburne ; so that it rests just as I could wish, and I certainly will not decide on that employment, till the Duke is thoroughly satisfied.

Draft, written on Lord Shelburne's letter of same date.

No. 3706—*Mr. Knox to the King.*

Mr. Knox most humbly intreats Your Majesty to pardon his presumption in making this last use of his key of the Box of the American Department to express his gratitude to Your Majesty for your great goodness to him, and humbly to assure Your Majesty that he shall ever hold his health and life which your goodness has restored and preserved, devoted to Your Majesty's pleasure, in whatever situation Your Majesty may be pleased to command his service. And as he has now been informed by Lord Shelburne that his attendance is no longer necessary at the Office, he proposes if Your Majesty does not disapprove it, to employ his leisure in digesting for Your Majesty's use, such Memorandums as he has made of Secret Causes, which produced or governed many of the important events which fell out while he was in office and are only known to himself, and which he will never communicate, but to Your Majesty.

SOHO SQUARE. *1st May,* 1782

No. 3707—*Lord Keppel to the King.*

Admiral Keppel has the honour to transmit to Your Majesty Captain Berkeley's letter of ye 20th April from Plymouth, giving an account of his having brought into Plymouth the Actionaire, a French Ship, prize to the Queen.

ADMIRALTY OFFICE. *May 1st,* 1782. 30 *minutes past four o'clock*

Endorsed by the King.

No. 3708—*The King to Lord Keppel.*

It is pleasing to find by the Account Lord Keppel has transmitted, that the Actionaire is safely arrived; the French but seldom arm en flute Capital Ships; I suppose therefore she will not be fit for all services, but may prove an useful addition to the Home Fleet.

QUEEN'S HOUSE. *May 1st,* 1782. *m.* 42 *past* 6 P.M.

Draft, written on a page of Lord Keppel's letter of same date.

No. 3709—*Lord Buckingham to the King.*

May ye 1st, 1782

SIR—It is with extreme reluctance that my own feelings are indulged in claiming one moment of Your Royal attention.

Nothing is more distant from my thoughts than the soliciting; at a juncture similar to the present, any immediate testimony of your favour, I am only solicitous to submit to the recollection of your leisure the Outlines of my publick situation.

It is now twenty six years since my first appointment to the Privy Council, of which I am one of the very oldest members. I was nearly three years Embassador in Russia, a Court upon the which the eyes of Europe were, at that time fixed, and I think it may be asserted that my conduct was not deemed anywhere to have disgraced my country, or her interests, in any instance to have been neglected. You must remember, Sir, the Negotiations of that period, and the unconditional tender of Naval assistance which I was authorised to make immediately from the Empress to Your Majesty.

Those who were the most competent to judge of the political transactions during my Mission did not think me totally undeserving of that approbation by which it was your gracious pleasure to distinguish me. I have since been honoured with the important Government of Ireland, where, during four years, I experienced as much anxiety as human nature could support. In difficultys such as, during that period, occurred, it would be presumptious, even to insinuate that my endeavors for your service might have been always judiciously exerted, yet Your Majesty's enemys (as my Foreign Correspondents assure me) gave me some little credit for disappointing their sanguine expectations in maintaining the tranquility of that Kingdom. Seven years is no small proportion of human life, such an absence cannot but have a most disagreeable operation upon any Man's connections and private affairs ; mine certainly have, in some instances, been inconveniently affected. It has not often happened to persons who have passed through similar situations to sink into retirement without any mark of distinction whatsoever, nor will it, perhaps be deemed presumptuous to suggest, that such pretensions are at least, equal with those of Men whose walk has been confined to offices of emolument rendered by far more desirable from conveying the honour of approaching Your Royal Person, divested also from every species of trouble or responsibility.

Any mark of your approbation will be received with the highest gratitude, though such would be the most valuable as could least be considered as lucrative objects. Permit me, Sir, further to mention that if at any time my support was withdrawn from Your Majesty's Ministers, a sense of obligation to Mr. Grenville and an esteem and veneration contracted from my earliest youth must plead my excuse. Nor did my Opposition, one or two instances excepted, extend beyond American Questions.

Should you have condescended to notice my conduct, You must have distinguished that I have never been dragged into any disrespectful Factious Flippaways, but through all the various, peculiar and delicate circumstances of the times, uniformly studyd to prove that attentive deference with which I have the honour to be, Sir, Your Majesty's most faithfull and most devoted subject and servant,   BUCKINGHAM.

No. 3710—*Mr. Fox to the King.*

The enclosed Papers were given to Mr. Fox by Mons. Simolin last night, merely as notes of the conversation. Your Majesty knows too well the uncertainty and inconstancy of the Court of Petersburgh, or otherwise things seem to have taken the very turn there that could be wished, and to be just ripe for receiving the proper impression from the accounts which must have since [been] received from the Hague and from hence.

ST. JAMES'S. *m.* 20 *past* 12. 2 *May,* 1782

Endorsed by the King.

No. 3711—*The King to Mr. Fox.*

ST. JAMES'S, *May 2nd,* 1782
m. 32 *past one* P.M.

My opinion of the papers Mr. Fox has sent to me entirely coincides with his, and the fluctuation of the Court of Russia alone prevents my feeling certain of the conduct of the Dutch meeting from thence with the reception it deserves.

Draft, written on Mr. Fox's letter of same date.

No. 3712—*Lord Shelburne to the King.*

Lord Shelburne has this moment received the dispatches from Ireland, which he has the honour to send to Your Majesty with the private letters which he received by the same conveyance.

4th May, 1782. 50 *m. past* 6 A.M.

Endorsed by the King.

No. 3713—*The King to Lord Shelburne.*

I cannot return the Dispatches arrived from Ireland without just expressing that they cannot be less comfortable. I neither admire the matter nor the reasoning they contain.

QUEEN'S HOUSE. *May 4th*, 1782. *m. 43 past* 7 P.M.

Draft, written on a page of Lord Shelburne's letter of same date.

No. 3714.

MEMORANDUM.

[Apparently in the handwriting of Mr. Robinson.]

May 1782

Memorandum. The additional £1,000 a Month to His Majesty's Privy Purse commenced for the month of November, 1777.

1778. January. His Majesty paid Lord North for the Months of November and December 1777	2,000	0	0
6th February. Received for January and Febry.	2,000	0	0
26th June. Received for 4 Months, April, March, May and June, ...	4,000	0	0
1779. 17th Sept. Received for 12 months from July 1778 to June 1779 inclusive . .	12,000	0	0
1780. 21st August. Received for 14 Months from July 1779 to August 1780 inclusive.	14,000	0	0
1781. 6th March. Received for 6 months from September 1780 to Febry 1781, inclusive	6,000	0	0
Total Received from His Majesty .	40,000	0	0
Received by Lord North otherwise as contributions towards the expenses of the several Elections	30,010	17	0
Total Received, .	£70,010	17	0
Disbursed as by the General Account, .	103,765	15	2
Deduct Receipts as on the other side .	70,010	17	0
Balance due to Lord North, . .	£33,754	18	2

For which expense Lord North on the 7th December 1780 borrowed of Messrs Drummond £30,000, and by His Majesty's orders gave to Messrs Drummond a Promissory Note for that sum . . . .

To make up which sum there rests with His Majesty from the month of March 1781 to the present month of March, inclusive, the sum of .   13,000   0   0

AND

There is yet to be paid by Lord Bute by agreement towards the expense of bringing his Son, Col. Jas. Stuart into Parliament, the sum of .   1,000   0   0

But, besides the above disbursements actually paid, as stated above, there are claims made for expenses for the Surry Election, beyond the sum which has been already advanced, and for the Liverpool, and the last Election and Petition for Colchester.

Endorsed, "Most Private State," *in the hand of the writer; and in the King's hand,* "Received from Ld North. May, 1782"

No. 3715—*The King to Lord North.*

Printed. Donne II. 428.

The shortest and clearest method that I can devise of closing the account of Secret Service Money with Lord North is to allow him to state the £3983. 8. 11 which he did not receive of the £20,000 I gave him leave to take for the discharge of his debts, which is ballanced by his paying an Article that never was stated to Me, and therefore for which I cannot stand indebted the £3250 to that worthless man, Mr Bates, which sum with the remaining money in Lord North's hands £712. 13. 4½ will give Lord North a clear claim to a ballance in his favour of £20. 15. 6½ which I therefore enclose.   G. R.

QUEEN'S HOUSE. *May 5, 1782*

Two copies, both in the King's hand, one endorsed by him.

No. 3716—*Lord Shelburne to the King.*

SIR—Before I received the Inclos'd [*wanting*] from Lord Rockingham, I had enquired after the present Lord Talbot, as Your Majesty will see by Lady Talbot's message to Mr. Ord, who has since seen Dr Talbot. His intention was to have brought it as soon as the late Lord was buried, which is to be tomorrow, the present Lord being in the Country, but that he could not with any propriety attend Your Majesty to-day with it. In the meantime the Staff is ready to be delivered to whomever Your Majesty will direct.

I have lost no time in communicating the dispatches from Ireland, and shall attend Your Majesty to-day in regard to them, and to the Letters prepared to be sent to the Towns and Cities, the drafts of which I have the honour to inclose for Your Majesty's consideration.

I have the honour to be, with the highest respect, Your Majesty's dutyfull subject, SHELBURNE.

5th May, 1782. 35 *m. past* 10

Endorsed by the King.

No. 3717—*Lord Shelburne to the King.*

[The enclosure is a printed copy of the Bill for restraining any person concerned in any contract, commission or agreement for the public service from being elected, or sitting or voting in the House of Commons ; with marginal notes in manuscript of amendments and of the divisions on the first section.]

SIR—I should not have thought it necessary to intrude the enclosed upon Your Majesty, if the Duke of Richmond and Lord Derby, the latter much more particularly, had not left the House under an idea that the essence of the Bill was lost by admitting the Amendment. The words were moved by Lord Ashburton upon the suggestion both of the Friends and Enemys of the Bill. I should have voted notwithstanding against it, if the genuine sense of the House had not been with it, and the Majority contained the most independent people, such as Lord

Spencer, Lord Coventry, Lord Ravensworth, and all the Lawyers. The Duke of Grafton spoke for it, without any communication with me. I forbore speaking from management for the Duke of Richmond, and on account of the triflingness of the Debate. I cannot conceive that so immaterial an event can produce the least consequence, if the turn of Debates in the House of Commons and other circumstances did not give too much room to suspect intended confusion.

The Cabinet is to meet to-morrow at eleven on the business of Ireland. Lord Rockingham continues so much indisposed that it's doubtfull whether he can attend.

I have the honour to be, with the highest respect, Your Majesty's dutyfull subject and faithfull servant, SHELBURNE.

Monday 6th May 11 o'clock P.M.

Endorsed by the King. Rd. May 7, 1782. m. 40 pt 6 A.M.

No. 3718—*The King to the Archbishop of Canterbury.*

MY GOOD LORD—The best measures if not duly attended to frequently serve as precedents to those of a very different tendency, to do good and at the same time obviate bad consequences is the cause of my giving you this trouble ; not to delay you unnecessarily I shall briefly state the business I wish to entrust to your care. I have learnt that Dr. Balguy whose diffidence of his health made him the last year decline being promoted to the See of Gloucester labours under the misfortune of a severe complaint on his breast, which at times disables him from going through the strict Residence required by the Statutes of the Chapter of Winchester, and that He has once at least been obliged to renew his Attendance : I wish therefore in the case of so valuable a Scholar as well as Man You would consult the Bishop of Winchester whether He has any objection to my granting Dr. Balguy a Dispensation from that strict Residence ; I am certain He will attend as much as he possibly can, but this indulgence will relieve his mind from the anxiety of being obliged to recommence his Residence if confined during that attendance by illness, and you must be sensible of the wonderful effect the mind has on the body, and that probably this indulgence will enable Him to go through his Duty without using it. His having declined a Bishoprick and his tallents are not common ; therefore I should hope the addition of No Dispensation being granted till you, the Primate of the Province have consulted the Bishop of the See will prevent this Indulgence from being a precedent in favour of non-Residence of the Clergy which is an evil I shall ever wish to be the foremost in preventing.

No. 3719—*The King to Lord Shelburne.*

WINDSOR, *May 7th*, 1782
m. 55 *past* 7 A.M.

I take very kindly Lord Shelburne's attention in communicating to me a Copy of the Contractors Bill, with the Amendment moved and carried by Lord Ashburton and the heat of the Duke of Richmond and Lord Derby in quitting the House of Lords upon it under an idea of its altering the essence of the Bill. I shall copy the Article as amended that I may see its tendency better than one not in the habit of amending Bills can at first sight ; but so many Independent Lords voting for the Amendment and all the Law Lords is a convincing proof to Me that the idea was rather capcious than founded. I cannot help commending the prudence of Lord Shelburne in forbearing speaking, for if the Duke of Richmond shall try to stir up any heat in the Ministry on this occasion, the conduct of Lord Shelburne will enable him to act with more dignity than if he had at the first hour stood forth.

I owne I begin to think that there is a plan of bringing things if possible into confusion ; the ill Success all their hasty negotiations have as yet met with ; the inutility of so openly avowing American Independency which is an article in all Mr. Fox's letters to the Ministers abroad and his adoption of all the wild ideas of Russia concerning the Neutral League give but too much reason to authorize such an idea.

Draft, endorsed by the King.

No. 3720—*Lord Keppel to the King.*

Lord Keppel has the honour to transmit to Your Majesty Vice Admiral Drake's letter of the 6th instant, with one from Captain McDougal of the Flying Fish, giving an account of the Dutch Squadron.

Lord Keppel has also the honour to transmit to Your Majesty a minute considered and taken at noon this day by Your Majesty's Servants, In consequence of the above Intelligence which is humbly offered to Your Majesty.

ADMIRALTY OFFICE, *May 7th,* 1782.
½ *past* 2 *o'clock* P.M.

No. 3721.

MINUTE OF CABINET.

[In Lord Keppel's handwriting.]

May 7th, 1782

Present :—Lord President, Lord Privy Seal, Duke of Richmond, Lord Shelburne, Mr. Fox, Lord John Cavendish, Lord Ashburton, General Conway, Lord Keppel.

It is humbly recommended to Your Majesty that Lord Viscount Howe should be ordered not to proceed to Brest as he was before directed, but that His Lordship should be ordered to repair with as much dispatch as possible with such ships of the line as he is able to collect at Spithead to the Downs, and to make the Dutch Squadron now supposed to lie at anchor off of the Texel the object of his service and exertion, as soon as his force is sufficiently collected, and His Lordship obtains Intelligence to direct his Motions. In addition to what is above recommended to Your Majesty, It is further recommended that Lord Viscount Howe should if possible send a ship of ninety or eighty guns, as a reinforcement to Rear Admiral Kempenfeldt where he is now employed and with fresh Orders from Lord Howe not to expect his immediately joining of him as he was to believe at the time of his sailing.

No. 3722—*The King to Lord Keppel.*

The opinion of the Cabinet Meeting this day that Lord Howe ought to be directed to repair to the Downs with as much dispatch as possible with such Ships of the Line as He can collect at Spithead, that he may use his best exertions against the Dutch seems a very proper measure. I trust Lord Keppel will issue the orders in consequence with the utmost celerity.

WINDSOR. *May 7th,* 1782. *m.* 4 *past* 6 P.M.

Draft, written on a page of Lord Keppel's letter of same date.

No. 3723—*Mr. Fox to the King.*

8*th May,* 1782

When the House met yesterday, Mr. William Pitt moved and Mr. Alderman Sawbridge seconded a Motion for a Committee to inquire into the state of the Representation of the Commons in Parliament, to report the same to the House, and what steps it might be proper for Parliament to take thereupon. Upon a division the question was lost by twenty, the numbers for it appearing to be one hundred and forty one, those against it one hundred and sixty one. The Principal Speakers were

For the Motion.	Against.
Mr. William Pitt.	Mr. Powys.
Mr. Alderman Sawbridge.	Mr. Thomas Pitt.
Sir George Savile.	Sir Horace Mann.
Sir Charles Turner.	Mr. Rosewarne.
Mr. Baker.	Lord Advocate.
Mr. Fox.	Mr. Rigby.
Col. Murray.	Mr. Rolle.
Mr. Sheridan.	Mr. Philip Yorke.
Mr. Ald. Townsend.	
Lord Surry.	
Mr. Dempster.	

GRAFTON STREET. *m.* 32 *past* 11 A.M. 8 *May,* 1782

No. 3724—*Lord Shelburne to the King.*

Lord Shelburne has the honour to acquaint Your Majesty that the Cabinet determined nothing yesterday relative to Ireland, the consideration of which was deferred to another Meeting.

8th May, 1782. 10 *m. past* 12.

Endorsed by the King.

No. 3725—*Mr. Fox to the King.*

The House went yesterday into the Committee upon the Bill for securing the property of Sir Thomas Rumbold and the other persons accused. A debate arose whether the *whole* of their property should be secured or only a given summ, and after a very long debate the House divided, and the numbers were, for the Bill as it stood, thirty six ; against it thirty three. The Principal speakers were,

For the Bill.	Against.
Lord Advocate.	Mr. Attorney General.
Mr. Powys.	Mr. Solicitor General.
Mr. Fox.	Mr. Rigby.
Mr. Mansfield.	Mr. James Lowther.
Mr. Jenkinson.	Mr. Rumbold.
Mr. McDonald.	Mr. Sawbridge.

When the Report comes on, on Monday next, Mr. Fox will be better able to inform Your Majesty what seems to be the real temper of the House, when in all probability it will be fuller. If a Judgement were to be formed from yesterday, it must be that there was much tenderness for the Persons accused, which if it be the real temper of the House at large, must make it impossible to carry on the prosecution with effect, in which case Mr. Fox thinks it his duty to submit to Your Majesty most humbly his opinion, that there are no hopes of Reform in India, or of treating Possessions there in any manner advantageous to this Country.

GRAFTON STREET. *m. 14 past twelve,* 10 *May,* 1782

Endorsed by the King.

No. 3726—*Lord Shelburne to the King.*

Lord Shelburne is honoured with Your Majesty's Commands relative to Doctor Balguy, and will take particular care to forward Doctor Balguy's Dispensation, and to write to him signifying Your Majesty's favour, in consequence of Your Majesty's Opinion of his Conduct and Character.

May 10*th,* 1782. ½ *past* 7 P.M.

Endorsed by the King.

No. 3727—*Lord Shelburne to the King.*

Lord Shelburne wishes the Dispatches from Ireland were more worthy Your Majesty's perusal. He will have the honour to write to Your Majesty as soon as he has seen the several persons appointed to be with him this morning.

11*th May,* 1782. 40 *m. past* 8 A.M.

Endorsed by the King.

No. 3728—*The King to Lord Shelburne.*

I lose no time in returning to Lord Shelburne the Dispatches arrived from Ireland ; I cannot say either the Matter or Manner edifies Me. He may choose to communicate them to some persons before they go in circulation, therefore I thought it best to send them back before I went out this morning.

QUEEN'S HOUSE. *May* 11*th,* 1782. *m.* 13 *past* 9 A.M.

Draft, written on a page of Lord Shelburne's letter of same date.

No. 3729—*Lord Shelburne to the King.*

Sir—The Lord Mayor, Aldermen Turner, Creichton and Townsend with the Town Clerk have been with General Conway and me, and I have the satisfaction to assure Your Majesty that business is in as proper a road as can be desired, so as to answer every good purpose without any Novelty. Their present plan is to incorporate their late Associations with the Regular Militia, which depends upon the Commission of Lieutenancy.

I have had several Hours' conversation with the Duke of Richmond first upon the subject of Lord Rockingham and his right to all Patronage, next upon his Plan of Parliamentary Reform, and his desire of some strong steps to be taken in regard to the Finances of the Kingdom. There was nothing which pressed in any part of his conversation, and which may not therefore be communicated to Your Majesty at leisure. He has laid me under very strict injunctions of Secresy as to the circumstance I hinted to Your Majesty,—but in truth it is of no sort of moment.

I have enquired very particularly of Col. Barré, Lord Advocate and others about Sir Thomas Rumbold's business. There is no reason which I can find for believing as yet anything improper is meant. His Defenders are Mr. Rigby, Sir James Lowther, and very unexpectedly the Solicitor General, who was his Council, but the Advocate has no doubt of a better attendance the next day it comes on.

Lord Ashburton promises me to be very attentive to the Attorney and Solicitor's conduct about the Civil List Bill.

I am going to Streatham where I hope to have a conversation to-morrow with the Chancellor, which I find very necessary. But Your Majesty may remain assur'd that neither Indolence nor Family nor any other avocation shall prevent that total Devotion of myself to Your Majesty's affairs, which they undoubtedly demand, and which Your Majesty has every right to expect from

Your Majesty's most Dutyfull subject and faithfull servant,

11*th May*, 1782 35 *m. past* 3 P.M.   SHELBURNE.

Endorsed by the King.

No. 3730—*Lord Shelburne to the King.*

Lord Shelburne hopes Your Majesty will forgive his troubling you from hence with the inclosed letter [*wanting*] from the Duke of Grafton, least so just an account of the meeting should not reach Your Majesty. The latter part of it refers to a Note Lord Shelburne had from His Grace in the morning, with an account of his being much out of order.

Lord Shelburne has proposed to Lord Rockingham to have the adjourned Meeting on Irish Affairs either Monday or Tuesday evening, presuming it agreeable to Your Majesty.

STREATHAM. *Saturday* 11*th May*, 1782. 11 P.M.

Endorsed by the King.

No. 3731—*General Conway to the King.*

LONDON, 12 *May* 1782

SIR—Imagining it might be agreeable to Your Majesty to have an early account of the inclosed intelligence [*wanting*] respecting the position of the Dutch Fleet, I have taken the liberty of sending it herewith. If in this I should have exceeded my duty, I beg Your M. to forgive it, and to honour me with your Commands how I should behave under similar circumstances for the future.

Gen. St. John who sends me this says he received it at ½ past 12 yesterday noon.

He had thrown two companies of the East Essex into Landguard, which make the Garrison there and close at hand 400 Men.

He was executing diligently the directions he had received of bringing on all the Corps in the Artillery Exercise and calling on the Inhabitants to do the same, but seems uncertain of his success, with the latter unless they are paid.

I am, Sir, with the greatest submission, Your Majesty's most dutiful Servant,   H. S. CONWAY.

No. 3732—*Lord Keppel to the King.*

Admiral Lord Keppel has the honour to transmit to Your Majesty Admiral Viscount Howe's letter of yesterday's date, off of the South Foreland; also Vice-Admiral Drake's letter of the same date from the Downs, A paper of Intelligence Lord Keppel likewise has the honour to send to Your Majesty the person that brought it, Admiral Lord Keppel examined himself, and has reason rather to credit it.

ADMIRALTY OFFICE. *May 12, 1782. 30 m. past 4 P.M.*

Endorsed by the King.

No. 3733—*The King to Lord Keppel.*

I am glad to find by the Dispatches I have received from Lord Keppel that Lord Howe arrived yesterday off the South Foreland; I should hope by the steps V. Ad. Drake has taken that a sufficient number of Pylots will have been got to prevent the Fleet being detained there, for every delay is detrimental to the design, as intelligence will undoubtedly soon reach Holland of the Force coming on that Coast.   G. R.

QUEEN'S HOUSE. *May 12th, 1782. m. 48 past 5 P.M.*

Draft, written on a page of Lord Keppel's letter of same date.

No. 3734—*The King to General Conway.*

Gen. Conway has acted very properly in transmitting to Me the account he has received from Major Gen. St. John of the proposition [*sic*] of the Dutch Fleet; it is a Military communication and could not therefore come so properly as from the Commander-in-Chief. I fear that Fleet will have sailed before Ad. Howe arrives on that coast.   G. R.

QUEEN'S HOUSE. *May 13th, 1782. m. 5 past 9 A.M.*

Draft, written on a page of General Conway's letter of 12 May.

No. 3735—*Lord Shelburne to the King.*

The House of Lords sat till half hour past eight upon the Second reading of the Cricklade Bill. The House was thin for a considerable time not having been summoned by the Treasury. The Debate turned on one side, considering the Bill as a Bill of Pains and Penaltys. On the other side, it was considered as a mere Bill of Regulation. Nothing Political passed except that the Duke of Richmond wished to pin Lord Shelburne to his professions of desiring a Parliamentary Reform, no particular detail of which, however, was entered into.

The Speakers were

Lord Mansfield, against the Bill.
Lord Portchester, who spoke only for the purpose of asserting his own innocence.

Duke of Richmond,	for
Lord Chancellor,	against.
Lord Ashburton,	for
Lord Loughborough,	against.
Lord Grantley,	for
Lord Shelburne,	for
Duke of Richmond,	to explain.
Lord Chancellor	to explain.

Contents, 47, Proxies, 5 ; Not contents, 22, Proxies, 3.

BERKELY SQUARE *Monday, May 13th,* 1782.

Endorsed by the King.

No. 3736—*Lord Rockingham to the King.*

Lord Rockingham humbly acquaints Your Majesty that the Earl of Scarborough, lately appointed one of the Vice Treasurers of Ireland, died last night. His Family Lord Rockingham fears, are left in very distressful circumstances, and that the natural source of bounty and affection towards them in Sir George Savile has in these times already brought difficulties upon him, and may prevent his being able to assist them to the extent of what may be necessary.

Lord Rockingham hopes to be able to pay his duty in attending Your Majesty on Wednesday, and will have obtained the best information he can, in order to lay the full state before Your Majesty's Royal mind.

Lord Rockingham humbly suggests to Your Majesty that the Office of one of the Vice-Treasurers of Ireland now vacant, would be highly acceptable to Lord Robert Spencer. There are also other and well deserving candidates but in the present moment, Lord Rockingham humbly requests that Your Majesty would be graciously pleased to suspend your Determination till after Wednesday.

GROSVENOR SQUARE. *Monday 12 o'clock, May ye 13th, 1782*

Endorsed by the King.

No. 3737—*The King to Lord Rockingham.*

I am sorry to find the Earl of Scarborough died last night. I shall certainly be open to any suggestion Lord Rockingham may be inclined to make in favour of his family, who I believe are left but scantily.

I shall certainly suspend any determination as to the Successor to Lord Scarborough till I have seen Lord Rockingham ; but I should think the removal of Ld Chas Spencer by the suppression of his employment and his family gives him a better pretension than his Younger Brother.   G. R.

WINDSOR. *May 13, 1782. m. 20 past 3 P.M.*

Draft, written on a page of Lord Rockingham's letter of same date.

No. 3738—*Lord Shelburne to the King.*

SIR—I received the inclosed letter last night from Lord Rockingham, and have been at His Lordship's House from 12 o'clock till this moment.

The Irish Business is further adjourned till to-morrow evening.

It appears that there are a number of applications in favour of Luke Ryan. It was arranged that if he were pardon'd, it would be unjust to condemn the other man with equal pretensions to mercy, and Lord Keppel insisted upon the hardship in such case of condemning the mutineers. Upon the whole it was agreed to submit it to Your Majesty, at the humble desire of the Cabinet that the whole might be respited for ten days, with a view of examining further into the several cases, understanding always that at least one of the Mutineers should in all events be executed for the example.

I defer troubling Your Majesty upon the temper Lord Rockingham discovers in his letter, till I have the honour of attending Your Majesty.

I have the honour to be, with the highest respect, Your Majesty's most Dutyfull subject and Faithfull servant,

SHELBURNE.

BERKLEY SQUARE. 13 *May*, 1782. ¾ *past* 3 P.M.

Endorsed by the King.

No. 3739—*Lord Keppel to the King.*

Lord Keppel has the honour to transmit to Your Majesty the different dispatches from Lord Howe and Vice-Admiral Drake received from them this morning, as well as a letter from Captain Bayley of the Cameleon at sea, dated the 10th instant, giving an account of the Dutch Squadron; other papers relative to the same force Lord Keppel has also the honour to convey to Your Majesty.

ADMIRALTY OFFICE, *May* 13th, 1782. 15 *m. past* 5 *o'clock.*

Endorsed by the King.

No. 3740—*The King to Lord Keppel.*

As Lord Howe was to sail this morning, I am not without hopes he will arrive in time to attack the Dutch Fleet; should he be able to give a good account of them it will greatly aleviate our situation for some time, and probably render that Republic rather more reasonable than has of late been experienced.

WINDSOR. *May 13th, 1782. m. 40 past 7 P.M.*

Draft, written on a page of Lord Keppell's letter of same date.

No. 3741—*The King to Lord Shelburne.*

The sooner some arrangement with Ireland can be formed the better, but if the same spirit which seems to direct the foreign Negociations is adopted in that business, this poor Island will be no great gainer.

I cannot say I admire the re-examining the opinion formed on mature deliberation for the execution of Men flying in the face of the Laws of their Country ; but as the Cabinet beg for a respite for ten days, I will consent to it.

I enclose the letter I have received from Lord Rockingham and my answer, which I trust I shall find returned when I come to town on Wednesday.

WINDSOR. *May 13th, 1782. m. 25 past 7 P.M.*

Draft, endorsed by the King.

No. 3742—*Lord Shelburne to the King.*

SIR—I have this moment been honoured with Your Majesty's commands inclosing Lord Rockingham's Note. His Lordship seems to referr to the Candidate whom Your Majesty more expressly names in your answer to succeed to the Vice-Treasureship of Ireland, and it is certain that I shall find myself most excessively embarrassed with the Duke of Marlborough in consequence of the conversation I had with His Grace, which I communicated to Lord Rockingham, in case that Office should be otherwise disposed of.

I have the honour to be, with the highest respect, Your Majesty's Most dutyfull subject and faithfull servant,

SHELBURNE.

BERKLEY SQUARE. *13th May, 1782. ½ past 11 P.M.*

Endorsed by the King.

No. 3743—*Lord Shelburne to the King.*

Sir—The Messenger who attended Mr. Grenville being arrived within this hour from Paris, I have the honour to send Your Majesty everything he brought me. I have likewise the honour to send Your Majesty a Letter I received this morning from Prince Ferdinand of Brunswick.

I will endeavour to have such a communication with Lord Rockingham upon the subject of the Vice-Treasurership, as may prevent the necessity of Your Majesty's further Interference, if it be possible. I have in the meantime, seen the Bishop of Bangor, and stated to him my apprehensions of a Family competion [*sic*], in consequence of what Mr. Fox stated to me some time since as his opinion and wish. The Bishop enters fully into all the disagreeable consequences of it, and I hope will be of use. I hope Your Majesty feels me truly sensible of your very gracious recollection of what passed between the Duke of Marlborough and me.

Of all the subjects depending, Ireland gives me most pain. Such is the difficulty of it, that I find myself depriv'd of the assistance in great measure, which I have in every other part of Your Majesty's affairs. It is the only subject through which I do not see some sort of way. However Your Majesty may depend upon its being never off my mind.

I have the honour to be, with the highest respect, Your Majesty's Most dutyfull subject and faithfull servant,

WHITEHALL, 14*th May*, 1782. 3 *o'clock* P.M.   SHELBURNE.

No. 3744—*The King to Lord Shelburne.*

Mr. Oswald's correspondence carries the mark of coming from a man of sense. As Dr. Franklin wishes he should remain at Paris, and as M. de Vergennes has intimated as much I should think it best not to let him, at least at present, come home.

By the letter Mr. Grenville has wrote certainly appearances are not favourable ; the Peace of Paris is refused to be the basis of a new one, and he insinuated that we ought to reduce our Possessions in India to Bengal.

Prince Ferdinand's letter is certainly very civil more could not have been expected.

I trust Lord Shelburne will be able to arrange the competition in the Spencer family.

Undoubtedly the affairs of Ireland are so embroyled that it is most difficult to suggest what can satisfactorily be done; I trust Lord Shelburne sees the magnitude of the question, and that to obviate future evils is as material as to remove those of the present hour.

WINDSOR. *May 14th, 1782. m.* 40 *past* 7 P.M.

Draft, written on a page of Lord Shelburne's letter of same date.

No. 3745—*Lord Shelburne to the King.*

SIR—Lord Rockingham was too ill yesterday to have the Council at his house, which was therefore deferred till this evening. He on the same account declin'd seeing me last night and I have receiv'd no answer to my desire of seeing him this morning, which I am however determined to do if possible. In the meantime, the Bishop of Bangor, whom I have seen three times, and is this moment left me, has not been able to bring the Spencer Family as yet to any good understanding. In this Situation, if I fail in all my endeavours, and Lord Rockingham presses Your Majesty further on the subject, of Lord Robert Spencer, I would submit to Your Majesty whether You would think it improper to mention to Lord Rockingham my claim in favour of Lord Charles Spencer, intimating as much as you think proper of Your Majesty's own Inclination, your dislike of competition among the great familys of your Kingdom, and particularly the Spencer Family, on account of Your Majesty's great Regard and Consideration of the Duke of Marlborough, and your desire that Lord Rockingham or Lord Shelburne should wait on the Duke of Marlborough to know his mind in regard to his own family. I mention'd it to the Duke of Richmond yesterday, who on my account professed himself dispos'd to give way, but I found it at the same time a party measure.

There has a matter just discover'd itself relative to the Paris correspondence which I will have the honour to state to Your

Majesty, the time not admitting of the possibility of doing it now.

While I write Lord Rockingham sends word that he is better and ready to see me. He proposes to attend Your Majesty.

I have the honour to inclose Your Majesty a letter I have received from the Irish Speaker.

I have the honour to be, Your Majesty's dutyfull subject,

15th May, 1782. 20 m. past 12   SHELBURNE.

Endorsed by the King.

No. 3746—*Lord Shelburne to the King.*

After a great deal of dispute about Commissioners to be appointed either by Your Majesty or by Parliament, the point was given up, and the Minute agreed to, which Lord Shelburne has the honour to send to Your Majesty.

Lord Rockingham persists in regard to Lord Robert Spencer, but agrees not to press Your Majesty upon it, till some proper communication can be had with the Duke of Marlborough and his Brother.

Lord Shelburne request Your Majesty's Commands, whether you would be pleased to be waited on to-morrow with the Inclosed Address [*wanting*] and whether it may be presented to Your Majesty at the Levee by the Field Officers of the Artillery Company and such other Officers as wish particularly to have the honour of attending the Presentation of it.

BERKLEY SQUARE. 16 *May*, 1782. ½ *past* 8 A.M.

Endorsed by the King.

Enclosure.   MINUTE OF CABINET.

[In Lord Shelburne's handwriting.]

15th *May*, 1782

Present :—Lord Chancellor, Lord President, Duke of Richmond, Marquis of Rockingam, Lord Kepple, Lord Ashburton, General Conway, Lord John Cavendish, Mr. Fox, Lord Shelburne.

It is humbly submitted to His Majesty as the opinion of the Lords present, that the following Resolutions should be proposed on Fryday next to both Houses.

That it is the opinion of this House that the Act of the 6 of George the 1st entitled an Act for the better securing the Dependancy of Ireland, Kingdom of Ireland [sic] upon the Crown of Great Britain, ought to be repeal'd.

That it is the opinion of this House that it is indispensible to the Interest and Happiness of both Kingdoms, that some solid and permanent connection should be established between them by mutual consent, and that an Humble Address shall be presented to His Majesty, that His Majesty will be graciously pleas'd to take such measures, as His Majesty in his Royal Wisdom shall think most conducive to this Important End.

No. 3747—*The King to Lord Shelburne.*

I am glad to find Lord Shelburne has fought off the idea of Commissioners who could only be the cause of further concessions, or of some *private* negotiation, by which the Public could not be a gainer. The Resolutions proposed seem to meet the situation of the business.

I feared Ld Rockingham would be obstinate as to Lord Robert Spencer, but Lord Shelburne has now put it into a train that will oblige the D. of Marlborough, and that is what I wish may be effected, by his knowing who are his friends and who are not.

The Address of the Artillery Company of the City is very proper ; the Field Officers of that Corps may bring it to-morrow to the Levee.

QUEEN'S HOUSE. *May 16th,* 1782. *m.* 2 *past* 9 A.M.

No. 3748—*Lord Shelburne to the King.*

BERKLEY SQUARE. 16th *May,* 1782

Captain Ball is just arrived with Dispatches from India, which I have the honour to send Your Majesty. I humbly beg leave to congratulate Your Majesty on their contents. He has left the Colours with me, that I may receive Your Commands concerning them.

Endorsed by the King.

No. 3749—*Lord Keppel to the King.*

Lord Keppel has the honour to transmit to Your Majesty Vice-Admiral Sir Edward Hugh's dispatches from the East Indies, of the 15th and 17th January, giving an account of the surrender of Negapatam upon the Coromandel Coast, to Your Majesty's Ships and the East India Company's Land forces, under the command of Sir Hector Munroe, and also of Your Majesty's Ships under His Command having taken Trincomolay from the Dutch, and its Fort by storm, on the Island of Ceylon.

May ye 16th, 1782. 35 *m. past four o'clock* P.M.

Endorsed by the King.

No. 3750—*The King to Lord Keppel.*

The news come this day from the East Indies I should hope will prove a very fortunate event, and if it does not make the Enemies of this Country more tractable, that it will at least make their attempts in that part of the Globe less successful.

QUEEN'S HOUSE. *May* 16th, 1782. *m.* 15 *past* 8 P.M.

Draft, written on a page of Lord Keppel's letter of same date.

No. 3751—*Lord Shelburne to the King.*

Lord Shelburne has been prevented attending Your Majesty by the Irish Business, which has taken up his whole time.

16 *May,* 1782. 5 *o'clock* P.M.

Endorsed by the King.

No. 3752—*The King to Lord Shelburne.*

The success of the Fleet and Troops under the command of Sir Charles [*sic*] Hughes and Sir Hector Munro by the taking of Negopatam is most fortunate, and seems to promise being very detrimental to any views France may have of making some attack in the East Indies, I should think the Colours had best remain at Lord Shelburne's Office.

The answers from the Lord Lieuts. of Counties and from some of the Magistrates of Towns, show that the plan proposed by Gen. Conway will not meet with approbation in this Country.

QUEEN'S HOUSE. *May* 16*th*, 1782. 3 *m. past* 9 P.M.

Draft, written on a page of Lord Shelburne's letter of same date.

No. 3753—*Lord North to the King.*

Lord North has been desired by Lord Brudenell to explain to His Majesty the hesitation of Messrs Drummond respecting the form of the receipt which he has given for the £7,000 sent to him by His Majesty. His Majesty will remember that the sum which Lord North was authorized to borrow of Messrs Drummond was £30,000, for which Lord North gave his own note of hand ; Mr. Drummond was afraid that if he signed a receipt in the form delivered by Lord Brudenell, He should be thought to acquit Lord North of the remainder of the Debt. Lord North, having no money, and not being able to give Mr. Drummond any security, is endeavouring to arrange his affairs in such a manner as to be able to apply the whole income of his office to the gradual extinction of the Debt, and was afraid that if he had stated the whole of the case to Mr. Drummond before the necessary arrangements were settled, he might have alarmed him with respect to the safety of the Debt. He therefore did not press him on that subject especially as the Note of Hand is signed by Lord North, and consequently His Majesty is liable to no legal demand in whatever form the receipts are given. If His Majesty, however, should think it right to require a receipt in another form, Lord North must explain the whole of the case immediately to Mr. Drummond, and trust in the generous and liberal spirit of that gentlemen that he will not distress him for the payment of the money, until the Note can be gradually discharged, in the manner above mentioned.

Thursday, May 16, 1782

Endorsed by the King.

No. 3754—*Lord North to the King.*

Lord North has the honour of informing His Majesty that Lord Fauconberg has desired him to signify to His Majesty his request that he may be indulged with a further time for the repayment of the £1,600 His Majesty was so good as to advance to him some time ago. He was obliged to borrow it to defray a part of the expense of raising the Yorkshire Regiment, and will not be able to repay it till he shall have received the Off-Reckonings which are due to him.

Thursday, May 16, 1782

No. 3755—*Lord Shelburne to the King.*

The House of Lords sat till forty minutes past eight on the Irish Resolutions. There was no opposition to any part of them except from Lord Loughborough, who objected to the mode of Repeal by a Resolution, which in great measure precludes the consideration, which a Bill of Repeal as well as every other Bill ought to have, in the different stages of its progress. He likewise objected to its being totally unqualified, and declared himself for retaining the Jurisdiction of the English Lords. He doubted as to the modification of Poynings's Bill, and was against the Repeal of the perpetual Mutiny Bill. He was answered by Lord Camden, Lord Townsend, Lord Ashburton, Duke of Chandos, Duke of Leinster, Duke of Richmond.

17th May, 1782

Endorsed by the King.

No. 3756—*Mr. Robert Day to [Lord Shelburne ?].*

17th May, 1782

MY LORD—I had the honour a few days ago to pay my respects at Your Lordship's door upon my arrival from Ireland. Had I not received some marks heretofore of personal condescension from Your Lordship, still I should have thought it my duty, having recently arrived from that Country, and knowing as I do the present sentiments of the people, to have taken an opportunity of stating frankly those sentiments to a Great Minister, the undoubted friend of both countries ; and as I only just now understand that the important subject Your Lordship did last Wednesday give the House notice of for this day is to be the Irish business, I trust Your Lordship will pardon my taking this, the only mode which now remains to me of submitting, however hastily and crudely, to Your Lordship what occurs to me.

The people of Ireland conceive they ask only for *Right*— Exclusive Legislature and Exclusive Judicature are their rights, and they will not consent to pay for them, or to negotiate upon them. They can not put in a train of Treaty what is already decided in both their Houses of Parliament, and what the Nation has pledged itself to stand by ; a question which they conceive to be already carried. The 16th April 1782 is styled in Ireland the Day of its redemption. We wait only to *thank* England for an immediate unsuspicious Repeal of the 6 Geo 1st., and not to negotiate.—such a proposition, I have not a doubt, would end in nothing but disappointment.

Your Lordship must be aware that the Powers Legislative and Judicative of this Kingdom over Ireland are become impracticable. No English Law or Judgment or Duress can be executed without the concurrence or consent of the Officers of the Irish Courts—they will never consent—they dare not consent, because they, in common with the rest of the Nation even to His Majesty's Attorney General, are covenanted to stop and resist the execution of such things. All then we ask of England (for we have of ourselves accomplished everything else) is that she will withdraw a barren claim ; a claim which *now* takes away our confidence, but cannot affect our Liberty.

The Claim then being unproductive to England, Ireland will not pay to get clear of it. But another very strong argument occurs against negotiation, that we have nothing to yield in negotiation. We can't negotiate away the freedom of our Trade or of our Constitution. As to Trade that is a fluctuating subject, and must be governed, not by perpetual regulation, but occasional laws. We can't give Revenue to England for our rights, for *we have it not*—the Irish Parliament have for eight or ten years past regularly made unsuccessful efforts towards equalizing the National revenues and expenses—every New Tax has fallen short infinitely of the Estimate, and there is no question that the Commerce of Ireland, in its present infant, puny state, is not a subject of further Taxation. As to a Land Tax, Your Lordship knows too well how obnoxious at all times such a proposition would be to that country, but certainly very justly obnoxious if demanded in retribution for withdrawing a claim which cannot be enforced.

In truth, the enormous expenses of England would derive but little aid from such an Irish subsidy as would stop the growth, inflame the passion, and totally banish that glow of affection with which Ireland impatiently awaits to embrace Great Britain for ever.

We can give nothing but affection—which is more valuable to England than any stinted reluctant revenue, wrung from a Country who asks for nothing but her right, and must be in the exercise of that right for some time before she can be in the possession of affluence. If we are unable to pay for the recovery of that right, it is because we have been so long deprived of it.

I have heard it asked with some triumph what resources Ireland hath in case England should put our right in a train of negotiation. But Your Lordship certainly has contemplated the subject with peculiar advantages, with equal knowledge of both countries, and therefore must easily see the error of such reasoners. We have only to retire within ourselves—preserving the most entire allegiance to the Crown, as annexed to England, and in perfect obedience to all the Laws of Ireland ; but we don't execute English Laws or English Judgments, we keep to our Covenants and Associations, consume our own Manufactures ; keep on terms of amity with England under the Law, but with that diffidence which an impotent claim, pointed however against our Liberty, must necessarily inspire. All this is consistent with the Law of the Land, though not with the Interests of England, nor with the cordiality of both Countries.

Your Lordship I trust will see through the freedom I have presumed to exercise in this address, a very honest object. My object is to put an end to, or rather, prevent that painful state of mind and alienated sentiment which a Negative, or even a Negotiation founded on the ultimate requisition of Ireland would inspire. As a friend of Ireland, I wish to eradicate for ever all jealousies, disputes and subjects of settlement with the British Nation. I wish above all things, next to the liberty of my own country, not to accustom the Irish mind to a diffident, suspicious habit with regard to Great Britain. I know that Ireland will not Negotiate upon Rights to which she is now committed, and I know she has nothing effectual to give except Affection. I do therefore, with infinite humility, but the most ardent conviction, submit to Your Lordship that the unqualified, unconditional Repeal of the Declaratory Act is the only wise and brilliant measure which can be adopted ; and I confess, entertaining as I do no less zeal for Your Lordship's personal interests than reverence for your great Public Virtues, I cannot help feeling the most anxious wish that the measure may proceed in the first instance from Your Lordship.

I have the honour to be, with infinite respect, my Lord, Your Lordship's most faithful and obedient servt.

No. 7. CLARGES STREET. 17 *May*, 1782. ROB. DAY.

No. 3757—*Mr. Fox to the King.*

Mr. Fox has the honour of transmitting to Your Majesty the Minute of the Cabinet Council assembled this morning at Lord Rockingham's. Mr. Grenville will no doubt make a proper use of the very important news received this day, upon which Mr. Fox takes this opportunity of congratulating Your Majesty, but in general Mr. Fox thinks it his duty to submit it to Your Majesty, that Your Majesty's Servants have proceeded upon this occasion rather upon the supposition that the present negotiation for Peace will fail, and that the measures which they humbly recommend to Your Majesty upon this occasion are directed more with a view to the use that may be made of them for the purpose of detaching from France her Allies, and of conciliating the Powers of Europe to this Country, than the object of success in the present negotiation with the Court of Versailles. If Mons. de Vergennes should reject Mr. Grenville's proposals, and should either decline to make any on his part, or make such as should be evidently inadmissible, Your Majesty's servants cannot help flattering themselves that such a conduct on the part of the Court of Versailles may produce the most salutary effects with regard both to Europe and America, and possibly to the exertions of Great Britain herself.

Mr. Fox takes this opportunity of informing Your Majesty that the Irish Business passed yesterday in the House of Commons unanimously.

St. James's. *m.* 1 *past* 10 P.M. 18 *May*, 1782.

Endorsed by the King.

Enclosure.

MINUTE OF CABINET.

[In Mr. Fox's handwriting.]

GROSVENOR SQUARE, 18 *May*, 1782

Present :—Lord Chancellor, Lord President, Duke of Richmond, Lord Rockingham, Lord Shelburne, Lord John Cavendish, Lord Keppel, Lord Ashburton, Gen. Conway, Mr. Fox.

It is humbly submitted to Your Majesty that Your Majesty will be pleased to direct Mr. Fox to order full powers to be given to Mr. Grenville to treat and conclude at Paris, and also to direct Mr. Fox to instruct Mr. Grenville to make propositions of Peace to the belligerent Powers upon the basis of Independence to the thirteen Colonies in N. America, and of the Treaty of Paris— and in case of such proposition not being accepted, to call upon Mons. de Vergennes to make some proposition on his part, which Mr Grenville will of course report to Mr. Fox.

Endorsed by the King.

No. 3758—*Lord Shelburne to the King.*

Lord Shelburne begs to lay every congratulation which a gratefull and faithfull servant is capable of, at Your Majesty's Feet on the glorious news arrived this day. Lord Kepple is anxious to know Your Majesty's Inclinations in regard to Admiral Sir George Rodney, that he may write accordingly some time to-morrow to him. He tells Lord Shelburne, that Your Majesty had deferred coming to any resolution on that

head, till Lord Shelburne attended Your Majesty, which mark
of Your Majesty's condesc[ens]ion makes an impression on his
mind which he has not words to express. He presumes that
Lord Kepple appriz'd Your Majesty of the contents of the private
Letters.

The Irish Drafts have been delayed by Mr. Ord's having
been taken Ill the night before last, of which Lord Shelburne
was not distinctly appriz'd till late last night, and by several
interruptions which Lord Shelburne has had in the course of the
Day.

BERKLEY SQUARE. 18 *May*, 1782. 7 *o'clock* P.M.

Endorsed by the King.

No. 3759—*The King to Lord Shelburne.*

QUEEN'S HOUSE. *May* 18*th*, 1782
m. 32 *past* 8 P.M.

I take very kindly the congratulations of Lord Shelburne on
the most compleat Victory that has occurred this War. It would
be a great ease to my mind if all those with whom I am obliged
to transact Public Business were as exact in reporting and
understanding what is said by Me, as he is. Lord Keppel said
this morning, He thought it absolutely necessary that some
ostensible reward should be bestowed on Sir George Rodney,
the more so as he did not wish this event should stop Admiral
Pigot's being sent to relieve him ; I told him I should be willing
to forward any recommendation he, in conjunction with you
and the rest of the Cabinet, might authorize him to propose to
me. When he came at three this day, with the two Officers, he
told me nothing had been at the Meeting decided on that head.
He has shown me no private letters.

I am very ready to say Sir Geo. Rodney deserves a reward,
and wish one may be proposed, but considering that his Victory
on the 12th owes its existence to Sir Samuel Hood having on
the 9th, with 18 ships of the Line obliged 34 French ships of the
Line to retire, I think his merit deserves also a public Mark of
Approbation, the more so as he has for the second time the
misfortune of being superseded in the Command of a Fleet with
which he has thrice proved victorious.

As to the dispatches to the Lord Lieutenant of Ireland, I have perused them with the greatest attention, and wish no addition except that He should be acquainted that He will see the justice of making an immediate and fair compensation to Sir John Irwin, for what I have never done during my Reign —the removing a General from a Government.

Draft, endorsed by the King.

No. 3760—*The King to Mr. Fox.*

It would not be doing justice to the penetration of those that composed the Meeting at Lord Rockingham's this day, to suppose they could seriously, after reading the Letter Mr. Grenville has written, expect that the Court of France has any intentions at present of making Peace upon such terms as this Country can accept : I certainly do not mean to object to the proposed plan, but I neither expect M. de Vergennes to speak out, nor do I imagine if He does, any Court in Europe is inclined to step forth to our assistance.   G. R.

Queen's House. *May 18th,* 1782. *m.* 10 *past* 11 P.M.

Draft, endorsed by the King.

No. 3761—*Lord Shelburne to the King.*

Sir—I called on Lord Kepple in my way out of town. He apprized me positively that he had not seen a single private letter from the West Indies. The fact is that there are several which accuse Sir George Rodney in the strongest terms for not pursuing the Enemy the day following the Action, and I have great reason to believe, it is the general opinion of the Fleet, that a great deal more might have been done. On the other hand, I have seen private letters of Sir George Rodney's, full of the most extraordinary Bombast, and condemning Sir Samuel Hood for his conduct before St. Christopher's. I trust Your Majesty will do me the Justice to believe that I have no pleasure in conveying Ill-natured particulars to Your Majesty, but I shall always think it my duty to lay Truth before You. Lord Kepple is anxious however that Your Majesty should conferr some immediate and considerable mark of Favour on Sir George Rodney. He repeated what I had the honour to mention to Your Majesty, his Inclination to propose to Your Majesty the creation of a Naval Order of Merit, an Idea which I combated a good deal, and endeavoured to convince him of its being at present an Ill-timed Measure. I spoke to him at the same time of the Indispensible necessity of taking some notice of Sir Samuel Hood, which he acknowledged after some discussion of his Merit and Conduct. I found upon the whole his mind went to the proposing a Peerage for Sir George Rodney, an Irish Peerage for Sir Samuel Hood, and that Admiral Drake and Commodore Affleck should be created Baronets. If Your Majesty agreed to a promotion of Admirals, his idea would be to give the Marines to Captains Leveson and Jervis, leaving the remaining one between Captains Allan Falkener and Fielding, with an Inclination to preferr Captain Fielding, which he seemed to think might be agreeable to Your Majesty, and in the meantime to accept Your Majesty's gracious Offer of a Red Ribband for Captain Jervis. I presume to mention this which pass'd as conversation without any reference whatever on my part to Your Majesty. I desir'd him to talk to Lord Rockingham about Sir George Rodney between this and Tuesday, when I am to see him again and when it will be easy for me to give the above propos'd arrangements any turn Your Majesty may choose, by giving them more or less encouragement. I am persuaded a Majority of the Cabinet would be for advising Your Majesty to conferr a Peerage on Sir George Rodney, to meet the Public Impressions of his Success. Lord Kepple likewise proposes that the thanks of both Houses should be given him, which he apprehends, if not done by some of Your Majesty's Servants, will be proposed from some other quarter.

I have the honour to be, with the highest respect, Your Majesty's most dutyfull subject and faithfull servant,

SHELBURNE.

STREATHAM. [*Sunday*] 19 *May*, 1782. ½ *past* 10 P.M.

Endorsed by the King.

No. 3762—*The King to Lord Shelburne.*

QUEEN'S HOUSE. *May 20th,* 1782
m. 22 *past* 9 A.M.

The decisive Action in the West Indies certainly has decided the safety of Jamaica for this season ; it has been not only the most decisive of this War, but the conflict of the largest Fleets ever engaged ; I think, therefore, however Sir Geo. Rodney may not have pursued his advantage so far as his next in command probably would, that He deserves great marks of approbation. I should have thought an Irish Viscount enough, but that would not have opened the City of Westminster which I take it for granted is Lord Keppel's reason for advising an English Barony. Should that still be proposed I do not intend to object to it, but must declare it must not open the door for other English Peerages. An Irish Barony for Sir Samuel Hood I highly approve of, as well as Patents of Baronets for Rear-Admiral Drake and Commodore Affleck. The promotion of Captains to the Rank of Rear-Admiral I shall approve of, provided the Rear-Admirals of the Red are made Vice-Admirals, which will include R. Admirals Digby and Ross. I shall consent to Captains Leveson and Jarvis succeeding to the Colonelcys of Marines provided Capt. Fielding has the remaining one ; He is both an excellent Officer and a Gentleman. Falkener ought certainly to give way to Him. Captain Jarvis shall certainly have the Vacant Red Ribband.

I am glad Lord Shelburne fought off a Naval Order. It was dropped to me on Saturday, but I remained silent on the subject seeing the intention.

When the Civil honours are finally determined, it will be right either for Ld Shelburne to write a Public letter to the Admiralty, conveying my intentions, with handsome compliments on the Persons concerned, or to write separate letters to the Gentlemen themselves.

Draft, endorsed by the King.

No. 3763—*Lord Keppel to the King.*

Lord Keppel has the honour to transmit to Your Majesty the dispatches received this morning from Lord Howe, off of the Texel, and also Rear Admiral Kempenfelt's letter by express from Torbay. Lord Keppel joins in opinion with Rear Admiral Kempenfelt that the three ships he chased on the 30th instant, was the Medway and two India Storeships under her convoy.

ADMIRALTY OFFICE. *May 20th*, 1782. 30 *m. past three o'clock* P.M.

Endorsed by the King.

No. 3764—*The King to Lord Keppel.*

The letters Lord Keppel has transmitted from Lord Howe and Rear Admiral Kempenfeldt show both are acting as from their reputation it is natural to expect.

WINDSOR. *May 20th*, 1782. *m. 55 past* 8 P.M.

Draft, written on a page of Lord Keppel's letter of same date.

No. 3765—*Lord Shelburne to the King.*

SIR—I shall see Lord Kepple between three and four o'clock tomorrow and will have the honour to apprize Your Majesty what his sentiments are about Sir George Rodney after his talking with Lord Rockingam and others. I do not conceive that he or his connections can desire an opening in Westminster, as Mr. Pitt will probably be the Member, who is certainly hostile to them, and is already felt so. There is another part of Your Majesty's administration, who might wish it on that account, but I hope Your Majesty believes, while Your Majesty honours me with your confidence, Your Majesty is undoubtedly the first person to whom I would expose any wish. In case of such an Event, I own I should desire very much that Mr. Pitt should feel himself somewhat oblig'd to Your Majesty, and I think it material to your Service. I see no objection to it, except in case of re-election, which I should hope might not be one with proper management. But I should hope I might give this last matter any turn Your Majesty wished in the course of to-morrow.

I have the honour to be, with the highest respect, Your Majesty's most dutyfull subject and faithfull servant,

SHELBURNE.

STREATHAM. *20th May*, 1782. 11 *o'clock* P.M.

Endorsed by the King.

No. 3766—*Mr. Fox to the King.*

Mr. Fox cannot but feel very happy on transmitting to Your Majesty Sir James Harris's dispatch received this evening Notwithstanding the levity of that Court with which Your Majesty is so well acquainted, Mr. Fox humbly submits to Your Majesty that it seems almost certain that the Empress will take some decisive step to bring the Republic to reason, especially as everything that has since passed both here and in Holland must, when known at Petersburgh, tend to confirm those favourable sentiments which appear in Sir James Harris's accounts.

Mr. Fox proposes, if it should meet with Your Majesty's approbation, to write to Lord Mountstuart tomorrow merely that his letters are received, as Mr. Fox humbly submits to Your Majesty that the answer to be sent to His Lordship may require some consideration.

ST. JAMES'S. *m.* 13 *past* 11 P.M. *20th May*, 1782.

No. 3767—*The King to Mr. Fox.*

WINDSOR. *May* 21, 1782
m. 2 *past* 7 A.M.

Undoubtedly the appearances in Russia are as favourable on the Dutch affairs as the most sanguine mind could expect, and the levity of the Court alone gives distrust as to the final issue. I have also some fear that Mr. Grenville's negociation at Paris will cause some disgust as the joint Mediation at Vienna is one of her favourite Projects.

The whole conduct of Sir James Harris has been most able on this occasion, and it is impossible for anyone to deny that He has done all that could be wished. I trust Mr. Fox will by this night's post acknowledge the receipt of his dispatches, and give him the commendation He so justly deserves.

Lord Mountstuart's letters certainly must be well considered before answered, and I should think time should be given to hear how the King of Sardinia's Minister states the Audience before an opinion is formed on the report on one side, and that of the person concerned.

Draft, written on a page of Mr. Fox's letter of 20 May, 1782.

No. 3768—*The King to Lord Shelburne.*

WINDSOR. *May 21st*, 1782
m. 13 *past* 8 A.M.

If Lord Shelburne can secure the election of Westminster in favour of Mr. Pitt, I shall think that a sufficient reason to prefer Sir George Rodney being an English Baron to an Irish Viscount : if He can at the same time prevent His becoming too much dipped in with measures by representing a popular place.

The draughts to Mr. Oswald and Dr. Franklin do honour to the Pen that has framed them, and do ample justice to my sentiments.

Draft, endorsed by the King.

No. 3769—*Mr. Fox to the King.*

Mr. Fox has the honour of transmitting to Your Majesty a copy of the letter which came by Lord Mountstuart's servant, directed to Monsieur de Cordon, and which Mr. Fox judged prudent to have opened.

Mr. Fox humbly begs Your Majesty's pardon for having again omitted to take a copy of the Minute of the Cabinet which he sent to Your Majesty, by which omission he is obliged to trouble Your Majesty to return the Minute in order that a copy may be taken of it for the use of Lord Shelburne, who is to send the substance of it to Sir Guy Carleton.

It will be quite in time if Your Majesty is so good as to give it to Mr. Fox to-morrow at St. James's.

A Dutch Mail is just come in, but no accounts are yet come to this Office.

St. James's. *m.* 48 *past* 3 P.M. 21 *May*, 1782.

Endorsed by the King.

No. 3770—*The King to Mr. Fox.*

Windsor. *May* 21st, 1782. *m.* 50 *past* 7 P.M.

By the Copy of Mr. de Hauteville's letter to M. de Cordon, the K. of Sardinia takes the language of Lord Mountstuart with more temper than I should have done if held to me by any foreign Minister; undoubtedly Mr. Fox will not toutch on this subject with the Sardinian Minister; therefore nothing will now on either side be mentioned; but I think it will, if it should end as I now expect, be very proper for Mr. Fox to point out to Lord Mountstuart that the taking so much on himself as to ask an Audience, and be so unguarded on the occasion, could not fail of meeting with my disapprobation.

I shall certainly bring the Minute of the Cabinet to St. James's tomorrow, that Mr. Fox may have a copy taken for the use of Lord Shelburne, after which I shall expect to have it returned to me.

Draft, written on a page of Mr. Fox's letter of same date.

No. 3771—*Mr. Fox to the King.*

As the Courier for Paris was just ready to set out when Mr. Oswald arrived with the inclosed Dispatch, Mr. Fox thought it would not be advisable to detain him any longer than was necessary for the writing of a letter to acknowledge the receit [*sic*] of the Dispatch and the arrival of Mr. Oswald.

Mr. Oswald's conversation confirms all that Mr. Grenville hints in his letter, and what induced him to come over at this moment was the desire of impressing Your Majesty's Servants with the favourable disposition of Dr. Franklin toards Peace with this country, even without the concurrence of France, much more without that of Spain and Holland.

Mr. Fox is satisfied that Your Majesty's penetration must see in a moment the incredible importance of this object, and the sanguine hopes which might reasonably be entertained with respect to the ensuing Campain [sic] in the West Indies after the important Victory which has been gained there, if we could come to such an understanding with America as to enable us to avail ourselves of Sir Guy Carleton's Army for the purposes of Military Operations in the Autumnal Season in the West India Islands.

Mr. Fox humbly entreats Your Majesty's pardon if he has gone too far in troubling Your Majesty with these ideas which have suggested themselves to his mind upon reading Mr. Grenville's letter, and hearing Mr. Oswald's conversation ; from both of which he forms more flattering hopes for the affairs of Your Majesty than he had hitherto allowed himself to conceive.

St. James's. *m. 3 past* 11 P.M. 21 *May,* 1782

Endorsed by the King.

No. 3772—*The King to Mr. Fox.*

I do not see anything in the Dispatch from Paris that should make the detaining the full Powers prepared for Mr. Grenville necessary. Till I have seen Lord Shelburne and heard from him all Mr. Oswald has related of Dr. Franklin, I cannot form any hope that He is ready to conclude a Peace without the concurrence of France.

Peace is the object of my heart if it can be obtained without forfeiting the Honour and Essential Rights of my Kingdom ; I do not think myself at liberty to hazard any opinion ; I must see my way clear before me.

Windsor. *May 22nd,* 1782. *m. 59 past* 6 A.M.

Draft, written on a page of Mr. Fox's letter of 21 *May.*

No. 3773—*Lord Shelburne to the King.*

SIR—I came to Town yesterday intending to see Lord Kepple, but not finding myself very well, I was afraid to trust myself to talk on business, particularly where Persons are concerned. I have however just now seen him, and found he had been conversing with Mr. Fox, who I suppose had shook him about Sir Samuel Hood. But after a good deal of conversation, we agreed upon the inclosed Memorandum, without committing Your Majesty's Name upon any one article, the whole to be submitted to Your Majesty's judgment and consideration for as long a time as you think proper. Lord Kepple wishes some consultation should be had with Lord Rockingam, whom he has not seen being in the Country, and Mr. Fox, upon the subject of them. There is less reason than ever for opening the Door to English Peerages at present, and infinite prejudice must result to Your Majesty's affairs, if you do it, till Your Government is perfectly settled. I do not conceive Sir George Rodney's Peerage can do it. Sir James Lowther however, having sent to desire to see me, it may possibly be with that view. I humbly submit it to Your Majesty as a Measure, which cannot be too cautiously nor too determinedly guarded against. This measure out of the question, the expectations of the Publick seems to go very strongly to the granting him this Honour. I suppose if Your Majesty commands me to acquaint his son of Your Majesty's intentions, it will answer every purpose, but Your Majesty will have time to consider what mode will best guard the door against other Pretensions for the present.

Admiral Pigott is gone, otherwise I own I think there is great inconsistency in rewarding and recalling.

I have been much surprised on coming to town this morning to find the letters inclosed from Mr. Oswald and Doctr. Franklin. I sent immediately for Mr Oswald, but he is not yet come.

I have the honour to be, with the highest respect, Your Majesty's dutyfull subject, SHELBURNE.

WHITEHALL. *22nd May*, 1782. *3 m. past* 12 P.M.

Endorsed by the King.

No. 3774.

MINUTE OF CABINET.

[In Lord Keppel's handwriting.]

May ye 23rd, 1782

Present :—Lord Chancellor, Lord Privy Seal, Lord Rockingham, Lord Shelburne, Mr. Fox, Lord John Cavendish, Lord Ashburton, Gen. Conway, Lord Keppel.

It is humbly recommended to Your Majesty, the Object of the Fleet's sailing from Spithead, under the Command of Lord Howe to the Coast of Holland, being at an end, by the Dutch Squadron getting into the Texel, that Lord Howe be directed to leave a respectable force under the Command of Rear Admiral Sir John Ross, and to proceed himself with the rest of the Ships under his Command to Spithead or Torbay, as His Lordship may judge best to effect the junction of the other ships under his Command now with Rear Admiral Kempenfelt.

Endorsed by Lord Keppel.

No. 3775—*Lord Shelburne to the King.*

Lord Shelburne has the honour to send Your Majesty a letter he has received from Lady Hood and to acquaint Your Majesty that the Archbishop of Canterbury has sent him a message by the Chancellor, that he conceived it would be decent and regular to have a Thanksgiving proclaimed for the Victory which Admiral Sir George Rodney [*sic*], and that he has one ready, which he would have proposed to Your Majesty, if the Gout had not prevented him.

BERKLEY SQUARE, 25 *May*, 1782. 20 *m. past* 9

Endorsed by the King.

No. 3776—*Lord Keppel to the King.*

Lord Keppel has the honour to transmit to Your Majesty Dispatches of the 20th of April from Sir George Rodney, and of the 22nd of April from Sir James Wallace, off Warrior giving an Account of an Action under the detached command of Sir Samuel Hood, and the Surrender of two more french ships of the line and a frigate, which Dispatches are brought home by Captain Courtenay of the Eurydice, who informs that one of the french ships was the St. Esprit of 80 guns ; the other had several masts on board for the ships at St. Domingue. The French ships of war surrendered to the Valiant and Monarch, After an Action of about half an hour.

Lord Keppel has also the honour to send to Your Majesty letters from Lord Shuldham in Hamoze, Rear Admiral Kempenfelt, and from Captain Pole, after his looking into Ferrol.

GREENWICH, *May ye 23rd*, 1782. ¾ *m. past twelve* P.M.

No. 3777—*Lord Shelburne to the King.*

SIR—I have lost no time to signifye Your Majesty's Commands to the Archbishop of Canterbury.

I humbly thank Your Majesty for mentioning the particulars of the news arrived from the West Indies, and humbly congratulate Your Majesty upon the same. I receiv'd a general account from the Admiralty of it, which I immediately forwarded to the Lord Mayor.

I have the Honour to send Your Majesty a Draft of my answer to Dr. Franklin, and have just finished a very long conversation with Mr. Oswald, at which I desired Lord Ashburton to be present, that in case of any misunderstanding, in consequence of the general terms of the Minute drawn up by Mr. Fox, I might be perfectly understood, and I have the satisfaction to apprize Your Majesty that Mr. Oswald goes away fully impressed of the propriety of making *Peace* either general or separate the Price of Independance, and that Your Majesty will not be bound by the propositions if Peace is not the consequence.

I have the honour to be, with the highest respect, Your Majesty's most dutyfull subject and faithfull servant,

SHELBURNE.

BERKLEY SQUARE. *25th May*, 1782. ½ *past* 5 P.M.

Endorsed by the King.

No. 3778—*The King to Lord Shelburne.*

QUEEN'S HOUSE. *May 25th*, 1782
m. 10 *past* 6 P.M.

The letter to Dr. Franklin seems very proper. I am glad Lord Ashburton was present at Lord Shelburne's interview this day with Mr. Oswald, as it is of the greatest importance that Gentleman should be fully apprized of what must be obtained at the dreadful price now offered to America, and that it is very material Lord Shelburne should have a witness to prove if necessary the exact extent of the proposition now sent.

Draft, endorsed by the King.

No. 3779—*Lord Chancellor Thurlow to the King.*

SIR—The Business of this day consisted entirely in voting Thanks to Sir George Rodney, and other Officers for the late action in the West Indies.

It was moved by Lord Keppel and agreed to by every Lord who spoke ; with more or less comments on His recal, and more or less advice as to the Honours which should be the reward of Their services.

Some thought an Earldom or Viscounty at least for Rodney, and an English Peerage for Hood.

The Speakers were :—Lord Keppel, Lord Sandwich, Duke of Manchester, Lord Loughborough, Duke of Richmond, Lord Stormont, The Chancellor, Lord Hawke, Lord Bathurst, Lord Ashburton.

Then a Motion was made to congratulate Your Majesty on the success of Your Majesty's Arms *in that particular instance* . . . to which were added some other words ; which seemed to have reference to the observations which were made on the recal, and to the advice about Honours. These, as tending to interfere with a matter in Your Majesty's pleasure, were left out.

Lord Shelburne has been seized with the prevailing disorder of a cough and fever, which so many people are disabled with ; and desired me to send Your Majesty an account of the proceedings. I am afraid it is not so perfect as He would have given. In truth I had almost forgot, that there was a division on the Amendment to the Address of five to thirty seven.

I am, Sir, Your Majesty's most dutiful subject and faithful servant,   THURLOW.

HOUSE OF LORDS. 27 *May* [1782].

Endorsed by the King.

No. 3780—*Lord Shelburne to the King.*

SIR—I have been in doubt whether Your Majesty might have recollected, when the Chapter of the Bath was order'd for to-morrow that it was the day of the Restoration. I have been for some Hours enquiring, to save Your Majesty the trouble of a Messenger. At the Chamberlain's Office and at St. James's they are positive Your Majesty will have a Levee ; Mr. Frazer is positive Your Majesty will not. As I have so much reliance on his punctuality, I take the liberty of troubling Your Majesty.

I have the honour to be with the Highest Respect, Sir, Your Majesty's dutyfull subject and faithfull servant,

BERKLEY SQUARE. 28 *May*, 1782. ¾ *past* 7 P.M.   SHELBURNE.

Endorsed by the King.

No. 3781—*The King to Lord Shelburne.*

WINDSOR. *May* 28*th*, 1782
2 *m. past* 10 P.M.

It is easy to explain the Servants at St. James's expecting a Levee to-morrow and Mr. Frazer being of a contrary opinion ; the 30th January being a Fast day, I ought if I appeared to go to Church and wear mourning, for which reason I always skip this day, but I appear as usual on the 29th May that being an Holyday, if it falls on a Court day. Lord Shelburne was quite right in writing to me for an explanation which Authority is the true one.

I hope Lord Shelburne is getting better of the influenza. The Chancellor mentioned his sending the account of the Debate arose from that indisposition.

Draft, written on a page of Lord Shelburne's letter of same date.

No. 3782—*Lord Shelburne to the King.*

29 *May,* 1782

SIR—I am truly sensible of Your Majesty's great condescension in mentioning my Health. I find myself so much worse this morning, in consequence of seeing people yesterday, that I am oblig'd to request Your Majesty's permission to attend to it, more than I could wish—but with a little quiet I know I shall be able to return to my Duty in a very short time.

I had a long conversation with the Duke of Richmond yesterday upon the Government of Portsmouth, upon which he will desire the honour of an audience of Your Majesty this day. Your Majesty knows that He is too close a Reasoner to omit the shadow of an Argument in his own Favour, without regard to any person. It is impossible therefore for me to apprize Your Majesty of what may occurr to him in addition to a great variety which he us'd to me, but for want of better, I imagine he will detain Your Majesty on the impropriety of my obtaining Your Majesty's promise in favour of Lord Pembroke, when I declared against Your Majesty's making any, and as to its being in the first formation of the Ministry, that I had not communicated it to Lord Rockingam. My answer to this is that I communicated it to General Conway, as soon as he had kissed hands, and that he agreed to it, and that if I omitted it to Lord Rockingam, it was not intentionally but owing to the difficulties which his Grace very well knew attended all communications between Lord Rockingam and me. Nor had Lord Rockingam been so punctilious to me as to give him any right to complain. The Duke of Richmond acknowledg'd this to be wrong, and I can plainly see is not inclined to be irrevocably out of humour. Old Regards and kind dispositions to me, upon which he dwelt, might make the conversation take a more good humour'd turn, but Your Majesty will naturally think, that the probability of obtaining his Object, when the Government of Plymouth drops, and securing it if he can in all possible events (for none seems to escape his Grace's foresight) have their full weight in his manner ; however I avoided any engagement as to myself, and said nothing to lead him to believe Your Majesty would commit yourself prior to the Vacancy.

Lord Kepple likewise desired to see me yesterday. He is rather sore with what passed in the House on Monday which I would have attended if I could have held up my head, and has renewed a former idea of proposing to Your Majesty the appointment of a Major General of Marines in favour of Admiral Barrington, to which I find Lord Rockingam has agreed. I find he is embarrass'd about Admiral Parker, who has been with him, the circumstances of whose case I am a total stranger to, except what has appeared to the Publick.

I was much shocked with seeing in Saturday night's Gazette the appointment of Mr. Flood to the Privy Council of Ireland, which was intended in the correspondence to have lain dormant. I find it was owing to the Deputy Gazette Writer taking these appointments from Mr Shadwell without the knowledge of any other person in the Office. Mr. Nepeane wrote on Monday to explain the matter to Mr. Fitzpatrick, thro' whom the appointment is to proceed, and I have taken very distinct measures to prevent such mistakes in future.

There are several Letters from Ireland upon the receipt of the Resolutions, but not a line from the Castle to the Office. I should scarce know how to communicate to Your Majesty the inclosed private letter, if Your great goodness had not already led Your Majesty to see that subject in so reasonable a view. It is of use however to be early appriz'd of the intention of confounding the Hereditary and Temporary Revenue. There can be no difficulty of checking such a project for the present, and it gives time for preparing against it's ever being brought forward with success. I have accidentally seen a private letter from Ireland, which mentions considerable Law changes having taken place there, and given satisfaction, but not particularizing them.

Lord Camden is just taken Ill, and desires me to make his humble excuses to Your Majesty for being obliged to put off a Council summoned at St. James's this day, and another at the Cockpit.

Captain Jervis will attend Your Majesty's Levee with Lord Kepple.

I have written to the Lord in Waiting to apprize him of Your Majesty's intention of conferring the honour of Knighthood on the Mayor of Lewis.

I am ashamed of troubling Your Majesty with so long a Letter, and shall be very unhappy till I can return to the most acceptable duty of my Office—that of attending Your Majesty's Person. In the meantime, I would wish Your Majesty's permission to propose a Meeting of Your Servants to Lord Rockingam upon East Indian Matters, when I may be to propose Lord Cornwallis, as I find the Resolutions against Mr. Hastings passed yesterday. I have mentioned Lord Cornwallis's name to none of the Cabinet except in very great confidence to Lord Ashburton.

I have the honour to be, with the highest respect, Your Majesty's most dutyfull subject,   SHELBURNE.

BERKLEY SQUARE. 29 *May*, 1782. 16 *m. past* 12 P.M.

Endorsed by the King.

No. 3783—*The King to Lord Shelburne.*

Lord Shelburne is perfectly right in keeping quiet a day or two which will probably reinstate him without much Physical assistance.

The Duke of Richmond will I suppose be very pressing but I shall certainly tell him that I do not chuse to bind myself by promises ; that they are ever inconvenient and often detrimental. Undoubtedly the recall of Rodney after so brilliant and unexampled a success is not popular. I am not therefore surprised that Ld Keppel feels the Debate on Monday could not be advantageous to Him. I have not heard a word of re-establishing a Major General of Marines ; the creating of fresh offices will also not increase his popularity though it may his dependents. The Gazette writers are certainly very negligent. I trust that in future more attention will be shown by them.

Mr. Perry's letter is couched with all the complacency and Art that seems very natural to him.

The Meeting on East India Regulations cannot be too soon, and the appointment of Lord Cornwallis known, which must meet with Universal applause.   G. R.

QUEEN'S HOUSE. *May 29th*, 1782. 20 *m. past one* P.M.

Draft, endorsed by the King.

No. 3784—*Lord Shelburne to the King.*

1 *June*, 1782

Col. Pringle, an Officer upon whom the Defence of New-foundland entirely depends who ought therefore never to have quitted it, and whose return Lord Shelburne has been con-tinually pressing since the beginning of April, now waits for some Commissions lying with Your Majesty for signing a week since. Lest any objections should have occasion'd it, Lord Shelburne has the honour to enclose General Conway's deter-mination concerning Col. Pringle's engagements, which he entered into with the Inhabitants upon the authority given him by the late Ministry and by the Admiral on the spot. It was referr'd by Your Majesty's orders to General Conway, Lord Shelburne exercising no judgment upon it, but was and is very anxious to get this Gentleman to his Post. Lord Shelburne has taken the liberty to desire Admiral Campbell on no account to give any Land Officer Leave of Absence from thence in future, without knowing Your Majesty's pleasure. He sets out this afternoon.

BERKLEY SQUARE. 1 *June*, 1782. 50 *m. past* 8

Endorsed by the King.

No. 3785—*Lord Shelburne to the King.*

1 *June.* 1782

SIR—I have the honour to send Your Majesty a Letter from the Duke of Portland. As I received it while Your Majesty was out of town, I took the liberty of carrying it to the Cabinet. After a good deal of undecided conversation on it, I propos'd, if Your Majesty approv'd, sending it to Lord Kepple officially, and that he should in the meantime prepare an answer explaining the necessary Detail for receiving the Men wanting to compleat Seamen and Marines, to which the first supply must naturally go : It will remain to be considered afterwards what encouragement to hold out in the nomination of Officers for raising the remainder.

I am very much afraid Your Majesty will be disappointed, as to the Effect of Lord Cornwallis's name towards settling East India Controversy. Lord Rockingam first dwelt upon the right of the Treasury to recommend—Lord Cornwallis was afterwards personally objected to, on account of Facility of Temper, etc. Mr. Francis was much recommended by Mr. Fox. It is left to be further considered, and I have thought it indispensible to send Mr. Ord to acquaint Mr. Gregory the Chairman of the India Company of my most earnest Wishes in regard to Lord Cornwallis, and of my having proposed him to the Cabinet. The rest of the time pass'd in altercation not worth troubling Your Majesty with the particulars ;—Lord Rockingam objected to my dispatches to Ireland precluding all possibility of Commissioners from thence. He then complained about Lord Rodney's Peerage being settl'd without him, there being, it seems, a good deal of difficulty in point of Form, about vacating his seat without his express acceptance, and I believe still more about finding a Member to represent Westminster upon the *mere* nomination of the Westminster Committee. Captain Jervis has unexpectedly declined it upon those Terms.

I have the honour to be, with the highest respect, Your Majesty's most dutyfull subject and faithfull servant,

BERKLEY SQUARE. 1*st June*, 1782. 7 *o'clock* P.M. SHELBURNE.

Endorsed by the King.

No. 3786—*The King to Lord Shelburne.*

Lord Shelburne will, I am persuaded, not doubt my candour when I state that the manner as yet pursued by the Duke of Portland does not seem to Me such as conveys any clear idea on any point He transmits from Ireland : I very much approve this new proposal being sent to Lord Keppel who I hope will suggest the mode of making it of some Utility.

I owne for the credit as well as good of the Nomination, I am hurt any rub should be thrown in the way of appointing Ld. Cornwallis Chief of the Supreme Council in India ; undoubtedly the Secretary of State for the Colonies and East Indies as well as Home Affairs is the proper person to settle this, and not the

Head of the Board of Treasury, who is not responsible for that business ; I am glad Lord Shelburne has lost no time in sending Mr. Ord to convey to Mr. Gregory the having proposed Lord Cornwallis as the properest person to the Cabinet this day.

I do not chuse to harbour ungrounded suspicion but it has the Appearance as if the many grievances broached this day were meant to offend Lord Shelburne, and perhaps have thrown him off his guard : but I know he is too well aware of their arts to be ever surprised by them.

QUEEN'S HOUSE. *June 1st, 1782. m. 48 past 7 P.M.*

Draft, written on a page of Lord Shelburne's letter of same date.

No. 3787—*Lord Keppel to the King.*

Lord Keppel has the honour to transmit to Your Majesty dispatches received this morning from Lord Howe from before the Texel, and from Sir Thomas Pye, from Portsmouth.

ADMIRALTY OFFICE. *June 3rd, 1782. Noon*

Endorsed by the King.

No. 3788—*Mr. Fox to the King.*

Mr. Cavalli has desired Mr. Fox to ask Your Majesty's permission that he may pay his respects to Your Majesty to-morrow, although he has taken his regular leave.

ST. JAMES'S. *m. 5 past 12. 3 June, 1782*

Endorsed by the King.

No. 3789—*Lord Shelburne to the King.*

The House of Lords sat till six o'clock. Nothing material passing except some questions from Lord Hillsborough regarding the Repeal of the Act 6 George 1st, and the Bill commonly called Mr. Yelverton's Bill now lying before the Council, which were answered by Lord Shelburne. There was afterwards a very short Debate on the Revenue Officer's Bill, to which Lord

Mansfield objected in terms of great moderation. He was answered by Lord Bishop of Peterborough and Lord Rockingham. The House divided Contents 34 ; Not contents 18.

HOUSE OF LORDS. *3rd June*, 1782. ¼ *past* 6 P.M.

Endorsed by the King.

No. 3790—*Lord Shelburne to the King.*

The House of Lords sat till half hour past eight hearing Council on Sir Thomas Rhumbold's [*sic*] first Bill, when the Chancellor mov'd its being committed for Tuesday.

Duke of Hamilton's claim was previously decided in his Favour. Lord Shelburne finding no other Minister attend it yesterday, did not think it proper for him.

The Duke of Richmond means, Lord Shelburne understands from him, to apply to Your Majesty, first through Lord Rockingam and afterwards himself, for a promise of Plymouth for Lord George Lennox, and that he shall not be remov'd from the command at Portsmouth after this campaign. Lord Shelburne endeavour'd to dissuade it, but he left him persisting in an intention of doing it to-morrow.

BERKLEY SQUARE. 6 *June*, 1782. 9 *o'clock* P.M.

Endorsed by the King.

No. 3791—*The King to Lord Shelburne.*

I am certain Lord Shelburne cannot think me wrong in declining both to the D. of Richmond and Ld. Rockingham to give any assurance in case Ld. Waldegrave should die that Ld. Pembroke shall obtain the Government of Plymouth, that Lord George Lennox may obtain Portsmouth ; no time but so extraordinary an event as the total rout of Ministry in March, could have made me promise that Government to Lord Pembroke, therefore it must not be drawn into precedent for future vacancies.

QUEEN'S HOUSE. *June* 6, 1782. *m.* 42 *past* 10 P.M.

Draft, written on a page of Lord Shelburne's letter of same date.

No. 3792—*Lord Shelburne to the King.*

Nothing pass'd in the House of Lords. The Irish Repeal was read a second time and committed for Tuesday next.

Lord Ashburton requests Your Majesty will understand the Inclos'd to be a mere precis of the Bill in question, very hastily taken.

BERKLEY SQUARE. *7th June.* 12 *o'clock at night*

Endorsed by the King.

No. 3793—*The King to Lord Shelburne.*

WINDSOR. *June 8th,* 1782
m. 20 *past* 7 A.M.

It seemed rather improbable that Ld. Hillsborough should chuse to oppose the Irish Repeal Bill, however he may not approve of the Measure ; I suppose it will not now meet with much delay in its future progress.

The Duke of Richmond and Lord Rockingham wanted to have a specific promise of Portsmouth by the removal of Lord Pembroke to Plymouth, whenever the latter should become vacant ; all I said was that I should consider Lord George Lennox on the vacancy of Plymouth, but kept clear of naming more ; but I am certain I am to be supposed to have consented to their plan, though I carefully avoided the word Portsmouth.

Lord Ashburton's attention to the business of the Civil List is very agreeable to Me ; I suppose when it is quite drawn, that the Chancellor as well as Him will read it over ; it is certainly slovenly constructed, but I believe it is best to let it go without much discussion which might render the sting worse.

The First Ld. of the Treasury without the Board was before this production never avowed. The powers of the Lord Chamberlain are much increased, and He placed above the Lord Steward when the Act of K. Henry VIII if of equal rank gives precedence to the latter. It would be more proper that the powers of the Green Cloth should remain in the Lord Steward, the Treasurer, Comptroller and Master of the Household ; this suggestion might perhaps without much difficulty be established, and prevent quarrels between future Stewards and Chamberlains.

Draft, written on a page of Lord Shelburne's letter of same date.

No. 3794—*Mr. Fox to the King.*

Your Majesty will observe by the intercepted letters from the King of Prussia that Mons. Luri did not at all exceed his authority in the conversation which Mr. Fox reported to Your Majesty, but what degree of advantage is to be hoped from His Prussian Majesty's good offices in Holland is what Mr. Fox cannot presume to judge.

It cannot escape Your Majesty that at the very time that Prince Kaunitz tells Sir Robert Keith that nothing is fixed in regard to Count Belgioioso's successor, he acquaints that Minister in his intercepted letter that Count v. Kagenek is actually named for the employment.

GRAFTON STREET. 12.50 P.M. *9th June,* 1782

Endorsement by the King.

No. 3795—*The King to Mr. Fox.*

The K. of Prussia is too political for me to pretend to guess at His intentions unless I at the same time can see what his interest should decide. Prince Kaunitz continues to hold a conduct towards Sir Robert Keith the very opposite to the character of rectitude that he has always been said to deserve.

WINDSOR. *June 9th,* 1782. *m.* 14 *past* 6 P.M.

Draft, written on a page of Mr. Fox's letter of same date.

No. 3796—*Lord Shelburne to the King.*

SIR—I have the honour to enclose to Your Majesty Dispatches, which arrived about an hour since from the Duke of Portland, together with a copy of a private Letter, which I immediately wrote in answer to His Grace's secret Letter, conceiving that Your Majesty would approve of no time being lost in giving all possible encouragement to His Grace's last proposal.

I have likewise the honour to enclose Your Majesty one of the Drafts to the Duke of Portland, a paragraph having been inserted by mistake in the copying the second page, and which I had expung'd, and which is not inserted in the Letter.

Your Majesty I presume knows that Lord Kepple is gone to Portsmouth and the Duke of Richmond to visit Portsmouth and Plymouth.

I have the honour to be, with the highest respect, Your Majesty's most dutyfull servant and faithful subject,

BERKLEY SQUARE, 9th June, 1782. 20 m. past 3 P.M.   SHELBURNE.

Endorsed by the King.

No. 3797—*The King to Lord Shelburne.*

WINDSOR, *June 9th*, 1782
m. 14 past 6 P.M.

The appearances in Ireland are certainly, by the D. of Portland's dispatch and private letter much better than there was reason to expect ; Ld. Shelburne was very right in not losing a minute in answering the private one. I found on Friday that the Duke of Richmond meant to go to Portsmouth and Plymouth, and Lord Keppel to Portsmouth. I hope Lord Shelburne will get the relief of Gibraltar discussed by the Admirals whilst at Portsmouth ; if the Navy do not clearly declare that it cannot be succoured, I am certain great blame will be due if that Fortress should fall.

Draft, endorsed by the King.

No. 3798—*Lord Shelburne to the King.*

SIR—The Chancellor cannot take upon him to answer for the Lord Advocate. I have since sent for Mr. Andrew Stuart who states the Advocate's determination to be, to accept of nothing without the Clerk of the Signet's being given for Life, and quotes the example of Sir Gilbert Elliott having the Clerk of the Signet for Life, together with the Treasurer of the Navy. I likewise take the liberty of enclosing to Your Majesty the Advocate's letter to Mr. Ord, which tends to that or more. Your Majesty knows his Importance, which has been confirmed to me by every person of every description. It must encrease as the Session of Parliament approaches. I would therefore submit to Your Majesty whether it would not be better to send for the Advocate and agree upon the best terms we can. I understand that he will not suffer much inconvenience by his Election being kept open during the summer, and that he may therefore accept without any regard to his Writ, in which case, if your Majesty approves the intention of contenting the Advocate, Mr. Barré need not hold both offices above eight or nine days, and may have the honour to kiss Your Majesty's hand to-morrow, as first intended.

I have the honour to be, with the highest respect, Your Majesty's dutyfull subject and faithfull servant,   SHELBURNE.

BERKLEY SQUARE. 10th June, 12 o'clock [1782].

Endorsed by the King.

No. 3799—*Lord Shelburne to the King.*

Lord Shelburne having had several applications on account of the Convicts sentenced for execution to-morrow thought it proper to send to the Recorder, that his opinion might be submitted to Your Majesty along with the Petitions.

The Recorder thinks that *Mary Balster's* case deserves attention, the declaration in her favour having preceded the conviction, which, so far as respects her, remains upon the sole testimony of the Prosecutrix.

WHITEHALL, 11th June, 25 m. past 2 P.M.

Endorsed by the King.

No. 3800—*The King to Lord Shelburne.*

There is no manner of utility in having the Recorder make the full Report of the Convicts at the end of each Old Bailey

Session, and the Law Lords attend for their opinion if subsequent applications are, without some new matter, attended to ; as the Recorder, by Lord Shelburne's account thinks the case of Mary Balster worthy of attention, as the declaration in her favour preceded the conviction, I therefore consent to her being respited, but the law must take its course on the other convicts already ordered for execution.

WINDSOR. *June 11th, 1782. m. 46 past 5 P.M.*

Draft, written on a page of Lord Shelburne's letter of same date.

No. 3801—*Lord Shelburne to the King.*

Lord Shelburne thinks it may be proper to apprize Your Majesty that there is an apprehension of some disagreeable consequences arising from the publication of Lord Rawdon's correspondence with the Duke of Richmond in the Morning Herald of yesterday. There is a doubt whether it should be taken up by the Chancellor in the House of Lords or mentioned to Your Majesty. Lord Shelburne dissuaded the latter until it was previously consider'd, as the moment it was mentioned in the Closet, Your Majesty would probably order both Lords under arrest. Lord Rockingam was to see General Conway upon it last night, who is the fittest person on many accounts to decide about it.

BERKLEY SQUARE, *12th of June. 35 mins. past 12 P.M.*

Endorsed by the King.

No. 3802—*Mr. Fox to the King.*

Mr. Fox takes the liberty of sending to Your Majesty a private letter from Sir James Harris to him, as it may tend to throw light upon the public letters accompanying it, and as the principal part of it relates to Public Matters.

ST. JAMES'S. 1 A.M. *15 June, 1782*

Endorsed by the King.

No. 3803—*The King to Mr. Fox.*

There is no doubt but the Empress of Russia seems to continue in better humour, but there are points in the communication of so serious a nature, and that must affect so much in futurity, that I am certain Mr. Fox must see the propriety of laying the dispatch of Sir James Harris before the Cabinet before He offers me any opinion on the subject, and consequently takes any step on it and on the communication Mons. de Simolin will make.

WINDSOR. *June 15th*, 1782. *m.* 55 *pt* 7 A.M.

Draft, written on a page of Mr. Fox's letter of same date.

No. 3804—*Lord Keppel to the King.*

Lord Keppel has the honour to transmit to Your Majesty The Addressed, sent from New York in the hands of Captain Montagu in the Pearl, from Rear Admiral Digby. Captain Montagu has directions to attend at St. James's at the Levee this day.

ADMIRALTY OFFICE. *June 14th*, 1782. *noon*

Endorsed by the King.

No. 3805—*Lord Keppel to the King.*

Lord Keppel has the honour to transmit to Your Majesty dispatches received this day from Lord Rodney at Jamaica, of the 5th of May, by the Ceres Sloop, Captain Dowsett.

Lord Keppel likewise sends to Your Majesty Lord Hood's private letter to Mr. Stephens, as it is very Informing of his situation off the west end of Hispaniola, and the Measures he was pursuing in consequence of Intelligence he had met with, as particularized in his letter.

The Ceres formerly taken by the French proves one of the two Frigates taken by Lord Hood in the Monu passage, after the action of the 12th of April.

ADMIRALTY. *June 16th*, 1782. 50 *mins. past one o'clock* P.M.

Endorsed by the King.

No. 3806—*The King to Lord Keppel.*

The Dispatches from Sir Geo. Rodney by the Ceres but too clearly prove the judiciousness of Lord Keppel's opinion that only two Ships of the Line and two Frigates had been taken subsequent to the glorious 12th of April.

The private letter of Rear Admiral Hood to Mr. Stephens is a fresh proof of the propriety of his conduct, and I trust it will be the cause of our hearing of some further success in that part of the globe. I am sorry Lord Rodney will have so many ships to send home, as by the intelligence he has sent there seems to be a large combined Fleet in the West Indies when the French disabled ships return to Europe.

WINDSOR. *June 16th, 1782. m.* 40 *pt.* 5 P.M.

Draft, written on a page of Lord Keppel's letter of same date.

No. 3807—*Lord Shelburne to the King.*

17 *June,* 1782

SIR—Major Ross, whom Lord Cornwallis sent to Paris to solicit his Exchange, return'd this morning with the letters, which I have the honour to send Your Majesty.

I find Lord Cornwallis very desirous that the particular Form of his Discharge may be communicated as little as possible, that his conduct may not be subjected to impertinent comment. I presume, as this is so very personal a matter, there will be no impropriety in letting the Form remain entirely with himself. He is naturally anxious to attend Your Majesty, and proposes having that honour on Wednesday, if Your Majesty does not disapprove of it.

I consider Mr Oswald's letter, marked Private, as merely so. He must have consider'd his conversation with Dr. Franklin about Gibraltar as well as the communication of it as entirely so. Your Majesty will easily believe he could have nothing from me, which tended to it, and I will take care to guard him against touching with Dr. Franklin on any part of the Peace which does not distinctly regard America.

The American Peace Bill will be read a third time this day

after which I will see the Chancellor, and I hope by Wednesday to be ready to lay before Your Majesty a Plan for a new Commission.

Major Ross brings no Intelligence except that Count D'Estaing is likely going, if not gone to take the command in the West Indies, That Monsr. de Fayette must be gone by this time to America, both the one and the other in Frigates or single ships ; that they were still uneasy about their West Indian Fleet, not having received satisfactory accounts from thence ; that they were displeased with Monsr. de Guichen's delay at Cadiz, who had been expected at Brest ; that the object of the Campaign was to be Gibraltar, and that both the Count D'Artois and Count of Bourbon were setting out for the Siege.

I have the honour to be, with the highest respect, Sir, Your Majesty's most dutyfull subject and faithfull servant,

WHITEHALL.   17 *June*, 1782.   ¼ *past* 3 P.M.   SHELBURNE.

Endorsed by the King.

No. 3808—*The King to Lord Shelburne.*

WINDSOR.   *June* 17*th*, 1782
15 *m. past* 7 P.M.

Till the receipt of Lord Shelburne's letter I was ignorant that Major Ross had been sent by Lord Cornwallis to Paris to solicit his Exchange ; there is no reason for wishing the mode of his Exchange to be known, and indeed it is a very equivocal one and resembles much the conduct I always expect to find from Dr. Franklin. I shall with pleasure receive Lord Cornwallis on Wednesday.

Lord Shelburne will certainly act very proper in directing Mr. Oswald not to hazard opinions on parts of the Peace to which he cannot have had any ministerial information, but being employed He may be supposed not to speak without foundation.

I desire Lord Shelburne will have a very clear opinion previous to my seeing him on Wednesday as to the new Commission that may be prepared in consequence of the American Peace Bill.

I cannot help adding that I greatly dislike the opinion now thrown out for the first time by Dr. Franklin that though the separate Peaces may be negotiated apart, that they must in the end be consolidated in one General one ; the idea can only add Difficulties.

Draft, written on a page of Lord Shelburne's letter of same date.

No. 3809—*Mr. Fox to the King.*

Mr. Fox trusts Your Majesty never could suppose him indiscreet enough to venture to give Your Majesty an opinion upon so important a point as the general recognition of the principles of the armed Neutrality without previously consulting the rest of Your Majesty's confidential servants. But Mr. Fox cannot avoid with all humility observing to Your Majesty that there appear at this moment (as well from the interceptions as from the dispatches from Your Majesty's Ministers at the respective Courts) dispositions in several of the Northern Powers highly favourable to this Country, and such as may possibly be improved to the great advantage of Your Majesty's affairs.

St. James's. 17 *June*, 1782. m. 32 *past* 10 P.M.

Endorsed by the King.

No. 3810—*Lord Keppel to the King.*

Lord Keppel has the honour to transmit to Your Majesty Dispatches from Rear Admiral Sir John Ross of ye 9th and 11th instant and of the 17th, received this morning, giving an account of his arrival in the Downs with the Squadron under his Command, the crews of the ships in a very sickly state.

Admiralty, *June* 18*th*, 1782. 5 *m. past one o'clock* P.M.

Endorsed by the King.

No. 3811—*The King to Lord Keppel.*

Windsor, *June* 18*th*, 1782
m. 55 *past* 3 P.M.

The account of Sir John Ross being from the Sickness of his Squadron obliged to quit his Station and come into the Downs is particularly distressing, as the Convoys from the Elbe and the

Weser, with this wind, must be on their passage : it is to be hoped that the Dutch Fleet is not exempt from this disorder.

Draft, written on a page of Lord Keppel's letter of same date.

No. 3812.

MINUTE OF CABINET.

[In Lord Shelburne's handwriting.]

CLARGES STREET
Thursday, June 20th, 1782

Present :—Lord Chancellor, Lord President, Duke of Grafton, Lord Keppel, Lord Ashburton, Lord John Cavendish, General Conway, Lord Shelburne.

It is humbly recommended, that His Majesty shall order Lord Shelburne to signifye his approbation of Admiral Digby's conduct, and that there can be no question as to the Legality or Policy of the Captures mentioned by him.

In regard to Canada, It being impossible to send any reinforcements from Great Britain or Ireland this year, It be recommended to Sir Guy Carleton to take the best measures possible in favour of that Province, consistent with a due attention to his former orders, which must likewise necessarily depend on the several circumstances of the War and the Negotiation.

That a new Commission be immediately ordered upon the plan of the present Act of Parliament, and varied from the other in such respect as the present Act of Parliament requires.

Endorsed by Lord Shelburne.

No. 3813—*Lord Shelburne to the King.*

SIR—Mr. Fitzpatrick arrived yesterday while I was attending Your Majesty, and not finding me at home then, different accidents prevented my seeing him till very late last night. He is come over to answer questions or give any information, which may be requir'd, and talks so sensibly and with so much good humour upon both men and things in Ireland that it's impossible to remember that he has been a principal actor in all the absurdities which have been passing there. He acknowledges that he brings no satisfactory particular whatever, except that there is an end of Evil for the present, by the Parliament's being adjourned to the 15th of next month, and understood then to meet for no other purpose except that of passing the Bills now with the Council here. Nothing further is to be expected, nor would any demand from hence have been complied with, nor any good whatever in his Judgment have been obtained by the appointment of Commissions, or any species of Negotiations but very much the contrary.

Captain Macbride expects about 6,000 men in two months, but very few seamen among them.

Mr. Fox acknowledges the impropriety of Inserting Mr. Grenville's name in the American Commission, which is now with the Attorney and Solicitor General. The Instructions are likewise preparing, and I hope to have both finish'd by Tuesday.

I have the honour to send Your Majesty the most interesting of Mr. Galloway's Papers.

I have the honour to be, with the highest respect, Your Majesty's most faithfull subject,   SHELBURNE.

LONDON. *22nd June*, 1782. 10 *o'clock*

Endorsed by the King.

No. 3814—*The King to Lord Shelburne.*

WINDSOR. *June 22nd*, 1782
m. 15 *past* 4 P.M.

The Account Lord Shelburne gives of Lt. Col. Fitzpatrick's language on Ireland shows what indeed but too often appears in life—that men may be able to discuss points with apparent judiciousness, and when called into Action, be totally void of good conduct.

I am glad the omission of Mr. Grenville in the new American Commission will create no more words ; certainly it is every way highly proper He should not be mixed in that business.

The papers received from Mr. Galloway are certainly very curious ; He seems to be an active man and it may not be unwise for Lord Shelburne to show him some civility ; time alone can decide whether it would be right it should proceed to anything further.

Draft, endorsed by the King.

No. 3815—*Mr. Fox to the King.*

Your Majesty will perceive from Prince Staremberg's letter that Mr. Fox will soon be applied to by Count Belgioioso upon the subject of the Duke of Gloucester. Mr. Fox takes it for granted that it will be his duty to say that he will take Your Majesty's orders upon the subject. Mr. Fox has humbly submitted this to Your Majesty because he is likely to see the Austrian Minister to-morrow.

St. James's. *m.* 50 P.M. 22 *June,* 1782

Endorsed by the King.

No. 3816—*The King to Mr. Fox.*

WINDSOR, *June 22nd,* 1782
m. 29 *pt.* 6 P.M.

If Count Belgioso should apply to Mr. Fox according to the directions He has received on the subject of the D. of Gloucester, the answer is very obvious that any civilities personally to the Duke cannot but be kindly felt by me ; but that as he does not here come to Court, I cannot suppose he will appear publickly at that of Brussels ; that Count Belgioso knows when I received my Brothers, I declared it made no alteration as to their Wives.

Draft, written on a page of Mr. Fox's letter of same date.

No. 3817—*Lord Keppel to the King.*

Lord Keppel has the honour to transmit to Your Majesty the latest Intelligence of the sailing of the combined Fleet the 4th instant from Cadiz ; and to submit to Your Majesty that it has been judged expedient to lose no time in apprizing Lord Howe that he may receive sudden orders for his sailing. It has also been judged expedient to direct Sir John Lockart Ross to despatch four ships of the line to join Lord Howe at Spithead, and to acquaint His Lordship of the same, with final orders for his sailing with the Squadron under his Command for the purpose of preventing the Enemy getting into Brest ; Lord Howe's

Squadron when joined by the four ships from the Downs will be twenty ships of the Line together, exclusive of the Vigilant cruising in the Bay within reach of being called for junction. Lord Howe's orders must necessarily depend upon circumstances and the force of the Enemy, If he should meet them. Lord Keppel humbly submits, the whole that he has the honour to have related to Your Majesty for Your Majesty's approbation.

ADMIRALTY, *June 24th*, 1782. *52 mins. past* 4 P.M.

Endorsed by the King.

No. 3818—*Mr. Fox to the King.*

24 *June,* 1782

Your Majesty cannot but observe from Mons. de Vergenne's answer how infinitely material it has been thought at the Court of Versailles to *appear* at least not averse to treaty, since they accept of the Treaty of Paris as a Basis, at the same time that they seem inclined to object to almost every article of it. Mr. Fox humbly submits to Your Majesty his conjecture that this conduct must be owing either to direct Insinuations that have been made from the Courts of Berlin and Petersburgh, or at least to the fear which they entertain of the blame of the continuance of the War lying at their door. Mr. Fox also humbly submits to Your Majesty that it appears from Mr. Grenville's dispatch that there is great inclination in Your Majesty's enemies to evade or at least to delay and protract this negotiation, from whence it might possibly be inferred that they are very apprehensive of the consequences which may attend a positive Refusal on their part, in regard to the effect of such Refusal both in Europe and America. Mr. Fox therefore humbly submits to Your Majesty that it will be the duty of Your Majesty's Ministers to take care that this country does not incur those disadvantages which the House of Bourbon seems so studious to avoid, but Mr. Fox will certainly not presume to take any step in this matter till he has had an opportunity of consulting upon it the rest of Your Majesty's confidential servants.

ST. JAMES'S. *m.* 50 *past* 11 P.M. 24 *June,* 1782

Endorsed by the King.

No. 3819—*The King to Mr. Fox.*

The dispatch from Mr. Grenville and its enclosure as well as the intercepted letter from Paris transmitted by Mr. Todd seem to confirm the opinion of Mr. Fox that the Court of France does not mean Peace, but wish the failure should not appear to lay at Her door.

WINDSOR. *June 25th, 1782. m. 5 pt 9 A.M.*

Draft, written on a page of Mr. Fox's letter of 24 June.

No. 3820—*The King to Lord Keppel.*

I do not doubt of Ld. Keppel's giving very proper directions to Lord Howe concerning the Combined Fleets of France and Spain, and that He will see the propriety of getting the Fleet for the North Sea out as soon as possible for the Defence of our Northern Trade as well as of the Eastern Coast.

WINDSOR. *June 25th, 1782. m. 10 pt 9 A.M.*

Draft, written on a page of Lord Keppel's letter of 24 June.

No. 3821.

MINUTE OF CABINET.

[In Mr. Fox's handwriting.]

CLARGES STREET. *26 June,* 1782

Present : — Lord Chancellor, Lord President, Lord Privy Seal, Duke of Richmond, Lord Shelburne, Lord John Cavendish, Lord Keppel, Lord Ashburton, General Conway, Mr. Fox.

It is humbly recommended to His Majesty to direct Mr. Fox to acquaint Mons. Simolin that His Majesty is desirous of entering fully into the ideas of the Empress and to form the closest connections with the Court of Petersburgh and that His Majesty is willing to make the principles of Her Imperial Majesty's declaration of the 28 February 1780 the Basis of a Treaty between the two Countries.

It is further humbly recommended to His Majesty to direct

Mr. Fox to acquaint Mons. Simolin with the substance of the Instructions to Mr. Grenville, as the best method of letting the Court of Petersburgh know that Ultimatum which she asks.

Endorsed by Mr. Fox.

No. 3822—*Mr. Fox to the King.*

It appears to Mr. Fox so necessary to inform Sir James Harris of what has passed between Your Majesty's Ministers and the Court of Berlin, and at the same time so improper to send the papers that contain these transactions either by the Post or by a Russian Messenger, that Mr. Fox humbly submits to Your Majesty his opinion that it will be advisable to send an English Messenger shortly, as mentioned in the draught to Sir James Harris.

ST. JAMES'S. *m.* 17 *past one* P.M. 29 *June*, 1782

Endorsed by the King.

No. 3823—*The King to Mr. Fox.*

It would be certainly highly incautious to send Sir Jas Harris either by the Post or by a Russian Courier the papers that have as yet passed between this Court and that of Berlin ; and indeed as yet no foundation of just expectation can be placed whether they will produce anything beyond civil expressions ; whenever anything more solid appears, it will certainly be right to transmit the whole to Sir James Harris, and probably to direct him to inform the Empress of Russia of it.

WINDSOR. *June 30th*, 1782. *m.* 19 *past* 9 A.M.

Draft, written on a page of Mr. Fox's letter of 29 June.

No. 3824—*Lord Shelburne to the King.*

30 *June*, 1782

SIR—I received the Inclosed account of Lord Rockingam in my way to a Cabinet summoned for this day by Mr. Fox on Mr.

Grenville's letter. There came more favourable accounts from the Family at the same time, and Mr. Fox talked of the case as by no means desperate, but I have seen Morn since, and there can be no doubt that his account is the true one. The Cabinet sat very late, but came to no final Resolution, and though I was enjoined Secrecy as to part of what has passed, It is my duty to apprize Your Majesty that there are two points which require to be taken into Your Majesty's speedy consideration. The first regards the propriety of declaring the Colonies Independent without any Peace. The second respects the weight which Your Majesty would think it proper to give Mr. Fox in case of any new arrangement. I have since Fryday seen the most material Persons. I have had I think a satisfactory conversation with Mr. Pitt, and a long and confidential one with the Speaker, among other things upon the subject of Mr. Jenkinson, whose assistance I wish for sooner or later, in my Government. But I find it the opinion of *all* that no Price is too great to obtain the continuance of that description of Men, if it be but for the present, who I very plainly see are too open to be operated upon by Mr. Fox's Habits, Assiduity and Address. I mention the opinion of others rather than my own, least my Temper which I suffer to govern me too often in my own Interests should mislead me in those of Your Majesty, Particularly in this Instance.

The American Commission, Instructions and Draft to Mr. Oswald have been all ready to be laid before Your Majesty since Fryday, but I have withheld them seeing the other correspondence at a stand.

I presume Your Majesty having approved of Col. Parr as Governor of Nova Scotia, and Major Parry Governor of Barbadoes will approve of their having the honour to kiss Your Majesty's hand on Wednesday, and of a Commission being made out to appoint Col. Campbell Governor of Jamaica.

I have the honour to be with the highest respect, Your Majesty's most dutyfull subject and faithfull servant,

SHELBURNE.

STREATHAM. 30 *June* 1782. ½ *past* 11 P.M.

Endorsed by the King.

No. 3825—*The King to Lord Shelburne.*

WINDSOR. *July* 1, 1782
m. 21 *past* 7 A.M.

Lord Shelburne must see I am certain with resentment the total ignorance that those who have governed Lord Rockingham cautiously try to keep both Me and Him as to the desperate state of that Lord, which certainly is with a view to some arrangement of their own.

I am apprised Lord Shelburne though He has gone great lengths at the expense of his opinion in giving way as to American Independence, if it can effect peace, would think He received advice in which his Character was not attended to, if it tended to give up that without the price set on it, which alone could make this Kingdom consent to it Besides, He must see that the great success of Lord Rodney's Engagement has again so far roused the Nation, that the Peace which would have been acquiesced in three months ago would now be matter of complaint.

From the language of Mr. Fitzpatrick it should seem that Lord Shelburne has no chance of being able to coalesce with Mr. Fox ; it may not be necessary to remove Him at once, but if Ld. Shelburne accept the Head of the Treasury, and is succeeded by Mr. Pitt as Secretary for the Home Department and British Settlements, that it will be seen how far He will submit to it ; the quarrelling with the rest of the Party as a party would not be wise, if they can be got to remain, it would be advisable, but it would not be right if only to be obtained by Lord Shelburne's being placed in the shoes of Lord Rockingham, that is, the head of a party when in reality he would be the Slave of it, He must be the Minister placed on a broad bottom.

The New Governors should be presented on Wednesday.

Draft, written on a page of Lord Shelburne's letter of same date.

No. 3826—*Lord Shelburne to the King.*

SIR—I write to acquaint Your Majesty that Lord Rockingam died this morning at half hour past twelve.

I have gone as far in collecting the opinions, which Your

Majesty might desire to be appriz'd of, as I can with any degree of prudence, without having the honour to see Your Majesty. I shall go in the Evening, where I shall wait the honour of Your Majesty's commands.

I have the honour to be with the highest Respect, Your Majesty's dutyfull Subject and devoted Servant,

WHITEHALL, *1st July*, 1782. **6 m. past 3.**   SHELBURNE.

Endorsed by the King.

No. 3827—*The King to Lord Shelburne.*

WINDSOR, *July 1st*, 1782
9 m. past 6 P.M.

Lord Shelburne must remember that when in March I was obliged to change my Ministry I called upon Him to form a new one and proposed His taking the Employment of First Ld. of the Treasury which He declined to accommodate Lord Rockingham ; the Vacancy of that Office makes me return to my original idea and offer it to Him on the present Occasion and with the fullest political confidence, indeed He has had an ample sample of it by my conduct towards Him since His return to my Service. I desire He will therefore see the Ld. Chancellor, the D. of Grafton, and others either in or out of Office, and collect their opinions fully that He may be able to state something to Me on Wednesday ; He is at liberty to mention my intentions with regard to Him and to set forward in forming a Plan for my inspection ; the letter I wrote this Morning, and the Conversations I have held with Him previous to it are the fullest instructions I can give on the subject.

Draft, written on a page of Lord Shelburne's letter of same date.

No. 3828—*Lord Keppel to the King.*

Lord Keppel has the honour to acquaint Your Majesty that Lord Howe after putting to sea with the Squadron under his Command, was necessarily obliged from the blowing westerly winds to return to St. Hellens, which cannot but be considered unfortunate, as this wind that has operated so unfavourably to Your Majesty's fleet may have enabled the Combined fleet entering the port of Brest unmolested ; after their having fallen in with Vice Admiral Campbell and the Newfoundland Convoy, a misfortune much to be regretted, tho' Inconsiderable both in value, size and numbers, a material disappointment. Lord Keppel has the honour to transmit to Your Majesty Vice Admiral Campbell's dispatches of 24th of last month. Lord Keppel hopes from the conversation he has had with Captain Lumesdaine of the Merlin that more of the Convoy may have escaped than the Vice Admiral seems to have imagined.

ADMIRALTY, *July 2nd*, 1782. 30 *m. past twelve* A.M.

No. 3829—*The King to Lord Keppel.*

WINDSOR, *June* [*sic, July*] 2nd, 1782
59 *m. past* 7 A.M.

The Account of V. Ad. Campbell having fallen in with the Combined Fleet and loosing part of his Convoy brought by Captain Lumesdaine of the Merlin is very unpleasant particularly if the Camp Equipage for Quebec should make part of it. I suppose the Combined Fleet will soon show what their Operations tend to, and that the Dutch will if possible get out at the same time.

Draft, written on a page of Lord Keppel's letter of same date.

No. 3830—*The King to Lord Shelburne.*

KEW, *July 3rd*, 1782
m. 53 *pt.* 6 P.M.

Lord Shelburne having wished to be apprised of what might arise in the Closet this day, on the late Death, as it might afford him some light as to the conduct he might hold towards the persons concerned ; it will be stated as briefly as possible the D. of Richmond on being told that Ld. Shelburne having been offered the Treasury in March had declined to accommodate Ld. Rockingham that He therefore naturally became entitled and as such is intended for that Office ; the Duke waved entering on the subject but said that none of the Ministers would choose to give any opinions till they had consulted together, that their advice would certainly be to place the Person best qualified to conciliate the Most Minds ; that the Public Affairs both within and without the Kingdom required unamity [sic] which alone he had in view.

Mr. Fox brought the Subject forward himself. He seemed much out of humour on being told the same as had been said to the D. of Richmond. He avowed that Administration would not be supported unless the first Ld. of the Treasury was one who agreed entirely in principles and lived in habitudes with the friends of Ld. Rockingham in which predicament he could not reckon Ld. Shelburne.

Ld. John Cavendish was mild on being told He could not be expected to remain under a new first Lord but that it was wished to place him in an office that might suit him. He seemed to take the offer kindly but inclined rather to retire which would probably be the case if the others remain which does not seem probable ; Gen. Conway seems well inclined but wishes appearances may be kept with the Rockingham's wishes Ld. John might succeed Ld. Shelburne as Secretary of State in which case the whole is an arrangement not a change.

Ld. Keppel did not get one word on the subject ; it could have been of no service.

Draft, endorsed by the King.

No. 3831—*Lord Shelburne to the King.*

Sir—The House of Lords sat till near seven o'clock, when they divided 44 against 9. Lord Chancellor Lord Stormont and Lord Loughborough oppos'd the Bill agreeing to the Principle of it, but setting forth the absurdity and confusion of most of the Clauses, which cannot be alter'd in the House of Lords on account of its being a Money Bill, and that the whole therefore should be rejected for this year. The Bill was supported by the Duke of Richmond Lord Coventry the Duke of Manchester and myself on general principles, except the Duke of Manchester, who spoke upon some of the Clauses. I have the honour to send your Majesty the Printed Bill.

I have nothing new to lay before your Majesty upon the head of negotiations. I am to see the Duke of Richmond to-morrow morning between 8 and 9—and their Meeting is talked of for tomorrow. It appears to me evidently taking the turn of their continuing, in which case I expect endless Stipulations will be insisted on—among others I am under no small apprehension of Mr. Fox's proposing Lord Temple instead of Lord John Cavendish for the Home Department. Your Majesty may depend on my taking the greatest pains to avert it.

I have the honour to be with the highest Respect, Your Majesty's Devoted Subject and Faithfull Servant,

BERKELEY SQUARE, 3rd July, 1782. 20 m. past 7   SHELBURNE.

Endorsed by the King.

No. 3832—*Mr. Jenkinson to the King.*

ADDISCOMBE PLACE,
July 3rd, 1782

SIR—I think it proper to inform Your Majesty that I have lately received two messages from Lord Shelburne, to the last of which I have returned an Answer. I place so much Confidence in his Lordship's honour and Candour that I entertain not the least doubt of his having reported faithfully to your Majesty every Sentiment that I convey'd to Him ; Being fearfull, however, that your Majesty might think me negligent and wanting in due attention, if I was wholly silent on this occasion, I will so far presume as to assure your Majesty that the answer I gave was dictated by those Sentiments of Attachment and Devotion which I shall ever bear to your Majesty's Person and Government and by no other Motive or Consideration whatsoever.

I am with the most profound respect, Your Majesty's Dutyfull Subject,   C. JENKINSON.

No. 3833—*Lord Shelburne to the King.*

SIR—On my return this moment from the House of Lords, I have been honour'd with Your Majesty's commands, accompanied with the Seals of the Foreign Department.

Nothing passed in the House of Lords except a tedious conversation upon the Clauses of the Establishment Bill, supported by the Chancellor and Lord Stormont on one side, the Duke of Richmond and myself on the other very shortly.

The Duke of Richmond condemns in very strong terms Mr. Fox's precipitate and unadvis'd conduct ; he promises support upon condition that he is allowed to consult with those Friends who remain about the Persons, who may be to fill up the vacant Offices, to which I have agreed provided he does not put me under the difficulty of a Negative on any particular Man, and that it does not interfere with conversations which I have already had. Lord Keppel does not seem ill dispos'd.

I have the honour to be with the highest Respect, Your Majesty's most Dutyfull & most Devoted Subject,

SHELBURNE.

BERKELEY SQUARE, 4 *July*, 1782. 5 *m. past* 9

Endorsed by the King.

No. 3834—*The King to Lord Shelburne.*

KEW, *July* 4*th*, 1782
30 *m. pt.* 10 P.M.

I think it right not to send back the Messenger without mentioning that Lord Keppel owned to me that the Duke of Richmond greatly disapproved of Mr. Fox's resignation and dissuaded him Ld. Keppel from thinking of retiring ; Mr. Townshend reprobates the idea of him quitting if Measures are right because they cannot fill offices to their wish, and owned it was the obliquy always thrown out against Ld. Rockingham and his friends that he always deny'd but would not say so now as far as regards Mr. Fox after the part He had acted this day, Ld. Shelburne if He can keep the D. of Richmond is right but he must not at the same time throw himself into His power.

G. R.

Draft, endorsed by the King.

No. 3835—*Lord Keppel to the King.*

Lord Keppel has the honour to transmit to your Majesty a dispatch received this morning from Sir Thomas Pye, the winds being Easterly prevents the ships off the Nore from sailing ; a Messenger will be immediately sent to Plymouth to hasten the suffolk and also another Messenger to the Downs to send the panther to join Lord Howe. Lord Keppel has the honour to assure your Majesty that no attention shall be wanting in collecting the force in port that was not in readiness or condition to sail with Lord Howe.

ADMIRALTY, *July 8th* [? *7th*] 1782. 30 *m. past* 9 *o'clock*

Endorsed by the King with date 7 *July.*

No. 3836—*The King to Lord Keppel.*

Ld. Keppel will undoubtedly enforce every mode of strengthening Ld. Howe as much as possible ; by the intelligence it seems as if the Combined Fleet mean to lay at least off of the Channel not put into Brest ; the 10 or 12 ships seen going into Brest under Convoy of Frigates, must be some of the captured Merchant Ships.

WINDSOR, *July 7th,* 1782. 13 *m. pt.* 2 P.M.

Draft, written on a page of Lord Keppel's letter of same date.

No. 3837—*Lord Shelburne to the King.*

SIR—The Duke of Richmond and Lord Keppel insisted upon my not proceeding in the arrangement, till the Event of a meeting at Lord Fitzwilliam's was known, which was not till late on Saturday night [6 July]. The time has been since taken up in conversing and waiting the Decision of those whom I applied to.

The Meeting at Lord Fitzwilliam's consisted of between thirty and forty, where the Duke of Richmond Lord Temple and Mr. Pelham resisted a monstrous scene of violence on the part of Mr. Fox and his particular Friends. The Duke of Richmond has* been much interested in consequence for Lord Temple, whose point was to be Secretary of the Home Department. I have been obliged to a great deal of management and in a very particular manner to the assistance of Mr. James Grenville to get him to go to Ireland in the stead of it.

I have left no stone unturn'd about a Chancellor of the Exchequer, but it's not to be described the difficulty I have met with in regard to that particular Employment. Mr. James Grenville declin'd in the most positive manner both that and Secretary of War. Mr. Hamilton's view goes to no active Employment whatever, but looks to some sinecure Situation. Upon the whole the arrangement which I have the honour to enclose to your Majesty I hope is the best of which the times and means admit.

I am still under a considerable difficulty about a Secretary at War, not being able to find anybody in Office to promote to that Employment except Sir George Young, about the propriety of which I have great doubts. Mr. Powis declin'd Employment three months since, and has appear'd very intimately connected with those who have lately resign'd, and I find great personal aversion to Lord Beauchamp, independent of going into another Line, without obtaining much efficiency by it, except in point of numbers.

I wait your Majesty's approbation to send to Lord Grantham.

Mr. Fox declar'd at his meeting that he intended taking all advantages, and to have no managements in his Language. He has given a proof by summoning every person possible to Town, with a view to bring a question on American Independance tomorrow in the House of Commons. I hope it will be properly resisted, and that I have neglected nothing, but being as yet totally ignorant about the House of Commons, I cannot answer for the Event in the manner I could wish to.

Lord Duncannon and Mr. John Townsend have resign'd to Lord Kepple, who has agreed to my recommendation of two Lords, upon condition of some future arrangement for his private Secretary, whom he had thought of bringing to the Board. Lord Robert Spencer having desir'd his resignation to be laid before your Majesty, I have taken the liberty to offer his employment to the Duke of Marlborough for Lord Charles Spencer. I hear of no further resignations except that of Mr. Burke, who has not as yet signified his Intention.

There are several particulars which I defer troubling your Majesty with till I have the honour of attending you.

I have the Honour to be with the highest Respect, Your Majesty's most Dutyfull Subject and Faithfull Servant,

SHELBURNE.

BERKELEY SQUARE, *9th July*, 1782.   2 *o'clock* A.M.

Endorsed by the King.

Enclosure.

[In Lord Shelburne's handwriting.]

Chancellor of the Exchequer
Mr. William Pitt.

Commissioners
Mr. James Grenville
Mr. Jackson—not decided
Mr. Eliot Junr.

Foreign Secretary
Lord Grantham.

Home Secretary
Mr. Thomas Townsend.

Secretary at War

Lord Lieutenant of Ireland
Earl Temple.

9th July, 1782.

Vice Treasurer
Lord Charles Spencer.

Admiralty
Mr. Pratt—certain
Sir Robert Smyth⎰
Sir Gilbert Eliot ⎱doubtfuls
Mr. Aubrey
Mr. St. John.

Pay Office
Mr. Barré.

Treasurer of the Navy
Lord Advocate of Scotland.

The Garter
The Duke of Rutland.

No. 3838—*The King to Lord Shelburne.*

The language of the D. of Richmond on Friday convinced Me that He would expect so much management towards himself in the Arrangement that I was not surprised at not hearing from Ld. Shelburne till this Morning. I do not doubt that Ld. Fitzwilliam is now intended to be the apparent head of the

Violent Party, the meeting at His House too clearly shews it, and his temper inclines to go any lengths.

Lord Shelburne has acted very properly in turning Ld. Temple from the Office of Secretary for the Home Department to Ld. Lieut. of Ireland. I am glad Mr. Jas. Grenville has been of use, I hope he will be cultivated; He is certainly a worthy man.

I am sorry Mr. Pitt cannot be Secretary of State but undoubtedly he may take the lead as Chancellor of the Exchequer, which Mr. Townshend cannot object to and perhaps considering his youth the arrangement may appear better as necessity has decided it.

It is impossible for Me to give any opinion as to the propriety of appointing Sir George Yonge Secretary at War as I am totally unacquainted with him, but I shall undoubtedly cordially receive anyone that may best suit the present Arrangement.

Ld. Grantham I should suppose is in Yorkshire, I perfectly agree to his being instantly summoned.

I am glad Mr. Fox is to try a question on American unconditional Independance; I do not believe the Nation at large willing to come into it and great credit will therefore attend the Party that proposes [opposes] it; the conduct of Ld. Shelburne and those who have acted particularly with him have ever held uniformly is known by the Public who will rejoice at seeing the question decided against the Leaders of Sedition.

I am glad Ld. Keppel consents to the two gentlemen coming to the Board of Admiralty Ld. Shelburne proposes, and looks to some future arrangement for his private Secretary; I am surprised he thought of a Seat at that Board for Him; he is son to a Domestick Servant of Ld. Keppel's father who lately died one of the Pages in my outward Room; this pretty clearly shews his intentions of resigning have vanished.

Ld. Chas. Spencer very properly succeeds his Brother.

Those agreeable to the enclosed Paper that can attend tomorrow ought to have notice to attend at St. James tomorrow.

I do not know whether the Minute of Cabinet in the Box was for my use I therefore return it but approve of the Measure.

WINDSOR, *July 9th*, 1782. 58 *m. pt.* 7 A.M.

Endorsed by the King.

No. 3839—*Lord Shelburne to the King.*

SIR—Sir George Yonge desires me to lay him at your Majesty's
Feet, and to say that he feels so much apprehension about accepting an office of so much business, as not to be overcome by
anything but his Devotion to Your Majesty.

I believe it will be necessary for Lord Keppel to attend Your
Majesty before Your Majesty's Dressing with the Resignation
of Lord Duncannon and Mr. Townsend, that Mr. Aubrey and
Mr. Pratt may have the honour to kiss Your Majesty's hand at
the Levee.   It will be necessary that Lord John Cavendish
should attend at the same time on the same account if Your
Majesty does not disapprove it.

I will at the same time lay before Your Majesty the List of
those who are to kiss hands.

I have the honour to be with the Highest Respect, Your
Majesty's most Dutyfull Subject,   SHELBURNE.

BERKELEY SQUARE, 10th *July*, 1782.   10 *m. past* 12 P.M.

Endorsed by the King.

No. 3840—*Lord Shelburne to the King.*

SIR—I have the honour to send Your Majesty the Speech.

I have a letter from Mr. Fox acquainting me that Lord Derby
is to call upon me this day for an explanation of what I said
yesterday relative to his Resignation, but it cannot admit of
a long discussion.

I have the Honour to be with the highest Respect, Your
Majesty's most Dutyfull Subject and Faithfull Servant,

SHELBURNE.

BERKELEY SQUARE, 11th *July*, 1782.   10 *m. past* 12 [A.M.]

P.S.   There has been no alteration in the Speech, except a
small transposition of Words, in the paragraph about America,
and the insertion of the word colonies.   The Fair copy will be
ready for Your Majesty at the Queen's House.

Endorsed by the King.

No. 3841—*The King to Lord Shelburne.*

KEW, *July* 11, 1782
m. 16 *pt.* 7 A.M.

The Chancellor's declining to answer for the Ld. Advocate and the opinion given by Mr. Andrew Stuart makes the line I have to take on the present occasion very obvious. Ld. Shelburne has my full authority to offer the Treasurership of the Navy to the Ld. Advocate, and to assure Him that if He will come to Town and accept it, He shall at the same time have His Office of Clerk of the Signet secured to Him for life. Mr. Barré's appointment to the Pay Office should be notified this day and his Writ moved.

The enclosed papers Ld. Shelburne left Yesterday in my hands, the one from Sir Geo. Saville may be fine Metaphisical Reasoning, I am the avowed enemy of that ingenious nonsense, therefore no judge of its supposed merit ; but common sense tells me that if unconditional Independance is granted, we cannot ever expect any understanding with America, for then we have given up the whole and have nothing to give for what we want from thence. Independance is certainly an unpleasant gift at best, but then it must be for such conditions of Peace as may justify it. Lord Camden yesterday said to Me that under the present Act He thought any Minister would risk his Head that advised granting Independance but as the boon for Peace.

Lord Clarendon may have an Audience tomorrow as he wishes it ; he seems much pleased with the K. of Prussia's personal attention to Him.

Draft, written on a page of Lord Shelburne's letter of same date.

No. 3842—*Lord Shelburne to the King.*

SIR—On coming out of your Majesty's closet I found a note of great anxiety from Lord Temple. I call'd upon him and found him under great appearances of distress in consequence of his accounts from Paris, lest his brother should take such a part on Mr. Fox's resignation, as would either occasion a Family

Breach, or oblige him Lord Temple to retire from any publick Situation. I hope and trust he has not chang'd his mind about going to Ireland, and in my conversation would not suppose it possible. It ended by my agreeing to submit to Your Majesty, out of Your Majesty's regard to Lord Temple, that a Messenger may be sent tomorrow to Mr. Grenville with leave to return, and directing him to acquaint the French Minister that it is for the purpose of receiving further Instructions. Lord Temple imagines he has a much better chance of governing him when he sees him, than at a distance, and promises to write to him by the same Messenger, recommending the utmost propriety of conduct.

I found Lord Grantham under, I am sure, a very unaffected apprehension of his own unfitness to fill the Situation design'd for him, and begs to be understood by Your Majesty, as undertaking it from entire Devotion to Your Service and Duty to Your Person, without any bargain or hesitation except what results from his knowledge of himself.

I have the honour to enclose to Your Majesty a Letter of the Lord President's. The course expected bears on the question entirely of *Free Ships Free Goods*. No Judgement has yet been given upon this principle. At the same time Your Majesty knows that all negotiation has been lately carried on with a view of gaining the Northern Courts by acknowledging it. For this reason it seems the opinion of those of the Cabinet which I have seen to put off the cause for further consideration. If Your Majesty thinks it proper, I will give the Lord President's Letter to Mr. Townsend, who will be to speak to the Danish Minister in as general Terms as possible to that effect.

I have the honour to be with the highest Respect, Your Majesty's most Dutyfull Subject and Faithfull Servant,

SHELBURNE.

BERKELEY SQUARE, 12*th July*, 1782. ½ *past* 11 P.M.

P.S. Since writing the above I have received a Note from Lord Temple, which I have the honour to send Your Majesty.

Endorsed by the King.

No. 3843—*The King to Lord Shelburne.*

The language of the Earl of Temple might have given rise to suspicion had not his subsequent note clearly shewn that his private not public sentiments were the cause of it ; I consent to Mr. Grenville's having immediate leave to come home.

Lord Grantham I flattered myself would conduct Himself as He does and as every honest Man unwarped by connections must ; I trust He will be diligent and practicable ; I am certain to the Corps Diplomatique His Nomination will be agreeable.

Undoubtedly it is best to put off the Danish Cause ; Mr. Hardynge is the Council for the Danes ; I should think the Lord President may induce him to forward a good humoured acquiescence in the delay.

WINDSOR, *July 13th*, 1782.   20 *m. pt.* 7 A.M.

Draft, written on a page of Lord Shelburne's letter of 12 July.

No. 3844—*Mr. Townshend to the King.*

WHITEHALL, *Saturday*
July 13th, 1782, 3 P.M.

Mr. Townshend has the honour of transmitting to His Majesty a minute of the Cabinet, which he was directed to lay before His Majesty for his approbation.

Enclosure.   MINUTE OF CABINET.

[In Lord Keppel's handwriting.]

ADMIRALTY, *July* 12, 1782

Present :—Lord President, Lord Privy Seal, Duke of Richmond, Lord Shelburne, Mr. Townshend, Lord Ashburton, General Conway, Mr. Pitt, Lord Keppel.

It is humbly recommended to your Majesty that Lord Howe upon his return to St. Helens in case he should not have fallen in with the Combined fleet which sailed from Cadiz and is supposed to be destined for the port of Brest, be Instructed to proceed again off Brest with the Squadron under His Command, and such others of your Majesty's ships of the line as can be Instantly collected for the purpose of joining his Lordship, taking with him under his care, the Bristol of 50 guns and the East India Ships under her convoy, and after his Lordship has satisfied himself that the Combined Fleet is in the port of Brest, directing the Captain of the Bristol to proceed with his Convoy, Agreeable to the Orders he shall have received from the Admiralty for his conduct and future destination, That his Lordship do then continue to Block up the Enemy in their port, till such time as he judges the Bristol and her convoy may be out of danger of the Enemy's getting up with them. When this service is performed, It is Humbly recommended to Your Majesty, that Lord Howe be Ordered to dispatch with as little loss of time as possible, Vice Admiral Milbanke and Sir Richard Hughs with ten or eleven ships of ye Line off the Texell, delivering to Vice Admiral Milbanke the Admiralty Orders for his conduct in the North Seas, And that his Lordship be ordered to repair himself with the remainder of his fleet to Torbay or St. Helens, as he may judge most convenient for his assembling such additional force as may be brought forward in his absence.

No. 3845—*The King to Mr. Townshend.*

Mr. Secretary Townshend's note accompanying the Minute of Cabinet is just received, the measure for the safe Convoying the East India Fleet through the Channel seems very proper, He is therefore to give such directions as may be necessary for putting this into Execution.

WINDSOR, *July* 13*th*, 1782. 51 *m. pt* 6 P.M.

Draft, written on a page of Mr. Townshend's letter of same date.

No. 3846—*Mr. Jenkinson to the King.*

ADDISCOMBE PLACE, *July* 13*th*, 1782
12 A.M.

SIR—I have this moment received Your Majesty's commands to which I will not fail to pay implicit obedience, and I will accordingly give every support and assistance in my power to

Lord Shelburne. Of this I will take a proper method of apprizing his Lordship. My Attachment has ever been to your Majesty and ever will be ; and for this reason I did not think it right to enter into any new Engagement till I had received Your Majesty's Commands on this subject.

I am with the most profound Respect, Sir, Your Majesty's Dutyfull Subject,   C. JENKINSON.

Endorsed by the King.

No. 3847—*The King to Mr. Jenkinson.*

WINDSOR, *July* 13th, 1782

Mr. Jenkinson's constant Assurances of personal Attachment to Me is the cause of my writing to Him on so extraordinary a position of Affairs as the present ; the mask is now certainly cast off it is no less than a struggle whether I am to be dictated to by Mr. Fox, who avows that He must have the sole direction of this Country ; Lord Shelburne certainly must and shall have my fullest support ; I therefore desire Mr. Jenkinson will give him every degree of Assistance. The Speaker has explained the very good disposition, but that the knowledge of my wishes was necessary to decide such a step. Lord Shelburne is apprised that I mean to write on this head.

Draft, endorsed by the King.

No. 3848—*Lord Keppel to the King.*

Lord Keppel has the honour to transmit to Your Majesty Admiral Drake's letter from the Downs July 12th, with two enclosed, one from Sir J. B. Warren and the other from Captain Douglas.

Lord Keppel has also the honor to send Your Majesty a letter from Captain Shirley of ye 15th of April received this morning, with one from Captain Trotsham late of the Aligator sloop, dated ye 1st instant.

ADMIRALTY, *July* 13th, 1782.   20 m. pt. 4 P.M.

Endorsed by the King.

No. 3849—*The King to Lord Keppel.*

The account Ld. Keppel has sent of the Dutch Fleet being out of the Texel on the 10th shews the intelligence I mentioned having received yesterday from Holland was founded ; I suppose by this steering they mean to go along our Coast and perhaps some of their line of Battle Ships may go North about to join the Combined Fleet.

The Dutch will feel this fresh blow on the Coast of Guinea.

WINDSOR, *July* 13th, 1782. 46 *m. pt.* 7 P.M.

Draft, written on a page of Lord Keppel's letter of same date.

No. 3850—*Lord Keppel to the King.*

Lord Keppel has the Honour to transmit to Your Majesty two dispatches from Plymouth of the 13th instant received this day forwarded by Lord Shuldham, And in consequence of the Information Lord Keppel has the further honour to acquaint Your Majesty that as time has pressed so materially for determination and dispatch he has presumed to send Orders to Portsmouth and Plymouth to get every ship that is in readiness and fitt, to sea as hastily as possible that Lord Howe's Squadron may be strengthened by every possible means, Lord Keppel has also the honour to send to Your Majesty Captain Lutterel of the Mediators journal, arrived at Portsmouth from a cruise in the bay.

ADMIRALTY, *July* 14th, 1782. 10 *m. past* 10 P.M.

Endorsed by the King.

No. 3851—*The King to Lord Keppel.*

Lord Keppel seems so aware of the necessity of strengthening Lord Howe's Squadron as much as possible that I have left nothing to say but that undoubtedly Lord Keppel is the best judge what exertions can be made and how short of Complement the ships can go on so short a service as the present ; I trust therefore soon to hear that the Western Squadron is increased.

WINDSOR, *July 15th*, 1782. 2 *m. pt.* 7 A.M.

Draft, written on a page of Lord Keppel's letter of 14 *July.*

No. 3852—*The Bishop of Worcester to the King.*

SIR—I have received with great pleasure the German Latin books, which Your Majesty was pleased to order for me, I am impatient to return my humble thanks to Your Majesty for so kind and agreeable a present. I shall not have it in my power to look into these Volumes, till I return from my Visitation which I enter upon this week, but I see from the titles of them the entertainment I am to expect especially from such as have been composed at the University of Göttingen, which has deservedly grown into great eminence under Your Majesty's generous encouragement and protection.

Having taken the liberty to trouble Your Majesty with this Letter, Your Majesty will forgive my adding one word on the subject of poor Dr. Arnald. He was with me an entire month, and during almost the whole of that time seemed in perfect health, so that he examined for me and assisted at my Ordination, and performed the Service of my Chapel. But a day or two before he left me, he appeared out of spirits, and was not well. However, he returned to Loughborough at his time, under the care of his servant, but with some difficulty. He there grew much worse, and, as I conclude from the information I received last night, is at this moment under confinement. This is a sad tale to entertain your Majesty with, but I thought it necessary to mention it, as I doubt it shews how little expectation there now can be of his perfect recovery.

I am, Sir, With the utmost gratitude and respect, Your Majesty's most faithful & obedient subject & servant,

R. WORCESTER.

HARTLEBURY CASTLE, *July 16th*, 1782

No. 3853—*Lord Shelburne to the King.*

Sir—I have just received the Inclos'd from Powis by Potter. The contents must decide on Mr. Fox's character with the Publick, if they are ever call'd for by Parliament. I am afraid Mr. Fox has none to lose with Your Majesty.

I have been detain'd here by a long and very satisfactory conversation with Mr. Jenkinson.

I have the honour to be with the highest Respect, Your Majesty's most Dutyfull Subject, Shelburne.

Streatham, 16th *July*, 1782. 3 *o'clock* P.M.

Endorsed by the King.

No. 3854—*The King to Lord Shelburne.*

The dispatches by Potter certainly are very unpleasant and show very clearly that Mr. Fox does not deserve to be better thought of than I have uniformly done. I flattered myself by the answer I received to the letter I wrote to Mr. Jenkinson that Lord Shelburne would have every reason to be satisfied with any conversation he might have with him.

Windsor, *July* 16th, 1782. 57 *m. pt.* 6 P.M.

Draft, written on a page of Lord Shelburne's letter of same date.

No. 3855.

Minute of Cabinet.

[In Lord Keppel's handwriting.]

Admiralty, *July* 17, 1782

Present :—Lord Chancellor, Lord Privy Seal, Mr. Townshend, Duke of Richmond, Mr. Pitt, Lord Keppel

Intelligence having arrived late last night at the Admiralty by Lieutenant Vancourt of the Mackerel Cartel transport from the Coast of Africa, who gave Information that he had seen the Combined Fleet at 3 a.m. on the 14th Instant wher[e] the Lands

End bore About North 8 or 9 Leagues the wind at W.N.W. A Spanish frigate had spoke to him before 10 o'clock, he was directed to go under the Admiral's Stern and was a little after twelve permitted to depart, Lieutenant Vancourt describes the Combined Fleet to consist of seven ships of three deck and thirty three of two Decks making in the whole forty ships of the line and Lord Howe's letter received this morning at 7 a.m. dated off Scilly 12th instant giving an Account of his having seen the Combined Fleet very early in the Morning consisting of thirty six ships of the Line, and that he had thought proper to avoid coming to Battle with them as then circumstanced, and therefore steered to the Northward to pass between Scilly and the Lands End, his purpose therein has been to endeavour to get to the Westward of the Enemy, both for protecting the Jamaica Convoy, and to gain that Advantage of situation for bringing them to Action, which the difference in his numbers renders desirable.

It is Humbly recommended to Your Majesty that the Admiralty should be directed, to pursue every method in their power to Encrease Lord Howe's force and to convey to him every Information upon the subject and State of the Ships intended to reinforce his Squadron with, and to cooperate with his Lordship for their safe junction with him, and when his Lordship shall judge his force, within four or five ships of the Line to that of the Enemies Combined Fleet, it is humbly recommended to your Majesty that he should be ordered to proceed in quest of them, and If his Lordship should meet with them to use his endeavours the first favourable ocasion he has, to bring them to battle when his Skill and Experience give him hope of doing it with success.

No. 3856—*Lord Grantham to the King.*

The Flanders Mail being opened while Your Majesty's Confidential Servants were assembled in Council, the Contents of the Dispatches from Russia confirmed the Resolutions stated in the Minute.

Lord Grantham begs to submit to your Majesty whether he should not dispatch a Messenger to Brussels to apprize Mr. Fitzherbert of your Majesty's gracious Intention of commanding his Services at Paris, and submits also the Draft for that purpose for Your Majesty's approbation.

Mr. Grenville arrived this afternoon.

St. James, 20*th July*, 1782

Enclosure.   MINUTE OF CABINET.

[In Lord Grantham's handwriting.]

St. James's, 20 *July*, 1782

At a Cabinet Council held this morning at ten o'clock.

Present :—Lord President, Lord Privy Seal, Duke of Richmond, Earl of Shelburne, Viscount Keppell, Lord Ashburton, Mr. Townshend, Mr. Conway, Mr. Pitt, Lord Grantham.

Upon consideration of M. de Vergennes Proposal, and Insinuation Verbale from the Courts of Vienna and Prussia, referred by Your Majesty, and of the Answer to be given to them it was agreed

To call upon France for a more explicit Answer and to communicate to M. de Simolin the Situation of the Negotiation now unavoidably depending at Paris and consult upon the best Mode of giving the written Answer to the Insinuation Verbale.

It was further agreed to make the same Communication in the fullest manner to the Court of Russia, assuring the Empress that there is not an idea of abandoning the Mediation but on the contrary, the greatest Confidence and Reliance on her Assistance for the most effectual Manner of procuring Peace.

No. 3857—*The King to Lord Grantham.*

The dispatches from Russia are certainly of a nature to confirm the propriety of the Minute transmitted to Me by Ld. Grantham. I ever looked upon the Negociation at Paris as very likely to displease both the Mediating Courts, the one it has most completely, the other I hope by the judicious opinion now given will be prevented.

The draft to Mr. Fitzherbert meets with my fullest Approbation.

Windsor, *July* 21*st*, 1782.   50 *m. pt.* 7 A.M.

Draft, written on a page of Lord Grantham's letter of 20 *July.*

No. 3858—*Lord Keppel to the King.*

Lord Keppel has the honour to transmit to Your Majesty Captain Bertie's letter to Lord Shuldham, upon his return to Plymouth after seeing a french Convoy of great numbers supposed from the West Indies under the protection of four ships of the Line. Lord Keppel also has the honour to send Your Majesty Captain Bertie's private letter to him.

ADMIRALTY, *July 25th*, 1782. 15 *m. past* 5 P.M.

No. 3859.

MINUTE OF CABINET.

[Copy, in Lord Grantham's handwriting.]

Thursday, 25th July, 1782

Present :—Lord Chancellor, Lord President, Lord Privy Seal, Earl of Shelburne, Duke of Richmond, Lord Grantham, General Conway, Lord Ashburton, Mr. Pitt, Mr. Townshend.

It is humbly recommended to Your Majesty that a Commission be made out to pass Your Majesty's Great Seal, for appointing Richard Oswald, Esq. a Commissioner to treat with any Commissioner or Commissioners &c. of the Colonies or Plantations, as mentioned in the Act of the last Session of Parliament.

No. 3860—*Lord Keppel to the King.*

Lord Keppel has the honour to transmit to Your Majesty Dispatches received this morning from Lord Hood at Jamaica of the 10th and 12th of last month, & those from Commodore Sir Richard Bickerton of the 29th of April and 20th of May the one from Rio Janeiro the other after leaving that place.

ADMIRALTY, *July 29th*, 1782. 30 *m. past* 12 P.M.

No. 3861—*Lord Keppel to the King.*

Lord Keppel has the honour to transmit to Your Majesty the Dispatches received this morning from Lord Shuldham from Portsmouth from Sir Peter Parker and from Vice Admiral Drake in the Downs.

ADMIRALTY, *July* 30*th*, 1782.　45 *m. past* 2 P.M.

No. 3862—*Lord Shelburne to the King.*

SIR—I have the misfortune to be confin'd with a sore throat, and to be prevented attending Your Majesty—I hope to be well enough to have that honour on Fryday.

I have the honour to enclose Your Majesty a Letter from Lord Kepple. I saw the Comptroller of the Navy last night, whose opinion I find is to send Orders to Admiral Pigott to go with the whole or part of the Fleet during the Hurricanes to New York, which would answer the double purpose of Escort and Transport, and appears to me after many enquiries the only means of ensuring the Removal of the Garrison. As to the Relief of Gibraltar I find the Comptroller against waiting till September, and inclines much to the detaching ten Ships. This depends so much upon local as well as naval knowledge of the entrance of the Bay and other circumstances, that I dare not offer to decide and I am apprehensive the Cabinet not being naval men will find a good deal of difficulty in doing so. It appears to me that a great deal should depend upon the experience and convictions of the Officer, who commands in either case.

I don't care to trouble Your Majesty further about Lord Temple, who has written to me a long and impatient letter upon his pretentions to Rank. I shall see him and endeavour to satisfye his mind with what Your Majesty has already said upon that subject.

Dr. Jackson will attend this day to kiss your Majesty's hand for the Prebendary of Westminster. Dr. Dodsworth is in the South of France with an only daughter, but expected shortly.

I have the honour to be with the highest Respect, Your Majesty's most Dutyfull Subject,　SHELBURNE.

BERKELEY SQUARE, 31*st July* [1782].　½ *past* 12 P.M.

Endorsed by the King.

No. 3863—*The King to Lord Shelburne.*

I trust that Ld. Shelburne will soon get well but must insist that if He is not quite recovered on Friday that He will not come out, a few days care may prevent many days illness.

I return Ld. Keppel's note I owne I concur much in the opinion of the Comptroller of the Navy that Adm. Pigott ought to go for the hurricane Months to N. America which will forward the Evacuations. I also think the Relief of Gibraltar ought not to be delayed till September, the way to keep up the spirits of the men is to shew they are not neglected, the Enemy avow that is the time they mean to make their Attack therefore our succours ought to be there before that time.

Lord Temple is now appointed Ld. Lieut. of Ireland He cannot [with] decency press me any further but if he does I must only repeat what I have already said.   G. R.

St. James's, *July 31st*, 1782.   48 *m. pt.* 3 p.m.

Draft, endorsed by the King.

No. 3864—*Mr. Townshend to the King.*

Mr. Townshend has the honour to transmit to Your Majesty two Minutes of your Cabinet of last night for Your Majesty's inspection and direction.

Whitehall, *August the 3rd*, 1782.

Endorsed by the King.

Enclosure.   I

MINUTE OF CABINET.

[In Mr. Townshend's handwriting.]

August 2nd, 1782

Present :—Ld. President, Lord Shelburne, Duke of Richmond, Lord Keppel, Mr. Pitt, General Conway, Mr. Townshend.

It is humbly represented to Your Majesty, that Sir Guy Carleton should prepare his Garrison for Embarkation against the arrival of Admiral Pigot at New York ; that part of it which is capable of serving in the West Indies should go to Barbadoes, where they will be to receive further orders from home ; the other part to go to Halifax according to former Orders.

It is further recommended to Your Majesty, that the Island of Providence should be attacked by such a detachment of Land and Sea Forces as shall appear to Sir Guy Carleton and Admiral Digby to be sufficient for that service.

II

MINUTE OF CABINET.

[In Lord Keppel's handwriting.]

August 2nd, 1782

Present :—Lord President, Lord Shelburne, Duke of Richmond, Mr. Townshend, General Conway, Mr. Pitt, Lord Keppel.

It is humbly recommended to his Majesty that Admiral Pigot should have orders sent to him to employ the Fleet under his Command during the Hurricane season in the West Indies, upon the Coast of North America leaving a sufficient force at the Leeward Islands for their safety during his Absence, he is to proceed to New York when there if Applied to by General Sir Guy Carleton to receive on board the ships of his Squadron any part of that garrison, He is to comply with such request directing as many of the troops to be received as the ships can conveniently take without endangering the health of the Ships crews, but although this service is recommended Admiral Pigot should be directed to get back to the Leeward Islands by the time the season is safe for Acting, a duplicate of these directions should be sent to New York, in case Admiral Pigot should have proceeded there In consequence of his General Instructions.

It is further recommended to Your Majesty that should Admiral Pigot leave New York before the Army there should embark for other services, he is nevertheless to receive the troops before mentioned If applied to by Sir Guy Carleton to do it and convoy them to Barbadoes there to land them.

No. 3865—*The King to Mr. Townshend.*

I approve of the two Minutes of Cabinet and authorise Mr. Secretary Townshend to prepare the necessary Orders agreeable to them. Not knowing whether he has kept copies of them I return them, but when he has done that, He will of course send them back.

WINDSOR, *Augt. 3rd*, 1782. *58 m. pt.* 3 P.M.

Draft, written on a page of Mr. Townshend's letter of same date.

No. 3866—*Mr. Townshend to the King.*

Mr. Townshend humbly presumes to represent to Your Majesty, that he is apprehensive that the delay in forwarding the Commission to Mr. Oswald, which is now occasioned by the Attorney General's absence from London, and which will be increased by the Chancellor's being at present at Trentham, may have materially bad consequences in the negotiation, which it is to authorize.

To prevent these, he wishes to receive your Majesty's Permission to send the Instructions to Mr. Oswald and a copy of the Commission to Paris immediately. In which case, he will write to Mr. Oswald to account for the delay, to prevent the jealousys, which he understands to be now arising from it.

WHITEHALL, *August the 3rd*, 1782. *55 m. past* 12.

Endorsed by the King.

No. 3867—*The King to Mr. Townshend.*

WINDSOR, *Augt. 3rd*, 1782
2.55 *m. pt.* 3 P.M.

Nothing can be more proper than the suggestion of Mr. Secretary Townshend that the delay in forwarding the Commission to Mr. Oswald may materially affect the Negotiation at Paris and that it is expedient to prevent it by sending Mr. Oswald a copy of the Commission immediately and stating that the delay of the Original is occasioned by the Chancellor being at Trentham and the Attorney General in Wales.

Draft, written on a page of Mr. Townshend's letter of same date.

No. 3868—*Lord Keppel to the King.*

Lord Keppel has the honour to send to Your Majesty letters received this morning from Lord Howe and Lord Shuldham.

ADMIRALTY. *August 6th*, 1782. 45 *m. past* 3 P.M.

No. 3869—*The King to Lord Keppel.*

I am glad to find by the dispatches Ld. Keppel has sent to Me, that Lord Howe is safely arrived at Torbay, and his Squadron healthy ; by the intelligence that accompanied them received from Falmouth I should hope the passage is now open for the Leward Islands trade, which must hourly be expected.

WINDSOR, *Augt. 6th*, 1782. 3 *m. pt.* 7 P.M.

Draft, written on a page of Lord Keppel's letter of same date.

No. 3870—*Mr. Robinson to the King.*

Mr. Robinson has had the honour to receive your Majesty's Commands on the Road as he was going to pay a Visit to Mr. Jenkinson before he goes into Huntingdonshire ; Mr. Robinson turned back immediately to acknowledge Your Majesty's Orders ; He begs leave to assure Your Majesty that he will take all possible care to forward safely the Pacquet to Lord North, and most humbly requests to be permitted to add, that as it is his bounden Duty, so it will be the Happiness and Pleasure of His Life to obey Your Majesty's Commands to the utmost of His Power, and to render every Service, which he can, in Support of Your Majesty's Government and the Constitution.

SYON HILL, *7th August*, 1782. 30 *m. p.* 2 P.M.

No. 3871—*The King to Mr. Robinson.*

Mr. Robinson is desired to send the enclosed [*see next letter*] to Ld. North. I cannot at the same time avoid expressing My Approbation of his having undertaken to furnish Ld. Shelburne an Accurate State of the House of Commons and the Connections of each individual as far as can be ascertained ; this will be very material to counteract the Activity of Mr. Fox, who every honest Man and those the least interested in the support of their Constitution must wish to the utmost to keep out of Power.

WINDSOR, *Augt. 7th,* 1782.

Draft, endorsed by the King.

No. 3872—*The King to Lord North.*

WINDSOR, *Aug. 7th,* 1782

Lord North has so often whilst in Office assured me that whenever I would consent to his retiring He would give the most cordial support to such an Administration as I might approve of, that I should not think I either acted properly to my own Affairs or placed that confidence in His declarations if I did not express my strongest wishes that He will give the most active Support the next Session of Parliament to the Administration formed with my thorough approbation on the death of Lord Rockingham, and that during the Recess He will call on the Country Gentlemen who certainly have great attention for Him to come early and shew their countenance by which I may be enabled to keep the Constitution from being entirely anihilated, which must be the case if Mr. Fox and his Associates are not withstood. Many strange scenes have occurred in this Country, but none more so than the present contest, it is no less than whether the sole direction of My Kingdoms shall be trusted in the hands of Mr. Fox ; Lord North has long known my opinion of that gentleman, which has been if possible more rivited by three Months experience of Him in Office, which has finally determined Me never to employ Him again consequently the contest is become personal and He indeed sees it also in that point of view. Lord Shelburne is acquainted with my intention of writing to Lord North and will I am confident be desirous of shewing every mark of attention for the assistance my Administration may desire in consequence of this letter.

Draft, endorsed by the King.

No. 3873—*Lord North to the King.*

[10 *August*, 1782 ?]

Lord North has received the honour of His Majesty's Commands.

While Lord North was at the head of the Treasury he certainly received from several independent country gentlemen a very steady, disinterested and effectual support and Lord North flatters himself that he still possesses their friendship in a considerable degree : He does not, however, know whether he can venture, in his present situation, to call upon them for their early attendance in Parliament, and their support of Government and he is afraid that he may give them some offence if he were to attempt it ; he will nevertheless take every opportunity of learning their inclinations and hopes to be able to inform His Majesty of their disposition before the meeting of Parliament.

No. 3874—*Lord Keppel to the King.*

Lord Keppel has the honour to transmit to Your Majesty Admiral Pigots letter of the 29th of June from Antigua received this day.

ADMIRALTY, 10*th August*, 1782.   15 *m. past* 10 P.M.

No. 3875—*Lord Grantham to the King.*

Lord Grantham sends the King Mr. Fitzherbert's Dispatch upon his arrival at Paris, and his first Conferences with the Minister.

Laujun the Messenger was detained by the wind being contrary thirty hours.

ST. JAMES'S, 11 *Aug.* 1782.

Endorsed by the King.

No. 3876—*The King to Lord Grantham.*

The dispatch which opens Mr. Fitzherbert's correspondence from Paris does Him credit, but the whole manner of Ct. de Vergennes clearly shows that the Negociation will prove abortive.

WINDSOR, *Augt.* 11*th*, 1782. 8 *m. pt.* 6 P.M.

Draft, written on a page of Lord Grantham's letter of same date.

No. 3877—*Lord Shelburne to the King.*

SIR—I have the honour to send Your Majesty the Inclos'd Letters from Paris. One is merely private, but I have great satisfaction in keeping nothing conceal'd from Your Majesty— I consider the being allow'd this liberty, as the most satisfactory circumstance of an arduous situation.

I consider the Treaty mention'd upon the point of conclusion between Spain and America, as the effect of Mr. Fox's precipitation on the head of Independancy.

I had a very long conversation yesterday with the Count de Grasse, perfectly open upon his part, but manners resembling those of the plainest of our Seamen. He stated his anxiety about his own Situation to turn more upon the general execution of his orders, than upon his conduct in regard to the Action. He is very desirous of laying the foundation of a Peace, and mention'd several particulars of his orders, which convinced him that the French Ministry look upon the Independance of America, and the retention of Santa Lucia and Dominique as the Essential points to be insisted on, and every thing else as very negotiable. I assur'd him of Your Majesty's disposition to Peace, and of the Sincerity of your Ministers without entering into particulars— that the great point to be obtained was mutual Confidence. I endeavour'd to give Mr. Fitzherbert and Mr. Oswald all the consideration I could, adding however that any communication made to myself thro' any channel should if requir'd be only known to Your Majesty.

I have been oblig'd to have a very grave conversation with Lord Kepple upon the Relief of Gibraltar and upon the damp thrown by the Admiralty upon the Spirit shewn by the County of Suffolk, the City of London and other places. Lord Kepple alledges the Indispensible necessity of seeing the Baltick Fleet home in the first instance, and the futility of any exertions beyond the very moment. The Comptroller is unluckily out of town till Monday—I shall see him on Tuesday, and shall have the honour of submitting the result to Your Majesty on Wednesday.

I have the honour to be with the highest Respect, Your Majesty's most Dutyfull Subject and Faithfull Servant,

HIGH WYCOMBE, 11th *August*, 1782.   10 *o'clock* P.M.   SHELBURNE.

Endorsed by the King.

No. 3878—*The King to Lord Shelburne.*

WINDSOR, *Augt.* 12th, 1782
m. 20 *pt.* 9 A.M.

I have read the two letters Lord Shelburne received yesterday from France and shall fairly owne that by what I have seen from the Correspondence of Mr. Vaughan I have but little opinion of his tallents, yet it confirms my opinion that Dr. Franklin only plays with us and has no intentions fairly to treat ; Mr. Oswald seems very sensible and the present letter before Me shews He is now not in the least inclined to be indiscreet, the treaty negotiating with Spain is the strongest proof of the insincerity of Dr. Franklin ; I agree with Ld. Shelburne that Mr. Fox's precipitation on the head of Independency has probably forwarded this additional stumbling block. I am sorry to say it but from the beginning of the American troubles to the retreat of Mr. Fox this Country has not taken any but precipitate steps whilst caution and system have been those of Dr. Franklin which is explanation enough of the causes of the present difference of Situation.

Lord Shelburne's language to Count de Grasse has been just what I could have wished.

Nothing could be more proper than Lord Shelburne's holding a serious Conversation with Ld. Keppel for when his conduct is so inimical it would be wrong for him not just to feel that though Ld. Shelburne is not rash, yet He is not blind. I am glad the Comptroller of the Navy is to be with Ld. Shelburne on Tuesday

I think He can clearly give the best opinion on the best conduct with regard to Gibraltar.

Mr. Fitzherbert's first Dispatch which arrived by the Messenger does him credit but the language of Ct. Vergennes gives me no hopes of a Speedy Peace.

Draft, endorsed by the King.

No. 3879—*Lord Keppel to the King.*

Lord Keppel has the honour to transmit to Your Majesty dispatches received this day from Lord Rodney and Lord Hood from Jamaica, which Lord Rodney has sent by Captain Wells of the Volcano fire ship.

ADMIRALTY, *August 12th*, 1782. *56 m. past 3* P.M.

No. 3880—*Mr. Townshend to the King.*

WHITEHALL, *August the 15th*, 1782
20 m. past four P.M.

Mr. Townshend has the honour of transmitting to Your Majesty two Minutes of Cabinet for Your Majesty's Commands upon them, copys of them have been taken.

The Box which Your Majesty was obliged to break open, and returned to Mr. Nepean, Mr. Townshend understands to have been sent from the Treasury having been made use of by Mr. Ord, when in this Office.

Endorsed by the King.

Enclosure. I

MINUTE OF CABINET.

[In Lord Keppel's handwriting.]

August 14th, 1782, A.M.

Present :—Lord Shelburne, Lord Grantham, Mr. Townshend, General Conway, Mr. Pitt, Lord Keppel.

It is humbly recommended to Your Majesty that Lord Howe, as soon as he has completed for sea the Fleet under his Command, should be directed to proceed off of the Texel with a Squadron from twenty to thirty three ships of the Line in quest of the

Dutch Squadron and not finding them there, to proceed as far to the Northward as the Nase of Norway, In order to meet them and give security to the Navigation in the North Seas, and particularly to the Valuable Convoy ready to sail with stores from the Baltick and other Convoys bound thither, and his Lordship having in his judgment rendered the appearances favourable for the safety of the before mentioned trade, to return to Spithead as soon as possible, In Order to proceed upon other very material and Important Service. And it is humbly recommended that Lord Howe should be at Liberty to detach before him off the Texel a division of his Fleet if he judges it necessary.

It is further humbly recommended to Your Majesty that as many of your ships as possibly can be got in readiness should be collected at Spithead In order to join Lord Howe upon his return from the Service of the North Sea.

Should it be advisable to send two ships of the Line to Convoy the East and West India trade Into the Sea before Lord Howe's getting back to Spithead, it is Humbly wished to recommend to Your Majesty that it may be directed If at the time it is judged Expedient.

II

MINUTE OF CABINET.

[In Lord Keppel's handwriting.]

August 14th, 1782, P.M.

Present :—Lord Shelburne, Lord Grantham, Mr. Townshend, General Conway, Mr. Pitt, Lord Keppel.

It is humbly recommended to Your Majesty in Addition to that which was to be offered for Your Majesty's Approbation this morning that Lord Keppel be Empowered to Advise with Lord Howe at portsmouth how probable it may be for the Measure that directs his Lordships going into the North Seas being performed in time, so as to enable the Fleet to again join force at Spithead, in Order to proceed at latest in the first week in September, with the Necessaries and Supplies for the relief of the Garrison of Gibraltar, and that Lord Howe proceeding to the Northward should depend upon the probable certainty of his getting back to Spithead by the time mentioned.

No. 3881—*The King to Mr. Townshend.*

This first Minute of Cabinet transmitted to Me by Mr. Secretary Townshend has my approbation by the very good appendix to it the Second Minute ; He is therefore to give the proper Orders agreeable to both.

WINDSOR, *Augt. 15th*, 1782. 15 *m. pt.* 7 P.M.

Draft, written on a page of Mr. Townshend's letter of same date.

No. 3882—*Mr. Robinson to the King.*

Mr. Robinson has the honour to transmit to Your Majesty the inclosed which he has just received from Wirksworth near Matlock. Mr. Robinson presumes to take the same channel to send it, through which he had the honour to receive Your Majesty's Commands, thinking it may be the proper one, and he hopes that he shall not have erred. Mr. Robinson has sent the Cover it came under to him, as the Wax of the Seals adheres, lest in taking off the one, he shall injure the Seal of the other.

SYON HILL, 19*th Augt.* 1782. 40 *m. p.* 4 P.M.

No. 3883—*The King to Mr. Robinson.*

Mr. Robinson has acted with his usual punctuality in using the same Channel to convey the answer by which He had the letter to which it relates.

WINDSOR, *Augt.* 19*th*, 1782. 46 *m. pt.* 8 P.M.

Draft, written on a page of Mr. Robinson's letter of same date.

No. 3884—*The Bishop of Worcester to the King.*

HARTLEBURY CASTLE. *Aug.* 17, 1782

SIR—I was extremely happy to receive Your Majesty's gracious Letter ; wch. contains the justest reflections on the present temper of the times, and the necessity there is of infusing a better spirit into the rising generation. Your Majesty has done your part in the great work, and it is one of the disgraces of our degenerate age, that the effect of it is not everywhere conspicuous. By degrees however this country must feel the influence of the Royal countenance and example ; and a time will come when your enlarged views for the good of all your subjects, in all parts of your Dominions, will be remembered with honour, while the furious passions of those who disturb and deform God's world, will be held in execration.

Sir, I humbly thank Your Majesty for designing me a further addition to your valuable present of the German Latin books. I am providing a decent Repository for them, and am proud to think what a distinction it will be to this See to have such an obligation to Your Majesty.

Your Majesty's humanity, I perceive, was much affected by the melancholy story I had to tell of Dr. Arnald. He was removed to Leicester, and commited to the care of a skilfull person. I have seen some letters from this person and one of a late date, which was sent me by yesterday's post. By these I learn that his Patient has been, and still is extremely ill, worse, I believe, than he was before : At least the fit is more obstinate, and likely to continue much longer. It was agreeable to your Majesty's usual delicacy to make a secret of this Relapse. But it is scarce possible it should be concealed. And, perhaps, it is not desirable that it should be so. For the notoriety of his case may dispose him to come to such resolutions about his future plan of life, as are most fit and reasonable ; and his being aware that his infirmity is well known will deliver him from a great anxiety in labouring to conceal it.

The very kind, &, I presume to think, just sentiments wch Your Majesty entertains of the unhappy man's virtues, will be a comfort to him when he is made acquainted with them, as he shall be one of these days, but not till he is enough recovered to bear the communication of this intelligence without too much emotion.

I presume to trouble Your Majesty at present with but one word more. The birthdays that have so lately been celebrated at Windsor cannot escape my recollection. And I cannot pay my compliments to the Princess or to Your Majesties better,

than by wishing, as I sincerely and fervently do, that as their
R. Highnesses advance in years, they may advance in filial Piety
and true wisdom.

I am with the deepest sense of Duty and gratitude, Sir,
Your Majesty's most faithfull and most obedient Subject &
Servant,   R. WORCESTER.

No. 3885—*The King to Lord Shelburne.*

LORD SHELBURNE—There is no kind of probability that my
Youngest son can survive the day, I cannot think therefore of
leaving the Queen tomorrow but trust that Religion which is
the only solid assistance to those who are in affliction, will so
far compose her mind that I may on Friday [23rd] as usual be
at St. James's. I desire You will acquaint the other Ministers
of this and that any business that requires being communicated
to Me may be sent ; for I should be sorry that at so critical a
time any business should be in the least suspended.

WINDSOR, *Augt. 20th,* 1782

Endorsed by the King.

No. 3886—*Lord Shelburne to the King.*

SIR—I pray to God, if the melancholy Event Your Majesty
apprehends should have taken place that he will enable both
Your Majesty and the Queen to submit to this first Domestick
Loss with Fortitude and Resignation.

I have obey'd Your Majesty's Commands to the other Ministers,
and have the honour to enclose to Your Majesty a Letter
from Lord Kepple. I had taken care on Saturday to expedite
the several Ships from the different Offices, and have now the
satisfaction to acquaint Your Majesty, that all the Ships are
gone down, except two which the Comptroller assures me this
Evening will certainly be ready on Thursday.

I have been much alarm'd this evening with a flying Report
of some differences on board the Fleet, and Admiral Barrington's
name being mentioned. The Comptroller has heard of it, but

imagines it was confin'd to some of the youngest Captains. I have the honour to send Your Majesty two letters from Captain Jervis, one to Mr. Barré and the other to me, which makes me hope that nothing material can have pass'd, else he would have explained it more particularly.

I am sorry to find Sir James Lowther very much agitated with the delay of the Court of Enquiry appointed to examine into his conduct, and bent upon resigning, and at the same time to request your Majesty's acceptance of a 74 Gun Ship fitted and compleatly mann'd at his own expence. I have endeavour'd to dissuade him from resigning, at least for the present on his own account, and have had recourse to every means possible to bring his business to a proper Issue. As to his intended Offer of a Ship, I told him as a Minister that Your Majesty on the part of the publick might think it too much to accept, at the same time I hop'd I did not do wrong in telling him as a Private Man how much honour such a Step must do him, but that I did not think it proper to carry such an offer hastily to Your Majesty, and should not therefore do it, till he had time to consider it well, and would mention it again.

I take the liberty of adding a Letter of Mr. Baring's, which it was my intention to have laid before Your Majesty tomorrow.

I ask pardon for intruding so much upon Your Majesty at such a time.

I have the honour to be with the highest respect and Attachment, Your Majesty's Devoted Servant and Faithfull Subject,

SHELBURNE.

BERKELEY SQUARE, 20th July, 1782.   12 o'clock at night.

Endorsed by the King.

No. 3887—*The King to Lord Shelburne.*

It is quite right that the Baltick Service should be suspended, as it can be only additional expence, to have the relief of Gibraltar executed with the utmost dispatch, which alone can render the measure effectual.

I am sorry to find that Lord Howe's desire of restoring discipline in the Navy should have caused some ill Humour but

I am clear He must be supported, and that once done that for the future the Service will be mended by this struggle.

I spoke strongly the other day to the Adjutant General of the expediency of preventing the Court Martial on Sir Jas. Lowther; he seemed to think that Gentleman disgraced if not allowed an opportunity to clear himself; I took the Line of only looking to the hartburns it might occasion in the Militia, and therefore it ought to be prevented. If Ld. Shelburne thinks I ought to take any further step I am ready to write to General Conway on the Subject.

Sir Jas. Lowther's offer is so unexpected that Ld. Shelburne has certainly acted properly in advising him to reconsider it.

I am glad to see the spirit that seems to actuate the Gentlemen in Devonshire.

WINDSOR, *Augt. 21st*, 1782. 35 *m. pt.* 9 A.M.

Draft, written on a page of Lord Shelburne's letter of 20 August.

No. 3888—*Lord Grantham to the King.*

Lord Grantham sends Your Majesty a Dispatch received this morning by a Messenger from Mr. Fitzherbert.

May Lord Grantham be permitted to express in the most dutifull manner, his deep concern at the Cause which prevents his receiving Your Majesty's Commands, at St. James's.

ST. JAMES'S.   *Aug. 21.* 35 *m. past* 1 P.M.

Endorsed by the King.

No. 3889—*The King to Lord Grantham.*

The Dispatch Ld. Grantham has received from Mr. Fitzherbert confirms the good opinion his former address had given rise to; I cannot say the conduct of the Comte de Vergennes makes me expect any good; perhaps the wretched State of the French Finances may some months hence be a more powerful cause of Peace than the good inclination of the present Minister of that Court.

I feel very sincerely Ld. Grantham's language on the event that has happened in my family ; I suppose as others that arise of a more pleasant kind, it will be proper to notify it to the different Courts ; if so, Ld. Grantham will order the letters to be prepared and sent for my signature here.

KEW, *Aug. 26th*, 1782. *m.* 18 *past* 3 P.M.

Draft, written on a page of Lord Grantham's letter of same date.

No. 3890—*Lord Grantham to the King.*

ST. JAMES'S. 21 *August*, 1782

As it is not Your Majesty's intention to order a Publick Mourning, Lord Grantham humbly submits a Draft of a Circular Letter to be written to Your Majesty's Ministers abroad ; and which if it meets with Your Majesty's approbation will be despatched on Friday.

Endorsed by the King.

No. 3891—*Mr. Townshend to the King.*

WHITEHALL, *August the* 21, 1782
m. 55 *past one* P.M.

Mr. Townshend humbly presumes to lay before Your Majesty the inclosed Dispatches from Mr. Oswald at Paris. As they contain matter of the utmost importance, upon which as speedy a decision as is possible may be necessary, Mr. Townshend wishes to receive Your Majesty's Commands upon the subject of summoning a meeting of your Cabinet as soon as from their distance they can be easily assembled. The Lord Chancellor being in Staffordshire and Lord Ashburton in Devonshire, this day seven night seems to be as early as they can be expected to attend.

Mr. Townshend hopes he may be allowed respectfully to express the deep concern which he feels for the heavy loss which Your Majesty and the Queen have sustained.

Endorsed by the King.

No. 3892—*The King to Mr. Townshend.*

KEW, *August 21st*, 1782
m. 22 *past* 4 P.M.

The Dispatches from Paris are undoubtedly very unpleasant, and authorize the doubt I have uniformly expressed of any inclination of Dr. Franklin in favour of this country, which I think is now very clear, as also that Mr. Jay is in the same sentiments, but avows them more openly. Before Mr. Townshend can wish to form any opinion to lay before Me on these Papers it is very natural that He should wish to have the sentiments of the whole Cabinet, which cannot be assembled, as they are at such a Distance, before this day seven night. I trust he will therefore send to the Absent Ministers and summon them for that day, and send them a short precis of the business He will then have to lay before them.

Mr. Townshend's expressions on the loss I and the Queen have sustained have the more weight, as he has but too strongly felt similar misfortunes and at more advanced years.   G. R.

No. 3893—*Lord Shelburne to the King.*

21 *August*, 1782

SIR—It grieves me more than I can express that, in a moment when Your Majesty and the Queen suffer under so much Domestick affliction, any advices from abroad should add to Your Majesty's uneasiness.

Mr. Oswald's Dispatches to Mr. Townshend and Mr. Fitzherbert's to Lord Grantham make it almost unnecessary to trouble Your Majesty with the Inclos'd, the reports attempted to be convey'd being evidently and foolishly calculated to alarm and mislead, tho' I know the Writer to be incapable of such Intentions. I perceive Dr. Franklin has taken every advantage of my communication to his Friends and Correspondents. They were made deliberately, and will prove at all times the soundness and fairness of Your Majesty's Proceedings, which will not appear to less advantage when contrasted with those which in their present state at least wear every appearance of Insolence and Craft. As to the Issue to which it is now brought, it is not for me to presume to Judge of Your Majesty's Feelings by my own. I shall consider it merely as a Political Question, and devote my mind to collect every Material which may enable Your Majesty's better Judgment to decide finally upon a matter, which is of itself highly important but render'd infinitely more so by its being complicated with every other question both at home and abroad now depending.

I hope it will be unnecessary to give Your Majesty any further trouble about Sir James Lowther's Court Martial, which is at last I hope in a fair way to be terminated as he wishes.

I have the honour to enclose to Your Majesty another letter from Lord Kepple. I hear nothing further about the Fleet, and hope everything is quiet for the present, which I hope may be the case till Gibraltar is reliev'd. I am very happy to know Your Majesty's determination as to the future discipline of it.

There is an account received of the Duke of Portland's having had a bad Fall from his horse. His Collar Bone has been dislocated, and one of his ribs broke, which is likely to confine him for six weeks at Your Majesty's House in the Phoenix Park. Lord Temple of course means to defer his departure to attend Your Majesty on Wednesday.

I have the honour to be, with the most Dutyfull anxiety for Your Majesty's and the Queen's Health, Sir, Your Majesty's Devoted Subject and servant,   SHELBURNE.

BERKLEY SQUARE. 21 *August*, 1782. 45 *m. past* 3.

Endorsed by the King.

No. 3894—*The King to Lord Shelburne.*

KEW, *Aug.* 21*st*, 1782
m. 5 *past* 6 P.M.

The dispatches from Mr. Oswald which Mr. Townshend has sent to Me fully shew that all Dr. Franklin's hints were only to amuse, for now He through Mr Jay allows that Independence cannot be admitted as sufficient reason for France to make

Peace, that the Dutch and Spaniards must also be satisfied before America can conclude ; that America dislikes G. Britain, loves France, yet that in this strange view we must decidedly grant Independence and retire all Troops prior to any treaty, consequently give everything without any return and then receive Peace if America will grant it, besides an hint that America is to Guarantee the General Peace. I think this must be the Machination of some of those who were lately in Employment ; I do not possibly see how the present Ministry can consent to Independency but as the price of a certain Peace.

These are my hasty thoughts on taking the various Dispatches of Mr. Oswald and the private letters of Mr. Vaughan into one view.

Draft, written on a page of Lord Shelburne's letter of same date.

No. 3895—*Lord Keppel to the King.*

Lord Keppel has the honour to acquaint Your Majesty that he left Portsmouth yesterday ; that he found upon his arrival there the 16th instant the weather so remarkably bad that almost every work became at a Stand and continued so the following day, but since that time there has been great dispatch in refitting the fleet, and now very little left to do, except getting the Ships' Companies paid their wages. Lord Keppel thinks he may venture to assure Your Majesty that Lord Howe will be in readiness to proceed wherever Your Majesty shall approve of his being directed, with at least thirty-two ships of the line, If not more, in a day or two.

Lord Keppel has further the honour to acquaint Your Majesty that there is great reason to hope that the different Victuallers and Ordnance Ships, Loaded in the river for Gibraltar will be assembled in the Downs, if the wind continues Westerly, by ye 28th or 29th, so as to proceed to Spithead as soon after as the wind may come Easterly.

ADMIRALTY. *August 22nd,* 1782. 30 m. *past* 5 P.M.

Endorsed by the King.

No. 3896—*The King to Lord Keppel.*

The assurances Ld. Keppel gives me that Ld. Howe will have in a day or two thirty two ships of the line at least ready for any Service, gives me great satisfaction ; but I am sorry the different Victualling Ships for Gibraltar cannot be assembled in the Downs before the 28th or 29th of this Month.

KEW. *August 22nd,* 1782. *m.* 35 *past* 6 P.M.

Draft, written on a page of Lord Keppel's letter of same date.

No. 3897—*Lord Keppel to the King.*

Lord Keppel has the honour to transmit to Your Majesty Dispatches received by the packet from Jamaica, from Lord Rodney of ye 9th and 10th of July ; From Admiral Pigot of the 10th of July, and from Rear Admiral Rowley of the 9th of July ; Also Captain Bromedge, of the Princess Caroline, letter from off Cork, dated the 7th of this month.

ADMIRALTY. *August 22nd,* 1782. 30 *m. past* 4 P.M.

Endorsed by the King.

No. 3898—*Lord Grantham to the King.*

Baron Nolken out of a very proper Respect to Your Majesty will not trouble Your Majesty with allowing him an Audience, but has remitted the letter of Notification of the Death of the Queen Dowager of Sweden to Lord Grantham, who with Your Majesty's Leave, will direct the usual answer to be given.

ST. JAMES'S. *22nd August,* 1782.

Endorsed by the King.

No. 3899.

MINUTE OF CABINET.   23rd August, 1782
                       m. 35 past 11 A.M.
Copy taken for Mr. Townshend's use.   25 August
The Minute of Cabinet meets with my thorough concurrence,
Mr. Townshend therefore to prepare the proper Orders agreeable
to it.

KEW, August 25th, 1782. m. 47 past 1 P.M.

In the King's hand.

A scrap of paper, referring to the Minute which follows.

[In Lord Keppel's handwriting.]

Present :—Lord President, Duke of Richmond, Lord Shelburne,
Mr. Townshend, Lord Grantham, General Conway, Mr Pitt,
Lord Keppel.

It is humbly recommended to Your Majesty that notwithstanding Lord Howe's former Orders of 15th inst. His Lordship
may be directed to proceed to Gibraltar for the relief of that
Garrison, with as great a force of ships of the line as can be
collected in time as soon as the Ordnance and Victualling Ships
that are to Accompany His Lordship are Arrived at Spithead.

His Lordship is to cause two Battalions of the King's troops
to be received on board the Ships of War under his Command,
distributing of them in the Manner he may judge proper in order
to their being disembarked upon his Arrival at Gibraltar.

His Lordship should be directed to take under his protection
the East and West India Convoys and Accompany them as far
as their ways may lay Conveniently together.

As soon as Lord Howe Arrives within the Straits of Gibraltar,
His Lordship is to use his Exertions and Abilities to effect the
relief of the Garrison, in Landing the Ammunition, provisions
and other necessaries with him for that purpose, As well as the
two Compleat Battalions embarked on board the King's Ships,
and His Lordship is to render every other Assistance to the
Garrison which may appear to him necessary, and which Circumstances will admit of.

It should be recommended to Lord Howe's consideration how

far it may be Advisable to order one of his Ships of the Line of sixty guns to remain at Gibraltar, when he leaves it, for the better defence of the place, as well as to assist in succouring partial reliefs that may be sent by ships running without Convoy. As soon as Lord Howe judges his remaining before Gibraltar of no further Temporary utility to the Garrison, he is, if no Objection appears to it at the time, to leave another Ship of the Line of sixty guns and a Frigate to watch an Oportunity of bringing through the Gutt the Emptied Ships. And His Lordship is to return to England, first detaching to Barbadoes, at the time he judges it most prudent, six ships of the line, Three of seventy-four guns and three of sixty four guns, Compleating their provisions and stores from his other ships in the best manner circumstances may enable him to effect, and directing their Commander on their Arrival at Barbadoes to put themselves under the command of the Senior Officer upon that Station ; And it may be of Importance to have a small detachment stationed to intercept the Enemies Convoys sailing from the French ports in the Bay for their Colonies. Lord Howe should be directed to leave at sea for that purpose two or three Ships of the Line with a frigate or two, ordering the Senior Officer of them to repair to Spithead at the Expiration of one month. No particular directions are offered regarding Lord Howe's meeting the Combined Fleet, but it is humbly recommended to Your Majesty that His Lordship should at all times be directed to use his judgment and discretion upon events and circumstances that cannot be provided for so well as he may determine, when the Object is before him.

No. 3900.

MINUTE OF CABINET.

[In Lord Keppel's handwriting.]

August ye 24th, 1782

Present :—Lord President, Lord Shelburne, Duke of Richmond, Lord Grantham, Mr. Townshend, General Conway, Mr. Pitt, Lord Keppel.

It is humbly recommended to Your Majesty that Lord Howe should be directed to Dispatch Vice Admiral Milbanke as soon as possible if the winds continue westerly with as many Ships of the Line as will make the number Already with Commodore Ho'tham in the Downs fifteen, and such Frigates as His Lordship may think proper ; Vice Admiral Milbanke To be instructed by Lord Howe to proceed off the Texel, where being satisfied that the Dutch are in port, Vice Admiral Milbanke should dispatch a Frigate to Elsineur to apprize the Convoy there of the necessity of their using every exertion in putting to sea and bringing the trade to the different ports of their destination or proceeding North About through the Irish Channel.

Notwithstanding the above wish'd service, Lord Howe should direct the Vice Admiral to allow nothing to divert him from rejoining the Fleet at Spithead with the fifteen ships and frigates put under his Command the first Easterly wind after his leaving Spithead.

No. 3901—*Mr. Townshend to the King.*

WHITEHALL. *August the 24th,* 1782

Mr. Townshend humbly presumes to transmit to Your Majesty the Instructions to the Governor of Nova Scotia as settled in the Committee of Your Majesty's Privy Council to-day. The reason for troubling Your Majesty with them for your signature now is, that Governor Parr is under the necessity of Leaving London to embark for his Government immediately.

Endorsed by the King.

No. 3902—*The Bishop of Worcester to the King.*

HARTLEBURY CASTLE. *Aug.* 24, 1782

SIR—I have the honour of Your Majesty's kind and affecting letter on a late unhappy event. Your Majesty has prevented me in those sentiments of pious resignation which are the only refuge of humanity in its distresses, and wch I could not have expressed so well. Yet the voice of Nature will be heard on these occasions, and I cannot wonder at Your Majesty's anxiety for the Queen, whose parental tenderness will be much affected. I know I can add nothing to what Her Majesty's true sense of religion will suggest to her ; yet I shall hardly forbear, in a day or two, to take the freedom of addressing a few words to Her Majesty, if it be only to express my duty at such a moment, and to testify the sincere part I take in her loss.

It is my pleasure, as well as duty, to put up my dayly prayers to Heaven for Your Majesty and the Queen and the whole Royal Family, wch I can do with redoubled fervour being, with infinite obligation, Sir, Your Majesty's most faithful and devoted subject and servant,   R. WORCESTER.

No. 3903—*Mr. Townshend to the King.*

WHITEHALL. *August the 24th*, 1782
m. 15 *past* 6 P.M.

Mr. Townshend humbly presumes to transmit to Your Majesty the Minutes of two Cabinet Councils held last night and this morning, for Your Majesty's Commands. [See Nos. 3899, 3900.]

No. 3904—*The King to Mr. Townshend.*

Mr. Townshend is to prepare the necessary Orders agreeable to the Minute of Cabinet He has transmitted to Me ; the other Minute I find by Lord Keppel's letter cannot be sent till to-morrow.

KEW, *August 24th*, 1782. *m.* 4 *past* 8 P.M.

Draft, written on a page of Mr. Townshend's letter of same date.

No. 3905—*Lord Grantham to the King.*

Lord Grantham sends Your Majesty a Dispatch from Mr. Fitzherbert ; The subject of which requiring due consideration, he submits to Your Majesty whether he should not take the opinion of Your Majesty's Confidential Servants, who being already summoned, will be in town on Wednesday. Lord

Grantham in the meanwhile, will write generally to Mr. Fitzherbert, preparing him to expect such Instructions as Your Majesty will direct.

RICHMOND. 9 o'clock A.M.   25 August, 1782

Endorsed by the King.

No. 3906—*The King to Lord Grantham.*

There cannot be the smallest doubt of the propriety of Ld. Grantham's idea that no answer can be sent to Mr. Fitzherbert on the proposition of M. de Vergennes concerning the Newfoundland fishery, till the opinion of the whole Ministry can be collected, and consequently that Ld. Grantham must write only generally to Mr. Fitzherbert explaining the reason that will prevent his sending an answer for some days.

I cannot conclude without just observing that it would have been more customary and perhaps liberal to have stated all the propositions, than to have sent but one over ; Mr. Fitzherbert's conduct seems very judicious, and I do not doubt that the Ministry will see the necessity of making France not have so large a part of Newfoundland, unless America is not permitted to have much on that Island ; otherwise between the two, poor England must have the worst share.

KEW. *August 25th*, 1782. *m.* 13 *past* 10 A.M.

Draft, written on a page of Lord Grantham's letter of same date.

No. 3907—*Mr. Townshend to the King.*

WHITEHALL, *Aug.* 30, 1782
m. 30 *past* 12 P.M.

Mr. Townshend humbly presumes to send Your Majesty a Minute of the Cabinet of last night, and likewise some dispatches and intelligence from General Elliot. There is another Dispatch decyphering at present, which shall be transmitted to Your Majesty immediately.

Endorsed by the King.

Enclosure.   MINUTE OF CABINET.

[In Mr. Townshend's handwriting.]

August 29, 1782

Present :—Lord Chancellor, Lord President, Lord Privy Seal, Earl of Shelburne, Duke of Richmond, Lord Grantham, Mr. Pitt, General Conway, Lord Ashburton, Mr. Townshend.

It is humbly recommended to Your Majesty that Mr. Oswald should be ordered to make the Concession of Independence pursuant to the Fourth Article of his Instructions, and to declare his readiness to conclude upon that, and the rest of the Four Articles stated to him by Dr. Franklin as mentioned in Mr. Oswald's letter to the Earl of Shelburne of the tenth of July last. But if the Commissioners should refuse to treat without the previous Acknowledgment of Independence, and should express themselves ready to declare themselves satisfied, with these Four Articles, provided the Independence should be irrevocably acknowledged, without reference to the final Settlement of the Treaty, Mr. Oswald should inform them that he has no Power under the Act of the last Session of Parliament to conclude upon that footing, but that Your Majesty will recommend it to Your Parliament to acknowledge the Independence of the thirteen Colonys absolutely and irrevocably.

No. 3908—*A. Gilmour to the King.*

August 30*th,* 1782

SIR—Your Majesty's known Humanity and Benevolence will, I flatter myself, plead my excuse for presuming humbly to make known to Your Majesty, the very distress'd situation in which I at present feel myself, owing most assuredly, in the first instance, to my own folly and imprudence, of which I can with great Truth assure you, Sir, I have sufficiently repented, and for which I hope Your Majesty will think I have been sufficiently punished, by having been four years banish'd in solitude from the society of the world. And before returning to it, I made every compensation to my Creditors which the settlement of my Estate would permit of. My present and immediate distress, I can with the same truth assure you, Sir, has by no means arisen from the same cause, but from my having been led into it, and by my believing myself to be possessed of an income which I never saw. It would be trespassing too much on Your Majesty's time for me to presume to enter into an explanation of that affair at large, but Mr. Townshend to whom I have long had the honour of being known, and who is perfectly informed of the whole transaction, will if Your Majesty is pleased to lay Your Commands on him, fully state it. And I hope after having had the honour of serving Your Majesty nine years in the Guards and fourteen at the Green Cloth, I believe I may add without vanity, with the approbation of those under whom I served, Your Majesty will be graciously pleased to take my melancholy situation into your consideration. I am very sensible, Sir, that an application of this nature to Your Majesty, ought in course to be made through Lord Shelburne, but as the intimacy I have had the honour of living in with Mr. Townshend makes my situation more fully known to him, than it possibly can be to His Lordship, I have taken the liberty of begging him to submit it, together with my humble request to Your Majesty, which deviation from the common course of business, will not I hope be deemed disrespectful either to Your Majesty or to Lord Shelburne, as I have followed that method of laying myself at Your Majesty's feet, merely for the reason which I have had the honor of mentioning. May I beg leave to assure Your Majesty that in every moment of my life, and on every occasion, you will ever find me, with the most sincere and profound respect, Sir, Your Majesty's most devoted and dutiful humble servant,

A. GILMOUR.

No. 3909.

MINUTE OF CABINET.

[In Lord Grantham's handwriting.]

4th September, 1782

At a Meeting of His Majesty's Confidential Servants, at the Earl of Shelburne's.

Present:—Lord Chancellor, Duke of Richmond, Earl of Shelburne, Ld. Vt. Keppel, Mr. Secry. Townshend, General Conway, Mr. Pitt, Ld. Grantham.

It was agreed humbly to submit to The King that Application should be made to the several German Princes, whose troops are in His Majesty's Service, for such extension of the stipulations of their Treaties with His Majesty, as shall entitle His Majesty to the Compleat Disposal of those troops, in any part of the world, as well as of any additional Corps, which may be taken into His Majesty's Pay.

Endorsed by the King.

No. 3910.

MINUTE OF CABINET.

[In Lord Keppel's handwriting.]

September 5th, 1782

Present:—Lord Chancellor, Lord Shelburne, Duke of Richmond, Lord Grantham, Mr. Townshend, Mr. Pitt, General Conway, Lord Keppel.

It is Humbly recommended to Your Majesty that Lord Howe should be directed to reinforce the detachment of Six Ships of the Line Intended as his Instructions point out for the West Indies, with the addition of one ship of ninety and one ship of eighty guns, of three Decks, at the time His Lordship judges it prudent to dispatch them from his fleet, to their destination.

No. 3911—*Lord Grantham to the King.*

Lord Grantham humbly lays before Your Majesty a Letter from the Officers of the Scots Brigade in the service of Holland.

At the same time he is to acquaint Your Majesty that by good authority there is reason to suppose that the Prosecution against them seems at present to be stopt.

¼ *past* 5 P.M. 7 *Sept.* 1782

No. 3912—*Lord Keppel to the King.*

Lord Keppel has the honour to send Your Majesty a letter just received by Express from Lord Shuldham, inclosing one from Captain Trollop, Commander of the Rainbow, employed upon the Coast of France under Commodore Elliot's Command, giving an account of her having taken a new French Frigate of forty guns.

ADMIRALTY. *Sept. 9th, 1782.* 30 *m. past* 4 P.M.

No. 3913—*The King to Lord Keppel.*

The Account Lord Keppel has sent of the capture of the Hebe by the Rainbow, is the more pleasing as she seems to be every way fit instantly to be taken into Service. I remember Captain Trollope has before distinguished himself, particularly whilst commanding the Kite Cutter.

WINDSOR, *Sept. 9th, 1782. m.* 30 *past* 8 P.M.

Draft, written on a page of Lord Keppel's letter of same date.

No. 3914—*Mr. Townshend to the King.*

WHITEHALL. *Thursday Sept. the* 12, 1782
m. 5 *past* 4 P.M.

Mr. Townshend humbly presumes to transmit to Your Majesty a Paper which was delivered to him this morning by a Person, who came lately from Holland, and says that he has a letter from the Emperor of Morocco, which he is ordered to deliver into Your Majesty's own hand. He is a Jew and has resided some years in Holland. He assigns as the reason for the singular manner in which he makes his appearance with this Letter, that the Emperor wished it to be conveyed to Your Majesty by this private Method, that the Spanish Court might not be apprized of his friendly Disposition. He gave Mr. Townshend to understand that as soon as the Packet was accepted, which he says contains his Credentials, he is to assume the character of Ambassador from the Emperor of Morocco. He was brought to the Office by Mr. Mendez da Costa, a Jew Merchant of reputation and credit in the City, who performed the Office of Interpreter, As this Person mentioned the necessity of secresy, and at the same time of delivering the Letter into Your Majesty's own hands, Mr. Townshend humbly begs to receive Your Majesty's

Commands upon the manner in which you would please to have him introduced to you.

Upon his being informed that in all probability he could not be presented to Your Majesty before Wednesday, he desired that his introduction might be on any day rather than that, as it is a Fast by his Religious Profession.

Endorsed by the King.

No. 3915—*The King to Mr. Townshend.*

WINDSOR, *Sept* 12th, 1782
m. 27 *past* 7 P.M.

This instant I have received Mr. Townshend's letter concerning the Jew the Emperor of Morocco has entrusted with a letter for Me from a desire of renewing the Peace, and giving assistance of Provisions, as formerly ; the mode is so new that I am under some difficulty of knowing how to give directions, though the wishing it may be conveyed privately assists me in the idea that the most suitable method will be to let Mr. Townshend introduce him at the Queen's House, for he could not properly be introduced at St. James's, unless he came in a public character ; Mr Townshend can therefore be at the Queen's House to-morrow at half hour past eleven and will bring the Jew and Mr. Mendez da Costa, the business may pass without any further preparation ; if Mr. Townshend cannot bring him then, if he will only [send] a box there by that hour acquainting Me that he cannot attend, I shall then go on as usual to St. James's.

Draft, written on a page of Mr. Townshend's letter of same date.

No. 3916—*Lord Grantham to the King.*

It is Lord Grantham's indispensible Duty to lay before Your Majesty a Copy of a Letter received by a Merchant by this day's mail, dated Perpignan, the 31st Aug.

At the same Time he must humbly submit to Your Majesty's Consideration, that if there is any Truth in the Advices which it contains, they must have been known at Paris by a Courier from Madrid, on the 28th of Aug. and even by the common Post on the 31st. And it is scarcely possible that such an Event known at Paris on either of those Days should not have found its way to England by this time.

It is to be added to this that the Journal of the Siege to the 18th of August in the Supplement to the Gazette de France of the 3rd inst., gives no Countenance to this Report, but in Effect contradicts it. And that a Gazette of the 6th inst. is totally silent upon it.

St. James's. 13 *Sept.* 1782

Endorsed by the King.

No. 3917—*The King to Lord Grantham.*

Though not sanguine on the Subject of Gibraltar, I owne I do not give more credit to the Account of the Surrender of Gibraltar than Lord Grantham does, but approve much of his having sent the Account.

Windsor. *Sept.* 13*th*, 1782. *m.* 58 *past* 8 P.M.

Draft, written on a page of Lord Grantham's letter of same date.

No. 3918—*Lord Shelburne to the King.*

13 *Sept.* 1782

Sir—I receiv'd the Letter which I have the honour to lay before Your Majesty from Monsr. de Rayneval on Wednesday night. In consequence of my answer, acquainting him that it was not my Intention to return until Tuesday next, but offering to go sooner, or receive him here, he came here this day with Monsr. de Vergennes' Letter. I have the honour to send Your Majesty the copy of a Paper containing Monsr. de Grasse's recollection of my conversation with him, previous to his departure from London. I return'd the original with the most distinct disavowal of every article, except what regarded

America, St. Lucie, Dominique and Dunkirk, which last was alluded to rather than mentioned. Monsieur de Rayneval stated it then as a mere memorandum between Monsr. de Grasse and Monsr. de Vergennes, and never intended to be communicated back to me, without pressing any of the other articles, as under my sanction.

I hope I shall not do Monsr. de Rayneval the same Injustice in stating for Your Majesty's Information, what I have been able to collect from some hours conversation with him, of Monsr. de Vergennes' disposition.

In regard to the Fishery, he repeated the Proposition laid before Your Majesty by Mr. Fitzherbert, but they appear disposed to relax as to the limits first stated, particularly to the Southward from Cape Ray to Cape May.

In the West Indies to Insist on St. Lucie and Dominique, and restore everything else.

In Africa, they desire Senegal and its dependencies or else certain means of being supplied with Negroes without our Intervention.

In the East Indies they expect to be restor'd to what they possess'd in 1749—as after the Peace of Aix in the end of 1748 they obtain'd grants of the Country Powers which they assert were intended to have been included in the Treaty of Paris, but were not for want of proper information, or if this is not agreed to, to have so much annex'd to each of their ancient settlements as may contribute to support them, without extending to provinces or to any Idea of Territorial Revenue, for supplying their Investment or return to Europe.

The Abrogation of all Articles respecting Dunkirk.

He states himself as no ways authoriz'd to treat for Spain, but alledges that no Peace can take place without Gibraltar, that in his opinion, supposing it taken or not, The King of Spain would be dispos'd to cede Oran and its dependencies to Your Majesty, which he affects to consider as a better harbour than Port Mahon. I upheld the impossibility of ever ceding it so strongly, that I could form no guess about their disposition regarding Porto Rico.

I could not discover any disposition to make a greater stand than Decency required in favour of the Dutch, after leaving nothing unsaid to ascertain so important a point.

Upon the whole, Monsr. de Rayneval appears a Well-Instructed, Inoffensive Man of Business, and makes the most decided Professions on the part of Monsr. de Vergennes, whom he states as desirous to expedite everything which can contribute to an Instant and final conclusion, as nearly as possible, upon these Ideas. The point of Independence once settl'd, He appears rather Jealous than partial to America upon other points, as well as that of the Fishery. He desir'd to be govern'd by my advice, and shew'd me a letter under a Flying Seal to Lord Grantham, which he was to deliver or not, as I should advise.

I have therefore taken the part of sending my Servant, who I hope will be at Windsor at seven o'clock to-morrow morning, and if I am honour'd with Your Majesty's Commands in the course of to-morrow, Monsieur de Rayneval, who stays here till Sunday morning may see Lord Grantham on Monday, if Your Majesty thinks it proper. I presume Your Majesty would not think it proper that this communication should be extended much further at present, as it is expressly stated to be reserv'd from any of the Ministers in France except the Comte de Vergennes.

I have the honour to be, with the highest respect, Your Majesty's dutyfull subject, SHELBURNE.

BOWOOD PARK. 13th September, 1782. 11 o'clock P.M.

Endorsed by the King.

No. 3919—The King to Lord Shelburne.

WINDSOR. September 14th, 1782
m. 40 past 9 A.M.

On returning from Chappel I have received Lord Shelburne's box ; the Paper containing M. de Grasse's conversation with him is an additional proof of a French Man of Quality even making his Imagination supply his Memory with what may be advantageous to his Country and very easily making Truth yield to that consideration ; I am therefore not surprised it has been so distinctly in most Articles disavowed.

By Lord Shelburne's account if we are not too eager to advance the Negotiation, I should hope as to the Newfoundland Fishery it may be settled to mutual advantage.

As to Africa, I am not sufficiently Master of the subject to know whether Senegal would not secure them the whole lead of the Slave Trade ; if it does not, it is getting rid of a Climate that certainly sweeps off a terrible number of my Subjects.

I am perfectly shocked as to the demands in the East Indies ; from thence and the West Indies we must alone, I fear after such a Peace as we are but too likely to make, to [sic] expect any Chance of putting this Country again into any flourishing State ; therefore if we are not very cautious, what concessions are made in those parts, nothing but eternal ruin can ensue.

As to what He alledges that more would have been done for France by the Treaty of Paris in the East Indies, had not information been wanting, is a fresh instance of the useful Memory those Negotiators are possessed of, and thoroughly void of truth.

Dunkirk certainly is of much less consequence than many other points, and therefore, if it can render other terms better, ought not to be in the least an object with us.

That Oran is a good port is quite new to Me, and I certainly doubt it, as it is offered as an equivalent for Gibraltar ; Porto Rico is the object we must get for that Fortress.

I hope Lord Shelburne is not deceived by the Appearance of Monsr. de Rayneval ; I owne the Art of Monsr. de Vergennes is so well known that I cannot think he would have sent him if he was an inoffensive Man of Business ; but that He has chosen him from having that appearance whilst well-armed with Cunning, which will be the more dangerous if under so specious a Garb.

Mons. de Rayneval ought certainly to see Lord Grantham, and the Communication ought certainly to go no further till it is sure whether anything can arise through this Channel.

I am ready to undergo any personal difficulties, but I owne I flinch whenever I think I may be in the end an instrument of effecting a bad Peace, which to prevent present difficulties may occasion lasting ones to my Country.

Draft, written on a page of Lord Shelburne's letter of 13 Sept.

No. 3920—*Lord Grantham to the King.*

Lord Grantham lays before Your Majesty a Dispatch from Mr. Fitzherbert. The French Minister in every respect but that of wanting to gain Time, seems plausible enough.

The Date of this Dispatch, added to the observation of the Dates—known yesterday, puts the Report about Gibraltar entirely out of the question.

6 P.M. 14 *Sept.* 1782

Endorsed by the King.

No. 3921—*The King to Lord Grantham.*

Perhaps I have so rooted an aversion to the duplicity of the French Court that I see with a jaundiced eye whatever comes from thence ; yet I cannot help acknowledging to Lord Grantham that the long Dispatch from Mr. Fitzherbert seems to contain nothing but the desire of gaining time. He is right in his information that Mr. Gerard de Rayneval is the person intended to transact with this Court ; indeed, he is arrived and is gone to Bowood. He has a letter for Ld. Grantham which he will deliver on Monday, and I have desired Lord Shelburne—as it is desired that as yet only Him, Lord Grantham and Myself shall be acquainted with this—that till some light is seen it may not be further communicated ; I thought it right to give this hint to Ld. Grantham, who I am certain however Mr. Gerard may be commended, will judge it right to speak very cautiously with so clever a man, and who I trust is not void of intrigue.

WINDSOR. *Sept. 14th*, 1782. *m.* 30 *past* 8 P.M.

Draft, written on a page of Lord Grantham's letter of same date.

No. 3922—*Lord Shelburne to the King.*

SIR—I have the honour to inclose to Your Majesty several Letters receiv'd mostly this morning from Paris. I have written to Lord Ashburton to know his opinion, how far the Act admits of what is desir'd, whether any expedient can be adopted, or any clause added, to provide against the consequences of the Negotiation's breaking off.

I have likewise the honour to send Your Majesty the Final Result of what passed between Mr. Rayneval and me previous to his leaving this. I made him write it to prevent again the Interposition of French Imagination.

I have held the point of Gibraltar so high that the alternative of Porto Rico may be catch'd at, I flatter myself whenever the time comes for it to be hinted by way of compensation or Exchange on the part of Your Majesty.

If any confidence is to be had in the Channell, I can speak much more positively as to the Harbour of Trincomalee the most valuable possession by every account in all the East but I lay this before Your Majesty as a point which requires the last degree of Secresy.

I have taken the best measures in my power to be precisely inform'd of the Northern and Western Coasts of Newfoundland ; likewise of the present state of the French Settlements in India from 1749 to 1754, and what districts may safely be allowed them. I propose going to Town without delay that all these facts may be laid before Your Majesty if possible on Wednesday.

As to the general Measure, I am as clearly of opinion against a Peace as I ever was against American Independence, till in fact the Resolutions of the House of Commons decided the point. I am very clear that Your Majesty has within your Dominions Resources of every kind, if they could be brought forth. But Your Majesty knows, what I am mortyfy'd to allude to, better than any of your subjects ; The State of both Army and Navy ; The few Subjects capable of supplying what is wanted in regard to both Services ; The State of Ireland, and that of the House of Commons, sufficiently exemplified in a Letter which Your Majesty has lately receiv'd. This obliges me in opposition to my own Temper, Conviction in many respects, and Interest, if I am capable of feeling any, separate from that of Your Majesty and Your Family, to state as clearly as I am able the other side of the question, least supposing Your Majesty could bring your mind still to risk so great a Stake on such weak abilitys, with the means I have stated, I may not be to reproach myself with consequences, which I may never be able to repair.

I presume to open my Heart to Your Majesty, meaning to do it with as much Personal Respect as I feel Devotion and Loyalty.

I have the honour to be, Your Majesty's dutyfull subject and faithfull servant, SHELBURNE.

BOWOOD PARK, 15th Sept. 1782. 11 o'clock P.M.

Endorsed by the King.

No. 3923—*The King to Lord Shelburne.*

WINDSOR. *Sept 16th,* 1782
m. 2 *past* 10 A.M.

Ld. Shelburne has acted very properly in writing to Ld. Ashburton concerning the new idea of Altering the full powers ; previous to any opinion whether it is right it is necessary to know whether it is legal.

The holding Gibraltar very high is quite judicious and if not taken I should hope Porto Rico may be got for it.

Certainly Trincomalee as represented seems a very desirable object, and as such cannot be kept too secret.

I am glad Ld. Shelburne is coming to Town more fully to investigate the bounds of Newfoundland and the East India points, that the interest of this Country in both may not wantonly be sacrificed.

As to the general question on Peace, I am too much agitated with the fear of sacrificing the interests of my Country by hurrying it on too fast, which indeed has been uppermost in my thoughts since the beginning of the War, that I am unable to add anything on that subject but the most fervent Prayers to Heaven to guide me so to act that Posterity may not lay the downfall of this once respectable Empire at my door ; and that if ruin should attend the measures that may be adopted, I may not long survive.

Draft, written on a page of Lord Shelburne's letter of 15 September.

No. 3924—*Lord Keppel to the King.*

Lord Keppel has the honour to transmit to Your Majesty Dispatches from Lord Rodney, who is arrived at Kinsale in the

Montagu. Lord Keppel also sends to Your Majesty Vice-Admiral Drake's letter of ye 14th from the Downs, and one from Hull of ye 14th inst, by which it may be hoped that the Dutch squadron is yet in the Texel.

BAGSHOT PARK. *September 16th,* 1782. *m.* 30 *past* 5 *o'clock*

No. 3925—*The King to Lord Keppel.*

Lord Keppel's Intelligence seems to prove the Dutch Fleet still in the Texel, and this may secure the passage for the Baltick Trade ; if Rear Adm. Greaves arrives as soon as expected, and that the Bombay Castle, Pegase, and Montagu can go to his Reinforcement, I should think Him fully able to meet the Dutch Fleet if they attempt to dispute the entrance of the Channel.

WINDSOR. *Sept.* 16th, 1782. *m.* 56 *past* 7 P.M.

Draft, written on a page of Lord Keppel's letter of same date.

No. 3926—*Lord Grantham to the King.*

Lord Grantham not being able to send Your Majesty the very long Dispatches from Petersburgh before three o'clock this day, did not presume to trouble Your Majesty with them in the evening, but directed the Messenger to be at Windsor early to-morrow morning.

The forwarding an Alliance, the Admission of the King of Prussia to a Share in the Mediation, and the Expectation of Support from Russia, seem at this time to be entirely suspended, as the Empress is wholly taken up with the Concerns of the Crimea.

ST. JAMES'S. 17th *September,* 1782. 9 P.M.

Endorsed by the King.

No. 3927—*The King to Lord Grantham.*

WINDSOR. *Sept.* 18*th*, 1782
m. 58 *past* 8 A.M.

I am glad Lord Grantham kept back the Dispatches from Petersburgh till this Morning, for I owne I can read papers of consequence to more effect in an early period of the day than in the evening.

The conduct of Sir James Harris has been exactly right, and the only result to be drawn from his well-digested Correspondence is that whatever is the object of the hour so fully engrosses the Empress that every other of ever so great consequence falls unheeded. We are, therefore, in the usual dilemma convinced that if less suspicious She is not more active in Her inclination towards Us, and that it is in the Emperor's power totally to guide Her in the affairs of Europe, if He will blindly follow Her in the Turkish dispute, or if He holds back to forfeit Her esteem, and then perhaps She may be brought to think the welfare of this Kingdom an object that regards her more nearly.

Draft, written on a page of Lord Grantham's letter of same date.

No. 3928.

MINUTE OF CABINET.

[In Mr. Townshend's handwriting.]

Monday Sept. 19, 1782

Present :—Lord President, Lord Privy Seal, Earl of Shelburne, Lord Grantham, Lord Keppel, Mr. Pitt, Mr. Townshend.

It is humbly recommended to Your Majesty that a new Commission be made out under Your Majesty's Great Seal for enabling Mr. Oswald to treat with the Commissioners appointed by the Colonys, under the title of Thirteen United States, inasmuch as the Commissioners have offered under that condition to accept the Independence of America as the First Article of the Treaty.

No. 3929—*Lord Shelburne to the King.*

Sir—I flatter myself Your Majesty will excuse the liberty I take in forwarding the inclos'd account the instant I have receiv'd it.

I have the honour to be, with the highest respect, Your Majesty's most dutyfull subject,   Shelburne.

Berkley Square, *21st September*, 1782.   25 *m. past* 11

Endorsed by the King.

No. 3930—*Lord Keppel to the King.*

Lord Keppel has the honour to transmit to Your Majesty Dispatches received this morning from Gibraltar from Captain Curtis, sent by Lieutenant Campbell of the Brilliant, who left the place the 5th inst. in an open boat with six seamen, and arrived safe in her at Faro. Lord Keppel also sends Your Majesty the account of The Dutchess of Richmond Ordnance return to Plymouth from damages received, having left Lord Howe's Fleet the 16th instant in the latitude of 48 ; 52 N. 10 ; 43 W, in a situation that may give hopes of His Lordship's soon reaching the coast of Cape Finister.

The appearance of the Baltick Convoy off Flamborough Head on Thursday last, the account of which came by express from Hull to town this morning, is a most pleasing information and Lord Keppel has much satisfaction in being able to convey to Your Majesty so Important an event.

Admiralty, *September 21st*, 1782.   *m.* 20 *past* 3 P.M.

No. 3931—*The King to Lord Keppel.*

By the dispatches Lord Keppel has communicated to Me, it appears that the good understanding between Gen. Elliott and Capt. Curtis continues, which is a most happy circumstance and that they are doing their utmost to counteract the Enemy ; I should hope Lord Howe will soon arrive to their assistance.

The news of the safe arrival of the Baltick Fleet off of the Yorkshire Coast is a most fortunate event.

WINDSOR. *Sept. 21st, 1782. m. 2 past 6 P.M.*

Draft, written on a page of Lord Keppel's letter of same date.

No. 3932—*Lord Grantham to the King.*

Lord Grantham would have sent Your Majesty the Result of his last Conference with M. de Reineval [*sic*], at which Lord Shelburne was present, as soon as it was over yesterday, if he had not thought that the Drafts which he now lays before Your Majesty, would serve to convey accurately and fully the substance of what passed on that occasion.

Lord Grantham proposes, with Your Majesty's leave, to send a Messenger immediately to Paris, in order that Mr. Fitzherbert's language may correspond to that which was used to M. de Raineval [*sic*].

RICHMOND. *22nd September, 1782. 11 P.M.*

Endorsed by the King.

No. 3933—*Lord Keppel to the King.*

Lord Keppel has the honour to send Your Majesty Dispatches from Rear Admiral Digby, sent from New York by the packet, and which were this day received.

ADMIRALTY, *September 22nd, 1782. m. 5 past 5 P.M.*

No. 3934—*The King to Lord Grantham.*

Lord Grantham's thinking his Drafts would be the most accurate method of laying before Me the Substance of what passed in his last Conference with M. de Rayneval, at which Ld. Shelburne assisted, was very judicious.

The Messenger ought directly to proceed to Paris that Mr. Fitzherbert may use suitable language to that held here, and that He may be properly prepared to treat with Cte. de Vergennes when called upon.

WINDSOR. *Sept. 23rd, 1782. m. 58 past 8* A.M.

Draft, written on a page of Lord Grantham's letter of same date.

No. 3935—*The King to Lord Keppel.*

I return the dispatches the Admiralty has received from R. Ad. Digby. I shall be glad when Lord Keppel can communicate that the West India Squadron or at least the greatest part of it is arrived off of New York, till which time I shall feel unpleasant, though I trust the shattered French ones must require some time to refit at Boston.

WINDSOR. *Sept. 23rd, 1782. m. 2 past 9* A.M.

Draft, written on a page of Lord Keppel's letter of 22nd September.

No. 3936—*Lord Grantham to the King.*

Lord Grantham receiving the enclosed Dispatches from Mr. Fitzherbert, sends them immediately to Your Majesty and humbly submits, that it not being expedient to delay the Messenger, he has taken upon himself to write to Mr. Fitzherbert in the Terms of the Draft sent now to Your Majesty.

1 P.M. ST. JAMES'S. *23rd Septr. 1782.*

Endorsed by the King.

No. 3937—*The King to Lord Grantham.*

Ld. Grantham has very properly wrote to Mr. Fitzherbert, the demand of the Dutch is the most preposterous, I have ever heard, what was perhaps lavishly offered to excite a separate Negociation cannot be admitted when they remain to come in at the fag end of a General Pacification.

I cannot help just remarking that Cte Vergennes' silence to Mr. Fitzherbert on having sent M. de Raineval and his Applause of the principles of the New Marine Code of the North which is quite contrary to what his Commis. declared, gives little room for his veracity or candour being relied upon.

WINDSOR. *Sept. 23rd*, 1782. *m.* 40 *past* 10 P.M.

No. 3938—*Mr. Townshend to the King.*

WHITEHALL. 11 P.M. *24th Sept.* 1782

Mr. Townshend humbly presumes to acquaint Your Majesty, that he has just received from Lady Algernon Percy a Letter for Your Majesty from His Royal Highness the Duke of Gloucester which she desired, might be conveyed as early as possible.

Mr. Townshend avails himself of this opportunity of mentioning to Your Majesty, that he has received the Commission from the Lord Chancellor, and has forwarded it to Mr. Oswald at Paris ; and of acquainting Your Majesty that Governor Franklin has desired him to receive Your Commands as to the time when you will please to receive the Address from the Loyalists and Refugees at New York, a copy of which was sent to Your Majesty with Sir Guy Carleton's last Dispatches.

The Commissions for Successions in the Army in Ireland will be immediately made out, if Your Majesty is pleased to signify your Approbation.

Endorsed by the King.

No. 3939—*Lord Keppel to the King.*

[25 *September*, 1782]

Lord Keppel has the honour to transmit to Your Majesty Admiral Pigot's letter of the 16th of July by the packet received this day, and to observe that the services proposed for the Fleet with him may occasion it being near the end of August before it will arrive at New York. Lord Keppel takes this opportunity of informing Your Majesty that many of the Leeward Island Convoy are arrived in the Downs, Spithead and Bristol Channel, with the Rotterdam, Orpheus and Tryton. The Janus of fifty guns that was with many of them when parted with off Cape Clear, and it may be hoped will be heard of in port to-morrow [sic].

No. 3940—*The King to Lord Keppel.*

I am sorry to find it is Ld. Keppel's opinion that the Fleet will not arrive off of New York before the end of August, as it must keep those there under very unpleasant suspense, and certainly, after the intelligence given by Sir Jas. Wallis, does not do great credit to the activity or decision of those that have and do command that Fleet.

The safe arrival of part of the Leeward Island Convoy in the Downs is most fortunate ; the rest I trust will soon follow.

WINDSOR. *Sept. 26th* 1782. *m.* 10 *past* 9 A.M.

Draft, written on a page of Lord Keppel's undated letter [25 *September*].

No. 3941—*Lord Shelburne to the King.*

SIR—The Letter from Lord Temple, which I have the honour to enclose to Your Majesty is the occasion of my presuming to trouble Your Majesty from hence.

I take the same opportunity of enclosing to Your Majesty a Letter from Lord Surry and one from Mr. Baring, observing what is mention'd in Mr. Fitzherbert's last Dispatch, touching a Treaty of Commerce as well as Peace, reminds me to acquaint Your Majesty that Monsr. Rayneval did throw it out in his first conversation. I told him that the Minds of the Publick here required first to be calm'd, and afterwards convinc'd on such subjects, before any such fundamental change could be thought of in our Commercial System. I gave him the British Merchant to read, a Book which has formed the principles of nine-tenths of the Publick since it was first written, and further told him as my own opinion that a Liberal Peace might perhaps remove many Prejudices, and could alone lay a foundation for a friendly discussion of reciprocal Commercial Interests. I satisfied him, as I thought, so entirely on this head, that I thought it unnecessary to detain Your Majesty with the particulars, till points which pressed for Immediate determination gave Your Majesty leisure to enter upon those which as yet cannot be considered as more than merely speculative.

I have the honour to be, with the highest Respect, Your Majesty's Dutyfull Subject and Faithfull Servant,

Bowood Park, 26th Sept. 1782. 8 o'clock P.M.   SHELBURNE.

Endorsed by the King.

No. 3942—*The King to Lord Shelburne.*

I am much obliged by Ld. Shelburne's Dispatch in sending the letter he has received from Lord Temple ; as Lord Bellamont is pretty rapid in his Motions, I should not be surprised if I found him this day at St. James's ; He certainly has for some years wished to meet with my approbation, and as I am now apprized of his intention of coming to Me, I shall not despair of putting Him into a better Channel than being an attender of Mr. Flood.

I have signed the Appointment of Lord Surry, and am glad He seems now heartily in the cause, indeed whoever does not mean confusion must take that part.

Mr. Baring by his account of Senegal and Goree fully answers the expectations in his favour Lord Shelburne has raised in my mind, and will I am confident prove very useful.

The last Conference Mr. Fitzherbert had with Cte Vergennes which Lord Shelburne's letter alludes to, does not raise one's opinion of his sincerity, the silence on the journey of Rayneval and the supporting the absurd claims of the Dutch but too clearly demonstrate it.

Lord Shelburne's answer to Mr. Rayneval concerning a new Commercial Treaty was very wise ; it is dangerous to be entering into that till we very clearly see our way.   G. R.

Windsor. *Sept. 27th,* 1782. *m.* 40 *past* 7 A.M.

Draft, endorsed by the King.

No. 3943—*Mr. Townshend to the King.*

WHITEHALL, *Sept. 27th*, 1782. *m.* 10 P.M.

Mr. Townshend humbly presumes to acquaint Your Majesty that he has seen Mr. Laurens, who pleading the dangerous state of his health has desired him to ask Your Majesty's permission to remain in England till the sailing of the November Packet, that he may have an opportunity of using the Bath Waters.

Endorsed by the King.

No. 3944—*Lord Grantham to the King.*

[The news alluded to is that of the relief of Gibraltar by Lord Howe.]

Lord Grantham humbly begs leave to express the satisfaction he feels at having the honour to convey the very important news sent herewith to Your Majesty.

ST. JAMES'S, *30th Sept.* 1782. *m.* 50 *pt.* 1 P.M.

Endorsed by the King.

No. 3945—*Lord Shelburne to the King.*

SIR—I have the honour to send Your Majesty, the Letters which I have just receiv'd from Paris.

I have the honour to be with the highest Respect, Your Majesty's Dutyfull Subject,   SHELBURNE.

STREATHAM, *3rd Octr.* 1782. ¼ *past* 2 P.M.

Endorsed by the King.

No. 3946—*The King to Lord Shelburne.*

Lord Shelburne does not I am clear admire the style of Mr. Vaughan's letters more than I do ; He seems to look alone to our placing implicit trust in the Americans, whilst Ld. Shelburne's ideas coincide with mine in thinking it safer to confide in France than in either Spain or America.

WINDSOR, *Nov.* 3rd [should be *Oct.* 3rd] 1782. 51 *m. pt.* 6 P.M.

Draft, written on a page of Lord Shelburne's letter of same date.

No. 3947—*The King to Lord Shelburne.*

Lord Shelburne having desired to have my opinion this day on the two first Collumns of the Abstract referred to in Mr. Gilbert's Report viz the former Sallaries of the Offices anihilated by the new Civil List Act and the Officers to be entered at the Exchequer as disallowed for the future. I consent to the second Collumn the first is by the highest Authority already fixed. Being uncertain whether the Papers are the originals or only Copies, I send the Report and the Schedule No. 1. Wardrobe Office, No. 4 Jewell Office, No. 6 Board of Works, No. 10 Ld. Steward's Office, to which that Second Collumn relates. At the time these reductions are made the Employments to be kept up to supply the business of the Wardrobe ought to be established as also of the Jewell Office, undoubtedly Mr. Egerton ought not to have less than 300 £ per Annum as He is now to be the Chief Officer in that department ; the Board of Works ought also to be instantly appointed agreable to Mr. Gilbert's proposal or even repair instantly stopps if the new regulation does not instantly take effect. I suppose the Ld. Steward will be acquainted what Offices are to be struck off at the Exchequer previous to effecting it.

I will make myself fully master of some of the other offices to be able to settle them on Wednesday ; I must have the report back before that time as I shall wish to have the Schedules I now send as soon as convenient.

WINDSOR, *Oct.* 7th, 1782. 10 *m. pt.* 9 A.M.

Draft, endorsed by the King.

No. 3948—*Lord Shelburne to the King.*

SIR—Immediately on receiving Your Majesty's Commands I have sent for Mr. Gilbert, and as soon as I can see him, I will have the honour to return to Your Majesty the Report and Schedules as directed together with the explanations Your Majesty desires, more distinctly that I can attempt to give them without his assistance.

I will take care to see Sir Francis Drake and always intended [to] communicate with the head of each Department, as soon as I know Your Majesty's pleasure in the general, to hear what observations they had to make, and if requisite to lay them before Your Majesty prior to a final Decision.

I have the honour to enclose to Your Majesty a Letter of Intelligence rec'd last night from Paris, and have the honour to acquaint Your Majesty that I likewise receiv'd last night a Note from the Chevalier Pinto to say, that he had good Intelligence from Holland imparting, that Ten Dutch Ships of the Line were upon the point of sailing to join 7 or 8 French ships assembl'd at Brythe and suspected to be intended against Jersey or Guernsey. Finding Mr. Stephens was not in town nor at Fulham, but at some distance from whence he is expected to return however this Forenoon, I sent a Messenger into Suffolk to Lord Kepple with this Intelligence.

I have not been able to find any port on the Map Spelt Brythe, and am not sufficiently acquainted with the French Ports to pretend to guess, whether it may be St. Brieux which is meant, and lyes on the Channell side of Brest.

I have the honour to be with the highest Respect, Your Majesty's most Dutyfull Subject, SHELBURNE.

BERKELEY SQUARE, *7th Octr.* 1782. *50 m. past* 1 P.M.

Endorsed by the King.

No. 3949—*Lord Shelburne to the King.*

SIR—I have the honour to enclose to Your Majesty the Report and Schedules, and to acquaint your Majesty, that the reason

Mr. Gilbert did not include in his second Column the Offices, which he proposes should be abolish'd under the Lord Chamberlain, is that they are not directed by the Act, whereas those in the first Column are particularly enumerated, and those in the secon'd tho' not particulariz'd are included under the general Terms of the Act as dependant on the former, and both order'd to be enter'd at the Exchequer before the 10th of this Month. I thought it would be more agreeable to Your Majesty to keep every further Reduction separate both for the purpose of giving Your Majesty more time for consideration, and that Your Majesty might not be deprived of the power of reviving them, if you thought fit, which will not be possible in regard to all those enter'd at the Exchequer.

I presume Your Majesty will have no objection to Mr. Arden having the honour to Kiss Your Majesty's hand on Wednesday as Solicitor General, as he waits in town for that purpose.

I have the honour to be with the highest Respect, Your Majesty's most Dutyfull Subject,   SHELBURNE.

BERKELEY SQUARE, 7th Octr. 1782. ½ past 11 P.M.

Endorsed by the King.

No. 3950—*The King to Lord Shelburne.*

The packet sent by Ld. Shelburne is safely arrived ; He may direct Mr. Arden to be presented tomorrow at St. James as Solicitor General.

WINDSOR, *Oct. 8th*, 1782. 50 *m. pt.* 7 A.M.

Draft, written on a page of Lord Shelburne's letter of 7 Oct.

No. 3951—*Lord Shelburne to the King.*

SIR—I have the honour to send Your Majesty the Letters which I have receiv'd from Paris this morning, together with the Copy of the Short Note, to which Mr. Oswald's is an answer.

The Schedule No. 4 belongs to those return'd to Your Majesty, It was left by mistake at the Treasury last night, where I had sent them to be copied.

I have likewise the honour to return Your Majesty's Box.

I have the honour to be with the highest Respect, Your Majesty's most Dutyfull Subject and Devoted Servant,

SHELBURNE.

BERKELEY SQUARE, 8th Octr. 1782. 25 m. past one P.M.

Endorsed by the King.

P.S. I have had the Duke of Manchester and Lord Carlisle who came to Town yesterday for a few days, and communicated with both upon what regarded their Departments.

No. 3952—*The King to Lord Shelburne.*

The letters Ld. Shelburne has received this day from Paris certainly bear much stronger marks of Peace being wished there, than had as yet appeared.

WINDSOR, *Oct. 8th,* 1782. 40 m. pt. 6 P.M.

Draft, written at the foot of Lord Shelburne's letter of same date.

No. 3953—*Lord Grantham to the King.*

Lord Grantham entreats Your Majesty's Pardon, for having kept the French & Spanish Papers so long.

He proposes, according to Your Majesty's Orders, laying them before Your Confidential Servants, as soon as they are all in Town.

In the mean while he has dispatched a Messenger to Paris, with the Letter of which Your Majesty receives the Draft herewith.

13th *October,* 1782

Endorsed by the King.

No. 3954—*Mr. Townshend to the King.*

Mr. Townshend humbly presumes to submit to Your Majesty whether it would not be proper for him to take the opinion of Your Majesty's Confidential Servants upon the Subject of the last Dispatches from Paris. As several of the Members of the Cabinet are at a distance Mr. Townshend ventures to propose Wednesday as the earliest day upon which it can easily be assembled.

WHITEHALL, *Monday* 11 P.M. *14th Oct.* 1782

Endorsed by the King.

No. 3955—*The King to Mr. Townshend.*

Mr. Townshend is quite right in wishing to have a Meeting of the Cabinet on Wednesday to lay before it the last dispatches from Mr. Oswald, as they require the maturest deliberation before they can be answered ; it will be right also to take under consideration the Secret and Confidential Dispatches from the Ld. Lieut. of Ireland, which are undoubtedly easier decided upon, as by the one now arrived He declares the not wanting an opinion which the former ones seemed to call for, but an Approbation of the part he has taken.

WINDSOR, *Oct.* 15*th,* 1782. 25 *m. pt.* 7 P.M.

Draft, written on a page of Mr. Townshend's letter of 14 Oct.

No. 3956.

MINUTE OF CABINET.

[In Mr. Townshend's handwriting.]

Oct. 17, 1782

Present :—Lord Chancellor, Lord President, Lord Privy Seal, Earl of Shelburne, Duke of Richmond, Lord Grantham, Lord Keppel, Mr. Pitt, General Conway, Mr. Townshend.

It is humbly represented to Your Majesty, that Mr. Townshend should send full instructions to Mr. Oswald at Paris either in writing or by some proper and confidential Person regarding the Boundarys to be fixed by the Treaty between Your Majesty's Colonys and those ceded to the Americans, That Mr. Oswald should be directed to insist upon as large an extension as can be obtained to the South West òf Nova Scotia on the side of Sagadahock to the Province of Main, and in the case of failure in these Claims, to refer them to Commissarys, as mentioned by the American Commissioners, rather than agree to a bad Boundary. That he should state Your Majesty's Right to the Back Country and urge it as a means of providing for the Refugees, saying however that Your Majesty is willing to recede from the same upon condition that the United States make a just provision for the Refugees, or in case other means shall occur in the Course of the Treaty with France and Spain.

That he should resist the Claim of drying fish on the Island of Newfoundland, on account of the danger of disputes and their own coast furnishing them sufficient convenience for drying.

That the Freedom of Navigation on the Mississippi should be agreed to, as proposed in the Fourth Article of the Treaty but that the remainder of that Article respecting Navigation can not at present be adopted, it appearing to be much more for the convenience of both Partys to refer it to a Treaty of Commerce, for which it is a proper subject, and that Mr. Oswald should assure the Commissioners, that Your Majesty is desirous of entering into such a Treaty.

The Discharge of Debts due to British Merchants before the War to be again urged strongly.

No. 3957.

MINUTE OF CABINET.

[In Lord Grantham's handwriting.]

At a Meeting of Your Majesty's Confidential Servants at the Earl of Shelburne's.　　　　　　　　　　　　　　*17th Octr.* 1782

Present :—Lord Chancellor, Lord President, Lord Privy Seal, Duke of Richmond, Earl of Shelburne, Ld. Vt. Keppell, Mr. Conway, Mr. Pitt, Mr. Sy. Townshend, Lord Grantham.

It is humbly submitted to Your Majesty that Lord Grantham should answer the French Paper delivered by M. de. Vergennes to Mr. Fitzherbert on the 6th of Octr. and should state Your Majesty's Intentions on each of the Articles of the Specific Propositions contained in the French Memorial.

The Conditions of Peace proposed by Spain, in a Memorial of the same date, delivered by M. D'Aranda to Mr. Fitzherbert, are such that it is humbly submitted to Your Majesty, that before they are answered, Mr. Fitzherbert should be instructed, to discover, whether they are meant by that Court to be ultimate Propositions.

No. 3958—*Lord Keppel to the King.*

Lord Keppel has the honour to send Your Majesty dispatches received this Afternoon by Captain Affleck of the Southampton, from Admiral Pigot who arrived off Sandy Hook the 5th of September with the fleet under his Command. Captain Affleck also brings Rear Admiral Digby's letters which Lord Keppel sends with those from Admiral Pigot, & Lord Keppel has much satisfaction in being able to Observe to Your Majesty, Admiral Pigot having Conducted His fleet to New York with much judgment and propriety.

ADMIRALTY, *October 18th*, 1782. 55 *m. past* 10 P.M.

Endorsed by the King.

No. 3959—*Lord Shelburne to the King.*

SIR—I have the honour to enclose to Your Majesty a Letter receiv'd this morning, which I sent immediately to Sir George Young, presuming that Your Majesty would have no time lost in attention to the application for Troops. I have some time past been apprehensive of the consequences of the badness of the Season on all the articles of Necessity, and have been very sorry to find that Parliament have not given proper discretionary powers to the Council. I have the honour to enclose to Your Majesty the result of some enquirys made by Mr. Baring. I am afraid by others that the present price of Wheat is principally owing to the lateness of the Season, and that as soon as the new crop begins to be thresh'd out, It will be lower'd.

I have the satisfaction to acquaint Your Majesty, that what Your Majesty said to General Conway, together with the letters receiv'd last night from New York, and some little discussion of the subject last night at Lord Kepple's has deferr'd the Measures propos'd regarding New York, till they can have due consideration, and I propose tomorrow or Monday having a particular conversation with General Conway on the subject of Sir Guy Carleton.

I have the honour to be with the highest Respect, Your Majesty's Devoted Subject and Faithfull Servant,

BERKELEY SQUARE, 19th Octr. 1782. 4 o'clock P.M. SHELBURNE.

Endorsed by the King.

No. 3960—*The King to Lord Shelburne.*

Lord Shelburne will I am convinced very easily discern on conversing with General Conway that the idea of recalling Sir Guy Carleton arose entirely from the D. of Richmond and as such *implicitly* adopted by Him ; I rather think the push for M. G. Dalling comes from the same quarter ; I hope therefore Ld. Shelburne will have a conversation with the General and *make* M. G. Grey go second in Command to Carleton ; it is fortunate that the troops were already ordered for Warwickshire before the letter now communicated arrived so that protection will soon be found there.

WINDSOR, *Oct. 19th*, 1782. 42 m. pt. 7 P.M.

Draft, endorsed by the King.

No. 3961—*Lord Grantham to the King.*

In consequence of the Opinion of Cabinet, to whom Lord Grantham had Your Majesty's Orders to communicate the French and Spanish Memorials, Lord Grantham has answered the Former, by stating, Your Majesty's Intentions upon each Article. And he has written to Mr. Fitzherbert with Instructions to discover, whether the exorbitant Demands of Spain are likely to be adhered to by that Court.

If the Answer to the French Specification and the Dispatches, of which Lord Grantham sends Your Majesty the Drafts, meet with Your Majesty's gracious Approbation, A Messenger will be immediately dispatched to Paris.

WHITEHALL, 20th Octr. 1782.   50 m. past 11 P.M.

Endorsed by the King.

No. 3962—*The King to Lord Grantham.*

It is certainly very painful to Me who had the honour to ratify the Peace of Paris in 1763 to be obliged to consent to such terms as the factions within my Kingdoms not the weight of my Enemies make necessary.

Ld. Grantham has drawn up the Instructions to Mr. Fitzherbert very clearly and cannot too soon dispatch the Messenger to Paris.

WINDSOR, Oct. 21st, 1782.   m. pt. 7 A.M.

Draft, endorsed by the King.

No. 3963—*Mr. Townshend to the King.*

Mr. Townshend humbly acquaints Your Majesty, that Dr. Watson, whom you have been pleased to promote to the See of Llandaff, is desirous of Your Majesty's Permission to pay Homage at St. James's tomorrow.

WHITEHALL, Oct. 22nd, 1782.   30 m. past 11 A.M.

Endorsed by the King.

No. 3964—*Lord Grantham to the King.*

It having been determined by Your Majesty's Confidential Servants that the Minute made at their Meeting of the 4th Sepr. and then humbly submitted to Your Majesty, should now be put into execution; Lord Grantham has appointed General Fawcett to meet him, in order to be prepared to receive Your Majesty's final Orders thereupon on Wednesday.

St. James's, 27th Octr. 1782. 11 p.m.

Endorsed by the King.

No. 3965—*Lord Shelburne to the King.*

Sir—I have the honour to send Your Majesty the Letters which I have receiv'd this morning from Paris. I mention'd to Lady Holdernesse, thinking she might have an opportunity of acquainting what Monsieur Limon mention'd concerning the suppos'd disgrace of the Marquis de Castries, and the probability of his being replac'd by the Count D'Estaing. Monsieur Limon likewise asserted to me with very great confidence the disposition of the Court of France to join us in everything which tended to open the Trade of Spanish America, provided it could be manag'd so, as that she might preserve appearances with Spain and the Letter of her Engagements. He spoke of his having been admitted to a considerable degree of confidence at Versailles, and as if he could be of considerable service to both Countries as he term'd it, in case the present Negotiation broke off. I communicated the whole of what he and Monsr. Saintfoix said on the present situation to Lord Grantham, and we agreed in thinking it could do no harm and might be of use to apprize Mr. Fitzherbert which Lord Grantham proposed doing in a private Letter by Mr. Townshend's Messenger, who was to go on Saturday night or Sunday morning.

I have the honour to be with the highest Respect, Your Majesty's most Dutyfull Subject and Servant,   Shelburne.

Streatham, 28th Octr. 1782. ½ past 3 p.m.

Endorsed by the King.

No. 3966—*The King to Lord Shelburne.*

The letters Ld. Shelburne has received this day from Paris do not give any new lights, the one from Him that accompanied them confirms what I ever suspected that Monr. Limon's journey is not entirely of private curiosity; his insinuation that the Court of France would join Us in whatever might open the Trade of Spanish America provided She could preserve appearances to Spain is so very singular a communication that I cannot venture to explain to myself what is meant by it; Lord Grantham having apprised Mr. Fitzherbert of this is very proper.   G. R.

WINDSOR, *Oct. 28th*, 1782. [50] *m. pt.* [6] P.M.

Draft, endorsed by the King, 50 m. pt. 6 P.M.

No. 3967—*Mr. Townshend to the King.*

Mr. Townshend humbly presumes to send Your Majesty the inclosed intelligence, which he has just received from Mr. Pulteney, who has called at the Office on his arrival from Paris.

WHITEHALL, *Oct. 31st*, 1782. 25 *m. pt.* 12.

Endorsed by the King.

No. 3968—*The King to Mr. Townshend.*

The intelligence Mr. Secretary Townshend has received from Mr. Pulteney of a Victory having been gained by Ld. Howe must give room to expect a Messenger from Mr. Fitzherbert every hour.

WINDSOR, *31st Octr.* 1782. 15 *m. pt.* 5 P.M.

Draft, written on a page of Mr. Townshend's letter of same date.

No. 3969—*Lord Macartney to the King.*

TO THE KING'S MOST EXCELLENT MAJESTY.

SIR—I humbly beg leave to throw myself at Your Majesty's feet & to entreat your Royal indulgence for the liberty of this address.

The late events here will, I flatter myself, in some measure plead my apology.

The ambition of Your Majesty's approbation & the fear of

your displeasure operate so powerfully on my mind that I can not resist the opportunity which now offers of conveying to your Royal hands, the enclosed paper, which is a copy of my last letter to the Earl of Hillsborough, whose friendship for me would have induced him to lay it before your Majesty. It contains a faithful representation of the impressions made upon me by the Nabob's conduct ; Mine, however, it may be represented, will I trust, be found to be such as becomes a good Englishman, a disinterested Servant of the East India Company & a most devoted and faithful Subject of Your Majesty.

Your gracious and repeated condescension to me encourages me to hope for Your Majesty's pardon on this occasion & for your favourable acceptance of those sentiments of the most profound respect & firmest attachment with which I am, Sir, Your Majesty's most humble & most dutiful Subject & Servant,

FORT ST GEORGE, *November 1st*, 1782.   MACARTNEY.

No. 3970—*Lord Grantham to the King.*

Mr. Fitzherbert's Dispatches give reason to think that Your Majesty will soon receive direct Advices from Lord Howe upon his Return thro' the Streights on the 16th Octr.

The French Minister (as appears by a Private Letter to Lord Grantham) is anxious that Spain should not continue to impede the Progress of a Pacification, as the American Commissioners declare publickly that they shall think themselves authorized to sign their Treaty, if France holds out upon any concerns but her own.

[*Nov.* 3, 1782.] WHITEHALL, 1 *o'clock* P.M.

Endorsed by the King.

No. 3971—*The King to Lord Grantham.*

By hearing nothing further from Mr. Fitzherbert than Lord Howe's having passed the jut on the 16th of October I doubt there having been any Action.

WINDSOR, *Novr.* 3rd, 1782. 51 *m. pt.* 6 P.M.

Draft, written on a page of Lord Grantham's letter of same date.

No. 3972—*Lord North to the King.*

Printed. Donne II. 433.

Lord North has the honour of informing His Majesty That, since he wrote to His Majesty from Derbyshire he has endeavoured to learn the dispositions of the gentlemen, who formerly gave him their assistance in the House of Commons, and finds that, in general, They are well inclined to concur in such measures as shall be necessary for the support of his Majesty's Government, in the present critical situation of the country. He finds them likewise, in general, very averse to any innovations in the Constitution.

Lord North believes That there will be a considerable appearance of members at the opening of the Session, but he thinks it probable That, as the meeting is fix'd on a day so near to Christmas, some Country Gentlemen will not chose to come to Town till after the Holydays.

BUSHY PARK, *Novr.* 4*th*, 1782.

Two copies ; corrected draft and fair copy.

No. 3973—*The King to Lord North.*

I have just received Lord North's letter acquainting me that those Gentlemen in general who supported the late Administration seem inclined to join in forwarding such Measures as may be necessary for the Support of Government ; the times certainly require the concurrence of all who wish to prevent Anarchy ; I have no wish but for the Prosperity of my Dominions therefore must look on all who will not heartily assist me as bad men as well as ungrateful Subjects.

WINDSOR, *Novr.* 4*th*, 1782.

Draft.

No. 3974—*Lord Grantham to the King.*

Lord Grantham is preparing the written Answer, and the Instructions to Mr. Fitzherbert which he hopes to lay before Your Majesty and to dispatch tonight.

WHITEHALL, *7th Novr.* 1782. 20 *m. past* 11 A.M.

Endorsed by the King.

No. 3975.

MINUTE OF CABINET.

[In Lord Grantham's handwriting.]

At a Meeting of His Majesty's Confidential Servants at the Earl of Shelburne's, on the 7th Novr. 1782.

Present :—Lord Chancellor, Lord President, Lord Privy Seal, Duke of Richmond, Earl of Shelburne, Ld. Vt. Keppell, Ld. Ashburton, Mr. Secy. Townshend, Mr. Conway, Mr. Pitt, Ld. Grantham.

It is humbly submitted to the King that a written answer should be given to the Spanish Memorial, in order to state that the Extent of the Terms offered by Spain, would render them inadmissible, if His Majesty's sincere desire of Peace did not induce His Majesty to declare His Readiness to adjust the several Articles of the said Memorial ; if they were not so connected with the Demand made by Spain of Gibraltar, for the Acquisition of which, notwithstanding the stress which is laid upon it, An Exchange so inadequate in every respect and so inadmissible has been offered.

It is also submitted to His Majesty that Mr. Fitzherbert be instructed to hold out to the Spanish Embassador that Regulations for the Cutting of Logwood on the Coast of Honduras and the Cession of West Florida to Spain, are points upon which the King may be more disposed to meet the views of that Court than upon any other stated in the Spanish Memorial.

And that Mr. Fitzherbert be further instructed to press as speedy and immediate a Communication of the Answer of Spain as can be obtained.

No. 3976—*Sir Charles Middleton to* [*the Lord Chamberlain ?*]

MY LORD—As Mr. Pocock who is the author of the drawings of the Action of the 12th of April wishes to begin the paintings that are intended to be taken from them so as to finish them by the time of the Exhibition—I must entreat the favor of Your Majesty's assistance in getting them from St. James's for that purpose, being with great respect,
    Your Majesty's most obedient & most humble Servant,
8th Novr. 1782.   CHAS. MIDDLETON.

No. 3977—*Lord Shelburne to the King.*

SIR—I have the honour to send Your Majesty the Letters which I have this moment receiv'd from Paris. Considering the very explicit Terms, in which Monsieur de Rayneval expresses himself, and the confidence undoubtedly due to that Gentleman, as well as that which the Court of France appears to have taken in Your Majesty, I think I may without presumption congratulate Your Majesty on the certainty of an honourable and I hope a lasting Peace, America out of the question, and at any rate a necessary one. It is impossible to foretell the good or bad consequences of that with America, but It must be the greatest consolation to Your Majesty to reflect, that any evils which may result to Great Britain from so great a Dismemberment or to America from the loss of so Essential a part of the English Constitution, as the Monarch has always prov'd, do not lye at Your Majesty's door, but at that of others.
    I would humbly submit to Your Majesty, whether it would not be expedient, as the Terms I suppose by the return of Mr. Strachey are brought to a Point with America, whether it would not be prudent to summon without delay a Cabinet, that we may come to a provisional agreement with them, and that their assistance may be obtain'd in settling with Spain, and the whole if possible brought together before Parliament.
    I will in the mean time make a private Enquiry concerning

the manner of putting off Parliament in case of necessity, and will take the liberty of recommending General Secresy to my Colleagues, which, if it can be now observ'd, as well as it has been in the progress of the Treaty hitherto must do Infinite Credit to Your Majesty's Government.

I have the honour to be with a zeal and attachment which can only end with my Life, Your Majesty's most Dutyfull Subject & Servant, SHELBURNE.

STREATHAM, 10th Novr. 1782. ½ past 2 P.M.

Endorsed by the King.

No. 3978—*The King to Lord Shelburne.*

Having read the letter Ld. Shelburne has received from Paris as well as the Official Dispatches to Lord Grantham and Mr. Townshend, I entirely coincide with the opinion that as all the Terms of France and America are now arrived, the Cabinet cannot too soon assemble that these may without delay be considered of. Lord Grantham's Dispatches being still on my table, I will write a few lines to him that the business may be brought forward as soon as possible.

I trust the same Secrecy which has done credit to the various parts of Administration during the early steps of the Negotiation, will continue now things seem to be drawing towards Maturity.

I cannot conclude without mentioning how sensibly I feel the dismemberment of America from this Empire, and that I should be miserable indeed if I did not feel that no blame on that Account can be laid at my door, and did I not also know that knavery seems to be so much the striking feature of its Inhabitants that it may not in the end be an evil that they become Aliens to this Kingdom.

WINDSOR, *Novr.* 10th, 1782. 55 m. pt. 6 P.M.

Draft, written on a page of Lord Shelburne's letter of same date.

No. 3979.

MINUTE OF CABINET.

[In Mr. Townshend's handwriting.]

Nov. 11th, 1782

Present:—Lord Chancellor, Lord President, Earl of Shelburne, Duke of Richmond, Lord Grantham, Viscount Keppell, Lord Ashburton, Mr. Pitt, General Conway, Mr. Townshend.

It is humbly submitted to Your Majesty, that a Counter Proposition be drawn up to Demand an explicit Declaration that the British Merchants shall be enabled to proceed for the Recovery of such Debts as were bona fide due to them before 1775, according to the full Value thereof in Sterling Money in the same manner and by the same legal means, that may be used by any of the Inhabitants or Citizens of any of the United States, and that all Lands that have been confiscated as belonging to Persons residing in Great Britain or Ireland shall be restored and the said confiscations reversed, and that likewise there shall be a full and complete Amnesty and oblivion of all acts done on either side in the Prosecution of the War, and that Mr. Strachey be sent with Instructions to insist on the Personal security of all those who have taken part with the Mother Country, and to obtain as much satisfaction as possible with regard to their Property.

It is also recommended that Mr. Strachey should object to any Privileges being granted to the Americans of drying Fish on the Shores of Nova Scotia.

No. 3980—*Mr. Townshend to the King.*

WHITEHALL, *Novr. 16th*, 1782, 5 P.M.

Mr. Townshend humbly presumes to acquaint Your Majesty that he has just received from the Recorder of the City of London a list of ten Prisoners, upon whom he is ready to make his Report, whenever it shall please Your Majesty to receive it.

Endorsed by the King.

No. 3981—*Lord Keppel to the King.*

Lord Keppel has the honour to send Your Majesty Dispatches received this day from Admiral Pigot and Rear-Admiral Digby, by the Packet from New York.

BAGSHOT PARK, *November 16th.* 1782. 45 *m. past* 10 P.M.

No. 3982—*Lord Grantham to the King.*

The Dispatch from Mr. Fitzherbert upon the French Claims after the Capture of St. Eustatia, not being ready in Time to receive Your Majesty's Orders upon it, before Mr. Townshend's Messenger was to set out Ld. Grantham humbly entreats Your Majesty's Indulgence for having presumed to forward it.

ST JAMES'S, 11 *o'clock* A.M. 19*th Novr.* 1782.

Endorsed by the King.

No. 3983—*Mr. Townshend to the King.*

WHITEHALL, *Nov.* 19, 1782
m. 10 *pt.* 6 P.M.

Mr. Townshend humbly presumes to send Your Majesty the copy of the Preliminary Articles intended to be transmitted to Mr. Oswald, which he has ventured to do without waiting for the Dispatches to Mr. Oswald and Mr. Strachey, as the latter though pretty nearly finished are not sufficiently accurate for Your Majesty's Perusal.

The Purport of these Dispatches is that after agreeing to the Independance and to the Boundarys, Mr. Oswald is to insist upon Personal Amnesty to all who have adhered to Your Majesty without any exception ; likewise upon payment of Debts due before 1775 and Restitution of Property to all Real British Subjects, taking care to obtain as clear and as favorable a definition of that Term as possible. With regard to the rest of the Articles, they are to be the subject of Negotiation ; Mr.

Strachey and Mr. Oswald being directed to use every effort to obtain the best terms possible. The Secret Article is not to be brought forward, but as a means of obtaining the full benefit of the Fifth Article without any of the Modifications. But even in that case all possible Pains are to be taken to have the Purport of it conveyed by private assurances, rather than by reducing it to the form of an article. Mr. Oswald is likewise directed not to sign, but with the full concurrence of Mr. Fitzherbert and Mr. Strachey given in writing.

Mr. Townshend humbly desires to receive Your Majesty's Commands, whether the Messenger should immediately set off for Paris with the Draught of the Preliminary Articles and the Dispatches, when the Draught returns from Your Majesty, or wait till your Majesty shall have seen the Dispatches.

WHITEHALL, *Novr. 19th*, 1782. 10 *m. pt.* 6 P.M.

Endorsed by the King.

No. 3984—*The King to Mr. Townshend.*

Mr. Townshend may send the Messenger to Paris with the draft of the Preliminary Articles and the Dispatches as soon as they are ready, without waiting for my seeing the latter ; He cannot be surprised at my not being over anxious for the perusal of them, as Parliament having to my astonishment come into the ideas of granting a Separation to North America, has disabled me from longer defending the just rights of this Kingdom. But I certainly disclaim thinking myself answerable for any evils that may arise from the adoption of this Measure as necessity not conviction has made me subscribe to it.

WINDSOR, *Novr. 19th*, 1782. 23 *m. pt.* 10 P.M.

Draft, written on a page of Mr. Townshend's letter of same date.

No. 3985—*Lord Shelburne to the King.*

SIR—I found on my return from Your Majesty, that Monsr. Rayneval was arriv'd at a lodging in this neighbourhood, which my Servant had indicated to him, when he was last here, to avoid the Inconvenience which attended him before at an Hotel, and I have just finish'd a very long conversation with him, the result of which has been, his sending a Courier, to acquaint Monsr. de Vergennes of the Impossibility of prevailing upon Your Majesty, to think of ceding Gibraltar, without a compleat restitution on the part of Spain, of every possession which she has taken, and the addition either of Porto Rico or Martinique and St. Lucie or Guadoloupe and Dominique. I take it for granted that his admitting the two last to come into question is founded upon a prospect of prevailing with Spain to cede to them the whole of St. Domingo. On the other hand they would meet our wants of a Harbour as well as Wood and Water among the Leeward Islands. I ventur'd to add that Your Majesty would expect the full value of all the Fortifications Artillery and Stores at Gibraltar. I found him dispos'd to agree to reasonable terms about the Logwood.

He is to be with Lord Grantham and me tomorrow at 10, and the whole will be submitted to Your Majesty after the Drawing Room.

I have the honour to be with the highest Respect, Your Majesty's Dutyfull Subject,   SHELBURNE.

BERKLY SQUARE, 20th Novr. 1782, ½ past one.

Endorsed by the King.

No. 3986—*Mr. Townshend to the King.*

WHITEHALL, *Nov.* 20th, 1782, 10 P.M.

Mr. Townshend humbly presumes to acquaint Your Majesty that in consequence of the information which he has received from Deal of the Distemper which seemed to have broken out among the Horned Cattle in that neighbourhood he has ventured to direct Mr. Cotterell to summon a council to meet at St. James's tomorrow, after the Drawing Room, that the same Orders may be given for preventing the spreading the Distemper which were issued in 1781 on the like occasion.

Endorsed by the King.

No. 3987—*The King to Lord Shelburne.*

QUEEN'S HOUSE, *Novr.* 21*st*, 1782
m. 42 *pt.* 9 A.M.

If any proofs were wanting of the sincerity of France to make Peace Mr. Reneval's sending off a Messenger the very Night of his arrival puts it out of further doubt ; and that arising from a single Conversation with Ld. Shelburne wherein the impossibility was shewn of ceding Gibraltar without the compleat restitution of every possession Spain has taken during the War and the addition of either Porto Rico, or Martinique and St. Lucie, or Guadaloupe and Dominique, and the full value paid of the Fortifications, Artillery and Stores at Gibraltar. I am ready to avow that I think the exchange of Gibraltar for either of the three valuable Possessions as now proposed is highly advantageous to this Kingdom.

Draft, endorsed by the King.

No. 3988.

MINUTE OF CABINET.

[In Mr. Townshend's handwriting.]

ST. JAMES'S, *Nov.* 21*st*, 1782

Present :—Lord Chancellor, Lord President, Lord Shelburne, Duke of Richmond, Lord Grantham, Lord Ashburton, Lord Keppell, Mr. Pitt, General Conway, Mr. Townshend.

It is humbly proposed to Your Majesty, that in consequence of the present State of the Negotiation for Peace that the Parliament be prorogued from Tuesday the 26th of this month to Thursday the 5th of December.

No. 3989—*Lord Shelburne to the King.*

SIR—Your Majesty's suggestion appeared to me so full of dignity and prudence, that I ventur'd after dinner to discuss it as my own with Monsr. de Rayneval, and after a conversation which lasted till very late at night set down the points enclosed as the result of it, which he had copied, to make the foundation of a Dispatch which he is to to send to the Count de Vergennes, the moment Mr. Ord acquaints him, that the Council have decided on the prorogation.

Lord Camden has undertaken to prepare everything for the Council without acquainting the Clerks. It may be worth consideration whether Your Majesty would have it before three o'clock as the Stock Exchange shuts at that hour, and opens at ten o'clock. It will therefore answer the purpose intended if the Notice goes to the Lord Mayor time enough to be publick very early tomorrow, and the inconvenience avoided of its being circulated thro' Europe by tomorrow night's Foreign Mail on account of Holland.

I have the honour to send Your Majesty a letter of Mr. Vaughan, which is a strong confirmation of what has passed with Monsr. de Rayneval.

I have the honour to be with the highest Respect, Your Majesty's most Dutyfull Subject,   SHELBURNE.

BERKLY SQUARE, 22nd Novr. 1782. ½ past 8 A.M.

Endorsed by the King.

No. 3990—*The King to Lord Shelburne.*

Nothing can be more proper than the manly manner in which Ld. Shelburne has brought the decision on Peace or War to a fixed point. Three o'clock will be a very proper hour for holding the Privy Council this day for proroguing the Parliament as it will prevent any Gambling in the Alley this day, and if the Lord Mayor gets the letter by eleven this night there will be time to prevent that to-morrow[:] might it not be proper for one of the Secretaries of the Treasury to write the same intimation to the Bank, and the East Company which will spread the account still faster.

The letter from Mr. Vaughan shews that France is sincere. I owne I still think St. Lucia and Martinique would sound better than Guadaloupe and Dominique.

QUEEN'S HOUSE, *Novr.* 22nd, 1782. *m.* 22 *pt.* 9 A.M.

Draft, endorsed by the King.

No. 3991—*Lord Shelburne to the King.*

SIR—Monsieur de Rayneval after much discussion yesterday morning and evening offer'd to follow his Messenger to Versailles, for the purpose of expediting the answer. Lord Grantham concurr'd with me in opinion that nothing could be more desirable. He came again to me this morning before he set out, desirous of being inform'd of Your Majesty's disposition regarding America and Holland.

I ventur'd to tell him that there would be little difficulty about Boundarys with the American Commissioners, provided the Article relative to the Loyalists was express'd in so comprehensive a manner as to acquit Your Majesty towards every description, which had a right to Your Majesty's protection. That in regard to the Fishery, Your Majesty wish'd nothing more than to avoid every possibility of future dispute and desir'd it upon their account as well as our own. I found him uninformed of what had pass'd. He stated the reserve of the Commissioners towards them, to be owing to their refusing to support them in a variety of unreasonable demands, which I perfectly believe. Lieutenant Lane came from Bristol yesterday, who gave the most distinct account possible of every circumstance relative to Newfoundland. It appear'd by what he said that Fogos would be a better situation for them than Pierre & Miquelon and more out of the way of Your Majesty's Fishery, but as it likewise appear'd that Pierre and Miquelon never can be fortified to the least advantage, and that the Island of Fogos may be made uncommonly strong, It was judg'd most prudent to say nothing further upon that head.

In regard to Holland I told him that I was not sufficiently instructed either of Your Majesty's disposition or Interests to hazard many particulars upon their subject, that in regard to the Commercial Article upon which he press'd me I could only say, that Your Majesty's went on the liberal side in all commercial questions, guarding however most explicitly against the principles of the Northern League, that in regard to the several possessions now in Your Majesty's hands, I could only say, that I was persuaded they would find in Your Majesty every generous principle which they could expect, that it was impossible to conceive the India Company could be brought to give back the several conquests now in their hands without Trincamolé or some better possession being confirm'd to them, and that as Demarera and Issequibo had been recaptur'd by them, the French, they would do well to keep it, for the purpose of throwing it into our scale, to allay the great Jealousies, which must arise if they should finally acquire the whole of St. Domingo. I would not upon any account flatter Your Majesty with the hopes of both acquisitions, or venture to convey to Your Majesty that there does not look some scheme on their part touching Holland, which has not appear'd, but I have great satisfaction in being able I think to assure Your Majesty that it does not extend to any Idea of keeping possession of the Cape having sounded him repeatedly on the subject of it.

I have the honour to enclose to Your Majesty my Letters to Count Vergennes and Mr. Oswald.

I have the honour to be with the highest Respect, Your Majesty's most Dutyfull Subject,   SHELBURNE.

BERKLEY SQUARE, 24th Novr. 1782.

Endorsed by the King.

No. 3992.

MEMORANDUM.

[In Lord Shelburne's handwriting.]   [Nov. 1782.]

The Bounds propos'd by Monsr. Rayneval to Ld. Shelburne were Aalemparve to the North and the River Shalambar to the South of Pondicherry and Gingi to the West. He declin'd any explanation regarding the other Settlements. See D'Anville's Maps.

No. 3993—*Mr. Townshend to the King.*

WHITEHALL, Nov. 24th, 1782
m. 10 pt. 2 P.M.

Mr. Townshend humbly presumes to send to Your Majesty a Petition in favour of Michael Ranton now under order for Execution on Wednesday next. He is one of the Persons included in the Recorder's Report of Wednesday last. General Conway presented a Petition to Your Majesty on Friday in favour of him, which he afterwards delivered to Mr. Townshend with your Majesty's commands to him to enquire into the Case. Upon making the best enquiry he finds no new Matters alleged relative to the Case itself. In Alleviation it has been said to him, that the Prisoner must have been but lately drawn into a vicious course of life, having within a few months past been entrusted with money and Plate to a considerable value, which he faithfully delivered to the Banker, to whom it was consigned.

Endorsed by the King.

No. 3994—*The King to Lord Shelburne.*

The proposal of Mr. de Reyneval to follow his Messenger to Versailles seems the most likely method of bringing things there to a quick decision, and as such I am glad Ld. Shelburne has encouraged him to put it into Execution ; the giving him on this occasion some insight into the Negotiations with Holland and America was also right, and it has much eased my mind that any Possession of the Cape of Good Hope is not secretly intended by France ; if She wounds the Dutch anywhere but in the East Indies I do not see they deserve our compassion. France I should hope will assist us in keeping the American Treaty less liable to be objected to on the score of Fisheries which certainly in its present shape is too loose and subject to much inconvenience.

WINDSOR, *Nov. 25th*, 1782. *m.* 40 *pt.* 7 A.M.

Draft, endorsed by the King.

No. 3995.

MEMORANDUM.   [? *Nov.* 1782.

The French before 1749 were in possession.

On the Coromandel Coast—only
> Pondicherry—Chief Settlement.
> Karrical a Comptoir ; and a Factory at Mazulipatnam and another at Ganaon.

On the Malabar Coast
>   A small Fort at Mahé and a Factory at Surat and another at Callicut.

In Bengal—
>   Chandenagar—Chief Settlement, with a small Factory or Residence at each of the 5 following places—viz— Balasore, Cossimbuzar, Patna, Jugdea and Dacca— merely to purchase goods.

In 1749 Chaunde-Saib ceded to the French the Lands of Villenour and Bahour adjoining to Pondicherry with 80 villages belongg. to them and their revenues at   Rs. 96,000

In 1750 Certain lands round Karrical were given them by Muzzifer Jung together with 81 villages belonging thereto, the revenues set at   Rs. 105,000

In 1751 Salabut Jung ceded or confirmed certain lands and Villages round Mazulipatnam with Nizampatnam— Condivir, Narsapour, Divi, &c. The revenues of these several districts the French estimated at   Rs. 14,00,000

In 1753 Salabut-Jung made a further cession to the French of the Four Circars nearest Mazulipatnam—viz—Raja- mundrie, Eloor, Mustafanagar, and Cicacole. These were given for the maintenance of the troops under Bussy in the Nizam's Service. The revenues set at
>   Rs. 30,00,000

The charge of the troops the French estimated
at   Rs. 25,00,000
so that a surplus remained on that calculation
of   Rs. 5,00,000

In the Company's returns from Fort St. George the revenues of Mazulipatnam and its Farms are valued at Pag. 1,24,000
>   or £   50,000

The revenues of Rajamundrie, Eloor, and Mustafanagar under Mazulipatnam are valued at   Pag. 6,20,000
>   or £   250,000

The Circar of Cicacole under Vezagapatam is valued
at   Pag. 2,10,000
                                            or £   80,000
Itchapore part of Cicacole Circar, but under Ganjam
    is valued at   Pag. 1,30,000
                                            or £   50,000

Truce signed end of December 1754 by the English and French Governments on the Coast and sent home for final determination.

The two Companies to renounce for ever all Moorish Governments and Dignity.

Mazulipatnam and Divi to be neutral. Each nation, as shall be determined from home, to have one with equal districts round them for Comptoirs, and an equal number of soldiers to guard them.

Marsapour River to be alike free to both nations, each a Factory on its Banks, and the districts to be equal &c. Commerce to be alike free to both Nations, and the Custom Houses to remain on the same footing as before the War, and no alterations made in the Duties paid on the importation, and exportation of goods. The produce or manufacture of the Coast.

[*No date nor sign of origin*]

No. 3996—*Mr. Townshend to the King.*

WHITEHALL, *Monday, Nov. 25th*, 1782, 1 P.M.

Mr. Townshend humbly presumes to transmit to Your Majesty a Letter, which he received yesterday in the afternoon by the hands of Mr. William Grenville, whom Lord Temple thought proper to send over to confer with Your Majesty's Ministers upon the Subjects of the Dispatch. Mr. Grenville in the very clear account which he gives of the present State of Ireland, confirms strongly the Opinions contained in the Dispatch of the Lord Lieutenant. Mr. Townshend humbly wishes to receive Your Majesty's commands upon the summoning a meeting of your Confidential Servants to consider of the State of Ireland, and of the Measures proposed by the Lord Lieutenant.

Endorsed by the King.

No. 3997—*The King to Mr. Townshend.*

WINDSOR, *Nov. 25th*, 1782
m. 24 *pt.* 6 P.M.

In consequence of Mr. Townshend's proposal, I approve of his summoning the Ministers and laying before them the letter from the Ld. Lieut. of Ireland, that the steps recommended may be duly weighed ; it will be right that Mr. Wm. Grenville should be called before them ; as he can state more fully those matters, than the extent of a letter would admit ; after which the deliberation should be held ; but probably most will wish as the matter is delicate, to put off any decision to a second Meeting.

Draft, written at the foot of Mr. Townshend's letter of same date.

No. 3998—*Lord Grantham to the King.*

Lord Grantham would be exceedingly concerned if anything of importance required, his paying his Duty to Your Majesty today, as he is still confined by the consequences of an accident which happened to him a few days ago.

He humbly hopes therefore to be indulged with Yr. Majesty's excusing him, hoping to avail himself of the first opportunity of receiving Your Majesty's Orders.

WHITEHALL, 27*th Nov.* 1782. ¾ *past* 4 P.M.

Endorsed by the King.

No. 3999—*Lord Shelburne to the King.*

SIR—I have this moment opened the Inclosed letter from Monsieur. De Rayneval. It came to my House this morning at half past two. Monsieur De Rayneval's Courier is a Boy, which my Servant sent to attend him from my House, upon his sending his own Servant with his Second Dispatch. The Boy mentions that Monsieur de Vergennes' son accompanies Monsieur De Rayneval. I have ordered him to be enjoined the strictest Secresy, being apprehensive that if such a circumstance transpires in the City, Peace will be looked upon as certain, and I cannot help submitting it to Your Majesty as a favourable Omen in all respects.

I have the honour to be, with the highest respect, Your Majesty's most dutyfull subject, SHELBURNE.

BERKLEY SQUARE. *2nd Decr.* 1782. ½ *past* 7 A.M.

Endorsed by the King.

No. 4000—*The King to Lord Shelburne.*

Lord Shelburne's Attention in immediately sending to Me the note he has received from Mons. de Reyneval is not thrown away. I cannot have a doubt though, there may be a strong push for some unreasonable demand, that Peace will be in the end obtained if Mons. de Vergennes' son is come to England ; therefore I trust Lord Shelburne will fight as strongly as possible. Is it not singular that not a line is yet received from Mr. Strachey.

WINDSOR. *Dec. 2nd*, 1782. *m.* 32 *past* 10 A.M.

Draft, written at the foot of Lord Shelburne's letter of same date.

No. 4001—*Lord Shelburne to the King.*

2nd December, 1782

SIR—I do not lose a moment to send Your Majesty Monsieur de Vergennes' answer to me. I have declined looking at the answer he has brought from Spain till Lord Grantham has seen it. The substance is an offer of Guadouloupe [*sic*] and Dominique for Gibraltar, Restitution of Minorca and the Bahamas, but Spain insists on keeping West Florida subject to certain limits and upon an arrangement, which he has brought relative to the Logwood. I have insisted with him in the most positive manner upon Martinique and Santa Lucia, and told him, that so far as I was concern'd I could not without it answer for Peace on the side of Your Majesty, much less for that Impression attending it, which could alone make it permanent. I dare not hazard to Your Majesty a guess, whether he will give way, as he affirms that it does not come within his Instruction, and he has hitherto preserv'd a line of great Sincerity. If he has not the power, it will be to be consider'd whether it's proper to take the chance of a favourable answer from France, and for that purpose to prorogue the Parliament for another Week.

I presume in all events, Your Majesty will approve of a Cabinet's being summoned by Lord Grantham if possible for this evening.

I have the honour to be, with the highest respect, Your Majesty's most dutyfull subject,   SHELBURNE.

SHELBURNE HOUSE. *2nd December*, 1782. 12 *o'clock*.

Endorsed by the King.

No. 4002—*The King to Lord Shelburne.*

The letter from Mons. de Vergennes is in the usual French style, from which no judgement can be formed on the fate of the Negociation ; but the Count's son I should think would never have been sent, had not Peace been the intention of that Court ; I therefore hope Mons. Reyneval has power to give St. Lucia and Martinique instead of Guadaloupe and Dominique, and that Spain will restore West Florida, but if he has not, after doing everything but putting off the Negociation, I think Peace so desirable, that as far as relates to Myself, I should not be for another Year's War.

WINDSOR. *Decr.* 2*nd*, 1782. *m.* 55 *past* 3 P.M.

Draft, written on a sheet of Lord Shelburne's letter of same date.

No. 4003—*Lord Grantham to the King.*

Lord Grantham having seen M. de Reyneval, and conferred fully with him upon the French and Spanish Propositions, has summoned Your Majesty's Confidential Servants to meet to-morrow morning.

2nd December, 1782. 11 P.M.

Endorsed by the King.

No. 4004—*The King to Lord Grantham.*

Lord Grantham is perfectly right in losing no time in calling a meeting this Morning on the French and Spanish Propositions; however unreasonable M. de Reyneval may be ordered to be in trying to make us yield all He can, yet I trust he has secret directions to give way rather than not have Peace, or Count de Vergennes would never have let him be accompanied by his Son; but should I be mistaken in my suggestion, after doing everything but letting them return to Paris to mend the Treaty, I think Peace so essential, and that the dreadful Resolution of the 27th of February last of the House of Commons has so entirely removed the real cause of the War to the utter shame of that branch of the Legislature, that it would be madness not to conclude Peace on the best possible terms we can obtain.

WINDSOR. *Decr. 3rd, 1782. m. 25 past 9 A.M.*

Draft, written on a page of Lord Grantham's letter of 2 December.

No. 4005—*Lord Grantham to the King.*

Lord Grantham will have the Preliminary Articles mentioned in the Minute of Cabinet ready for Your Majesty's perusal, on your Arrival in town.

The Cabinet sat eight hours upon the Articles and dispatches, which came from Mr. Fitzherbert. Lord Grantham will see Mr. de Rayneval to-morrow morning and do his Utmost to induce him to accept of the Alterations made in his Proposals. The signature of the American Treaty may perhaps facilitate this.

The Proposal of accepting Guadalupe for Gibraltar (as Dominica can scarcely be called a part of the exchange) was not unanimously agreed to; the Duke of Richmond and Lord Keppel will of course lay before Your Majesty their objections to it.

3rd December, 1782. 11 P.M.

Endorsed by the King.

No. 4006—*The King to Lord Grantham.*

I shall be glad to find the Preliminary Articles ready this Day ; whatever alterations in the proposals made by Mons de Reyneval Lord Grantham can get to our advantage, will undoubtedly be very servisable, and what I also value will do him personal credit.

When Lord Grantham mentions that the Duke of Richmond and Lord Keppel dissent from the Opinion of receiving Guadaloupe in lieu of Gibraltar, I thought Gen. Conway would of course have sided with them.

WINDSOR. *Decr.* 4*th*, 1782. *m.* 58 *past* 8 A.M.

Draft, written on a page of Lord Grantham's letter of same date.

No. 4007.

MINUTE OF CABINET.

[In Lord Grantham's handwriting.]

At a Meeting of Your Majesty's Confidential Servants at Lord Grantham's Office, 3rd Dec. 1782.

Present :—The Ld Chancellor, Ld Privy Seal, Ld President, Duke of Richmond, Earl of Shelburne, Ld Ashburton, Ld Vist Keppel, Mr. Pitt, Mr. Conway, Mr. Sy. Townshend, Ld Grantham.

Upon consideration of the State of the Negotiation with the Powers at War, and of the demands made by them as the price of Peace,

It is humbly submitted to Your Majesty, That if the Court of France will agree to the Preliminary Articles as now drawn up ; And that if Spain will besides Minorca restore the Islands of the Bahamas, and allow a well regulated Establishment on some Part of the Coast of Honduras, The Proposal of exchanging Gibraltar for Guadelupe may be accepted.

And it is further submitted to Your Majesty that in consideration of West Florida being kept by Spain, The Island of Trinidad should be ceded to Your Majesty in Addition to the above Offer.

Endorsed by Lord Grantham.

No. 4008—*Lord Shelburne to the King.*

SIR—I have had the honour to obey Your Majesty's commands in acquainting the Chancellor and Speaker that it is Your Majesty's Intention to be at the House at half past two to-morrow. There has been a meeting of sixty-two Peers to hear Your Majesty's Speech. No particular person except the Duke of Richmond absent, which I conceive from his conversation, after I attended Your Majesty must have been owing to accident. I have talked to the Duke of Grafton whose conversation now partakes more of caution than hostility.

Monsr. de Rayneval has sent his Courier, and I have great reason to believe that Your Majesty may on his return have either Santa Lucia or Trinidada in compensation for West Florida.

I have the honour to send Your Majesty a correct copy of the Speech for Your Majesty's use. I omitted to acquaint you that the reason for the expression concerning the Civil List Debt was to avoid as much as possible any Debate on that particular Subject.

I have the honour to be, with the highest respect, Your Majesty's most dutyfull subject,   SHELBURNE.

BERKLEY SQUARE. *4th Decr.* 1782.

Endorsed by the King.

No. 4009—*The King to Lord Shelburne.*

QUEEN'S HOUSE. *Decr. 5th,* 1782
m. 42 *past* 7 A.M.

Whether the absence of the Duke of Richmond last night at the reading of the Speech at Lord Shelburne's was purposely or accidental, nothing that He said in the Closet yesterday can authorize my hazarding an opinion. Indeed, He painted in the strongest Colours the whole negotiation of Mr. Oswald, and seemed to think that unless Lord Shelburne had some secret view, he, the Duke, could not fathom, he could not account for the not having long changed our American Negociator when every other Member of the Cabinet had long seen he plead only the Cause of America, not of Britain ; He reprobated the grant of fishing to that Country, and made use of the strangest Sophistry, that his sole idea in yielding to America had been to be the better able to be firm against France and Spain, to which a very obvious answer lies that timidity once shown others will take advantage of it. He blamed the Peace with France in the strongest [terms ?], thought some equivalent should have been obtained for giving up the Commissary at Dunkirk. He roundly asserted that he did not think anything could have been a compensation for Gibraltar which he termed *the brightest jewel of the Crown* ; but that Guadaloupe was nothing ; that He had no private View by his dissent that He is inclined to the present Administration, that He had shown it by consenting to be in a very secondary situation when he might have claimed the first. As I did not think it right to heat the coals at present, I seemed to acquiesce in opinion, being the only cause of his dissent.

Lord Keppel was less full but seemed to insinuate that if when the Messenger returned the terms of Peace were not greatly improved, and if Gibraltar did not remain in our hands, He should resign, and by what He dropped, He seemed to insinuate the Duke of Richmond as taking the same line ; He expressly added He should keep his dissent to himself till then ; but I am clear the Duke of Richmond dropped nothing that bore that interpretation, to Me.

Draft, endorsed by the King.

No. 4010—*Lord Grantham to the King.*

Lord Grantham thought it necessary—after both Houses of Parliament were up, to dispatch a Messenger to Mr. Fitzherbert with the enclosed Dispatch, in order that the Sentiments which were declared on all sides might, upon being represented, make a due impression on ye French Ministry.

5 *Decr.* 1782.   30 *m. past* 12 P.M.

Endorsed by the King.

No. 4011—*Lord Shelburne to the King.*

SIR—I have obeyed Your Majesty's Commands relative to the Lord Chancellor and the Speaker. The answer to the Address shall meet Your Majesty at St. James's. I see very plainly the vast Importance of expediting all the publick business thro' both Houses, and Your Majesty may depend upon my making it my Incessant Study, as long as I have the honour to serve Your Majesty.

The Chancellor wishes me to be at the House and to attend the Address to St. James's. It will be necessary on account of an Idea, which the Duke of Richmond and Lord Keppel have taken up, of thanking Lord Howe, in conséquence of what pass'd yesterday, and of adjourning the House to Monday instead of Fryday for that purpose. The Intention is much disapprov'd of by Your Majesty's Servants in the House of Commons. I have therefore determin'd to send Mr. Ord to Lord Howe, and if Your Majesty does not disapprove, I propose to leave it to be decided by his own Judgment.

I have great Satisfaction in acquainting Your Majesty that everything pass'd perfectly well in the House of Commons.

I have the honour to be, with the highest respect, Your Majesty's most dutyfull subject, SHELBURNE.

BERKLEY SQUARE. 6 *December*, 1782. 8 *o'clock* A.M.

Endorsed by the King.

No. 4012—*The King to Lord Shelburne.*

QUEEN'S HOUSE. *Decr.* 6th, 1782
m. 48 *past* 8 A.M.

It is rather hard that when so many weighty concerns are on foot, Ministry must be employed in healing the little evils which particular Members of it will be bringing forward ; if there was any Energy or Discipline in Government, a Master General of the Ordnance and a first Lord of the Admiralty ought not to be making Motions in one House of Parliament without the concurrence of the rest of the Ministers in both Houses. I trust that day will still come, or all my labours will continue to prove abortive.

In the present position Lord Shelburne can do nothing better than to send Mr Orde to Lord Howe, and leave it to his decision ; perhaps his *vanity* will make him lean to the Vote, and though Mr Orde has acuteness as well as civility, it will not be easy to show the Viscount that in this instance his brother blue Coat moves the Thanks to have it meet with some discredit in the other House ; I take it for granted if Lord Howe is thank'd, either Ld Shelburne or Ld Grantham will make a similar motion in favour of Gen. Elliott and the brave troops that have defended Gibraltar.

Draft, endorsed by the King.

No. 4013—*Mr. Townshend to the King.*

ALBERMARLE STREET. *Friday Dec. 6th,* 1782
m. 30 *past* 7 P.M.

Mr. Townshend humbly presumes to send Your Majesty the list of the Speakers in the Debate upon the Report of the Address. It was in general a repetition of the Debate of yesterday, except that the different passages of Your Majesty's Speech were more discussed.

Endorsed by the King.

Enclosure.

6 *December,* 1782

Mr. Minchin.	Mr. Hamel.
Governor Johnstone.	Mr. Burke.
Mr. Townshend.	Mr. Pitt.
Governor Johnstone.	Mr. Fox.
Mr. Luttrell.	Mr. Pitt.
Mr. Fox.	General Conway.
Mr. Townshend.	Mr. Burke.
Mr. Pitt.	Sir Richard Sutton.

No. 4014—*Lord Shelburne to the King.*

Sir—I have the honour to send Your Majesty the Letters which I have received this afternoon.

There was one awkward occurrence in the House of Commons yesterday, owing to Mr. Pitt's explanation of the Article which regards the Independence. He stated it as depending on a Peace with France, but irrevocable whenever that event should happen, though the present Treaty should prove abortive. Mr. Fox affected to consider this as a concession to the Opinion, which determin'd his resignation. It created some uneasiness, but will not I hope be attended with any bad consequence, as the Treaty with France is so nearly concluded, and Mr. Pitt undertakes that Mr. Fox will not carry through the deception. In this case the best must be made of it in the House of Lords.

I have the honour to be, with the highest Respect, Your Majesty's most dutyfull subject, Shelburne.

Berkley Square. *7th December*, 1782. 11 *o'clock* P.M.

Endorsed by the King.

No. 4015—*The King to Lord Shelburne.*

Windsor. *Dec. 8th*, 1782
m. 2 *past* 10 A.M.

By Ld. Shelburne's Account, it very clearly appears that Mr. Pitt on Friday stated the article of Independence as irrevocable, though the Treaty should prove abortive ; this undoubtedly was a mistake, for the Independence is alone to be granted for Peace. I have always thought it best and wisest if a mistake is made openly to avow it, and therefore Mr. Pitt ought if his words have been understood to bear so strong a meaning to say it is no wonder that so Young a Man should have made a slip ; this would do him honour. I think at all events it is highly material that Lord Shelburne should not by any language in the House of Lords appear to change his conduct, let the blame fall where it may. I do not wish He should appear but in a dignified light, which His station in my service requires, and which can only be maintained by his conduct in the whole Negociation of Peace having been *neat*, which would not be the case if Mr. Fox could prove that Independence was granted otherwise than as the price of Peace ; besides Mr. Vaughan's letter shows further demands are to come from Franklin, which must make us the more stiff on this Article.

Draft, written on a page of Lord Shelburne's letter of 7 December.

No. 4016—*Sir William Musgrave to [Lord Shelburne ?]*

PARK PLACE, ST. JAMES'S. 10th *December*, 1782

MY LORD—Enclosed I have the honour to send Your Lordship the Lists of Useless and Sinecure Offices, with the places of the Abodes of such of them as have thought proper to inform the Secretary to the Board of Customs where they are to be found, in case they should be wanted for the publick service.

And in perusing these Lists I am persuaded that it will not escape Your Lordship's observation

1stly. That very few of the Employments (exceeding £200 per annum) have been given to any persons for their Support of Government, but have rather been bestowed upon the Relations, Friends and Dependants of the Ministers for the time being (many of them Children at the time of their Appointment) as will appear by an extract of a few of them on the back hereof.

2ndly. That even those who obtained them by real services, know that their patents cannot be vacated at pleasure, but only by a tedious and expensive process at Law, upon proof of Misfeasance ; consequently that they are entirely independant, and many of them have engaged warmly in Opposition to His Majesty's Measures at different times, as may be instanced by the Duke of Manchester and others.

3rdly. That most of these patent Officers have many Deputies under their own Appointment ; for example the Customer of Plymouth promotes his own Substitutes, not only at that place, but also at Padstow, St. Ives, Penzance, Helford, Falmouth, Penrin, St. Mawes, Truro, Fowey, Looe, Saltash, etc.

consequently when the Principal is adverse to Government, the Deputies are ready to follow his dictates in obstructing Elections and operations of that kind.

4thly. That very few of these patent Officers reside upon their employment, so that they have no personal interest there to assist Government when they are so disposed, and it must even appear offensive to the Inhabitants of the different Towns, to find such large sums levied upon them and sent away for the benefit of an *Individual*, of whom perhaps they know nothing more than that he is amply provided for by other considerable appointments under Government ; as may be observed in the case of the Duke of Newcastle and of Sir John Burgoyne, the Comptroller of Chester ; which includes also Liverpoole, where the Deputy (beside his own extra gratuities) levies on the Merchants of that flourishing town upwards of £500 in what is called Legal Fees for his principal, and a still larger sum is collected for Mr. Pelham of Crowhurst, who is the patent Customer there, and also holds the office of Inspector of Imports and Exports in the Customs with a salary of £500 per annum.

I have mentioned Sir John Burgoyne, from this peculiar circumstance ; that he is now in the E. Indies, and as no person can appoint his Deputies but himself, the Port of Beaumaris is now without a Comptroller for want of his deputation, and in case his substitute at Liverpoole should die, the Board would have no Comptroller upon the collection of upwards of £200,000 per annum at that Port, and all the accounts must stand still for several years, till a fresh deputation can be sent out and be returned properly signed by him to authorize some person to officiate there.

Add to all this that many Patentees consider their employment only as so many farms, and let them out to Deputies very ill qualified to serve the Publick, merely because they are the highest bidders, and will send them the largest rents ; which compells such miserable substitutes to be guilty of unreasonable indulgences (to call them no worse) towards the Merchants that they may extort from them unlawful perquisites in return ;

I am sure that it requires no more than to have stated all these evils, for Your Lordship to see the necessity of putting a speedy end to them, if any regard is had to the satisfaction of the Merchants, the improvement of Trade, and the consequent

Increase and Safety of the Revenue. At the same time, it will strengthen and enlarge the proper influence that Government ought always to have. Because when the Useless and Sinecure Employments shall be abolished, and the business shall be conducted by efficient Officers resident on the spot, the Treasury will have the appointment of them at all these places where the Patentees now put in Deputies, so that instead of 23 patent Comptrollers, *they* will nominate 72 Efficient Comptrollers acting by Commission from the Board of Customs, with Salaries from 100 to 300 per ann ; who being entirely dependant, and at the same time resident at their posts, will always be ready to observe such directions as they shall receive for the good of His Majesty's Service and the Measures of Government.

There will be the same increase of real patronage in the number of Searchers, and so proportionately in the rest.

As a proof that the patents granting Offices in the Customs were formerly thought illegal, it is to be observed that there was alwaies inserted in them, a Clause of " Non Obstante " for the Statutes of K. Rich 2nd ; K. Hen. 4th, and K. Hen. 6th— so long as the Crown exercised a dispensing Power before the Revolution.

I have the honour to remain, with the greatest respect, My Lord, Your most obedient and most humble servant,

W. MUSGRAVE.

Enclosure.   I

An Extract from the Lists of Useless and Sine-cure Offices marked A and B.

Collector Outwards for two lives.	Geo. Duke of Manchester 1,500
Collector Inwards.	Robert Mann and his Heirs
N.B. Under this Grant, if the late	in trust, for the lives of the
Mr. Mann had left a daughter of	late Lord Walpole and Sir
two years old, she w'd have been the	Edward Walpole. 1,500
Collector to receive Two Millions	
and an half annually.	
	In reversion to Mr. Jenkinson.
Searcher.	Charles Churchill 600
Comptroller.	Henry Duke of Newcastle. 1,500
	(in reversion to Ld Guilford
	and his heirs for the lives of
	Messrs North)

Surveyor General.	Thomas Lord Pelham	950
Customer of Chester.	John Pelham	700
Searcher.	Henry Shelly	600
Customer of Milford.	James Piggot	350
Usher in the Long Room.	William Vary	600
Comptroller of Southampton.	Robert Stannard of Euston, Suffolk.	200
Surveyor of London.	Henry Lord Stawell	800
Inspector of Exchequer Books.	Heneage Legge	220
Register of Warrants	do.	250
Chief Searcher, London.	William Legge.	400
Searcher do	Fras. North	600
Comptroller of Chester.	Sir Jno. Burgoyne, in the Army.	450
Customer of Cardiffe.	John Osborne, Colonel in Militia.	200
Customer of Newcastle.	Richard Williams, in the Army	400
Comptr. of Customs on Wool	Richard Williams.	100
Searcher of Chester.	Jeremiah Robinson.	700
Inspector of Prosecutions.	William Poyntz. in Reversion to Mr. Robinson and Mr. Neville.	3,000
Customer of Southampton.	William Brummell.	430
Register of Seizures.	Brian Broughton.	320

The following Employments are of great publick utility, though the possessors of them have in a great measure converted them into Sine-cures, consequently their Salaries might be saved and the business be conducted by their Deputies and Clerks as at present.

But they may be left as they are if it shall be thought proper that the Minister for the time being should have some easy employments of that sort to bestow on his dependants.

Comptroller General.	Hugh V. Jones.	1,000
Receiver General.	William Mellish	1,500
Comptroller on do.	Henry Ellison.	400
Register General of Shipping.	Peter Shaw	500
Inspector General of Imports and Exports.	John Pelham.	500
Receiver of Forfeitures.	Richard Thompson	500
Accomptant of Petty Receipts.	John E. Freeman	1,300
Appraisers.	Thomas Pearse. Thomas Alderson.	

Enclosure.

II

Dead.		
Ld Hunsdon.		600
Daniel Miller.		400
Lord Willoughby		700
Edward Young		200
Geo. Marshe Dickenson		512
Sir Thos. Dennison		1,200
		3,612
Resigned. Ld Essex		1,000
		4,612

No. 4017—*Lord Shelburne to the King.*

SIR—Your Majesty will have been acquainted by Lord Grantham, of the arrival of Monsr. de Rayneval's Courier, and of the fresh Proposals called for by the Court of France, in consequence of our desiring an addition to the Equivalent propos'd by them for Gibraltar. It being impossible to think of any for Martinique, by which Your Majesty would not be a loser, and hazardous to return instantly to the former ground, especially as Gibraltar ceases to stand in the way of Peace, as has hitherto been understood to be the case ; there seems no power left except to make the roundest offer possible to Spain, to induce them to desist from that Pretension, and I would humbly submit to Your Majesty whether it would not be prudent to offer the Floridas, or at least West Florida, with an extended Boundary, and Minorca, provided the French will add Dominica to the other restitutions on their part, and If Spain does not agree to this, to get back as honourably as we can, to the last propositions made by France, without regard to the part, which the Duke of Grafton, General Conway and Lord Camden may take upon it. I wish that too much way may not already have been given to their hesitation, in truth more, than I could answer to Your Majesty, if Monsieur de Rayneval himself had not at the same time given us hopes of succeeding, which he now very fairly acknowledges. The last circumstances made me suspect that the French might possibly have chang'd their Plan, since he came away, in consequence of the signature of the American Articles or of good accounts from the East Indies. I took all the pains possible with him to discover this, but to no purpose, and I should hope Your Majesty will find them still sincerely dispos'd to Peace. It will however be Mr. Fitzherbert's business to spare neither pains nor money to ascertain this fact against the return from Spain.

I have the honour to be, with the highest Respect, Your Majesty's most dutyfull subject,   SHELBURNE.

BERKLEY SQUARE. 11th *December*, 1782. 8 *o'clock* A.M.

Endorsed by the King.

No. 4018—*Lord Grantham to the King.*

11 *December*, 1782

Lord Grantham has the honour of informing Your Majesty that he has presumed to call a Cabinet for this morning, upon having received from M. de Rayneval, two Propositions, of the greatest importance, brought over by a French Messenger, who arrived yesterday.

The first is, to give Guadelupe and Dominica for Gibraltar, adding thereto St. Lucia, but as in that case France would consider the Tenure of Martinico uncertain, that Island shall be added to the Exchange, provided an equivalent for it be given to France in the East or West Indies.

The second Proposition is founded on an Opening from Spain. It is, that if France shall be confidentially informed upon what terms Peace may be made with Spain, if the latter gives up the Thoughts of insisting upon obtaining Gibraltar, the French King will undertake the Negotiation with Spain.

In the former case an Equivalent for Martinico seems not easy to find, tho' if found the Peace might more speedily be signed.

In the latter, tho' accompanied with some Delay and Risque, there appears such a chance of keeping Gibraltar, that the Consideration deserves the most mature Deliberation.

The Result of it will be, as soon as it is formed, immediately sent to Your Majesty.

WHITEHALL. 45 *m. after* 8 A.M.

Endorsed by the King.

No. 4019.

MINUTE OF CABINET.

[In Lord Grantham's handwriting.]

At a Meeting of Your Majesty's Confidential Servants at Lord Grantham's Office on the 11th of Decr. 1782.

Present :—Lord President, Lord Privy Seal, Duke of Richmond, Earl of Shelburne, Ld. Vt. Keppell, Ld. Ashburton, Mr. Sy. Townshend, Mr. Pitt, Mr. Conway, Lord Grantham.

It is humbly submitted to Your Majesty that the Terms of Peace to be offered to Spain shall be, the Cession of Minorca and The Floridas.

That the Bahamas shall be restored to Gt. Britain, and the Right of cutting Logwood be preserved under regulations.

It is further humbly submitted to Your Majesty that the Restitution of Dominica be insisted upon from France.

Endorsed by the King.

No. 4020—*The King to Lord Grantham.*

QUEEN'S HOUSE. *Decr. 11th,* 1782
m. 25 past 10 A.M.

The situation of the Negociation certainly requires that there should be no unnecessary delay in answering the two Propositions now sent by France.

The 1st. Guadaloupe and Dominica for Gibraltar, in which case Martinico to be added and We to find an equivalent in the West or East Indies for the latter Island.

The 2nd. Gibraltar to be kept but an equivalent to be given to Spain to make Her conclude Peace.

Nothing can be more difficult than to decide on these two propositions ; as to the first I do not see any Possessions in the West Indies that could be given to France ; the only one I could think of would be the two Floridas, which they would certainly refuse, and giving Her more footing in the East Indies would be big with mischief.

As to the second I am ready to avow that Peace is not

compleat unless Gibraltar be exchang'd with Spain ; if it is to be kept I should think the two Floridas ought to content Spain, or else Shè should keep Minorca and restore West Florida.

G. R.

Draft, endorsed by the King.

No. 4021—*The King to Lord Shelburne.*

QUEEN'S HOUSE. *Decr.* 11*th*, 1782
m. 36 *past* 10 A.M.

When Lord Shelburne's note arrived, I had not heard from Lord Grantham that M. de Reyneval's Messenger was returned, and as it referred to the Propositions he had brought, I was under a difficulty to answer for want of precisely knowing them ; but fortunately I have just received one from Lord Grantham, begging to have a Cabinet Meeting this morning, and stating the two propositions.

1st. St. Lucia and Guadaloupe for Gibraltar, but that as this will entirely render Martinico useless to France, some equivalent must be found for that Island either in the East or West Indies, and Martinico be added to our Possessions.

2nd. Gibraltar to remain in our hands, but Spain be satisfied by some other acquisition.

I should vastly prefer the first Proposition if I could see any equivalent for Martinico in the West Indies that we could offer France ; to give Her further footing in the East Indies I should think big with mischief ; the two Floridas alone occur to me, and let France and Spain settle that to their own convenience.

As to the Second, I would propose if Gibraltar is kept, that Spain should have the two Floridas, or Minorca, but I would wish if possible to be rid of Gibraltar, and to have as much possession in the West Indies as possible ; for it has been my purpose ever since Peace has been on the Carpet to get rid of ideal advantages for those that by a good Administration may prove solid ones to this Country. Minorca I should not willingly give up, because if Port Mahon was made a free port, it might draw again into our hands the Mediterranean Trade.

One unpleasant addition to the great difficulties which arise from these Propositions is the enabling the Dukes of Richmond,

Grafton, Lords Camden, Keppel and Genl. Conway to fight the whole Peace over again, and to form fresh Cabals ; I also dread that delays will give time for France to receive accounts from the East Indies which cannot but add to Her demands.

This letter is less explicit than I wish to be, but the difficulties increase so much whichever way we turn that I think it necessary to conclude with just adding that I think Peace every way necessary to this Country, and that I shall not think it compleat if we do not get rid of Gibraltar but that I am not ready to chalk out anything fresh at so sudden and I owne, rather unexpected propositions.

Draft, endorsed by the King.

No. 4022.

MINUTE OF CABINET.

[In Lord Keppel's handwriting.]

December ye 11th, 1782

Present :—Ld. President, Ld. Privy Seal, Ld. Grantham, Mr. Townshend, Lord Shelburne, Duke of Richmond, Mr Pitt, Mr. Conway, Lord Keppel.

It is humbly recommended to Your Majesty that a Squadron of Large and smaller frigates with a ship of fifty guns be equipped with all expedition to accompany and act jointly with Your Majesty's troops intended for a secret undertaking.

No. 4023.

MINUTE OF CABINET.

[In Lord Keppel's handwriting.]

December ye 11th, 1782

Present :—Lord President, Lord Privy Seal, Lord Grantham, Mr. Townshend, Lord Shelburne, Duke of Richmond, Mr. Pitt, General Conway, Lord Keppel.

It is humbly recommended to Your Majesty that in addition to the eight ships of the line dispatched by Admiral Lord Howe after his repassing the Straits of Gibraltar to reinforce the Fleet in the West Indies under the Command of Admiral Pigot, a force of eight other ships of the line should be fitted, and proceed when ready as a further strength to that fleet.

And it is also recommended to Your Majesty that three ships of the Line be without loss of time dispatched to reinforce The Fleet in the East Indies and that as many more ships be sent there, with the East India Outward Bound trade as soon as they can be assembled at Spithead.

No. 4024—*Lord Keppel to the King.*

Lord Keppel has the honour to send Your Majesty a Note which is this moment received from Lloyd's Coffee House, and which If true is of much Importance, but would have been more so if the Marquis de Boille had been captured at the same time the French Ship Armé En flute is supposed to have been taken.

ADMIRALTY, 12 *December*, 1782. *m.* 35 *past* 3 P.M.

Endorsed by the King.

No. 4025—*Lord Shelburne to the King.*

14 *December*, 1782

SIR—I should not think it worth troubling Your Majesty with an account of what passed in the House of Lords yesterday, if I had not had a conversation with Monsr. de Rayneval, of which it may be satisfactory to Your Majesty to be apprised.

Nothing passed in the Lords except conversation, in consequence of a set of questions, which Lord Fitzwilliam had upon paper to put to me, contrary to all order or precedent. He was supported by Lord Derby and Lord Townshend. The Duke of Richmond took a very distinct part, in support of the order of the House, and of Your Majesty's present Administration. This led to some explanations, which I should think make it impossible for much cordiality to remain between that party and His Grace.

I have great satisfaction in acquainting Your Majesty that if Monsr. de Rayneval is not fundamentally deceiv'd, or the Comte de Vergennes disgrac'd, The Peace is still at Your Majesty's Command. He acknowledges the last offer to lay the foundation of not only an honourable but *fructueuse* Negotiation. He is most earnest that the Intermediate Time should be employ'd in finding some equivalent or fresh arrangement, that might satisfye us, in case the Spanish Obstinacy regarding Gibraltar should still prove invincible, for he quoted so many passages from Monsr. de Vergennes' private letters, and mention'd unnecessarily so many circumstances, that I have not myself the least Doubt that they are perfectly sincere in wishing Spain to close on any terms, and that the exchange of Guadouloupe for the Spanish part of St. Domingo is not an object of theirs, or at least a very secondary one.

He avow'd the separation of North America to be their principal Object, and that they considered everything else comme des Drogues. He consider'd I found the Independancy as entirely depending on the present Negotiation, and the Debates about it as ridiculous. He acknowledg'd that Monsr. de Vergennes was astonish'd at the Negotiation being so much advanced without their knowledge, as well as at the Articles, of which Monsr. de Vergennes has sent him a Copy. He said they could not enter into our conduct about the Fishery, and still less into our giving the back lands, which were the sole occasion of the War of 1755. Upon the whole they seem discontented with the conduct of the Americans but determin'd to put the best Face upon what has pass'd.

I am to ask Your Majesty's pardon for so long a detail, and likewise for omitting to take Your Majesty's Commands upon the subject of the Civil List Compensations, as stated by Mr. Gilbert.

I have the honour to be, with the highest respect, Your Majesty's dutyfull subject,   SHELBURNE.

BERKELEY SQUARE. 14*th December*, 1782. 9 *o'clock* A.M.

Endorsed by the King.

No. 4026—*The King to Lord Shelburne.*

The whole conduct of the Lords that chose to be troublesome yesterday shewed more spleen than sense, and gave an opportunity of registering Sentiments that cannot fail of being advantageous to the State.

The language of Mr. de Reyneval makes me flatter myself that peace is not in so desperate a situation as I imagined.

I shall bring the Papers Lord Shelburne sent me concerning the Compensations on the Civil List as stated by Mr. Gilbert on Monday that they may be finally settled.

WINDSOR. *Dec. 14th,* 1782. *m.* 20 *past* 7 P.M.

Draft, written at the foot of Lord Shelburne's letter of same date.

No. 4027—*Mr. Townshend to the King.*

WHITEHALL. *Dec. 15th,* 1782
m. 10 *past* 5 P.M.

Mr. Townshend humbly presumes to send Your Majesty a Minute of Cabinet relative to the Command of the Army in North America. The Cabinet did not think proper to come to any Resolution upon the affairs of Ireland, as the immediate subject before them related to the Decision of a Court of Justice, and the Lord Chancellor was absent.

Mr. Townshend has ventured to inclose to Your Majesty a letter which he has just received from General St. Leger, confirming the account of the capture of a very valuable Prize in the West Indies.

He has been pressed by General Cunningham to advertise Your Majesty of his arrival in England by the direction of the Lord Lieutenant, being apprehensive that his appearance at Your Levee to-morrow, without Your Majesty's leave of Absence might otherwise seem a defect in his respect and duty.

Endorsed by the King.

Enclosure.

MINUTE OF CABINET.

[In Mr. Townshend's handwriting.]

[General Grey, referred to below, was an officer who had greatly distinguished himself in the American War. He served in 1794 in the West Indies in company with Sir John Jervis (later Earl St. Vincent), with whom he was on most affectionate terms. He became later the first Earl Grey, being the father of the Earl Grey of the Reform Bill of 1832.]

WHITEHALL. *Dec. 15th,* 1782

Present

Lord President, Lord Privy Seal, Earl of Shelburne, Duke of Richmond, Lord Grantham, Lord Keppel, Lord Ashburton, General Conway.

It is humbly recommended to Your Majesty, that orders be immediately sent to Sir Guy Carleton to make a Detachment of Troops to the West Indies in case he should not have already embarked any on board any part of Your Majesty's Fleet for that purpose.

It is likewise humbly proposed that General Grey be immediately sent out to relieve Sir Guy Carleton, who has positively and repeatedly desired Your Majesty's permission to resign his Command, and that Your Majesty's Orders should be signified to the Admiralty to prepare a Ship of War to receive General Grey and his Retinue.

No. 4028—*The King to Mr. Townshend.*

WINDSOR. *Dec. 15th.* 1782
m. 40 *past* 9 P.M.

Mr Townshend may give the necessary Orders agreeable to the Advice offered in the Minute of Cabinet ; I am glad to find from the private letter of Major Gen. St. Leger that the Prize taken in the West Indies is so valuable.

Draft, written at the foot of Mr. Townshend's letter of same date.

No. 4029- -*Sir Guy Carleton to Lord Shelburne.*

NEW YORK.   16th *December,* 1782

MY LORD—I think it proper to address this letter to Your Lordship, rather than to convey it in a more official way to the Secretary of State. I have great confidence in the information it contains, but it comes to me so irregularly, that I have not chosen to hazard its being put into instant circulation, as I understand to be the case of Official Dispatches ; but in this manner it may notwithstanding be known under Your Lordship's discretion to The King's confidential servants.

An opinion prevails without the lines that proposals for a peace with America have been made from hence, and rejected by Congress ; this opinion occasions some discontent; I have been urged to repeat those proposals, with assurances that the changes made lately both in Congress and in the different Assemblies are favourable : that the new members are in general men of more property and better education, and from their influence 'tis expected that the true interests of America will be more attended to. I have also been informed that the French Minister at Philadelphia demanded of Congress that Rhode Island be delivered up as a pawn for the money lent them by France, and that it be declared the King's port, 'till the debt be paid, and then to be restored to its former state. The advice says that this demand was refused, and that it gave much uneasiness to the few who were informed of the proposal. I have not yet heard that the French Fleet has sailed from Boston, nor that any of their troops are embarked. They seem to have paid great attention to the people of Newport and Providence, not with great success, and there were some appearances of an intention to winter there, even when it was most strongly asserted they were to embark for the West Indies ; a little time will unmask their intentions. In the meantime the different parties, which became more conspicuous on the suspention of Military operations, and the holding out of Independency, are endeavouring to strengthen themselves. Most people among them think a second Revolution must take place after Great Britain gives them up. The party of Congress, Washington and France, though formerly one, seems now to separate, and form into three. Congress, many think will be overturned, that the notion of governing this country by a Republic is impracticable, and that a Monarchy must of necessity take place ; under this persuasion three ideas are formed, a Prince of the blood of England, one of France, and General Washington, to whom, 'tis added, the Monarchy has been offered, and by him refused. There are who suspect the two last to form but one interest, and to have but one common view, and conceive, that finally, from an inability and unwillingness to pay taxes and support an Independence, the country must fall into the hands of France or England. Perhaps a decided superiority by Sea might determine this important question.

I am, with much respect and esteem, Your Lordship's most obedient and most humble servant, 　GUY CARLETON.

No. 4030—*Lord Shelburne to the King.*

SIR—Some circumstances regarding Mr. Graham's health and private affairs make it material for him to prepare for going abroad as soon as possible, and makes him wish to kiss Your Majesty's hand to-morrow for the Honour Your Majesty intends him of Baronet. Mr Whalley Gardiner and Sir Peter Parker, whom Your Majesty was pleased of some time since for the same Honour may, if Your Majesty thinks proper, attend at the same time.

Upon examining Mr. Gilbert's papers I find that it is not his intention to propose any new person for Superintendant, but that it should make part of the Duty of Pay master, and that it is a confusion of Names, which I will take care shall be avoided in future.

I have the honour to be with the highest respect, Your Majesty's dutyfull subject, 　SHELBURNE.

Endorsed by the King.

No. 4031—*The King to Lord Shelburne.*

I am pleased to find that the favour I am conferring on Lord Chatham is so properly felt by His Mother.

I approve of the three new Baronets appearing tomorrow at St. James's. I believe it had never occurred to Lord Shelburne that Mr. Gilbert was to be a Member of the Board of Works ; it certainly would be in the teeth of the Act for the Members are declared to be bred to the Profession of building, which he certainly has not been.

QUEEN'S HOUSE. *Dec.* 17, 1782. *m.* 40 *past* 3 P.M.

Draft, written on a page of Lord Shelburne's letter of same date.

No. 4032—*Lord Shelburne to the King.*

[The Prince is Prince William, then serving in the Royal Navy.]

SIR—Col. Carleton is this moment arrived at my House. He has Letters for Your Majesty from Admiral Digby, and as he supposes from the Prince, and being in doubt about the proper manner of delivering them, I have presum'd to advise him to carry them without a moment's delay to the Queen's House, and to attend Your Majesty's Commands there.

I have the honour to be, with the highest respect, Your Majesty's most dutyfull subject,   SHELBURNE.

BERKLEY SQUARE. 18*th* December, 1782. ¾ *past* 10 P.M.

No. 4033—*Lord Grantham to the King.*

19*th December*, 1782

Lord Grantham has this moment received the enclosed Note. Ld Shelburne being at the Office, received his at the same time.

Ld Grantham proposes seeing Mr. de Rayneval as soon as the Cabinet is over, and till then takes no notice of this Information, but to Your Majesty.

ST. JAMES'S. 10 *m. past* 1 P.M.

Endorsed by the King.

No. 4034—*The King to Lord Grantham.*

I sincerely rejoice at Spain's acquiescing to our retaining Gibraltar, as it now I hope makes Peace certain, which the Want of Public Zeal and the deficiency of Army and Navy makes me think indispensable. I should have liked Minorca, the two Floridas and Guadaloupe better than this *proud Fortress*, and in my opinion source of another War, or at least of a constant lurking enmity. I trust we have condescended thus far that France is not to keep Dominique.

St. James's. *Dec. 19th, 1782. m. 14 past 1 P.M.*

Draft, written on a page of Lord Grantham's letter of same date.

No. 4035—*Lord Keppel to the King.*

Lord Keppel has the honour to transmit to Your Majesty Sir John Jervis's letter, commanding the Port of Plymouth, of the 19th instant, with two letters from Captain Lutterel of the Mediator, arrive at Plymouth, whose services seem to meritt much approbation.

Admiralty. *Decr. 21st, 1782. m. 45 past 11 P.M.*

Written below by the King as draft reply to Lord Keppel—

The skill as well as Bravery shown by Capt. Lutterell of the Mediator deserve much approbation.

Windsor. *Dec. 22nd, 1782. m. 37 past 8 A.M.*

Endorsed by the King.

No. 4036—*Lord Shelburne to the King.*

Sir—The Chancellor and Speaker have both promis'd to be at the respective Houses at one o'clock, and I hope that proper care will be taken to get Members enough down in due time to be ready for Your Majesty any time after two o'clock.

I have the honour to send Your Majesty the letters which I have received from Paris. I have been in some doubt whether it was worth while to trouble Your Majesty with reading Mr.

Vaughan's, but having hitherto taken that liberty and Your Majesty having been used to overlook the foibles of the Writer, I think it my duty to continue to lay them before Your Majesty.

I take the liberty of enclosing to Your Majesty the individual Letter to the City which preceded Monsieur de Rayneval's Courier and astonished him and us. I have found out both the Writer and Receiver, and Lord Grantham after considering the matter, agrees with me in thinking it would be for Your Majesty's Service to accept an offer made by the latter to go to Paris to-morrow morning, to assist Mr. Fitzherbert, and facilitate as far as the secret channell he is in possession of can be of use, the accomplishing what remains to be wish'd with Spain and Holland. I have liberty to acquaint Your Majesty of both the Names.

I have the honour to be, with the highest respect, Your Majesty's Dutyfull subject,   SHELBURNE.

BERKLEY SQUARE. *22nd December*, 1782. 4 *o'clock*.

Endorsed by the King.

No. 4037—*The King to Lord Shelburne.*

I have ordered my Equipages to be ready at half hour past two to-morrow at St. James's for going to the House of Lords which seems to answer very exactly with the arrangement Lord Shelburne has made with the Ld Chancellor and the Speaker. I suppose I shall see Ld. Shelburne at St. James's previous to my going to Westminster.

Mr. Fitzherbert continues to deserve the highest commendations, and had his hands not been tyed by the strange, undigested opening of the Negociation by Mr. Grenville under the direction of Mr Fox, the Treaty would have been more expeditiously concluded, and in some articles, more advantageously.

As to poor Mr. Vaughan, he seems so willing to be active and so void of judgment that it is fortunate he has had no business, and the sooner he returns to his family the better ; indeed the fewer engines are employed the better, and these should be of the most discreet kind.

WINDSOR. *Dec.* 22nd, 1782. *m.* 2 *past* 9 P.M.

Draft, endorsed by the King.

No. 4038—*Lord Grantham to the King.*

Lord Grantham having received the enclosed Dispatch and private Letter from Mr Fitzherbert this morning has the Honour of taking the earliest Opportunity of laying it before Your Majesty.

St. James's. *4 o'clock.* *22nd Dec.* 1782.

Endorsed by the King.

No. 4039—*The King to Lord Grantham.*

Mr. Fitzherbert's correspondence continues to deserve the utmost approbation. I shall be glad to find the Spanish Secretary enabled to fix the Logwood and Mahogany trade on such ground that the Treaty may be soon concluded.

Windsor. *Dec.* 22nd, 1782. *m. 2 past* 9 P.M.

Draft, written on a page of Lord Grantham's letter of same date.

No. 4040—*Lord Grantham to the King.*

M. de Heredia is come, and has brought three letters which Lord Grantham has the honour to send to Your Majesty.

That from M. D'Aranda is a temperate and reasonable paper, tho' it resists the idea of allowing any British Establishment on the Coast of Honduras, the right to which is established by the Treaty of Paris. Lord Grantham will be able to judge in another Conference with him, whether his Instructions are positive upon this point, and will be prepared with a variety of Plans for the arrangement of that Trade.

Lord Grantham also sends Your Majesty three letters which contain a very satisfactory Admission on the part of the French Ministry, that the Complaints brought some time ago, against some of Your Majesty's Naval Officers were groundless.

He proposes communicating these papers, with Your Majesty's leave, to the Admiralty.

The increasing abuse of the Neutral Flag is manifested in so many late instances that it would require the most strenuous resistance, if the Peace does not take place. At all events, Lord Grantham proposes to make the Ministers of the Neutral Courts sensible of these excesses.

The Master General of the Ordnance has suggested to Lord Grantham that as Your Majesty had been graciously pleased to meet the King of Naples's wish, with regard to some small pieces of Ordnance, it would enhance the value of Your Majesty's condescension on this occasion, if they were to be sent to Naples in Your Majesty's Name.

If this meets with Your Majesty's Approbation, Lord Grantham will acquaint the Neapolitan Minister with this great Mark of Friendship to His Sicilian Majesty.

Lord Grantham being uncertain when he may next have the honour of taking Your Majesty's Commands in person, finds himself obliged to trespass this much upon Your Majesty.

St. James's.   12 p.m.   24th December, 1782.

Endorsed by the King.

No. 4041—*The King to Lord Grantham.*

Windsor.   Dec. 24th, 1782
m. 33 past 6 p.m.

I do not deny the appearance of M. d'Aranda's language being temperate, but his ideas on the Logwood trade do not please Me ; Spain delivering to our ships that come in *Ballast* as much Logwood as we may require, will not do ; we must have the permission to cut it ourselves, consequently have persons for that purpose settled on the Coast.

The letters from the French Court in answer to our State of the Naval Complaints are very satisfactory.

Undoubtedly the abuses of the neutral Flags encrease daily, and require a serious notice from Lord Grantham to the Ministers of those Courts.

I approve of the Cannons being sent to the King of Naples in my name.

Draft, written on a page of Lord Grantham's letter of same date.

No. 4042—*Lord Keppel to the King.*

Lord Keppel has the honour to send to Your Majesty, Rear Admiral Rowley's letters with two to him from the Captain of the London, which Lord Keppel has delayed sending to Your Majesty In hopes that a more Intelligent account might arrive that would give more satisfaction.

Lord Keppel humbly begs to propose to Your Majesty that he may be permitted to appoint Sir John Jervis to the Command of the Intended Secret Expedition.

ADMIRALTY. *Dec. 25th,* 1782. *m.* 45 *past* 11 A.M.

Endorsed by the King.

No. 4043—*The King to Lord Keppel.*

I do not recollect ever to have heard before the name of Captain Kempthorne, but his account of the action is certainly far from clear, and the French ship cannot have been a match for the London, therefore it seems not a very creditable engagement for the British Flag.

Should War continue, I should imagine no Captain can be employed with more propriety to command the Secret expedition than Sir John Jervis.

WINDSOR. *Dec. 25th,* 1782. *m.* 20 *past* 3 P.M.

Draft, written on a page of Lord Keppel's letter of same date.

No. 4044—*Lord Grantham to the King.*

Lord Grantham has the honour to inform Your Majesty that M. de Rayneval's Messenger is returned. Lord Grantham has seen M. de Rayneval who insists that France never had a thought of giving up Dominica, and that if England wants it, it must be for some equivalent—any other Island, as he states it.

St. Vincent's if insisted upon, will be given up, as Lord Grantham conceives.

The French are strenuous in supporting the Dutch upon the subject of Trincomali.

Lord Grantham imagines, that a Cabinet must be summoned and by the Time that it can meet, presumes that all the other Articles can be finally arranged and fit for signature.

The Answer from M. de Aranda will be here in the middle of next week, and M. de Heredia thinks he will agree to Lord Grantham's Proposition, in the letter sent herewith, whereby the Right of Establishment and cutting the Logwood is preserved.

St. James's. 27 *December*, 1782. 11 P.M.

Endorsed by the King.

No. 4045—*The King to Lord Grantham.*

Windsor. *Dec.* 28*th*, 1782
m. 5 *päst* 9 A.M.

It is impossible to treat less above board than the French Court does, and indeed at all times it has been famous for losing nothing from too scrupulous a mode of Negociating : Dominica and Guadaloupe were offered for Gibraltar, which we very absurdly refused, and in return offered the two Floridas and Minorca for Gibraltar, and specified that though in that case we would not claim Guadaloupe, we must have Dominica restored to Us.

When the Messenger returns from Count D'Aranda it will be very proper to hold a Cabinet on the French and Spanish Propositions : I do not love to hazard an opinion on matters that essentially regard my Subjects without having certain grounds to build upon ; I therefore think Ld. Grantham ought to acquire all the information he can whether Dominica or St. Vincent is most advantageous to Us, both in point of Culture and in Situation.

Draft, written on a page of Lord Grantham's letter of 27 December.

No. 4046—*Lord Grantham to the King.*

ST. JAMES'S. 5 *o'clock* P.M.
28 *Dec.* 1782

Lord Grantham having consulted with some of Your Majesty's Principal Servants, proposes with Your Majesty's Leave to see M. de Rayneval to-night.

From the account which he gives of the situation of affairs in France, it is humbly conceived that no time should be lost, in trying whether an offer of Tobago will secure Dominica.

Or whether a District in the East Indies with Karical instead of Tobago will be satisfactory.

To prepare everything else to [be] ready against the return of the Messenger.

Endorsed by the King.

No. 4047—*The King to Lord Grantham.*

WINDSOR. *Dec.* 28*th*, 1782
m. 35 *past* 10 P.M.

The sooner Lord Grantham can bring the French Negociation to a certainty the better ; I therefore am glad he intends seeing M. de Rayneval this Evening ; in the morning St. Vincent seemed to be the equivalent proposed for Dominica—now either Tobago or an additional District in the East Indies with Karical.

Draft, written on a page of Lord Grantham's letter of same date.

No. 4048—*Lord Shelburne to the King.*

SIR—I have the honour to send Your Majesty the Letters which I have receiv'd from Paris late last night and this morning. I had a very confidential conversation with

Monsr. Rayneval previous to Lord Grantham's writing to Your Majesty on Saturday, which leaves me under no apprehension about the Peace, unless a change takes place in the French Ministry. He stated his own and Monsr. de Vergennes' Salvation as depending upon it.

I have the honour to be, with the highest respect, Your Majesty's most dutyfull subject.   SHELBURNE.

STREATHAM. *30th December,* 1782   12 *o'clock Noon.*

Endorsed by the King.

No. 4049—*The King to Lord Shelburne.*

WINDSOR, *Dec. 30th, m.* 6 *past* 4 P.M.

I wish I could think Peace as certain as Ld. Shelburne does ; the encreasing demands and Acrimony in drawing up their Papers indicate some change of Sentiments ; we have never known how to treat with that crafty Nation, chicane has always been an advantageous weapon in Her hands on such Occasions. If M. de Vergennes keeps his ground and that his safety depends on Peace, that may clear up the Picture and make things end as I most ardently wish.

Draft, written on a page of Lord Shelburne's letter of same date.

No. 4050—*The King to* [*Lord Bute ?*]

[1782.]

It gives me ever pain to answer any one in a dubious manner, and it must consequently much more so to my D. Friend, but I should think myself culpable if I did not convey the most secret feelings of my heart on this occasion ; whenever the promotion of Peers takes place from the time I have fought it off, and the many engagements the necessities of particular pinching moments have not in the most smooth times obliged me to consent to, made the number larger than I should have chosen ; this makes every addition to it still more unadvisable ; Lord Mount Stuart is certain of a Seat in the House of Lords ; I hope indeed it is far very far off, therefore it cannot be much an object to him ; besides the House of Commons is the Scene for a Man to exercise his tallents, and to acquire that facility which the Superior House never can give occasion to. That I may quite unburthen myself I must add, the cruel attacks You have met with, would not this give fresh handle for it, I only throw this out for consideration ; should You after all still desire to have the request publicly conveyed to Me, I should think Lord North the proper Channel, and will in that case duly weigh the case but cannot give any other answer at present as I wish to do what on the most mature consideration may seem most adviseable.

No. 4051—*Plan for a Naval Academy.*

[? 1782.]

Of the Academy.

if a suit of Uniform or all the Cloathing is to be allowed, the particulars and the whole charge to be specified.

Suppose fifteen Schollars Sons of Sea Officers to be admitted on the foundation, to be boarded and educated gratis, viz. ten sons of Captains and five sons of Lieutenants.

The choice of these to be so admitted to be determined by rules to be founded on motives of justice and compassion and encouragement to those officers ; for this end I would propose to divide the claimants into classes, and in the admission of them, those of the first class to be always preferred to those of the second, and so on to the rest for the first compleating the numbers to be allowed, and afterwards for filling every vacancy.

Of the Academy.

The Guardians or Executors of the Father, or the next of kin to those who claim under the 1st Class or 2nd Class to declare on oath that the Orphan is not left with a clear income of above £ per annum, & in every case the Guardian or Parent of the boy admitted to give proper assurances to receive him again in case of misbehaviour to deserve to be dismissed, also to provide his cloathing agreeable to the regulations to be established, and no Scholar to be cloathed in a more expensive way than shall be thought right to be prescribed as a rule of the Academy.

1st Class.

To be orphans whose Fathers were slain in battle, or who died afterwards of their wounds.

2nd Class.

Orphans whose Fathers died a natural death after 30 years' service in the Navy.

3rd Class.

The Sons of Captains or Lieutenants who are a burthen to their Mothers, that is whose circumstances are so low as to entitle them to the Widdow's Pension and whose Husbands were slain in battle, or died afterwards of their wounds.

4th Class.

Those who in like manner are a burthen to their Mothers, whose Husbands died of a natural death after thirty years service in the Navy.

When two or more claim under the same class, the Seniority of the Father to give the preference.

None to be admitted under twelve nor more than fifteen years of age.

I think the present plan might in many respects be altered for the better fulfilling the original institution & for making it of more general use and encouragement for Officers and others Gentlemen to send their Sons thither to be educated for the Sea Service.

This I think might be done if among other things, regulations were made to prevent the whole expence exceeding a certain reasonable sum, including the £25 per annum for board, all the Masters being paid by the Public, the expence ought not to exceed that of other reputable public schools.

The present plan of education, I think, is much too large, and seems more calculated for the purpose of keeping the boys there a long time for the benefit of the Master who boards them, than of use to the Schollars.

By curtailing the plan many boys might go through it in two years; three is too long a time to lose at that age from the practical part of the profession.

The time within which a boy may go through the plan to be admitted in his time of service.

This or any other alterations or additions should be first well considered by those who are better acquainted with such kind of business.

Unsigned.

No. 4052—*Mr. Townshend to the King.*

WHITEHALL. *m.* 15 *past* 1 P.M.
[*Jan.* 1783.]

Mr. Townshend humbly presumes in transmitting to Your Majesty the inclosed Dispatches which are all that he has received from General Elliott, to submit to Your Majesty whether it might not be proper, that the rest of Your Ministers should see them as early as Your Majesty can spare them, for the purpose of selecting such Parts as may be proper to be published in the Gazette of this night.

Endorsed by the King.

No. 4053—*The King to Lord Hood.*

QUEEN'S HOUSE. *Jany.* 2nd, 1783

LORD HOOD—Your letter in answer to mine on placing my son William under Your care was brought by Capt. Elphinstone, I owne I am anxious for the first Accounts from the West Indies after Your arrival, as I trust it will bring me a letter from You with an Account of the manner in which William has conducted himself in the new Scene he now is entered upon ; I should have been glad had the health of Mr. Majendie permitted him to have remained some time longer with him, as he knew so perfectly his disposition, and therefore might have continued very useful; the character I have received from V. Ad. Barrington and others concerning Capt. Napier makes me hope on further acquaintance that He will meet with Your approbation. I shall only add that a thorough conviction of Your private character, as well as of Your tallents as an officer makes me thoroughly convinced that I have acted the proper part as a Parent in placing my Son under You, and that I rely on Your keeping a strict eye over him, and remembering that He must act with civility and attention to all persons and avoid that familiarity which frequently borders on contempt.

Draft.

No. 4054—*Lord Shelburne to the King.*

SIR—I found a note from Monsr. de Rayneval on my return from Your Majesty, which determin'd me to stay in town for the purpose of seeing him, and such Members of the Cabinet as were in town, in consequence of what pass'd with the Duke of Richmond.

I have the satisfaction to acquaint Your Majesty from the style of Monsr. de Vergennes' letter, part of which M. de Rayneval read to me, and still more from his appearance and manner, that there does not appear the smallest room to doubt of the Sincerity and good dispositions of the French King and His Minister. Lord Chancellor, Mr. Townshend, Mr. Pitt and Lord Grantham are all clearly of opinion, that this great object is no longer to be trifl'd with, but that final orders should be sent to Mr. Fitzherbert, as soon as the French Courier returns. I have no apprehension of General Conway's giving any material difficulty, as he was very reasonable in a conversation which I had with him upon leaving Your Majesty. Neither the Duke of Grafton nor Lord Camden are in town. I will make it my business to see them as soon as they arrive.

I have the honour to be with the highest Respect, Your Majesty's Dutyfull subject,   SHELBURNE.

BERKLEY SQUARE. *4th Jany.* 1783. 8 *o'clock* A.M.

Endorsed by the King.

No. 4055—*The King to Lord Shelburne.*

WINDSOR. *Jany 4th,* 1783
m. 25 *past One*

Lord Shelburne's Attention in acquainting Me of the satisfactory completion of that part of Monsr. de Vergennes' letter which Mr. de Rayneval last night communicated to Him and that the Chancellor, the two Secretaries and Mr. Pitt are clearly of opinion that Peace must no longer be trifled with, but the final Orders sent to Mr. Fitzherbert as soon as the French

Courier returns, meets every way with my warmest thanks, for I was rather desponding as to the success of the Negociation.

I think it right just to give the heads of what dropped from the Duke of Richmond and Ld Keppel; the former said it was impossible he could continue a Member of the Cabinet after at a Meeting the Ultimatum had been settled, and that Ld Grantham had been authorized to offer Tobago in lieu of Dominica by a more intimate consultation; That he had found Ld Keppel and Gen. Conway equally ignorant of this transaction, that He did not mean that He could not attend Councils *He did not guide*, but He could not be a member of Council and consequently *answerable for Measures of which he was ignorant*; but that as the taking that step hastily might prevent Peace, he would abstain from taking this step till that great measure had one way or other come to a decision; that He did not mean to blame Lord Grantham, whose conduct had ever been polite and ingenuous; that he had attacked the late Ministry because He thought they *did not act in concert*; That on the same plan He must object to anyone acting as *Sole Minister*; that he had *no one measure to object to* but that the Country would never bear a Prime Minister, and that We did nothing but yield one point after another to France.

Ld Keppel complained of having been constantly slighted, that Duty to Me made him silent till Peace was decided, but that he is convinced France will not conclude one.

Gen. Conway was attentive to his own Department and did not drop one sillable on the above affair, therefore I am certain will not join the two others.

Draft, endorsed by the King.

No. 4056—*Lord Shelburne to the King.*

[7 *Jan.* 1783.]

SIR—No Messenger being arriv'd from Paris, I have the honor to enclose to Your Majesty a Letter from Monsr. Rayneval and some letters from the City, as they upon the whole prove the French Ministry still sincere in their desire of Peace. It's to be hop'd that He may arrive in the course of this Day, but if he does not, I hope the Cabinet who must necessarily meet this Evening, on account of the Lord Chancellor and the Duke of Grafton, will submit to Your Majesty, Definite orders to Mr. Fitzherbert to sign, leaving the more or less of everything that remains, to his discretion. I have been at the same time turning my mind to prepare such a Plan to be submitted to Your Majesty, in case of the worst that Government may in no event appear confounded or desponding.

If the Duke of Richmond had confin'd his remonstrances to the Inability of the person he alludes to, I can easily conceive the Publick might be of his side, and Your Majesty's Goodness be put to a very severe trial, but I am afraid his own conduct calls too plainly for a greater degree of the very Interference, of which he professes himself so jealous.

I have the honour to be, with the highest respect, Your Majesty's dutyfull subject,   SHELBURNE.

STREATHAM. 7 *Nov.* [*sic*] 1783. ½ *pt.* 11 A.M.

Endorsed by the King, Jan. 7, 1783, which is plainly the correct date.

No. 4057—*The King to Lord Shelburne.*

WINDSOR. *Jany 7th,* 1783
46 *m. past* 3 P.M.

Lord Shelburne is very right even if the French Courier should not arrive in the course of the Day in getting the Cabinet this evening to advise definite orders to Mr. Fitzherbert to sign, and leaving those who are to execute the Orders that discretion which is necessary to conclude the Treaty, without further meetings.

I thought it right to give Lord Shelburne the exact complexion of the D. of Richmond's language, and as nearly as possible his words, as it might be material to see how it corresponded with what He might say to others. I do not think it proves anything so clearly as his own inclination to be prying into every department, and which if it lasted would prove incompatible with any system.

Draft, endorsed by the King.

No. 4058—*Lord Grantham to the King.*

Lord Grantham has the honour of laying the Drafts of the Preliminaries with France and with Spain before Your Majesty.

The Article 20 with the French, and the Article 8 with Spain, are not yet drawn out, as Lord Grantham proposes to adjust them if possible with M. de Rayneval and M. de Heredia.

ST. JAMES'S, 9 *Jany.* 1783. 10 A.M.

Endorsed by the King.

No. 4059—*Lord Keppel to the King.*

Lord Keppel has the honour to send to Your Majesty letters of the 11th and 14th of December last from Rear Admiral Digby at New York, and likewise sends Your Majesty Sir Charles Knowles's letters from Gibraltar of the 21st of November and 19th of December last, by which Your Majesty will observe the situation of the St. Michael to be very critical and hazardous.

ADMIRALTY, *January 11th*, 1783. *m.* 40 *past* 11 A.M.

No. 4060—*Lord Grantham to the King.*

[13 *Jan.* 1783.]

Lord Grantham humbly begs leave to express the satisfaction which he feels at conveying the enclosed Dispatches from Mr. Fitzherbert. They open so fair a Prospect of signing the Preliminaries immediately, and upon Terms even more Advantageous than there was reason to expect in several Particulars that he will lose no time in preparing His Dispatches for Mr. Fitzherbert, communicating to him Your Majesty's Commands to conclude this important Business.

So that if upon the last Instructions which went the Signature has not actually taken place, there can scarce be a doubt of that Measure's immediately following the Arrival of the next Messenger from hence.

The Couriers were detained four days by contrary winds.

45 *mins after* 4 P.M. ST. JAMES'S. 13 *Dec.* [*sic,* should be 13 *Jan.*] 1783.

Endorsed by the King, Jan. 13, 1782 [*sic,* should be 1783].

No. 4061—*The King to Lord Grantham.*

WINDSOR. *Jany* 13*th,* 1782 [*sic,* should be 1783]
m. 15 *past* 9 P.M.

By the cursory view I have taken of Mr. Fitzherbert's Dispatch and of the alterations made in the project by the French Preliminaries, I should hope this arduous task may be easily accommodated and in some points more advantageously than by the Draft sent last Friday ; as the ending this business with correctness as well as dispatch is necessary ; I desire Lord Grantham will prepare the answer to Mr. Fitzherbert with all possible dispatch, but as four eyes sometimes see what two may omit, that He will communicate it to Ld. Shelburne before he sends off the Messenger, as it will be impossible to make any further amendment to the Articles when returned this time to Paris.

I think the Draft of a joint declaration to the two Imperial Courts will require some amendment before we can entirely consent to it, though the general idea may be eligible.

Draft, written on a page of Lord Grantham's letter of same date.

No. 4062—*Lord Hood to* [*General Sir William Fawcett ?*]

BARFLEUR OFF CAPE FRANCOIS
Jany. 16*th,* 1783

MY DEAR GENERAL—I give you many and sincere thanks for your affectionate letter of the 26th of June, which was brought me from Barbadoes a few days ago with above one hundred others, amongst which was a duplicate of one you had the goodness to write me on the 7th of August, addressed to New York. From these letters I was somewhat consoled for my ill fortune in not having mett with Vaudreuil, as I have received but one short letter from any part of my family of a later date than the end of April.

I do not yet despair of having an opportunity of paying my compliments to the noble Marquis, as I know he had not sailed from Boston on the 15th of last month.

I want words, my dear General, to express how much I think myself obliged for the very kind and truly salutary advice you had the goodness to give my dear Henry. I thank you again and again, and am very sensible I can never do it sufficiently ; you have saved me from ruin ; I feel it very forcibly.

Upon my arrival at New York, I was accidentally informed, that I had been put in nomination for Westminster but that my son had wisely withdrawn my name as a candidate. I instantly wrote him a few lines of the fullest approbation, without knowing at that time, how very much I stood indebted to your friendship ; if I had you would either have received my most gratefull acknowledgments, which I now beg you will be pleased to accept. Poor as I undoubtedly am, my good friend, I would sooner have given 500 pounds than have stood a contest, even had I been sure of succeeding, for a tenth part of the money ; a seat in the House of Commons, I have no ambition for, and will never offer myself *anywhere* ; if there is public spirit enough left in any corporation in England to make choice of me, as its representative from the free will of the Electors, *well* ; if not, I shall be full as well satisfied. Believe me, my dear General, I shall studiously steer clear, as far as I am able, of all suspicion of being a *party man*, for if once I shew myself of that frame of mind, whether for or against the minister, unbecoming a Military servant of our Royal and most gracious Master, I from that moment must expect to lose all consideration in the line of my profession, which ever has been and ever will be the first and greatest object of my wishes. I revere my King ; I have much affection for my Country, and the pride and glory of my remaining days, will be to assist both, with my feeble services, to the utmost extent of my abilities, and I have the vanity to think that I am in some small degree qualified to fight the Battles of my King and country, upon my own element, but confess myself totally unfit to fight the Battles of a Minister in either House of Parliament ; and even if I had the abilities equal to the task, I think it an employment derogatory to the character of a sea officer whose highest ambition is to stand well in the good opinion of his Sovereign and fellow-subjects in his professional line. These are my sentiments, and I hope and trust I shall have fortitude enough to adhere to them ; for had the free and unbiassed voice of the people carried my Election, against all Opposition, and without a shilling expense to myself, it would have distressed me beyond measure, with such a Colleague ; besides, the business of so large and populous a place as Westminster would have been more intricate and burthensome than I could have undertaken, and have loaded me with insupportable vexation and trouble.

I am, my dear General, in another strong instance very highly indebted to your kind advice ; I see the propriety and force of it, and hope I shall prove that it is not thrown away upon me. But my opinion of the *sad* finish of the business of April the 12th, is well and fully known to every Officer in the Fleet, and I am confident it is by no means irregular, but pretty unanimously concurred in. That gallant, good officer, Captn. Cornwallis, can give perhaps a better and more just account of the whole transactions of that day than any other officer, as his situation enables him to do so. There are two or three persons, of whose Friendship and attachment I have had such proof that I thought myself bound, *confidentially*, to make them acquainted with my sentiments ; but still, I see as fully and forcibly as you can wish, the very wholesome and candid advice you have had the goodness to honour me with, and which I trust I shall make a proper use of, and very much attend to.

It is with the greatest truth I can assure you that Prince William is perfectly well and attends Captain Knight very closely for two hours every morning at the mathematics and drawing, and His Royal Highness takes a pleasure in both. The Cold Bath seems to have been of great service to his shoulder, in which His Royal Highness now feels no kind of complaint.

I am grieved beyond expression to find that notwithstanding the sacrifice the King has made, by parting with his old and faithful servants, such a distraction still continues, which must infallibly, sooner or later, work our ruin. We have accounts of Peace from various quarters ; it is an event I shall have cause to rejoice at, with respect to myself, as my slender frame is so very much shook that I have much difficulty to keep upon my Legs, and could not possibly hold out beyond the end of the present year in this country ; but whether I shall have reason to do so, for my poor Country, I very much doubt, being clearly of opinion, considering *all things*, formidable as the combination is against us, we shall I fear never again be in so good a condition for recovering the nations's honour, as at this present moment nothing is wanting, I am very confident to effect it, but unanimity at home and a regard to whom the King's Fleets and Armies are trusted, and without that, all is over with us, as a great and powerful Kingdom, and it matters not, whether we have peace or war, it comes to one and the same thing, with this difference only, that by peace the evil will be at somewhat a greater distance, but according to my conception, sure and certain ; for if it should please God to prolong my life to another War, some years hence, I shall look to the event of it with fear and trembling, unless by the all powerfull interference of the Divine Providence, we become an united and rational people. After a very few years' peace, we shall have scarce any Lieutenants that will know their duty ; at present our situation is bad enough in that respect ; it will then be abundantly worse, as we have so many *ignorant Boys* in that character, which from being any time on shore, will become more ignorant, and probably not so well disposed towards improvement, and the few capable officers we now have, will then be past such active service as will be required of them.

At midnight on the 11th of this month, I was joined by the Acteon, one of Rear Admiral Rowley's ships, which I had taken upon me to station, to the northward of the Caycos Island, to look out for the enemy, whose Commander informed me, he had on the 8th in the afternoon seen a large fleet steering for the Caycos Passage, which was either French or Spanish, and that he counted fifteen very large ships, and afterwards saw a frigate, bear down to two neutral vessels, which he had spoken with in the morning, with French colours hoisted. I immediately examined how the winds had blown between the 8th and the 11th, and finding the Fleet could not fetch Cape François, I concluded it would steer for Cape Nicola Mole on the Bite of Leogane, and bore up for those places ; though I was pretty confident in my own mind (and told the Captain of the Acteon so) the Fleet seen was the Transports from Charles Town, going to Jamaica ; but he was so positive of its being either French or Spanish, and that fifteen ships were of the line, I was under the necessity of attending to the information. But neither seeing or hearing any trace of enemy's ships, and after ordering two Frigates to reconnoiter Cumberland Harbour on the Island

Cuba, as the only place they could take shelter in, I got back
to my station to windward of Cape François yesterday, and
very fortunately nothing had arrived while I was away but an
American Frigate from Europe.

Jany. 28th.   OFF CAPE TIBEROON

On the 19th instant at night I received certain intelligence
that the Marquis de Vaudreuil was off the Harbour of St. John's
Portorico on the 16th with ten sail of the line. I immediately
did my utmost to get to windward, but both wind and current
were so strong against me that I could gain but little ground.
On the 23rd I was informed that the enemy was still off St.
John's on the 23rd. On the 24th at three in the morning, when
I should have fetched the east end of Hispaniola a large French
ship with masts, and 250 soldiers on board came under the stern
of my repeater, taking us for the French Squadron. She sailed
from Portsmouth in Newhampshire on the 29th of last month,
with the Auguste and Pluton, and Amazon frigate, and parted
company with the two line of battle ships, three days after they
came out ; on the 22nd they got off St. John's, and were informed
by a Pilot that came out, that the Marquis de Vaudreuil had
bore away to leeward the night before, on being joined by the
Auguste and Pluton ; and upon the return of the Amazon's
Boat from the shore, she bore away also, after ordering the
Transport into St. John's, but on her working up to the harbour's
mouth, a sudden squall carried away her maintopmast, which
caused her to bear up for Cape François. Upon receiving this
intelligence, I made all possible sail to the Westward, taking it
for granted that Vaudreuil had gone through the Mona channel,
either with a design of harbouring at Port Louis on the south
side, or coming round the West end of the Island to Nicola Mole,
unless he should go to the Havana to join Don Solano, and
come up in great force together to the Cape, and though I was
well satisfied the enemy's squadron could not have passed me
unseen, I looked into Cape François and the Mole, as I came
down.

I have now but a small chance left for having a meeting with
Vaudreuil, but in order to enable the King's Squadron under my
command to keep the sea ten or twelve days longer, I availed
myself of a few hours calm yesterday to distribute a little water

and bread to those ships which were most short ; some had only bread for two days, but a few tons of water ; we have had no supply of the latter since the 14th of November, and when we reach Jamaica not a ship will have more than three days of Bread, Pease, Rum or water, but I thank God we are in general tolerably healthy in two or three ships the scurvy has taken root pretty strong.

On the return of the two frigates from Cumberland Harbour (where they saw nothing) they gott a certain account that I was right in my conjectures, for the fleet seen and reported to me by the Acteon, was the transports from Charles Town under the protection of three frigates. This will shew you what sad consequences may arise from a loose report of a Fleet's being seen, and not look'd at near enough to be sure and certain, whether it consists of men of war or merchant ships. I have ordered a ship to reconnoiter Port Louis, and shall wait here till she returns, unless I hear for certain that Vaudreuil is gone to the Havana or harboured elsewhere. As the refitting the King's Squadron will employ my whole time at Port Royal, I am preparing my letters while I have leisure.

If upon Sir Richard Hughes's arrival at Barbadoes from Lord Howe, [Admiral Pigot] had not seen it necessary to keep the reinforcement to windward, and have come with, or detached it, hither, St. John's in Porto Rico as well as Cape François might have been guarded, which must have secured Vaudreuil to us ; but doubtless Admiral Pigot had good and sufficient reason from his information from home against doing either. The force to windward is 23 of the Line and the Leander of 50 guns ; if therefore nothing was to be apprehended but from Vaudreuil ten sail might have been spared and a force left equal to him, but it was next to a certainty that his destination was for the Cape. However the Admiral might have strong and substantial reason for expecting a very formidable force at the Windward Islands, either from France or Spain : though I am free to confess my opinion, that let the enemy's force which will come from Europe, be more or less formidable, it will not touch at Martinique, but come directly to the Cape. But when an Officer in Command does that, which human prudence as well as sound judgment suggests, he ought to submit with all becoming fortitude, there is no guarding against *misfortune*.

Feby 5th, 1783. PORT ROYAL, JAMAICA

I am just anchored here and as many folks are coming on board and I have many things to do, I will close my letter, a Pacquet being about to sail.

I am, with most perfect regard and esteem, my dear General, Your most faithful and obedient humble servant,   HOOD.

No. 4063—*Lord Shelburne to the King.*

Lord Shelburne has the honour to inclose for Your Majesty's use the List of Naval Promotions, which he received from Sir John Jervis, together with a memorandum in answer to Lord Kepple's last argument against the Peace. He has likewise the honour to send yesterday's accounts from the City.

BERKLEY SQUARE. 19*th Jany*. 1783.

Endorsed by the King.

No. 4064—*The King to Lord Shelburne.*

QUEEN'S HOUSE. *Jany* 19*th*, 1783
m. 31 *past* 10 A.M.

The Names of the Officers promoted by Ld Keppel are in general I should hope for their merit, for undoubtedly I never heard scarce the name of two of them, therefore their families cannot have been their recommendation. Most of the Arguments in the paper Lord Shelburne has communicated to Me by way of answer to the last Opinion of Lord Keppel against the necessity of Peace are very forcible. I am sorry to see there has been so much business in the Alley yesterday. I trust tomorrow night or Tuesday morning will enable us to know that Peace is concluded.

Draft, written on a page of Lord Shelburne's letter of same date.

No. 4065—*Lord Keppel to the King.*

Lord Keppel has the honour to send Your Majesty Captain Cristie (late of the Hannibal taken by the french Squadron in the East Indies) his letters giving Information he has been Able to collect, relative to Events in the East Indian seas, & which Accounts he delivers himself, having taken his passage from the Cape of Good Hope In a danish East India Ship.

Lord Keppel Also has the honour to send Your Majesty, Admiral Sir Thomas Pye's letter in Answer to the Admiralties Messenger sent to Sir Thomas with your Commands as Signified to the board, by Mr. Secretary Townshend to delay the sailing of Commodore Elliot & Captain Elphinston.

ADMIRALTY *jany.* 19*th* 1783.
  m. 35 *past* 4 P.M.

No. 4066—*Mr. Townshend to the King.*

WHITEHALL. *Jany* 20*th*, 1783
m. 30 *past* 12

Mr. Townshend humbly presumes to send Your Majesty a Dispatch, which he received yesterday from the Lord Lieutenant of Ireland, with the Draught of his Answer to it. He finds himself under a necessity of explaining to Your Majesty, that the four Draughts upon which the Lord Lieutenant observes, were Papers which Mr. Grenville sent to Ireland in a private letter for the opinion of the Lord Lieutenant, and even without the knowledge of Mr. Townshend, who never saw three of them till since the receipt of the Dispatch ; the Lord Lieutenant seems to have mistaken these Papers for an Official Communication.

Endorsed by the King.

No. 4067—*The King to Mr. Townshend.*

QUEEN'S HOUSE. *Jany* 20*th*, 1783
m. 50 *past one* P.M.

I am sorry to find Lord Temple's anxiety to get the present difficulty as to Writs of Error from Ireland prevented for the future, does not allow him more coolly to view the conduct held on this Occasion by Ministers on this side of the Water when they are restrained by no consideration but the doing what He wishes in the least exceptional mode. The reality, not the Manner should alone interest him; besides as every Lawyer must coincide in Opinion that till such a Bill has passed that it has ever been the Law that these Writs of Error when applied for should be granted, consequently the taking away the power is all that can be done.

Draft, written on a page of Mr. Townshend's letter of same date. Duplicate copy in the King's handwriting.

No. 4068—*Lord Grantham to the King.*

Lord Grantham has seen M. de Rayneval this morning, who has had a Messenger from France with Letters from Paris of the 15th & 16th inst.

There is an English Messenger also on the Road.

The Letters from Paris inform M. de Rayneval, that everything between M. Fitzherbert, M. de Vergennes, and M. D'Aranda, was so far settled that the Preliminaries could have been signed on the next Day, but for the strenuous opposition on the part of Mr. Fitzherbert to the Restitutions to the Dutch.

Your Majesty however recollects the Latitude which Your Majesty has allowed to your Minister on that Subject, and that the Dispatches of the 14th would enable him to sign immediately.

Lord Grantham therefore conceives that the Signature will have taken place on the 18th and that Notice thereof may be expected almost hourly.

ST. JAMES'S. *20th Jany.* 1783. *5 m. past* 1 P.M.

Endorsed by the King.

No. 4069—*The King to Lord Grantham.*

By the note just received from Lord Grantham, I shall think myself authorized to expect hourly the Account of the Signature of the French and Spanish Preliminarys; I thank him for his Attention in preparing Me for so desirable an Event.

QUEEN'S HOUSE, *Jany 20th,* 1783. *m. 58 pt.* 1 P.M.

Draft, written on a page of Lord Grantham's letter of same date.

No. 4070—*Lord Grantham to the King.*

Mr. Oswald is returned from Paris, and has brought Mr. Fitzherbert's Dispatches of the 15th Instant, which confirm in every particular the Advices received yesterday by M. de Rayneval.

They shall be immediately laid before Your Majesty.

M. de Rayneval however has just received a private but certainly authentic Notice that the Preliminaries were signed on Saturday the 18th. This Information is surely not sufficient to justify any Notification of it at all, but authorises me humbly tho' cordially to congratulate Your Majesty on this important Event.

St. James's, *m. 25 past* 1 p.m. 21*st Jany.* 1783

No. 4071—*The King to Lord Grantham.*

Queen's House, *Jany.* 21*st*, 1783
m. 46 *pt.* 3 p.m.

As M. de Rayneval's intelligence is only from a private Channel He could not with propriety officially announce the intention of signing the Preliminaries on Saturday last; but I think this quite sufficient for me to thank Ld. Grantham for his communication of so important an event.

Draft, written on a page of Lord Grantham's letter of same date.

No. 4072—*Lord Shelburne to the King.*

Sir—Mr. Ord is this moment come from Monsr. De Rayneval, who had in the instant *seen a private Letter* from Paris dated Saturday, upon which he can entirely depend, which states that Mr. Fitzherbert receiv'd his last dispatches from hence on Fryday morning, that he immediately saw Monsr. de Vergennes, who took the King's Commands upon the whole of the articles the same night and that in consequence every thing was agreed on Saturday morning, before this Letter came away, and were certainly to be sign'd on Saturday Evening or at the farthest early on Sunday.

Monsr. Rayneval says that he cannot upon this authority make an Official communication to Lord Grantham, as it is not address'd to himself, but he is as sure of the fact, as if he had received it from the hand of Monsr. De Vergennes. I have therefore thought it my Duty to acquaint Your Majesty, and I beg leave most humbly to congratulate Your Majesty and the Queen upon the completion of this great Event.

I understood from Monsr. de Rayneval yesterday, that Negapatnam would occasion no difficulty.

I have the honour to be with the highest Respect, Your Majesty's Faithfull Subject and Devoted Servant, SHELBURNE.

BERKLEY SQUARE, 21 *January*, 1783. ½ *past one* P.M.

Endorsed by the King.

No. 4073—*Mr. Townshend to the King.*

WHITEHALL, *Jany* 21, 1783
m. 30 *past* 1 P.M.

Mr. Townshend humbly presumes to send Your Majesty a Letter, which he has just received from Lord Keppel for Your Majesty's inspection, and that he may receive Your Commands concerning the summoning a Cabinet.

The Business of the House of Commons may possibly detain Mr. Pitt and General Conway as well as Mr. Townshend a considerable time, but the urgency of the matters to be considered as stated by Lord Keppel seem to forbid any delay beyond this evening. Mr. Townshend at the same time presumes to inclose to Your Majesty a Letter, which he received yesterday from Lord Keppel containing two from Sir Thomas Pye, and likewise one which he has just received from Mr. Oswald.

No. 4074—*The King to Mr. Townshend.*

QUEEN'S HOUSE, *Jany* 21*st*, 1783
m. 46 *pt.* 3 P.M.

I should have thought Gen. Conway, Mr. Pitt, and Mr. Secy. Townshend so material persons at the deliberation Ld. Keppel wishes to have held that, I am certain if He knew they are not likely to be present at a meeting this Evening, that he will wish to have it postponed till tomorrow; but if the business will not afford that short delay, I authorize Mr. Secy. Townshend's sending summonses for this evening.

Draft, written on a page of Mr. Townshend's letter of same date. Duplicate draft in the King's handwriting.

No. 4075—*The King to Lord Shelburne.*

QUEEN'S HOUSE, *Jany.* 21*st*, 1783
m. 46 *pt.* 3 P.M.

Though Monr. de Rayneval is right in not thinking himself authorized to announce the Preliminarys being signed on Saturday as his intelligence does not come from Count de Vergennes; but as he looks on the Channel as authentic Ld. Shelburne is certainly well warranted to look on the Event as certain. The keeping Negapatnam is certainly an advantageous measure. By Mr. Fitzherbert's letters I find new demands are to be made by Dr. Franklin, but I trust if the other Treaties are signed they will meet with the treatment they deserve.

G. R.
Draft, endorsed by the King.

No. 4076—*Lord Keppel to the King.*

Lord Keppel has the honor of sending Your Majesty Rear Admiral Digby's letter from New York of the 18th & 22nd of last December also Captain Craven of the Adamant & two from Captain Surny of the Assurance.

ADMIRALTY, *January* 21*st*, 1783. *m.* 50 *past* 4 P.M.

No. 4077—*Mr. Townshend to the King.*

Jany 22, 1783
m. 30 *past* 9 P.M.

Mr. Townshend humbly presumes to send Your Majesty a Minute of Cabinet, which Lord Keppel wished to be transmitted to Your Majesty, as soon as the account of the Preliminarys being signed should arrive, that he might receive Your Majesty's Orders upon the subject contained in it.

Endorsed by the King.

Enclosure.

MINUTE OF CABINET.

[In Mr. Townshend's handwriting.]

ST. JAMES'S, *Jany.* 22, 1783

Present :—Lord Chancellor, Lord Privy Seal, Earl of Shelburne, Lord Keppel, Lord Grantham, Lord Ashburton, Mr. Pitt, General Conway, Mr. Townshend.

It is humbly recommended to Your Majesty that the Admiralty should be directed to stop the sailing of Commodore Eliot with his Squadron to the West Indies, and that Captain Elphinstone's sailing should also be stopped, and the troops on board the Transports relanded at Portsmouth.

It is also humbly recommended to Your Majesty that the West India Convoy with a proper number of ships, three Ships of the Line, should procede upon the Voyage, as soon as the wind becomes favorable without embarking Troops intended for the West Indies, and it is likewise recommended to Your Majesty, that the three Ships of the Line and two Frigates intended as Convoy to the East India Ships should sail as soon as the Embarkation intended to procede with them are on board, and that Commodore Eliot's Squadron should procede and protect the two Convoys for the East and West Indies a hundred and fifty Leagues into the Sea, and after having seen them in safety so far to be ordered immediately to return to Spithead, giving every possible protection and assistance to the Trade of Your Majesty's Subjects, they may fall in with.

Endorsed by the King.

No. 4078—*Lord Grantham to the King.*

Lord Grantham has just received Dispatches from Mr. Fitzherbert of the 19th Inst. in which he informs him that the

Preliminary Articles were definitely agreed upon on the 17th Inst. by M. de Vergennes & himself, were transcribed fair and (the Spanish Preliminaries having been likewise settled on the same Day and the principal points of the Dutch Treaty agreed upon on the 18th) were to be signed on the 20th.

¼ *past* 12 P.M. *22nd Jany.* 1783

Endorsed by the King.

No. 4079—*The King to Mr. Townshend.*

Mr. Secy. Townshend's Note Accompanying a Minute of Cabinet concerning the Squadrons ready for Sailing and proposing some alterations which the prospect of Peace rendered necessary and which the news arrived this Evening makes highly proper to be instantly put into execution. Mr. Secy Townshend will therefore issue the necessary Orders agreable to this Minute ; I cannot help observing that the Note is dated the last Evening though but just arrived.

QUEEN'S HOUSE, *Jany.* 23rd, 1783. *m.* 3 *pt.* 11 P.M.

Draft, written on a page of Mr. Townshend's letter of 22 January, 1783.

Duplicate in the King's handwriting.

No. 4080—*Lord Grantham to the King.*

ST. JAMES'S, 11 P.M.
23rd Jany, 1783

Lord Grantham sends Your Majesty the Dispatches & the Preliminaries received this Afternoon ; And humbly prays that Your Majesty would please to direct them to be sent to the Office tomorrow morning as Your Majesty's Confidential Servants are to meet before eleven o'Clock.

M. de Rayneval having received his Credential, Lord Grantham will have the honour of introducing him to his Audience to-morrow & of presenting M. de Vergennes and M. de Heredia at the Levee.

Endorsed by the King.

No. 4081—*The King to Lord Grantham.*

QUEEN'S HOUSE, *Jany 24th,* 1783
m. 17 *pt.* 10 A.M.

The more I reflect on the Want of Sailors and Soldiers to enable Us to carry on with any probability of advantage the War against so many Enemies, the total indifference at least of the other European Powers towards Us, and the inimical conduct of those who carry on any Trade and more particularly the ingratitude of Portugal, who owes her very existence to Us, the more I thank Providence for having through so many difficulties among which the want of Union and Zeal at home is not to be omitted, enabled so good a Peace with France, Spain and I trust soon with the Dutch to be concluded.

I desire Ld. Grantham will come with the Gentlemen He has to present this Day at St. James's as soon after half hour past twelve as He can ; indeed the D. of Richmond having retired from Council ; I trust the Meeting cannot last longer than the time necessary for reading the Preliminaries that have been signed.

Draft, written on a page of Lord Grantham's letter of same date.

No. 4082—*Dr. Hallifax to the Duke of Manchester.*

ALBERMARLE STREET, 24th *Jany.* 1783

MY LORD DUKE—I beg the favour of Your Grace humbly to represent to the King, the high sense I have of the honour & confidence His Majesty is graciously pleased to shew me by ordering me to provide proper persons to attend upon and supply His Majesty's Household with Medicines at Windsor and Kew as well as in London, and that I shall always be happy to shew my duty to the King by devoting myself to His Service in any respectable situation, & to be an instrument in reforming the expense of it, though to the further diminution of the value of my own appointment.

If the number of His Majesty's Servants who are to be allowed the benefit of Medicine, be limited according to the regulation of the late Duke of Grafton, and they are not to have the liberty of sending to the Apothecary for what Drugs or Medicines they think proper, which are not prescribed by the Physician to the Household ; I should hope that the expence of this supply might be reduced to £300 a quarter for all the services together. But I am certain, to whoever this contract is given, he must frequently give his personal superintendance over the Apothecaries and the Sick, wherever the Royal Family resides, or His Majesty's Service cannot be well executed, and bills would soon be brought in, equal to or exceeding this allowance.

I hope Your Grace will not think it an extravagant request, if I sollicit your recommendation to the King to be pleased to order the continuance of the Salary, as now established, in compensation for the trouble and expence of those journeys.

The expence in London alone is now £1158. I beg leave also to mention that my reliance on the emolument of the appointment I now have the honour of holding in His Majesty's Family, has been the occasion of my relinquishing all my other business ; and that Mr. Holdich is still quartered upon me, though his life indeed is now very precarious. The above calculation is made on the idea of the appointment being given to one person, free from incumbrance & deduction ; but if the salary be granted, an allowance might be made for it to Mr. Holdich for £100 a year during his life.

I have the honour to be My Lord Duke, Your Grace's most obliged & obedt. humble Servant, ROBT. HALLIFAX.

No. 4083—*Lord Grantham to the King.*

Lord Grantham has received the Papers which Your Majesty has had the gracious Attention to send him.

He is in hourly expectation of the Messenger from France, where the Roads are exceedingly bad.

Lord Grantham would not have troubled Your Majesty, but to make his respectfull Acknowledgments to Your Majesty's Condescension.

WHITEHALL, 24*th Jany.* 1783. *m.* 15 *past* 5 P.M.

Endorsed by the King.

No. 4084—*Lord Grantham to the King.*

Lord Grantham has the honour & satisfaction to acquaint Yr. Majesty, that the Preliminaries with France & Spain are arrived signed—A Dutch Secretary is coming over, & the Armistice between England and America is secured by a Declaration of yr. American Commissioners.

Endorsed by the King.

No. 4085—*The King to Lord Grantham.*

I am infinitely happy at the Receipt of Ld. Grantham's note with the wished for Notification of the Signature of the Preliminarys with France and Spain, with the other concurrent circumstances, which Ld. Grantham ought without loss of time to communicate to the Ld. Mayor ; the East India and South Sea Companies and the Bank ; a Cabinet should be held that the Ratifications may be made out without delay ; from the D. of Richmond's notification yesterday I should imagine he will not Attend.

QUEEN'S HOUSE, *Jany 23rd*, 1783. *m.* 9 *pt.* 6 P.M.

Draft, written on a page of Lord Grantham's letter of same date.

No. 4086

MINUTE OF CABINET.

[In Lord Grantham's handwriting.]

At a Meeting of His Majesty's Confidential Servants at Lord Grantham's Office on the 24th of Jany. 1783.

Present :—Lord Chancellor, Lord Privy Seal, Earl of Shelburne, Ld. Vt. Keppel, Lord Ashburton, Mr. Townshend, Mr. Pitt, Mr. Conway, Lord Grantham.

It is humbly submitted to His Majesty that he would be pleased to ratify the Preliminary Articles of Peace, between

Great Britain & France, & between Great Britain and Spain, which were signed at Versailles on the 20th Jany. by Mr. Fitzherbert & the Ministers Plenipotentiary of those Courts.

No. 4087—*Lord Grantham to the King.*

St. James's, 24*th Jany.* 1783. 11 P.M.

Lord Grantham notified to the House of Lords, that the Preliminaries of Peace with France & with Spain, were signed, & that he did not doubt receiving Your Majesty's Commands early in next week to lay them before the House.

In Conversation with the Marquiss of Carmarthen, Lord Grantham having observed His Lordship's Desire of offering his Service to Your Majesty, as Ambassador to France whenever it shall be judged expedient to name one, presumes to lay this Circumstance before Your Majesty, hoping that if it meets with your royal approbation, he may be permitted to acquaint the Marquiss of Carmarthen, with Your Majesty's gracious Approbation of his Readiness to serve Your Majesty in that important & honourable Commission.

Lord Grantham is further to acquaint Your Majesty that Lord Mount Stewart in a manner the most dutiful to Your Majesty, expressed his desire on this occasion to serve Your Majesty in either of the Embassies, to the Courts of France or Spain. Lord Grantham in consequence of the conversation above mentioned, & of Lord Carmarthen's name having been mentioned to Your Majesty this Day at St. James's, took upon himself to say, that he considered the Embassy of Paris, as already destined to another Person of high Distinction. Lord Mountstewart then desired Lord Grantham to lay him at Your Majesty's feet, & to request for him the Embassy to Spain. Upon the receipt of Your Majesty's Pleasure upon this Subject, Ld. Grantham will convey it to Lord Mount Stewart whose appointment if Your Majesty approves it, cannot but be very flattering to the Court of Spain.

Endorsed by the King.

No. 4088—*The King to Lord Grantham.*

WINDSOR, *Jany 25th*, 1783
m. 10 *pt.* 10 P.M.

Ld. Grantham seems to have judged very properly in not fixing the particular day for laying the Preliminaries of Peace with France and with Spain before Parliament but confining himself yesterday in the House of Lords but [to ?] declaring it would be early in the next week.

Ld. Grantham may acquaint both Ld. Carmarthen and Ld. Mount Stuart that their offers of going Ambassadors to the Courts of France and Spain are willingly accepted by Me ; I should think this [the] right moment for Ld. Grantham to settle with Ld. Shelburne the provision that is to be made for Sir Jas. Harris, and that when the Messenger carries him a copy of the Preliminaries He may know He has leave to prepare for returning home, and that Mr. Poole Carew is to succeed him.

Draft, written on a page of Lord Grantham's letter of same date.

No. 4089—*Mr. Townshend to the King.*

WHITEHALL, *Jany 28th*, 1783
m. 50 *past* 1 P.M.

Mr. Townshend humbly presumes to acquaint Your Majesty that he has received by Major Bailey an account of a dangerous Mutiny at Portsmouth of the 77th Regiment, who have wounded the Lieutenant Colonel of the Regiment & another Officer & have killed a Soldier of the 41st. & wounded several others who were on the Main Guard. Upon the representation of Major Bailey Mr. Townshend has ventured to send to the Lords of the Admiralty to desire that Admiral Pye may be ordered not to disembark the 68th & 81st Regiments but at the requisition of General Smith, that the General may judge of the propriety of Disembarking the latter of those Regiments, which being a Highland Corps, might be liable to catch the disposition of the 77th. or at least be unwilling to act against them. Mr Townshend humbly hopes that this step, which he has thought necessary to take upon this pressing emergency will not be disapproved by Your Majesty.

Endorsed by the King.

The last seven words are inserted in the King's handwriting.

No. 4090—*The King to Mr. Townshend.*

QUEEN'S HOUSE, *Jany* 28*th*, 1783
m. 54 *pt.* 2 P.M.

Mr. Secretary Townshend has acted very proper in sending the Orders that were necessary to the Admiralty on account of the Mutiny in the 77th Regt. I trust he has acquainted Gen. Conway with the Steps He has taken, who will undoubtedly send such Orders as may oblige the deluded Men to return to their Duty.   G. R.

The case of Dr. Magenise is too serious for Me to decide without knowing the sentiments of the Ld. Chancellor and of the Ld. President. I desire therefore the Papers on that Subject which accompanies this may be laid before them.

No. 4091—*General Conway to the King.*

LITTLE WARWICK STREET,
1 *Feb.* 1783

SIR—I had writ to inform Your Majesty of the reports I had received from Lord G. Lennox, M. Gen. Smith & M. Gen. Murray of the then Orderly State of the 77th Regt. owing much I believe to the proper spirit and good sense with which his Lordp. particularly had conducted himself, when Sir Hugh Dalrymple arrived with the very disagreeable account of Mutiny broke out in the 68th Regt. which he commands as General & as violent as that of the 77th, on the bare surmise that they might be ordered in lieu of the latter to the East Indies.

They seez'd their Arms, confin'd their Officers on board ship, threaten'd to cut their cables & with great difficulty the utmost mischief was prevented. They appeal to the Order published in 1775 and claim their Discharges, but declare positively against going to the East Indies.

In this extremity I have thought of absolute necessity to confirm the Provisional Assurance Lord George and their Officers had given relative to the discharges of those who had a just claim and that they should not be compelled to go, and also as the likeliest way to make them return to temper and obedience (their Officers being all in their power) that the Regt. should be disembarked ; which is to be on the Gosport side with power to Lord George to move them farther out of that place if he judges fit.

His Lp. is then ordered to try if the 83rd continue in the same orderly disposition and in that case to tell them that on being Re-attested for 3 years, or during the War in India, they shall receive a Bounty of 2, or if thought quite necessary of 3 guineas pr. man.

Lord Shelburne has approved of the Govt. giving One Guinea, & Sr. H. Fletcher has assured me the E. India Company will pay the rest.

And as the 81st. have hitherto declared the same disposition as the 83rd. I have recommended him to engage them in the same manner.

I shall be happy if these Measures shall in this exigency be approved by Your Majesty, no time was to be lost.

I have taken the liberty to enclose a Narrative of the transactions of the 77th sent by Gen. Murray which I thought Your Majesty might be pleased to see.

I am with the utmost zeal and respect, Your Majesty's most dutiful Servant,   H. S. CONWAY.

Endorsed by the King.

No. 4092—*The King to General Conway.*

WINDSOR, *Feby. 2nd*, 1783
m. 58 pt. 9 A.M.

Lord George Lennox is so thorough a soldier that I am not surprised his conduct on the Mutiny of the 77th Regt. deserves commendation ; but I am sorry to see the Men are not yet returned to some Sense of contrition for their inhumanity as well as disobedience to their Officers. The 68th Regt. having taken the Allarm makes me not sanguine as to the prospect of getting the 81st or 83rd Regts. to go to the East Indies. The fresh Enlisting there may perhaps engage part of them ; should not the whole consent might it not be wise to try to persuade any of the 77th. who may be willing to enlist in either of the last mentioned Corps to compleat the 2000 men.

If I am to credit the Accounts of the Debate in the House of Commons on Friday as stated in the different Newspapers of Yesterday, I should think that if the deluded Men should be acquainted with it, they will not prove more tractable. It is shocking that Self interest or pique will make Men any way wound their Country if it answers either of those mean objects.

Draft, written on a page of General Conway's letter of 1 *February,* 1783.

No. 4093—*Lord Grantham to the King.*

[2 *Feb.* 1783.]

The Dispatches from Paris of the 25th of Jany were detained at Calais five days by bad weather.

The Enclosures are kept by Lord Grantham in order that they may be communicated to the proper Offices. They contain full Directions to the French Generals, Admirals and Governors, to prevent, and to cease Hostilities. They bear date on the 22nd of January.

Lord Grantham thinks that M. de Mouttier is arrived.

The last Dispatches from hence were also detained four days at Dover, by which means the exchange of the Ratifications will meet with some small Delay.

m. 5 *past* 1 PM.

Endorsed by the King, 2 *Feb.* 1783.

No. 4094—*The King to Lord Grantham.*

WINDSOR, *Feb.* 2*nd,* 1783. *m.* 15 *pt.* 4 P.M.

The Dispatches from Paris are in general pleasant as they shew an inclination to be friendly. The new Appointment of

Mr Fitzherbert is quite agreeable to the proposal now made and consequently requires no further attention.

I like the sending Mr. de Moultier much better than if Count de Noailles had come, those who have had unpleasant Missions should not return upon a more favourable aspect, I suppose the ratifications of the Preliminary Articles cannot arrive till the end of the Week as the Messenger was detained four days at Dover.

Draft, written on a page of Lord Grantham's letter of same date.

No. 4095—*Lord Howe to the King.*

Lord Howe has the honor to submit for His Majesty's perusal the Papers received this morning by Express, from the Admiral Sir Thomas Pye ; relative to a claim made in the name of the Irish Volunteers, embarked in the Ships of War under Orders for the East Indies.

The claim is consonant to the Terms upon which the Irish Volunteers were entered to serve in the Fleet and, tho' Lord Howe sees no cause for uneasiness on this subject, he humbly submits for His Majesty's consideration the propriety of his going to Portsmouth tomorrow morning in his character of Commander in Chief of the Channel Fleet ; and by direction from the Admiralty to see (with the concurrence of Sir Thos. Pye) that proper attention is had to the just representation of the Claimants and that due order is preserved in the Division of the Fleet, at that Port.

If the Weather is favorable for Lord Howe to go off to Spithead on the day after he arrives at Portsmouth, he trusts he shall be able to return to Town on Friday. He understands that General Conway has taken all the necessary steps with relation to the circumstance stated in Sir Thomas Pye's letter concerning the conduct of the 83rd Regiment.

ADMIRALTY OFFICE, *4th Feby.* 1783. 3.45 P.M.

The limitation for the time of Service referr'd to in the Claim beforementioned, is expressed in a Proclamation not an Act of Parliament.

No. 4096—*The King to Lord Howe.*

The idea of going tomorrow to Portsmouth to see that proper Attention is had to the just representations of the Irish Volunteers, is very becoming of Lord Howe's Character, and cannot but be the most efficacious means of keeping the Fleet at Spithead in good Order, and I should immagine that He will be able by the end of the Week to return ; but the present is so much the most pressing business, that it certainly calls most essentially for his Attention.

QUEEN'S HOUSE, *Feby 4th*, 1783. *m.* 20 *pt.* 4 P.M.

Draft, written on a page of Lord Howe's letter of same date.

No. 4097—*Mr. Townshend to the King.*

ALBERMARLE STREET, *Saturday, Feby. 4th*, 1783
m. 5 *past* 10 P.M.

Mr. Townshend humbly presumes to send the enclosed Letter from General Conway & upon the pressing necessity mentioned in it has ventured to summon a meeting of Your Majesty's Servants at one today, that as immediate steps as possible may be taken to remedy the present, and prevent further mischief from the Mutinous spirit now prevailing among the Troops.

Endorsed by the King.

No. 4098—*The King to Mr. Townshend.*

QUEEN'S HOUSE, *Feby. 4th*, 1783
m. 50 *pt.* 2 P.M.

Mr. Secy Townshend has acted very properly in calling a meeting together this Day at the requisition of Gen. Conway on account of the Mutinous disposition that seems very rapidly to spread among the troops ; I shall be curious to receive as soon as possible the result of this Meeting.   G. R.

Draft. This draft has also been copied by the King on to a page of Mr. Townshend's letter of same date.

No. 4099—*Lord Shelburne to the King.*

SIR—I have the honour to send Your Majesty a Letter from Lord Carlisle resigning the Staff of Lord Steward. There are no names which immediately occur to me to submit for Your Majesty's consideration to succeed to it, except Lord Gower, the Duke of Marlborough, or the Duke of Rutland. I presume Lord Gower cannot wish to succeed immediately to so near a connection, and I am apprehensive that the Duke of Marlborough may hesitate, especially as there is no offering it to him except by Letter.

I have the honour to be with the highest Respect, Your Majesty's Dutyfull Subject and Faithful Servant,   SHELBURNE.

BERKELY SQUARE, 4*th Feby.* 1783. ½ *past* 5 P.M.

Endorsed by the King.

No. 4100—*Mr. Townshend to the King.*

HOUSE OF COMMONS, *Tuesday, Feb.* 4, 1783
m. 16 *past* 5 P.M.

Mr. Townshend humbly presumes to acquaint Your Majesty, that the Result of the Meeting of Your Majesty's Ministers was to direct an Advertisement signed by the Secretary at War to be inserted in the Gazette of tonight assuring Your Majesty's Troops, that no Soldier would be constrained to serve on any other Terms, but on those on which he was attested, and stating the Ratification of the Definitive Treaty of Peace as the Real end of the War.

General Conway has written to the same effect to Lord George Lennox & to the Commanding Officers of the several Regiments. The Troops Disembarked seemed quieter than before[,] the 77th in particular.

Endorsed by the King.

No. 4101—*The King to Mr. Townshend.*

The opinion given at the Meeting this Day that Sir Geo Yonge should sign an Advertisement in the Gazette of this night,

assuring that no Soldier would be constrained to serve any longer
than the Term to which he has been attested, and stating the
Ratification of the Definitive treaty of Peace as the real end of
the War, is highly proper, and so right that it seems wonderful
Gen. Conway did not propose it to have been done in last
Saturday's Gazette, which would have prevented the Mutiny
from having spread so much.

QUEEN'S HOUSE, *Feby. 4th*, 1783. *m. 2 past* 6 P.M.

Draft, written on a page of Mr. Townshend's letter of same date.
Another copy in the King's handwriting.

No. 4102—*The King to Lord Shelburne.*

After what passed last Year on the Subject of the Steward's
Staff, the D. of Marlborough would have reason to be displeased
with Ld. Shelburne if it was not offered to him. I cannot see
the smallest inconvenience to that being done by letter and
think therefore Ld. Shelburne ought immediately to write to
Him.

QUEEN'S HOUSE, *Feby. 4th*, 1783. *m. 24 pt.* 6 P.M.

Draft, endorsed by the King.

No. 4103—*Lord Howe to the King.*

Lord Howe has the honour to report for His Majesty's in-
formation, that the State of the Weather since his arrival at
Portsmouth yesterday, has prevented him from visiting the
Ships at Spithead.

He does not find there is any material irregularity to be
apprehended from the Irish Volunteers, or Seamen, in the Ships
under orders for the East Indies. He therefore proposes to wait
only for an opportunity for getting off to Spithead early tomorrow morning, before he sets out on his return to Town.

PORTSMOUTH, 10 P.M. *6th Feby.* 1783.

Endorsed by the King.

No. 4104—*Dr. Warren to the King.*

SACKVILLE STREET, *Feby.* 7, 1783

Dr. Warren presents his most humble duty to His Majesty & hopes His Majesty's goodness will pardon him for presuming to address His Majesty in this manner.

Dr. Warren's eldest son is very desirous of serving His Majesty in the Army, and particularly wishes to be honoured with a commission in the guards. Dr. Warren humbly lays himself at His Majesty's feet & begs that His Majesty will condescend to give the Dr's son an Ensigncy in ye guards.

Dr. Warren humbly hopes that the largeness of his family, having nine sons and two daughters, will plead for him to His Majesty for his presuming to solicit this mark of His Majesty's favour.

Lord Waldegrave has approved of Dr. Warren's son & has recommended him to His Majesty for ye ensigncy that will become vacant by the promotion in the room of Lord Delawarre. Dr. Warren's highest ambition is to owe this favour to His Majesty's goodness alone.   RICHARD WARREN.

Endorsed by the King.

No. 4105—*Lord Grantham to the King.*

Lord Grantham humbly presumes to apprise Your Majesty, that agreably to Your Majesty's Direction, M. de Rayneval will take his Audience of Leave, And M. de Moustier presents his Credentials today immediately after the Levee, and that M. de Vergennes who returns to Paris with M. de Rayneval will attend Your Majesty's Levee for the last Time during his stay in England.

WHITEHALL, *7th Feby.* 1783   11 *o'clock* A.M.

Endorsed by the King.

No. 4106—*Lord Grantham to the King.*

Lord Grantham has the satisfaction at informing Your Majesty That the French Ratifications arrived.

The Spanish ones will be here in a very few Days.

And the Dutch Plenipotentaries have received Instructions to accede to the suspension of Hostilities, agreed upon So that the Proclamation will now issue.

Your Majesty will see by the Dispatches, that M. d'Adhemar will be appointed Embassadour to Your Majesty as on to-morrow, so that Lord Grantham humbly presumes that he may acquaint Lord Carmarthen & Mr. Fawkener officially with their Appointments, and with Your Majesty's gracious Intention that they should kiss Hands on Monday.

St. James's, 8 : *Feb.* 1783. *m.* 30 *past* 3 P.M.

Endorsed by the King.

No. 4107—*The King to Lord Grantham.*

It is with infinite Satisfaction that I learn from Ld. Grantham's note the Arrival of the Ratification of the French Preliminary Articles, the expectation of the Spanish one in very few days and the Accession of the Dutch Plenipotentiaries to the suspension of Arms. I trust when either M. de Rayneval or M. de Moutier may try to have the Articles of the proposed Preliminaries with the Dutch made more palatable to that Republic, that Ld. Grantham will stand very stiffly to the Articles as they are already drawn up, which they must accept though with a bad grace.

As M. d'Adhemar is to be nominated Ambassador to this Court tomorrow, Ld. Grantham may certainly acquaint Ld. Carmarthen and Mr. Fawkener that they should be presented at the Levee on Monday.

Windsor, *Feby.* 8*th*, 1783. *m.* 41 *past* 6 P.M.

Draft, written on a page of Lord Grantham's letter of same date.

No. 4108—*General Hotham to the King.*

Hampton, *Feb.* 10, 1783

Sir—I beg a thousand pardons for troubling You again about my son Frederick. But when I took my leave of The Bench I received such marks of Your Majesty's Approbation together with your Royal Satisfaction with my Deserts, that I could not but feel the Importance of them, particularly when I had the honour of receiving from my brother the Admiral Your Majesty's kind approbation of my first letter in his favour. Your Majesty has been pleased to mark all my family with various distinctions, and we have all been proud of them, and have endeavoured to show ourselves worthy of them by the sincerest gratitude.

My son who has very little to brag of at present, has a heart that is large and open to any of Your Majesty's Royal favors. He [*illegible*] with impatience by a part of them, & would gladly accept whatever would do him so much honour, and give me so great a share of your Royal Bounty.

I have the honour to be Sir, Your most loyal and affectionate humble servant,   B. HOTHAM.

No. 4109—*Lord Shelburne to the King.*

[10 *Feb.* 1783.]

SIR—All negotiation between Mr. Pitt and Mr. Fox is broke off by an absolute Refusal on the part of the latter ; alledging no reason except, what could only be mention'd in a room, that neither he nor those he acted with would [enter] into no consideration of Men or of Measures seperate from that of the Minister, and accordingly there was scarcely another word pass'd. I am confident this Incident may be improv'd much to the advantage of Your Majesty's present and future Government, if other descriptions of Men will give the opposite principle fair play by a disinterested plain conduct. They will ensure their personal consideration, and lay the foundation of a Government in whatever hands Your Majesty chooses in a short time to place it. No Endeavours shall be wanting on my part to dispose men to each other.

I have the honour to be with the highest Respect, Your Majesty's Dutyfull Subject,   SHELBURNE.

Undated.   Endorsed by the King.

No. 4110—*The King to Lord Shelburne.*

I am not in the least surprised at Mr. Pitt's interview with Mr. Fox ended as abruptly as the hastiness and impoliteness of the latter naturally led me to expect, I shall certainly not object to any other quarter Ld. Shelburne may with the advice of Mr. Pitt choose to sound ; but I must insist that Ld. Shelburne's remaining in his present situation be the basis of any plan that may be prepared for my Inspection ; by this clear instruction Ld. Shelburne must feel himself at liberty to act as he may find it necessary, and I can trust his own Sentiments are too much exalted to think of suplicating any party ; but that whoever he treats with must be expected to feel obliged for any offer that is made.

QUEEN'S HOUSE, *Feb.* 11*th*, 1783. *m.* 20 *pt.* 9 A.M.

Draft, written on a page of Lord Shelburne's letter.

No. 4111—*Lord Grantham to the King.*

Lord Grantham is obliged to trouble Your Majesty with the Passports sent herewith in order that they may receive your Royal Signature.

He humbly presumes to trespass on Your Majesty's Leisure, now, rather than press them at the Moment, when they may be wanted to be interchanged.

ST. JAMES'S, 11*th Feby.* 1783. 10 *m. past one* P.M.

Endorsed by the King.

No. 4112—*Lord Shelburne to the King.*

SIR—The Duke of Rutland has agreed with some difficulty to accept the Lord Steward's Staff, desiring at the same time to succeed to the Duke of Richmond's place in the Cabinet. Lord Carlisle has likewise renew'd his application to Lord Grantham, being desirous of resigning before any business can come on in the House of Lords.

I have the honour to be with the highest Respect, Your Majesty's most Dutyfull Subject, SHELBURNE.

BERKLY SQUARE, 13*th Feby.* 1783. *m.* 20 *past* 9.

Endorsed by the King.

No. 4113—*The King to Lord Shelburne.*

I cannot say that I am edified at the D. of Rutland's accepting with some difficulty the Ld. Steward's Staff which has ever been anxiously wished for by Men of equal Rank and Property. Ld. Shelburne may acquaint Ld. Carlisle that he may attend after the Levee tomorrow and resign that Staff and the D. of Rutland to receive it.

QUEEN'S HOUSE, *Feb.* 13*th*, 1783. *m.* 27 *pt. one* P.M.

Draft, written on a page of Lord Shelburne's letter of same date.

No. 4114—*Lord Grantham to the King.*

The Spanish Ratifications are arrived, as also the Dutch Acceptance of the Suspension of Hostilities.

Lord Grantham will forthwith have the honour of sending Your Majesty the Dispatches.

The Passports are arrived.

WHITEHALL, 13*th Feb.* 1783. *m.* 55 *past* 9 A.M.

Endorsed by the King.

No. 4115—*The King to Lord Grantham.*

The arrival of the Spanish Ratifications is very agreeable, but I do not like the Bourbons acting as apparent Mediators in the Dutch business.

QUEEN'S HOUSE, *Feby.* 13*th*, 1783. *m.* 27 *pt. one* P.M.

Draft, written on a page of Lord Grantham's letter of same date.

No. 4116—*Dr. Robert Hallifax to the Duke of Manchester.*

ALBERMARLE STREET, 13*th Feby.* 1783

MY LORD DUKE—Dr. Gisborne has acquainted me with Your Grace's proposal of allowing me twenty shillings a head pr. ann. to supply His Majesty's Servants in London at Windsor and Kew with Medicines, and of a further allowance of £100 a year to defray the expenses of my necessary journeys to the two latter places.

It is with the greatest reluctance that I am obliged to decline any proposal Your Grace does me the honour to make to me ; but as the terms of this contract would put both His Majesty's Household and myself on so near an establishment, that my accepting it would materially injure my fortune, disable me from doing credit to His Majesty's Service, and disgrace the character and reputation that I have had the happiness honourably to acquire, I humbly beg the favour of Your Grace to excuse me.

I hope too that You will give me leave to acquaint You, that the appointment I have at present the honour to hold in the King's Family, is a Patent Office under the Great Seal ; and if it is Your Grace's pleasure I should be deprived of it You will be so good to do me the justice of procuring for me a compensation, equal to what is to be allowed to other Patentees, who have the misfortune to lose their Patents.

I have the honour to be, My Lord Duke, Your Grace's most respectful & obedient humble Servt,   ROBT. HALLIFAX.

No. 4117—*Dr. Robert Hallifax to the King.*

ALBERMARLE STREET, 13*th Feby.* 1783

SIR—I most humbly beg Your Majesty's gracious indulgence to permit me to lay before You with all submission and respect, a proposal that I have received from the Duke of Manchester for the provision of Medicines for Your Majesty's Household ; and the serious embarassment it gives me.

His Grace ordered me in the last month to give him a plan for this Service, which should reduce Your Majesty's expence, & comprehend the care and attendance on the Household at

Windsor and Kew as well as in London. After having represented in a longer detail the nature and duty of my present situation, I had the honour of sending the enclosed proposal on the 21st of Jany. Yesterday the Duke sent me a message by Dr. Gisborne, with an offer to allow me twenty shillings a head Pr. ann for the whole expence of medicines and attendance at Windsor, Kew and in London, with a further allowance of £100 a year to defray the expenses of occasional and necessary journeys.

With the most perfect sense of Your Majesty's own goodness and desire that I should not be placed, by any regulation, in a situation dishonourable to me ; it is with the utmost anxiety and regret that I feel myself compelled to submit to Your Majesty's benignity and judgment, how far it is possible for any Man of Character to accept of a Contract, that would endanger his fortune, ruin his reputation, and deprive him of the means to do justice or shew humanity to your Servants.

The happiest circumstance in my life has been the honour of being in Your Majesty's Service, and not being conscious of having neglected the duties of my appointment, which with more Liberality to the Household has been less advantageous to me than to any of my predecessors, I had flattered myself, when in consideration of this Patent Office being given to me jointly with Mr. Holdich, I had quitted other very reputable business, that I should not have been liable to this disgrace and ill usage.

By advice of several respectable friends, who were apprehensive for my welfare, I have accepted a Degree in Physick, that the Archbishop of Canterbury with great kindness conferred upon me, I am under a necessity to apply myself to business again in that Line.

If I have ever found grace in Your Majesty's sight, I have not by any act of my own ever brought reproach upon myself, I most humbly beg that Your Majesty will not suffer me to be dismissed Your Service without some Mark of your Royal Favour, and approbation of my past conduct ; on which my fame, character and prosperity now depend.

If Your Majesty would be graciously pleased to give me that honourable distinction of appointing me Physician Extraordinary to Your Majesty's Person or Household, and permit me to ask the Prince of Wales to confer the same honour upon me, Your Majesty will give me a rank and consequence, that I hope not to prove unworthy of, & which will establish my reputation and gratitude for ever.

I have the honour to subscribe myself, with the most profound respect, Your Majesty's most dutiful & devoted Subject & Servant,   ROBT. HALLIFAX.

No. 4118—*Mr. Townshend to the King.*

Mr. Townshend humbly presumes to send Your Majesty the Names of the Speakers on Lord Maitland's Motion for an Address to Your Majesty desiring, that you would be pleased to confer a Signal Mark of Honour upon Sir George Augustus Eliot. The Order of the Day being moved for by Lord Beauchamp, the second Motion was carried by 90 to 18.

There were two other short Debates before Lord Maitland's Motion, one of which was a Motion of Mr. Eden's for the Commissions and Powers by which the Provisional Articles were negotiated and signed. The Speaker put the Question on the Motion without supposing there would be a Debate, which took place in an extraordinary manner after the Decision.

ALBEMARLE STREET, *Friday, Feby.* 14*th*, 1782 [should be 1783]
m. 40 *past* 7 P.M.

Enclosure.

Lord Maitland moved.
Lord Parker seconded.
Lord Beauchamp moved the Order of the Day.
Mr. Townshend seconded.
Sir Charles Coxe.
Mr. Onslow.
General Ross.
Mr. Dempster.
General Conway.
Governor Johnstone.

No. 4119—*Lord Grantham to the King.*

Lord Grantham has the honour of informing Your Majesty, that it will be necessary to give Your Majesty the trouble of holding a Council today for the purpose of the Duke of Rutland's being sworn in.

The enclosed Dispatches from Mr. Fitzherbert arrived last night. Lord Grantham hopes the Mediators will refuse coming into the Close of the Negotiation, but presumes to think Your Majesty will in a great degree keep pace with France & Spain in the Offer.

The Declarations, explain as much as is necessary, the Omission in ye. Preliminaries.

10 m. past 10 A.M. 17th Feby. 1783.

Endorsed by the King.

No. 4120—*Mr. Townshend to the King.*

17th Feby. 1783

Mr. Townshend humbly presumes to send Your Majesty the names of the Speakers in the Debate upon the Address, which was moved with great ability by Mr. Thomas Pitt, and very well seconded by Mr. Wilberforce. Lord John Cavendish moved an Amendment, and was seconded by Mr. St. John, & supported by Lord North. Lord John's Amendment was carried by 224 against 208.

No. 4121—*Lord Shelburne to the King.*

SIR—I have the honour to enclose to Your Majesty a list of the Speakers and a Copy of the amendment propos'd by the Earl of Carlisle.

The Independance being agreed to on all sides made the rest of the Debate uninteresting. The article regarding the Loyalists was most dwelt upon. Lord Gower was on their account against the Address and the Amendment—the Duke of Richmond was likewise against both for reasons he would not explain from regard to the Cabinet. The House did not break up till Four o'clock.

The Chancellor expects Your Majesty's Commands, when the House may attend Your Majesty with the Address. Wednesday is thought of, if it meets Your Majesty's pleasure.

I have the honour to be with the highest Respect, Your Majesty's most Dutyfull Subject, SHELBURNE.

BERKLEY SQUARE, 18th Feby. 1783. m. 3 past 5 A.M.

No. 4122—*The King to Lord Shelburne.*

I am much concerned that Ld. Shelburne's note has not more comfortable intelligence to communicate than that the Address on the Peace was on a division carried by 14 in the House of Lords, which is undoubtedly the smallest Majority I ever remember in so full an House. I owne this made me expect that the Question would have been lost in the other House ; but Mr. Townshend has just acquainted me that it was carried by 16.

QUEEN'S HOUSE, Feb. 17th [mistake for 18th] 1783. m. 40 pt. 8 A.M.

Draft, written on a page of Lord Shelburne's letter of 18 February.

No. 4123—*The King to Lord Shelburne.*

QUEEN'S HOUSE, Feby. 18th, 1783
m. 40 pt. 5 P.M.

The disappointment at the very small Majority this Morning in the House of Peers made me omit desiring Ld. Shelburne to acquaint the Ld. Chancellor that I shall be ready tomorrow at two to receive the House of Lords ; an answer must be prepared to that Address.

On looking again at Mr. Townshend's note I find Ld. John Cavendish's amendment was carried, which is an event I had not understood when I wrote this Morning.

Draft.

No. 4124—*Mr. Townshend to the King.*

ALBEMARLE STREET, *Saturday, Feb.* 22*nd*, 1783
m. 30 *past* 4 A.M.

Mr. Townshend humbly presumes to send Your Majesty the names of the speakers in the two Debates today upon the Resolutions moved by Lord John Cavendish. Mr. Pitt's Speech in answer to Mr. Fox was generally agreed to be one of the finest that was ever heard. Lord John Cavendish's fourth Resolution, upon which the House divided, was carried by 207 to 190. The Words of the Resolution were, "that the Concessions made to the adversarys of Great Britain by the Provisional Treaty & Preliminary Articles, are greater than they were entitled to, either from the actual situation of their respective Possessions, or from their comparative strength."

Enclosure.

On the first opening.

Lord John Cavendish	Mr. Wallace
Mr. St. John	Sir William Dolben
Mr. Keith Stuart	Mr. Rosewarne
Mr. Townshend	Attorney General
Sir Peter Russell	Sir Francis Basset
Sir Cecil Wray	Attorney General
Sir Horace Man	Mr. Lee
Mr. D. Hartly	Sir Adam Ferguson
Mr. Onslow	Solicitor General
Lord North	Mr. Eden
Lord Newhaven	Lord North
Sir William Dolben	Governor Johnstone

On the 4th Resolution.

Lord John Cavendish	Sir Edward Ashley
Mr. Powys	Mr. W. Bootle
Lord John Cavendish	Mr. Pitt
Mr. Powys	Mr. Onslow
Sir Richard Sutton	Mr. Martin
Mr. Wilberforce	Mr. Wilmot

On the 4th Resolution.

Mr. Hill
Mr. T. Pitt
Mr. Wilberforce
Ld. John Cavendish
Mr. St. John
Lord North
Mr. Powys
Lord Mulgrave
Mr. Townshend
Mr. Burke
Lord Advocate
Governor Johnstone
Sir H. Fletcher
Mr. Sheridan
Mr. Townshend
Mr. McDonald
Mr. Fox
Mr. Pitt
Sir Cecil Wray
Lord North
Mr. Townshend

Mr. Pitt
Mr. Hartly
Mr. Banks
Sir William Dolben
Mr. Yorke
Mr. Smith
Mr. James Grenville
Sir Francis Basset
General Smith
Sir George Howard
Mr. Fox
Mr. Pitt
Mr. Sheridan
Mr. Lee
Mr. Norton
Mr. Pitt
Ld. Fred. Campbell
Attorney General
Mr. Lee
Mr. Rigby
Mr. Adam

No. 4125—*The King to Mr. Townshend.*

I cannot help on coming home and receiving Mr. Secy Townshend's note with the List of the Speakers and the Numbers of the Division this Morning, just to express that I am sorry it has been my lot to Reign in the most profligate Age and when the most unatural coalition seems to have taken place, which can but add confusion and distraction among a too much divided Nation.

WINDSOR, *Feby. 22nd,* 1783. *m. 47 pt. one* P.M.

Draft, written on a page of Mr. Townshend's letter of same date.

No. 4126—*Lord Howe to the King.*

Lord Howe has the honour to acquaint Your Majesty that by letters received this morning from Admiral Sir Thomas Pye, he finds, that amongst the Seamen in the Ships destined for foreign Service, more particularly, the impatience to receive their wages & discharge, appears to require early attention. He therefore proposes returning to Portsmouth to-morrow morning, and flatters himself he shall be able to prevent any inconvenient extension of those irregularities, by his presence : Tho' he apprehends his stay at Portsmouth must be continued, until the weather may prove sufficiently temperate for him to visit the Ships at Spithead.

The Messenger is directed to meet Lord Howe on the Road to Portsmouth, with any commands Your Majesty may be pleased to honor him with on this occasion.

ADMIRALTY, *22nd Feby.* 1783.

Endorsed by the King.

No. 4127—*The King to Lord Howe.*

Lord Howe acts on the present Occasion with his wonted activity and Propriety, his journey to Portsmouth consequently meets with my fullest Approbation. I cannot help just mentioning the extraordinary coalition that seemed to appear in the last night's Debate in the House of Commons, one that I cannot think honourable to either of the Parties and can tend to nothing but hurrying this Country still faster to Anarchy and Confusion.

WINDSOR, *Feb. 22nd,* 1783. *m.* 58 *pt.* 5 P.M.

Draft, written on a page of Lord Howe's letter of same date. Duplicate copy in the King's hand.

No. 4128—*Mr. Townshend to the King.*

WHITEHALL, *Feby. 22nd,* 1783
m. 25 *past* 4 P.M.

Mr. Townshend humbly presumes to desire Your Majesty's Permission to summon a Meeting of Your Majesty's Confidential

Servants tomorrow to consider on the Propriety of continuing to disarm in the present Crisis, as well as upon the general situation of Your Majesty's Government. Mr. Townshend likewise humbly solicits Your Majesty's Orders on the subject of summoning the Duke of Rutland to the Cabinet.

Endorsed by the King.

No. 4129—*The King to Mr. Townshend.*

Mr. Secy. Townshend has my thorough approbation for summoning a Meeting of the Cabinet tomorrow to consider of the propriety of continuing to disarm at a time when by the violence of faction the Powers who have just signed Preliminary Articles will be backward in following the Example. The D. of Rutland must be summoned on this and all future Occasions.

WINDSOR, *Feby 22nd*, 1783. *m.* 38 *pt.* 7 P.M.

Draft, written on a page of Mr. Townshend's letter of same date. Duplicate copy in King's hand.

No. 4130—*Lord Shelburne to the King.*

BERKLEY SQUARE, 22*nd* Feby. 1783
m. 20 *past* 5 P.M.

SIR—I am deeply concern'd to find it the universal sense of Your Majesty's Servants in the House of Commons, that any further attempt to carry on Government on the part of Your Majesty's present Servants would be vain and highly prejudicial to Your Majesty. The State of the Navy, the Disarmament, the Loan besides other important points cannot admit of further delay, and it will be impossible to prevail on Your Majesty's present Cabinet to decide on any of them, after all that has now passed the House of Commons. It is my Duty to lose no time in apprizing Your Majesty of the State of things, which I hope to have the honour to do more fully and with more convenience to Your Majesty upon Monday. The Secretarys of State Mr. Pitt and the Duke of Rutland wish to submit their sentiments to the same effect when they can do it most respectfully. Those of the House of Commons wish to have that honour on Monday on account of the State of that House. It is thought desireable that I should communicate with the Boards and some other Persons in both Houses which I propose doing tomorrow morning or evening with Your Majesty's permission.

I have the honour to be with the highest Respect and inviolable attachment, Your Majesty's most Dutyfull Subject & Faithfull Servant,   SHELBURNE.

No. 4131—*The King to Lord Shelburne.*

WINDSOR, [*Saturday*] *Feb.* 22*nd*, 1783
m. 30 *pt.* 9 P.M.

Lord Shelburne's letter containing the sentiments of the Gentlemen in High Office in the House of Commons on the unnatural and factious Coalition of adverse Parties to my Present Ministry, gives me real concern but after the event of last night it does not surprise Me. Had my immediate presence been necessary I should have instantly set out for Town but as I think it better for Ld. Shelburne to have seen all the effective Cabinet Counsellors before He speaks fully to Me, consequently my presence cannot be necessary till Monday. Ld. Shelburne has my consent to communicate to the Board and any others he thinks proper on this Subject. Mr. Pitt and Mr. Townshend may state what they have to say on Monday on this unpleasant Subject, as also the D. of Rutland. The Chancellor and Ld. Camden ought also to come and state what occurs to them for till I have seen all the Cabinet I shall not think of turning my thoughts to any mode of seeing what can be done ; I am again from necessity left to extricate myself, to the Assistance of Providence and the rectitude of my intentions I can alone hope for succour [*sic*] ; of one thing alone I can answer, that no consideration shall make me throw myself into the hands of any Party ; it must be a Coalition of the best of all not a narrow line that can prevent anarchy.

Draft.

No. 4132—*Lord Howe to the King.*

Lord Howe has the honour to submit to Your Majesty, that he does not see cause to believe, the object amongst the greater part of the seamen at this Port, extends farther than to obtain an exemption from foreign Service, in imitation of the Regiments first ordered to the East Indies. By others, an earnest desire for their wages, and immediate discharge is expressed. This impatience he hopes he shall be able to correct, if the weather will admit of his going off tomorrow to Spithead, as the present appearance of it renders probable, and he then proposes to pay his duty to Your Majesty on Wednesday morning.

Lord Howe has with much pain observed, the turn the Debates in Parliament have lately taken. He most humbly prays that his situation may not weigh in the infinite goodness he has experience, to impede any arrangement deemed most beneficial to Your Majesty's Service. At the same time, he begs permission to suggest, that he views the important charge he has lately had the honor to be vested with, in the light of a military Post, at which it is incumbent on him to wait for further Orders.

PORTSMOUTH, 24*th Feby.* 1783. *m.* 10 *past* 10 P.M.

No. 4133—*The King to Lord Chancellor Thurlow.*

MY LORD—I lose no time in acquainting you that on my mentioning to Mr. Pitt Your suggestion on the present crisis, that he received it with a spirit and inclination that makes me think he will not decline, though he has very properly desired time to weigh so momentous a step.

QUEEN'S HOUSE, *Feby.* 24*th,* 1783. *m.* 30 *pt.* 6 P.M.

Draft, endorsed by the King.

No. 4134—*Mr. Townshend to the King.*

Mr. Townshend humbly presumes to acquaint Your Majesty, that Sir George Yonge is just come in from the House of Commons, where there has been a Division on the Lord Advocate's Motion for an Adjournment till Friday. The Motion was carried in the Affirmative by 49 to 37. Lord North was in the Minority with Mr. Burke. Some others objected on account of particular Businesses, which had been appointed for the intermediate Days.

WHITEHALL, *Tuesday, Feby.* 25*th*, 1783. *m.* 30 *past* 4 P.M.

Endorsed by the King.

No. 4135—*Lord Grantham to the King.*

Lord Grantham humbly submits to Your Majesty the enclosed Commissions for Signature. They are for the Spanish Consuls, most of whom were actually resident in the Spanish Dominions at the moment of the Rupture, and the others all connected with the Commerce of that Kingdom.

Lord Grantham presumes to think it due to them to be restored, more especially as those Offices now reduced by the Loss of American Trade, are scarcely beneficial to any Persons, but such as have houses or Connexions in Spain.

Lord Grantham is ashamed to trouble Your Majesty for the Condescension of Your Name to a Nomination of a poor Brother of the Charter house and your Leave to name an Extra Messenger.

ST. JAMES'S, 26*th Feby.* 1783. 8 *o'clock* P.M.

No 4136—*Lord Bathurst to the King.*

[Undated]

SIRE—Considering myself as solely obliged to Your Majesty for the very honourable offices I have enjoyed, I never woud enter into any close connexion with any particular part of Your Ministers, tho' I flatter myself that none who may be in Your Majesty's Service woud have any personal objection to Me ; I wish however to be under no obligation to any one but Your Majesty, and I shall be happy in every opportunity of shewing my sincere attachment to your Royal Person and Government.

Perhaps in forming your Administration there may be difficulty in finding a proper Person to hold the Great Seal, putting it into the hands of the Commissioners is never eligible, unless in very quiet times, and perhaps at present no one woud be found to take it without stipulating for a Pension and other advantages, which might be inconvenient to Your Majesty. If my Service can be usefull, Your Majesty may command me just for as long or short time as shall be convenient, and Your Majesty may rest assured that I shall at all times think myself sufficiently recompenced by my having the Power of Shewing my Zeal for your Service, being with the greatest Veneration and Attachment, Sire, Your Majesty's most faithfull most obliged & devoted Servant, BATHURST.

Endorsed by the King, Rd. Feby. 26th, 1783.

No. 4137—*General Conway to the King.*

LITTLE WARWICK STREET, *28th Feby.* 1783

Gen. Conway with his most humble duty has the honour to acquaint his Majesty that by letters he receiv'd from Lord George Lennox yesterday every thing was then quiet among the Troops of his district and the Embarkation of the Regiments going on with no other interruption but from the absolute want of more money for the payment of the Bounty ; there being no specie to be procur'd there, but on application to the E. India Directors G. Conway immediately procured 2,000 guineas which he has sent down by an Officer this morning.

There has been a slight mutiny among the Yorkshire Volunteers, particularly among the Light Company at Wallingford, on account of their claim to be discharg'd having been contested during the War, no mischief nor bad consequence has its understood ensued. G. C. sent down an explanatory order as to their claims and situation and also sent down Sir Thos. Dundas whose influence, with the proper explanation it is hoped will put an end to the disorder.

Gen. Conway̕ has taken the liberty of sending the Returns of the Troops by Sir George Yonge ; and also a list of Recommendations which he hopes His M. will find unexceptionable— he is exceedingly mortified that a St. Anthony's fire which has fallen into his leg in consequence of a slight fever he had

immediately after the last long day in the House, has prevented
his being able to pay his duty to His Majesty in person ; though
he hopes his confinement will not be of long continuance.

Endorsed by the King.

No. 4138—*Mr. Fraser to the King.*

[? *Feb.* 1783]

Dr. Heberden did not return yesterday till within a quarter
of nine. Mr. Fraser called upon him immediately. He told him
Lord Suffolk had had another fit at Four in the Afternoon,
through which he had struggled notwithstanding his weak state,
but he was afraid, if he should have another, it would be fatal.
He said he left Lord Suffolk in extreme Danger but not quite
Hopeless.

Mr. Fraser is very happy in sending Your Majesty a letter
from Lady Aylesford just received, with the Accounts from
Mr. Carter to which Her Ladyship referrs.

m. 55 P.M.

Endorsed by the King.

No. 4139—*The King to Mr. Townshend.*

Mr. Secy. Townshend is desired to come here directly in the
Morning Dress He may happen to have on.   G. R.

QUEEN'S HOUSE, *March* 1st, 1783. *m.* 57 *pt.* 10 A.M.

Endorsed by Mr. Townshend.

No. 4140—*The King to Lord Chancellor Thurlow.*

MY LORD—I wish You would if not very inconvenient to call
as early as may be convenient to You this Morning, as I wish
to hear the result of Your enquiries, being desirous that no unnecessary delays may arise from Me in trying if possible to
counteract the most extraordinary Combination that the depravity
of such times as we live in could alone have given birth to.

QUEEN'S HOUSE, *March* 1st, 1783.

No. 4141—*Lord Chancellor Thurlow to the King.*

Saturday, 1 March, 1783

SIR—Mr. Jenkinson has thought much of the subject of possible arrangements ; he has some ideas on the matter, which perhaps I should be at a loss to explain ; and certainly it would be tedious. I submit it to Your Majesty that it would be useful to hear from Himself His Ideas ; which must at least furnish matter deserving of further discussion.

I am, Sir, Your Majesty's most Dutiful Subject and faithful Servant, THURLOW.

Endorsed by the King.

No. 4142—*The King to Lord Chancellor Thurlow.*

QUEEN'S HOUSE, *1st March* 1783. *m.* 57 *pt.* 2 P.M.

MY LORD—I cannot in the Smallest degree object to seeing Mr Jenkinson as You advise it, I desire You will therefore direct him to call here at seven this Evening, & shall certainly take no step till that is over except continuing to hear the want of means of carrying on the present Administration which all the Members of the Cabinet have suggested to me except Ld. Ashburton who has not been here, but who I expect every Minute.

Draft, written on a page of Lord Thurlow's letter of same date.

No. 4143—*The King to Lord Chancellor Thurlow.*

MY LORD—Nothing can be more handsome than the Sentiments Ld. Gower has entrusted you to communicate in his Name, and his disposition is as favourable as I could wish or his good sense authorize.

I have seen Mr. Townshend, he accepts a Peerage, and has my directions to acquaint Ld. Rawdon that he is at the same time to be placed in that House.

I find from Mr. Townshend that Ld. Shelburne will think himself unkindly treated if Mr. Jones is not sent to the East Indies on the vacancy of Judge which has subsisted some years ;

I shall take it as a personal compliment to Me if You will consent to it. Ld. Ashburton answers for his being competent as a Lawyer, and his knowledge of the Eastern languages is a very additional qualification.

QUEEN'S HOUSE, *March 1st,* 1783. *m.* 35 *pt.* [*sic*] M.

Draft, endorsed by the King. Lord Thurlow's letter, to which this is a reply, has been lost.

No. 4144—*Lord Shelburne to the King.*

SIR—Immediately upon receiving Your Majesty's Commands I took the necessary measures to forward the Warrant Your Majesty directed to be made out for the Lord Chancellor. I found it necessary to consult His Lordship upon it, and likewise Mr. Pitt, on account of a good deal of difficulty, which I have not troubl'd Your Majesty with, tho' it has prevail'd for some time past, on account, in my opinion, of an excess of apprehension, as to signing any Grant whatever, least those who do should be inconvenienced under the Civil List Act. However I have got Lord Grantham's settl'd and have the honour to send it to Your Majesty for signing—and I have got Lord Chancellor's settl'd with the assistance of Lord Ashburton, who desires that it may go to the Chancellor previous to its being sent to Your Majesty. This I hope will not prove a delay of more than an Hour or two more.

We have had a good deal of difficulty with Mr. Gilbert which I would not presume to trouble Your Majesty with adverting to, if it was not [to] prevent Your Majesty's attributing any delay, where in truth it does not belong.

I have had a very civil Visit from the French Minister at the desire of the Count de Vergennes, with many compliments, which I have answer'd by telling him, that I hop'd to preserve his good opinion by a firm adherence to every principle, and by proving myself in all situations

Your Majesty's most Dutyfull Subject and Faithfull Servant,

SHELBURNE.

BERKLEY SQUARE, 1*st March,* 1783. ¼ *past one* P.M.

Endorsed by the King.

No. 4145—*The King to Lord Shelburne.*

The Grants in favour of the Lord Chancellor and Ld. Grantham cannot be deemed new ideas the first has been in agitation ever since he has held the Great Seal and the latter deserves it from his foreign services. I know Ld. Shelburne does not love delay therefore cannot suppose in either of these cases or in that of Mr. Gilbert it can with any degree of justice be layed at his door.

QUEEN'S HOUSE, *March 1st,* 1783. *m.* 15 *pt.* 3 P.M.

Draft, written on a page of Lord Shelburne's letter of same date.

No. 4146—*Mr. Townshend to the King.*

ALBEMARLE STREET, *March 1st,* 1783
m. 30 *pt.* 6 P.M.

Mr. Townshend humbly presumes to propose the name of Sydenham of Sydenham in Kent for the Barony, which Your Majesty is pleased to confer upon him, as he finds that elder Branches of his Family think they may some time or other have claims upon such as had at first occurred to him.

Endorsed by the King.

No. 4147—*General Conway to the King.*

LITTLE WARWICK STREET, *1st March,* 1783

Gen: Conway presents his most humble duty to His Majesty. On receipt of His Majesty's Commands last night he immediately sent to Sir George Yonge but heard that on it's being found he could not attend St. James's the papers had been returned to G. Conway's, which he was not acquainted with till he had enquir'd this morning having concluded Sir George had on his note sent them to His Majesty.

The North Yorkshire Volunteers had been ordered on their March Northward which was the immediate cause or pretence of the disturbance, rais'd by some of the Southern men who were impatient of their Discharges.

The Lancashire Volunteers, unless His Majesty should be pleas'd to order otherwise, are for the present stopt on the Windsor Quarters that they may not arrive at Manchester till the Militia of that County are disembodied.

The difficulty about the money at Portsmouth cou'd not possibly have been foreseen here, as it arose from an occasional want of Specie in that Town.

The Five Lieut. Colonels recommended for Rank by Brevet are the Oldest on the List, and all men of distinguish'd service and character. Col. McKenzie was the only Lieut. Col. of the Gibraltar Garrison before omitted; Lieut. Col. Gordon of the 77th. had lost his Rank by accident and Lieut. Col. Straubenzie who is now embarking for the E. Indies is an excellent Field Officer and has on the present occasion added to his merits by his extraordinary exertions to augment and increase his Battalion.

Endorsed by the King.

No. 4148—*Mr. Townshend to the King.*

ALBEMARLE STREET, *March* 2, 1783
11 A.M.

Mr. Townshend humbly presumes to send Your Majesty a Letter, which he has just received from Lord de Ferrars as an apology, though perhaps a very insufficient one for the troublesome liberty he ventures to take. When he receives so high and valuable a mark of Your Majesty's gracious approbation of his endeavours to serve you, the consideration of the Title itself occupys his thoughts no farther than to avoid taking any one which might clash with the pretentions of any other family. The Hydes may have Views upon Rochester, and I believe the Female Branches of the Sydney Family former Claims upon the Barony of Lisle. If then Your Majesty approves of giving way to the anxiety of Lord de Ferrars, and will allow Mr. Townshend to change the title to Sydney of Chiselhurst or Somerford [?] of Chiselhurst, neither of which are claimed by any body, and to which he is allied, as Lord de Ferrars informs him, by the Sydneys and the Veres, Mr. Townshend hopes that His Relatives will be satisfied, and that he shall offend no one else.

Mr. Townshend humbly implores Your Majesty's forgiveness for this intrusion and importunity, and hopes Your Majesty is persuaded that the Paragraph to which Lord de Ferrars alludes was a matter in which he had no concern.

Endorsed by the King.

No. 4149—*Lord Shelburne to the King.*

SIR—Finding the Lord Chancellor dissatisfied with the manner in which his Warrant was express'd, and knowing Your Majesty's Intention of having it made perfectly agreeable to him, I have presum'd to direct another to be prepar'd, the words of which I have immediately with himself. The Alteration consists in Your Majesty's recital of Your Promiss of a Tellership to him at the time of his being appointed to the Great Seal, and Your Majesty's Intention to make it good, *Subject however to such Regulation and Provision as shall be made concerning the same in Parliament.*

I have the Honour to be with the highest Respect, Your Majesty's Dutyfull Subject, SHELBURNE.

BERKLEY SQUARE, *2nd March*, 1783. ¼ *past* 3 P.M.

Endorsed by the King.

No. 4150—*The King to Lord Chancellor Thurlow.*

MY LORD—I have seen Lord Guildford and sent him to Ld. North with the offer of placing him again in the Treasury and consulting him on the formation of a Ministry on the most comprehensive lines, that if he declines that particular Employment I am willing to place him in another suitable Cabinet Office to advise with him on the formation of a fresh Administration; but then reserving to myself the appointing a Peer not connected with any of the Strong parties that distract this Kingdom to preside at the Treasury.

Ld. Guildford has promised to use his utmost endeavours on this Occasion and to get Ld. Dartmouth, Lord Bagott and other sober minded men, who he is certain must rejoice at so generous an Offer from Me to assist in combating the natural indecision of his Son of which the intriguing Counsellors he is beset with take too easy advantage.

QUEEN'S HOUSE, *Mar. 2nd*, 1783. *m.* 10 *pt.* 10 P.M.

Draft, endorsed by the King.

No. 4151—*Mr. Townshend to the King.*

ALBEMARLE STREET, *Monday, March 3rd*, 1783
m. 17 *past* 9 A.M.

Mr. Townshend humbly begs to receive Your Majesty's Commands as to the time that Lord Rawdon and he should have the honour of kissing Your Majesty's hand.

Endorsed by the King.

No. 4152—*The King to Lord Townshend.*

Mr. Townshend has my consent to his kissing hands as well as Ld. Rawdon either this day or Wednesday. As yet I have had no answer of any kind to the message I gave yesterday to Ld. Guildford.

QUEEN'S HOUSE, *March 3rd*, 1783. *m.* 12 *pt.* 11 A.M.

Draft, written on a page of Mr. Townshend's letter of same date. Duplicate in the King's handwriting.

No. 4153—*The King to Lord Chancellor Thurlow.*

MY LORD—I have this instant seen Lord Guildford who acquainted Me that Lord North cannot bring his mind to returning to the Treasury, or accepting of any other office ; but is not disinclined to be talked to by me on the subject of forming an Administration and of being of the Cabinet ; I have therefore appointed him at Nine this evening but declared that my Resolution is taken that the Treasury must be in the hands of no head of a Party but an Independant Peer named by Myself.

QUEEN'S HOUSE, *Mar. 3rd*, 1783. *m.* 30 *pt. m.*

Draft, endorsed by the King.
Duplicate copy in Queen Charlotte's handwriting.

No. 4154—*Lord Weymouth to the King.*

ARLINGTON STREET, *March 3rd*, 1783

SIR—Upon an application to Your Majesty several years ago, to revive the Barony of Carteret in the person of my Brother who is become the representative of that family, I had the honour of receiving an answer from Your Majesty which I flatter'd myself was not unfavorable. As I hear that some promotions of that kind are to be now made, I hope Your Majesty will pardon me if I venture again to lay that matter under your consideration. I shall add nothing on the subject but submitt to Your Majesty's pleasure, and subscribe myself, in all events,

Your Majesty's most loyal Subject & devoted Servant,

WEYMOUTH.

Endorsed by the King.

No. 4155—*The King to Lord Weymouth.*

Lord Weymouth is not now to learn the real Satisfaction I feel whenever I am able to forward any of his Wishes, and therefore that I shall embrace the first proper Opportunity of conferring the Barony of Carteret on his Brother. On the advancing Mr. Townshend to the House of Lords I considered whether I could with propriety accompany him with some of the applications that had been made personally to Me, but I found that I should be making more than the present Moment seemed to authorize. I therefore have only added to Him Ld. Rawdon whose personal services stood on a Separate line from any one else and who had not solicited it therefore did not lay me under any difficulties. I have been thus extensive in my answer that Ld. Weymouth may see the motives of my conduct, and may be assured that I shall seize the first proper opportunity of complying with his wishes, which this Second application has certainly made the stronger incumbent on me. G. R.

QUEEN'S HOUSE, *March 4th*, 1783.

Draft, in Queen Charlotte's handwriting, endorsed by the King.

No. 4156—*Lord North to the King.*

Lord North has the honour of informing His Majesty That last night after he had left His Majesty, He had the inclosed conversation with Mr. Fox ; that, thinking it better in a matter of such importance, to trust to writing, than to verbal communication, He sent the inclosed note this morning to Mr. Fox, that he might judge whether Lord North had stated accurately the conversation which had passed between them. Mr. Fox has in a note he has just received from him, acknowledged the accuracy with which the note states the purport of what Lord North said to him, and of what he said in return. Lord North hopes that he has with equal correctness stated what His Majesty commissioned him to say to Mr. Fox and his friends. If he has made any error, he will correct it upon the signification of His Majesty's pleasure, and he hopes that, for the reason given at the beginning of the note, His Majesty will not disapprove of his having taken this method of conveying to His Majesty the sentiments of the Rockingham party.

March 4, 1783

Endorsed by the King.

No. 4157—*The King to Lord North.*

Lord North has very correctly understood what I said to him the last night ; I desire he will come at nine this evening.

QUEEN'S HOUSE, *March 4th,* 1783. *m.* 58 *pt.* 3 P.M.

Draft, written on a page of Lord North's letter of same date. Duplicate copy in the King's handwriting.

No. 4158—*Lord North to the King.*

Lord North has the honour of informing His Majesty that he has seen Mr. Fox, and that, in obedience to His Majesty's Commands, he desired to know, whether Mr. Fox and his friends would assist in forming an Administration, and in that view, would accept of distinguish'd, honourable and efficient offices in

His Majesty's service. Lord North acquainted him, at the same time, that it was His Majesty's intention to confer the office of First Lord of the Treasury on some Peer, who is not at the Head of any Party. In answer to this Mr. Fox, in the name of his friends, inform'd Lord North, That they could not form a part of any administration unless His Majesty should think proper to appoint the Duke of Portland First Lord of the Treasury.

March 4, 1783

Two copies, both in Lord North's handwriting, one endorsed by the King.

No. 4159—*Mr. Townshend to the King.*

ALBEMARLE STREET, *Tuesday, March 4, 1783*
m. 30 past 12

Mr. Townshend humbly presumes to acquaint Your Majesty, that in obedience to Your Commands he saw Mr. [William] Grenville yesterday, who informed him that he believed, that there were a number of Gentlemen whose names he apprehended, the Lord Lieutenant would humbly propose to Your Majesty to be made Peers of Ireland at the time of the Dissolution of the Parliament of that Kingdom. These Gentlemen are persons who will meet with Contests at their Elections in consequence of the support they have hitherto given to Your Majesty's Government, and are chiefly chosen for Countys, & have been recommended to Your Majesty for that honour by both Lord Carlisle and the Duke of Portland. Mr. Townshend thought it his duty to apprise Your Majesty of the Prospect of this Application.

Endorsed by the King.

No. 4160—*The King to Lord Temple.*

I trust Ld. Temple will be as sparing as possible in his list of Peers ; Mr. Grenville ought to apprise him that Mr. Pennington must be made a Peer at the same time and that if He proposes any advances in the Peerage—the Dowr. Lady Longford must be a Countess and if He proposed to advance any Peer junior to Ld. Dartrey that He will also recommend him for a similar promotion.   G. R.

QUEEN'S HOUSE, *March 4th*, 1783.   *m.* 30 *pt.* 4 P.M.

Draft, endorsed by the King.

No. 4161—*Lord North to the King.*

Lord North has the honour of informing His Majesty That, in obedience to His Majesty's Commands, He has re-consider'd the State of the Parties, and of the House of Commons with a few friends who are the best acquainted with them, and is confirm'd in the opinion he had the honour of submitting last night to His Majesty, that it is impossible to form a Ministry capable of conducting His Majesty's affairs in the House of Commons by a junction of Lord North's friends with the remainder of the Administration.

March 5 [1783].

Endorsed by the King.
Duplicate copy in Lord North's handwriting.

No. 4162—*Mr. Pitt to the King.*

Mr. Pitt humbly presumes, in the absence of the Secretary of State, to inform Your Majesty that a Motion has been made in the House of Commons by Mr. Powys for an humble Address, reciting the Clause of the Civil List Act, which restrains the Grants of Pensions after the Fifth of April, and expressing the Confidence of the House that the same œconomical Moderation will be adhered to in any Pensions which Your Majesty may be advised to grant antecedent to that period. It was moved to insert instead of the latter words That the same Restrictions will be observed in respect to any Pensions which Your Majesty may be advised to order to be granted antecedent to that Period. After some Debate in which Mr. Powys, Mr. Luttrell, Mr. Fox, Mr. Eliot, Mr. Burke, and Governor Johnstone spoke, the Motion so amended was carried without a Division.

Thursday, March 5th, 1783.   *m.* 25 *pt.* 3 P.M.

Endorsed by the King.

No. 4163—*Lord Sydney to the King.*

WHITEHALL, *Thursday, March 6th*, 1783
m. 22 *past* 3 P.M.

Lord Sydney humbly presumes to submit to Your Majesty a Petition of John Holden ordered for execution tomorrow. As the Prayer of the Petition is only for a Respite till the Report of the Judge can be received, Lord Sydney wishes to have Your Majesty's pleasure upon the granting such a Respite.

Endorsed by the King.

No. 4164—*Lord Sydney to the King.*

ALBEMARLE STREET, *Thursday, March 6th*, 1783
m. 16 *past* 6 P.M.

Lord Sydney humbly presumes to submit to Your Majesty a Dispatch which he has just received from the Lord Lieutenant of Ireland, and at the same time humbly to desire Your Majesty's Commands upon the subject of the Earl of Arran's being invested with the Order of St. Patrick's in the room of the Earl of Antrim.

Endorsed by the King.

No. 4165—*Lord Chancellor Thurlow to the King.*

5 A.M. 7 *Mar.* 1783

SIR—After having the honour of conversing with Your Majesty, I met Lord Gower, and some of His friends at Mr. Rigby's. I conversed with them a long while, as appears from the Date. My humble advice to Your Majesty is to send for Lord Gower, and to refer to Him the thinking of such an Administration, as may be sufficient to take on Them the conduct of Your Majesty's affairs.

I am, Sir, Your Majesty's most dutiful and faithful Servant,

THURLOW.

Endorsed by the King.

No. 4166—*The King to Lord Chancellor Thurlow.*

QUEEN'S HOUSE, *Mar.* 7*th*, 1783
m. 33 *pt.* 8 A.M.

MY LORD—I shall certainly with very great pleasure instantly send for Lord Gower agreable to your Advice and refer to him the thinking of such an Administration as may be sufficient to take on them the conducting of Public Affairs, and if He shall not be able to form such a Plan, I shall certainly still attempt to find whether there is no Man willing at this Crisis to stand by the Crown against a desperate Faction in whose hands I will never throw myself.

Draft, written on a page of Lord Thurlow's letter of same date.

No. 4167—*Lord Gower to the King.*

Lord Gower has the honour to inform Your Majesty that he has seen Mr. Pitt and that he will be ready to attend His Majesty when he receives his commands.

8 *o'clock* P.M. *Friday, March* 7*th*, 1783.

Endorsed by the King.

No. 4168—*The King to Lord Gower.*

By Ld. Gower's not expressing that Mr. Pitt has declined I trust he has the agreable intelligence to communicate that He accepts. I am ready to receive Lord Gower as soon as may be convenient to Him this Evening.

QU. H. *Mar.* 7*th*, 1783. *m.* 2 *pt.* 9 P.M.

Draft, written on a page of Lord Gower's letter of same date.

No. 4169.

MEMORANDUM BY MR. THOMAS PITT.

[In the King's handwriting.]

Minutes of a conversation with Ld. Gower at the House at Whitehall March 7th 1783.

His Ldp. began with telling me he had sent for Me in consequence of a conversation He had had the honour to hold that morning with the King upon the present strange and critical Situation of his Government ; that the King felt with indignation the violence done to himself and to the Country by the combination of opposite faction avowedly for the purpose of taking possession of His Government ; that He was *almost* determined *at any hazard* to resist it, to prevent the consequences that must necessarily be derived from it to Himself and His People, That He had called upon his Ldp. to form an Administration for Him which with much reluctance he had inclined to do, satisfied of the true picture the King had drawn of the posture of Affairs and convinced that such an undertaking was more practicable than he had at first imagined it to be, from such observations and informations as he had lately had upon the temper of the Public and the disposition of parties who seemed to support any Ministry rather than to submit to such a combination. That my relation (Mr. W.[illiam] P.[itt]) had been applied to by H. My. upon a former occasion and by his Ldp. in consequence in every mode offering assistance to him in place or out of place, or in any situation, that he had at first seemed to listen to it, but had finally declined it Altogether. That his Ldp. was sensible that unless he could have the assistance of some Man of character and abilities in the House of Commons it was in vain to undertake the business and that he had taken the liberty to state to H. My. that nobody stood so forward in both respects in that House and that therefore before he would engage in it he must first be assured that I would take that department upon Me in the Station of Secretary of State. That he had seen nobody since but the Chancellor for half an hour as it was impossible for him to proceed in the business till he knew my determination upon the subject.

After expressing the sense I had of the honour done me by his Ldp.'s favourable opinion and by the King's condescension in suffering such a proposition to be named to me—I assured him that no Man could feel a warmer indignation than myself at the unnatural Union that had taken place and at the disgrace which the success of such a conspiracy inflicted upon the Country. That I had ever thought the character of Mr. Fox dangerous to the public peace and from which everything might be apprehended—that when he came in with Lord Rockingham and many more who tempered and blended the System, I had hoped that there might have been checks upon his violence which might have kept him within the bounds, whilst the union of so many parties might give that strength and dignity to Government which might add weight to our counsels abroad whilst they obtained the confidence of the people at home. But when the Rockingham party flew off upon the death of the Marquiss because Ld. Shelburne would not a second time yield the Treasury to whoever they should please to nominate, that I thought them unjustifiable factions and indifferent to the good of the Country at the moment it the most wanted their assistance. That it was in vain now to talk of the D. of Portland ; it was directly *Mr. Fox's Administration* and as such if his shameless Union with those he had reprobated for so many Years were out of the question, I should still apprehend mischief from it. That as to Ld. North if anything could be wanting to render his Character compleat, it was such an unparaleled act of ingratitude to his benefactor and such a profligate surrender of all public principles. That thinking of these Gentlemen therefore as I did nothing could be more painful to my feelings than that the Country should be surrendered up into their hands.

And yet if H. My. had not taken an inflexible resolution upon this subject, I could not help wishing it were possible for him to revolve the consequences once more in his mind, before it was too late for him to recede. That no man had now so much experience before him in the art of governing this Country as H.M. that I was sure He could not but recollect how many mischiefs might have been avoided more than once by timely concessions which were rendered desperate by resistance. That if I could flatter myself that there was a chance of anything like a well supported firm and vigorous Administration to be formed in the present hour, I should be the last man in England to advise the smallest condescension towards the Union ; but that the contest was to be of short duration and must end in a surrender when Government would be still more disgraced and these factions rendered less odious by the natural effect of popular oppositions, the consequences would be only more humiliating and perhaps more fatal to the Country by all the inflammatory matter thrown out among the People. That I agreed perfectly in the disgust that their Union had universaly spread even in their own parties, but that in my poor judgements the only way that the King could avail himself of it, was by suffering them to reap the fruits of their perfidy. That as Opposition was in itself always popular, so the coming into Office was always unpopular especially when the means were peculiarly odious. That whilst they were out many of their interested followers would be kept together through hope but that the moment the arrangement was made, the posture which was already too much narrowed for one party, would certainly be too narrow for two. That the disappointed would revolt as well as those who disdained to have their public opinion made over to the Opposite faction by an agreement to which they had not given their assent and in which they in no way found their accounts, that thus the strength of the faction would be in great measure disbanded and their popularity lessened, perhaps totally overthrown, whilst, H. M's would be looked upon by His People as in thraldom and their indignation without doors assisted with the spirit within doors would shortly make way for such a Government in whom the People might have confidence whilst they were entitled to H.M.'s esteem. That besides these considerations the real difficulties of Government were such as I wished might rest upon the responsibility of those Gentlemen, that 2 or 3 million taxes would be a heavy load for his Ldp. to take upon himself that the concluding the Definitive Treaties which they had now so much embarrassed and in particular the Treaty with the Dutch, ought to be left in the hands of Mr. Fox ; that the failure in the Schemes of Representation, and all the other perplexities of their reform, they should be left to extricate themselves from as they could, and that as much of the difficult ground as they should rid away, would be so much more facility to any future Government, and that therefore I imagined that nothing could be so hurtful to the importance of these factions in every light as to give way to them in the present moment, or so likely to accomplish what was the wish of every honest man a future Administration supported by the weight of property and independence.

That when I presumed to advise His Majesty in His magnanimity to restrain his feelings for the good of His people, I was far from wishing him to conceal or dissemble them. He yields to necessity as to arrangements of Office and as to Public Measures, but as to favours, He has a right to reserve them within His own Breast, and that if they dared refuse their Services to the public upon personal questions of Honour and Emolument, it would only render them more odious in the eyes of all mankind and tend to revolt every man from them.

That after all if H. My. still persisted in his resolution to stand his ground against them, He should well weigh His decision, perhaps the most important of His Reign, that every symptom of a distempered State seemed to prognosticate the danger of some convulsions if the temper of the times was not managed with the prudence, and that this might prove a new Æra to H. My's Counsels. That to give the weight and dignity to such a system in the House of Commons (from which H. My. should not easily be tempted to recede) it would require the experience, the abilities and authority of a Ld. Chatham, or a Mr. Grenville at least if indeed they could be equal to the circumstances of the time worked up with all the acuteness and vehemence of Fox and all the cunning and ironical Arts of Ld. North. That I was by indolence and by many concurring circumstances totaly unequal to public business, but most certainly unequal to a task like this, that I beged his Ldp. therefore to express my most dutiful devotion to H. My. but at the same time to lay before him the reason why it was impossible for me to avail myself of the very partial and flattering representation that had been made him of me, whilst I should always esteem it as the highest honour that H. My's attention could have been ever drawn towards me at so important a Crisis.

Endorsed by the King.

No. 4170—*The King to Lord Ashburton.*

Lord Ashburton is desired to come here this Morning as early as may be convenient to Him, after having seen the Ld. Chancellor who means to wait on Him on his way to Lincoln's Inn Hall; of this Lord Ashburton need not mention being apprized, nor of his being to see Me subsequent to that visit.

QUEEN'S HOUSE, *Mar.* 10*th*, 1783. *m.* 40 *pt.* 7 A.M.

Endorsed by the King.

No. 4171—*The King to Lord Grantham.*

Lord Grantham is desired to acquaint those of the expiring Ministry likely to attend at St. James's this day, that I shall not appear there as usual being fully employed in attempting to form without further delay an Administration; it is not to my fault but to the knavery and indolence perhaps I might add timidity of the times that my incessant labours have as yet proved unsuccessful; things must speedily come to a conclusion. I shall be glad if Ld. Grantham will call here at one this day.

G. R.

QUEEN'S HOUSE, *Mar.* 10*th*, 1783. *m.* 40 *pt.* 7 A.M.

Draft, endorsed by the King.

No. 4172—*Lord Chancellor Thurlow to the King.*

Monday, 2 P.M. 1783
[10*th March*]

SIR—In obedience to Your Majesty's commands I have seen Lord Ashburton and I have found that His decision was that Lord Gower, Mr. Jenkinson, and Lord Advocate would be capable of forming a Bottom, on which the sentiment of the Publick might raise an efficient administration; but that he neither knew the mind of those Persons, nor had calculated on the particular accession, which They could promise themselves. I am equally ignorant of those particulars; and much less sanguine in the general expectation; and can only refer Your Majesty to the other alternative, I had the honour to state more at large to Your Majesty last night. The Time already taken and the urgent situation of publick affairs press the consideration, whether the absolute want of an Administration be not the worst state, in which Things can be left.

I have the honour to be, Sir, Your Majesty's most dutiful Subject and faithful Servant,   THURLOW.

Endorsed by the King.

No. 4173—*The King to Lord Chancellor Thurlow.*

MY LORD—I am hurt at finding that you only communicate to Me the Sentiments of Ld. Ashburton which are perfectly consonant to those he gave yesterday personally to Me, and that you have not added what past with the Ld. Advocate who was to breakfast with you this Morning. The Alternative you stated last night seemed so very similar to what I have uniformly declared I cannot submit to, that I most earnestly press You to weigh it and see whether you can mould it into a less revolting shape; no one is more anxious than I am to come to a final decision but I hear from Ld. Grantham that it is said the Opposition will bring on a question this day, it is highly material I should know the purport and fate of it before I take any step. I shall certainly from this hour not see or talk to anyone on this sad business till I meet you tomorrow; I shall not fail in the morning to write and fix the hour; I am really so ill this day I cannot add more.

QUEEN'S HOUSE, *Mar. 10th*, 1783. *m. 43 pt. 3 P.M.*

Draft, endorsed by the King.

No. 4174—*Lord Chancellor Thurlow to the King.*

10 *Mar.* 5 P.M. 1783

SIR—I humbly beg Your Majesty's pardon for having been so short in the Letter, I had the honour to write to Your Majesty this morning, but I fancied that the Advocate's opinion was included in that, I humbly submitted to Your Majesty. Lord Gower, had, I supposed, stated to Your Majesty, that he did not find it possible to hope for any solid plan being formed, unless He could have introduced into Your Majesty's Service some other description of Men, than that which would otherwise have been obvious; and the Advocate had then, as well as now, concurred; although both were extremely desirous to take any practicable part for setting the publick business forward. The Ideas I had the honour of submitting to Your Majesty were not without the view and hope of moulding the proposals to be laid before Your Majesty into some more acceptable shape, than it has hitherto appeared in; and I should think it the happiest moment of my life, if I could invent and suggest to Your Majesty any such Temperament. The House of Lords is adjourned till Wednesday, that I may be more at liberty to pay immediate obedience to Your Majesty's Commands.

I am, Sir, Your Majesty's most dutiful Subject and obedient Servant,   THURLOW.

Endorsed by the King.

No. 4175—*Lord Chancellor Thurlow to the King.*

[10 *March*, 1783 ?]

SIR—I have found Lord Gower in the same disposition, He has uniformly entertained; an earnest wish to see the Government of the Country upheld, and ready to take any part, which promises a fair expectation of attaining that end.

He professes to have no personal objection to Lord North; or any other objection, besides that, which the Rumour now abroad has created in the world in general. For the rest, it seems impossible to form a more specifick determination, without seeing the arrangement proposed, in order to judge of the practicability of it; and this He will be ready to consider with all the zeal for Your Majesty's service, which the utmost Duty can suggest.

I am, Your Majesty's most dutiful Subject and faithful Servant,   THURLOW.

No. 4176—*The King to Lord Chancellor Thurlow.*

MY LORD—I am sorry to find every description of Men equally unwilling to stand forth, I trust you will give the fullest attention to the great business before us, that you may when called upon tomorrow be able fully to give me Your Sentiments.

QUEEN'S HOUSE, *Mar.* 10*th*, 1783. *m.* 29 *pt.* 6 P.M.

Draft, endorsed by the King.

No. 4177—*Lord Sydney to the King.*

ALBEMARLE STREET, *Monday, March* 10*th*, 1783
m. 16 *past* 5 P.M.

Lord Sydney humbly presumes to transmit to Your Majesty a note from General Conway, which he has found on his return from the House, that he may receive Your Majesty's Commands upon the subject of it. He likewise ventures to send a Note from the Duke of Grafton, the contents of which he apprehends the Duke wished to have laid before Your Majesty.

Endorsed by the King.

No. 4178—*The King to Lord Sydney.*

QUEEN'S HOUSE, *March* 10*th*, 1783
m. 5 *pt.* 6 P.M.

Lord Sidney [*sic*] has judged very properly in transmitting to me without loss of time Gen. Conway's proposal concerning the Fensible Regts in Scotland, his proposal is very proper, he communicated it to me on Friday, I desire the order may instantly [be] given to that purpose.

The D. of Grafton's polite notice is not lost on Me, I desire he will go tomorrow to Northamptonshire, for though I do not certainly mean to lose unnecessary time it is not very easy to act right in so factious and unnatural times. G. R.

No. 4179—*Lord Grantham to the King.*

Lord Grantham has the honour of sending the enclosed Letter & Translation of it—by which it appears that an Embassador from Spain is fixed. And by the Dispatches which Lord Grantham has seen from C. Floridablanca to M. D'Aranda, it appears that this Employment is actually conferred upon M. Almodovar.

Lord Grantham therefore humbly submits it to Your Majesty, whether Lord Mount Stuart may not have the honour of Kissing Your Majesty's Hand, on the first opportunity.

St. James's. *30 m. past 4 p.m. 11 March,* 1783.

Endorsed by the King.

No. 4180—*The King to Lord Grantham.*

The Account from Paris fixing Almodovar as the Ambassador, there cannot be the smallest objection to Ld. Mount Stuart being tomorrow nominated Ambassador to Spain, and being presented at the Levee.

Queen's House. *Mar.* 11, 1783. *m.* 15 *past* 5 p.m.

Draft, written on a page of Lord Grantham's letter of same date.

No. 4181—*The King to Lord North.*

Lord North is desired to call here at twelve this day, that the Levee at St. James's may not be delayed by this interview.

Queen's House. *Mar.* 12, 1783. *m.* 30 *pt.* 8 a.m.   G. R.

No. 4182—*Lord Grantham to the King.*

St. James's, 12 *March,* 1783
36 *m. past* 10 a.m.

Lord Grantham having learnt from M. de Moustier that a Courier would be dispatched yesterday Evening, availed himself of it to write to Mr. Fitzherbert. Not having time to submit the Draft to Your Majesty, he ventured to take upon himself to send off the Letters immediately. The Drafts are now sent to yr Majesty.

Lord Galway being anxious to secure his Appointment humbly begs leave to kiss Your Majesty's Hand, as upon taking leave to repair to his Destination at Munich.

Endorsed by the King.

No. 4183—*Lord Shelburne to the King.*

Sir—I hope Your Majesty will excuse my presuming to lay before Your Majesty, the humble request of Sir John Jervis to succeed to the Command of Your Majesty's Yacht. Lord Howe is prepossessed with Your Majesty's preference of Captain Elphinston, which I could not remove, without repeating more of Your Majesty's conversation than I thought it became me to do. Captain Elphinston is a much Younger Officer, and has lately taken a part very opposite both to Your Majesty's Government and to the Sense of his own Profession on the subject of the Peace. Sir John Jervis is given to understand that, if the Department is chang'd, he has nothing to expect but resentment on the same account, and I believe besides being ambitious of it as a great honour, it is very material to his circumstances, which have suffer'd by the War, being upon the point of taking a Step in his private Life, which always carries more or less expense along with it.

I have the Honour to be, with the highest respect, Your Majesty's Dutyfull Subject and Faithfull Servant,

Berkley Square, 13 *March*, 1783. ½ *past* 10 a.m.   Shelburne.

Endorsed by the King.

No. 4184—*The King to Lord Shelburne.*

Ld. Shelburne is mistaken in the idea that Ld. Howe proposes to recommend Capt. Elphinston to the Command of my Yacht; I had on his first Appointment told Him Merit not favour must decide the Nomination, upon that plan alone He, above three weeks ago proposed Capt. Cornwallis whose merit no one can deny, and had therefore my Approbation : therefore I cannot now mention any other person to him for this favour ; if Ld. Howe could be persuaded to recommend a promotion of Rear Admirals, a Regt. of Marines might be vacated for Sir John Jervis.

QUEEN'S HOUSE. *Mar. 13th*, 1783. *m.* 30 *pt.* M.

Draft, written on a page of Lord Shelburne's letter of same date.

No. 4185.

CABINET.

[? *March* 1783]

Ld. North witht. Office; 1st Ld of ye Ty; D. of Portland : Sec: of State; Ld. Stormont: Chanr. of ye Exr ; Ld. J. Cavendh: Prest. of the Counl: Ld. Bathurst: Sec of State Mr. Fox: Privy Seel Ld. Dartmouth : 1st Ld of ye Adty: Ad. Ld. Keppell. Chancellor

Stewd of ye Household Ld. Hillsborough.

Ld. Sandwich Chamberlain.

Comptr. Ld. Hinchingbrook.

Post Office   Ld. Foley.
Treasurer of ye Household   Ld. Cholmondeley.
Treasurer of the Navy.
Paymaster.

Mr. Ellis.
Ld. Clive
Sr. T. Egerton.
Mr. Vyner

Rough draft, undated, not in the King's hand.

No. 4186—*Lord Sydney to the King.*

WHITEHALL. *March* 13, 1783
m. 39 *past* 11 P.M.

Lord Sydney humbly presumes to acquaint Your Majesty that upon being informed of a very dangerous disposition to

Riot and Disturbance at Newcastle under Line and in it's neighbourhood on account of the high Price of Corn, he has ventured to send the Letters, of which the inclosed are Draughts, to the Lord Lieutenant of the County of Stafford; to the Commander in Chief & Secretary at War, as the Necessity of giving immediate Orders appeared to him to be very pressing, he trusts that Your Majesty will not disapprove of his having made use of Your Authority without waiting for Your Commands upon the Subject.

Endorsed by the King.

No. 4187—*The King to Lord Sydney.*

Lord Sidney [*sic*] has given the proper Orders on the Account He has received of a very dangerous disposition to Riot and Disturbance at Newcastle under Line and its Neighbourhood on account of the high Price of Corn, which I trust will prevent any mischief. He forgot to send me at the same time the ground on which He has acted, I mean the Intelligence He has received.

QUEEN'S HOUSE. *Mar. 14th*, 1783. *m. 15 pt.* 8 A.M. G. R.

No. 4188—*Lord North to the King.*

Lord North humbly requests to know His Majesty's pleasure when He will permit him to wait upon His Majesty to lay before him what has passed in consequence of the Order he received from His Majesty on Wednesday morning.

Friday. 4 o'clock. [14 *March*, 1783]

Endorsed by the King, Mar. 14, 1783.

No. 4189—*The King to Lord North.*

LD. NORTH—As I am agoing to the Oratorio this Evening, I cannot see You till tomorrow Morning at Ten.

QUEEN'S HOUSE. *Mar.* 14, 1783. *m. 35 pt.* 4 P.M.

No. 4190—*Lord Sydney to the King.*

ALBEMARLE STREET. *March* 14, 1783.   12 P.M.

Lord Sydney humbly presumes to send Your Majesty the Letters, which he has received from Mr. Barré, & Sir George Yonge upon the subject of the Dismission of Mr. Powell from his various Offices. He humbly begs leave at the same time to mention to Your Majesty that he stated to Mr. Barré Your Gracious Predilection for Officers who had served in the Army to fill up the Vacancys. But as Your Majesty's orders upon that head were not positive, he presumes that the particular situation of Mr. Estwicks may make him appear not unworthy of that much of Your Majesty's Favour.

Lord Sydney has heard this afternoon from Lord Gower, that two of the Ringleaders of the Riot at Newcastle had been lodged in Stafford Gaol, where, from the approach of the Assizes, they were likely to be tried immediately.

Endorsed by the King.

No. 4191—*The King to Lord Sydney.*

Having read the Papers Lord Sydney left this Day with Me concerning the conduct of the Cashier and also of the Accomptant of the Pay Office, and that they have been removed by the Paymaster General of the Forces for their conduct ; He must acquaint the Secretary at War by a Public letter that in consequence of the information come from The Treasury I dismiss Mr. Powell from the Offices of Secretary and Register of Chelsea Hospital, and joint Agent to the Invalids, and He will privately direct to consult with the Paymaster concerning the proper Successors, those of Chelsea Hospital and the Agentcy to the Invalids might probably be very well held by different persons, and if they had been formerly in the Military Line, it might not be improper.

QUEEN'S HOUSE. *Mar.* 14, 1783.   *m.* [*sic*] *pt.* 5 P.M.

Draft, endorsed by the King.

No. 4192—*Lord Sydney to the King.*

WHITEHALL, *March* 15, 1783
m. 55 *past One* P.M.

Lord Sydney humbly presumes to submit to Your Majesty
a Letter, which he has just received from the Mayor of Liverpool.
The Object being of great importance, & the Request of the
Mayor very urgent, Lord Sydney ventures to express his humble
Wish to receive Your Majesty's Commands upon this subject,
that such Orders as you may deem necessary may be given for
the Security of the Town & Preservation of Peace and Order,
& that he may acquaint the Mayor with the Steps which Your
Majesty may order to be taken.

Lord Sydney likewise humbly submits to Your Majesty's
consideration a Petition which has just been delivered into the
Office in favour of a Person under Sentence of Death at Aylesbury.

Endorsed by the King.

No. 4193—*The King to Lord Sydney.*

I desire Ld Sydney will immediately see Gen. Conway and
settle with him that a Sufficient Military force may be assembled
at Liverpool to assist the Civil Magistrates if necessary ; perhaps
the Royal Lancashire Volunteers under the Command of their
Worthy Commandant Sir Thos. Egerton may be a proper Corps
for that purpose when arrived in that County, but till then the
Gen. Must collect even parts of Corps for so great an emergency.

I shall be glad to hear what is settled and that the Mayor
may have an answer to his letter dispatched this Evening.

The case of Davis should be referred to the Judge.   G. R.

QUEEN'S HOUSE. *Mar.* 15, 1783. *m.* 42 *pt.* 2 P.M.

No. 4194—*Lord Sydney to the King.*

WHITEHALL. *March* 15, 1783
m. 15 *past* 3 P.M.

Lord Sydney humbly presumes to transmit to Your Majesty
a Memorandum, which he has just received from Lord Surrey

& Colonel Harvey relative to the Behaviour of two Officers in the Militia of the West Riding of the County of York, commanded by the latter. The time for disembodying the Regiment being so near, they thought it would be impossible to have them tried by a Court Martial, especially as they are still absent, and not to be found. They therefore have desired Lord Sydney humbly to submit to Your Majesty their Proposal for the immediate dismission of the two Officers in such a manner as may mark Your Majesty's Disapprobation of their Conduct.

Lord Sydney has just received Your Majesty's Orders concerning the Letter of the Mayor of Liverpool, & in obedience to them is going immediately to General Conway.

Endorsed by the King.

No. 4195—*Lord Sydney to the King.*

ALBEMARLE STREET. *March* 15, 1783
m. 5 past 5 P.M.

Lord Sydney humbly presumes to acquaint Your Majesty that he has seen General Conway in obedience to Your Commands. The Regiment, which Your Majesty mentioned under the Command of Sir Thomas Egerton is now on it's march from Windsor & Hampton Court. The General sent immediately for the Quarter Master General to consider of collecting a proper body of Troops to march to Liverpool : & will himself immediately transmit to Your Majesty his Disposition of them. A Messenger is ready to set off for Liverpool as soon as Lord Sydney receives any intelligence from General Conway.

Lord Sydney humbly submits to Your Majesty's consideration a Letter he has just received from Sir George Yonge.

Endorsed by the King.

No. 4196—*The King to Lord Sydney.*

Lord Sydney will give Orders for the dismissing the two Officers of the 2nd Regt. of West Yorkshire Militia, agreable to the Memorandum that has been delivered to Him by the Lord Lieutenant, and the Colonel of the Corps.

He will also acquaint the Secretary at War that I approve of the two Persons He has proposed for succeeding Mr. Powell, the one in supplying the Garrison of Gibraltar with Coals and Fuel, and the other as Deputy Pay Master of the Widows Pensions till Col. Fox, the Patentee, can appoint a proper one.

The Measures Gen. Conway is taking for assistance to the Civil Magistrates at Liverpool shall meet with no delay when laid before me.   G. R.

QUEEN'S HOUSE. *March 15th*, 1783. *m.* 55 *past* 5 P.M.

No. 4197—*Lord North to the King.*

Lord North has the honour of informing His Majesty that he communicated this morning to the Duke of Portland His Majesty's Sentiments concerning the Lord Chancellor & Lord Stormont & has since had the honour of a visit from His Grace, who after mentioning the persons concern'd in terms of high respect, expressed, in the name of himself and his friends, his sorrow that it would not be in their power to enter into His Majesty's Service, if the two points mention'd by His Majesty were considered as essential to any arrangement for bringing them into office.

LOWER GROSVENOR STREET. *Saty. Evening March* 15.
m. 50 *past* 8 P.M.

Endorsed by the King. Copy of this letter in the King's hand.

No. 4198—*General Conway to the King.*

Saturday near 5 P.M. 15th *March*, 1783

Gen. Conway presents his most humble Duty to His Majesty & has the honour to acquaint His M. that in consequence of the communication made by Lord Sydney, Orders will be immediately dispatched to Manchester to His M.'s Regt. of Dragoons & Major

Elford's Corps to march on any Requisition from the Mayor of Liverpool. There are some Troops on the march that way but none as yet near enough to give immediate assistance.

Endorsed by the King.

No. 4199—*The King to General Conway.*

QUEEN'S HOUSE, *March* 15th, 1783
m. 10 *past* 6 P.M.

Gen. Conway seems to have proposed the most expeditious mode of giving Assistance if necessary to the Civil Magistrates at Liverpool, but attention must be had to so populous a Town as Manchester, where disturbances may also arise, if when the Troops are drawn from there, none are coming to replace them; The Lancashire Volunteers being chiefly raised at Manchester will be fitter to aid the Magistrates at Liverpool than at the former place.

Draft, written on a page of General Conway's letter of same date.

No. 4200—*The King to Lord North.*

Lord North is desired to be here at Seven this Evening.

QUEEN'S HOUSE. *March* 16th, 1783. *m.* 15 *past* 4 P.M.   G. R.

No. 4201—*Lord Sydney to the King.*

ALBEMARLE STREET. *March* 16th, 1783
m. 48 *past* 5 P.M.

Lord Sydney humbly presumes to transmit to Your Majesty a Letter, which he has just received from Mr. Grenville that he may communicate to Mr. Grenville Your Majesty's Orders concerning the time & manner in which You would please to receive the Ribband & Badge of the Order of Saint Patrick.

Endorsed by the King.

No. 4202—*The King to Lord Sydney.*

Lord Sydney should receive the Ribband and Badge of the Order of Saint Patrick this Evening from Mr. Grenville and transmit it to Me, and I shall privately Invest my Son with it : the Collar will, I suppose, as well as the Starr be sent over by the Lord Lieutenant.   G. R.

QUEEN'S HOUSE. *March 16th*, 1783. *m.* 5 *past* 6 P.M.

No. 4203—*The King to Lord·Weymouth.*

LORD WEYMOUTH—I have this instant seen Ld North, I convinced him that what I said yesterday to Him concerning my disapprobation to any idea of removing the Chancellor was for his private information, at an interview which I looked upon only to excuse himself for not being yet able to bring any Plan of a comprehensive Administration, and the inferior Arrangements consequent to it ; that therefore I recurred to the opening of the Negociation through him on Wednesday, that such a Plan must be drawn up and brought for my deliberation before I would give answer to separate Removals : He wished to decline going on from not seeing the smallest chance of bringing such a Paper, but I insisted on his going and trying, and if He cannot succeed that he must on paper acquaint Me how impossible it is for Him to get the Separate Parties to consent to such an Administration as He can term on a broad basis. I hope this has now thrown the onus on those who ought to bear it, instead of its being laid most unjustly on Me.

QUEEN'S HOUSE, *Mar.* 16, 1783. *m.* 50 *pt.* 7 P.M.

Draft, endorsed by the King.

No. 4204—*Lord Sydney to the King.*

ALBEMARLE STREET. *March 18th*, 1783
m. 39 *past* 8 P.M.

Lord Sydney humbly presumes to send Your Majesty a Letter, which he has just received from Mr. William Grenville, as well as Two Dispatches from the Lord Lieutenant of Ireland. The Importance of one of these Dispatches, as well as Mr. William Grenville's urgent request to be admitted to Your Majesty's presence, whenever you will be graciously pleased to allow him that Honour, inclined Lord Sydney to think it necessary to transmit these Papers to Your Majesty without Delay.

The other Packet which Lord Sydney presumes to transmit to Your Majesty, contains the Ribband, Badge and Star of the Order of St. Patrick.

Endorsed by the King.

No. 4205—*The King to Lord Sydney.*

QUEEN'S HOUSE, *Mar.* 16, 1783
m. 19 *past* 9 P.M.

Lord Sydney is desired to send Mr. W. Grenville immediately here, when I shall certainly try to get Ld. Temple at least not to think of quitting his present Situation till He sees how things are settled here, which by a conversation I have had this evening with Ld. North, seems farther from any chance of being settled than it has ever yet appeared.

Draft, written on a page of Lord Sydney's letter of same date. Another copy in the King's handwriting.

No. 4206—*Lord Grantham to the King.*

Lord Grantham has the honour of sending Your Majesty some Dispatches received this morning from Paris.

Lord Grantham took the Liberty once of suggesting to Your Majesty that Mr. Munro's Return to Spain with the Distinction of Knighthood might be of use to his Commission there & to himself personally. If Your Majesty approves of it, Mr Munro might attend the Levee and receive that Honour.

WHITEHALL. 17 *March*, 1783. 11 *o'clock* A.M.

Endorsed by the King.

No. 4207—*Lord Sydney to the King.*

WHITEHALL, *March 17th,* 1783
m. 15 *past* 3 P.M.

Lord Sydney humbly presumes to transmit to Your Majesty the request of Mr. Jones, lately appointed a Judge in India, to receive the honour of Knighthood from Your Majesty.

Endorsed by the King.

No. 4208—*The King to Lord Sydney.*

QUEEN'S HOUSE. *Mar.* 17, 1783
m. 51 *past* 5 P.M.

Lord Sydney may acquaint the new Judge at Bengal that if he attends at the Levee on Wednesday, He shall be Knighted.

G. R.

No. 4209—*Lord North to the King.*

SIRE—Being pretty much indisposed this evening, I trust in Your Majesty's goodness to excuse my taking this method of communicating a letter I have just received from the Duke of Portland. Your Majesty will perceive from thence that it is out of my power to form in concert with His Grace, such a Plan as Your Majesty seemed to wish that we should prepare & lay before you; Indeed, If the Duke were willing to concur in forming an arrangement before he has the honour of being admitted to Your Majesty's presence, It would not perhaps be easy for us to agree completely in any plan, although the necessity of speedily concluding some arrangement for the conduct of Your Majesty's affairs would induce me to acquiesce whenever Your Majesty should think it requisite for your service that I should recede from any opinions of my own.

Upon reconsidering the difficulties which have been made with respect to the nomination of Lord Stormont to the office of Secretary of State, it has occurr'd to me that as those difficulties still continue, it might not be disagreeable to Your Majesty to intrust the Seals of the Home Department to me.

Honourable, distinguish'd, and advantageous as this situation is, my unfitness for it & my love of ease render it less desirable to me than it ought to be. But, in the present emergency, I will chearfully undertake it, if it is Your Majesty's pleasure ; otherwise I should choose to remain, as I first intended, out of Office. Your Majesty's determination shall determine me, who will be guided entirely by Your Majesty's wishes.

I have the honour to be, with the utmost deference, Sir, Your Majesty's most dutiful servant and subject,   NORTH.

Endorsed by the King, Mar. 17, 1783. Two copies, both in Lord North's handwriting.

Enclosure.

The Duke of Portland to Lord North.

WHITEHALL, *Monday March 17, 1783*

MY LORD—I have very fully considered what Your Lordship has at different times communicated to me respecting The King's expectations relative to a Plan of Arrangement of a New Administration, & it is with the greatest pain that I must acknowledge the impossibility of fulfilling them until I shall have had the honour of being admitted to His Royal Presence & of Receiving his Commands for that purpose immediately from Himself.

If it is His Majesty's pleasure to place me at the head of the Treasury, it is impossible to suppose that He means to withhold from me any part of his Confidence, but it is very necessary that the Publick should be convinced of that circumstance, and that I should be authorized to speak to those whose assistance it may be thought necessary to apply for, in such a manner as may satisfy them of my being possessed of the means of fulfilling the engagements I may propose to them. I feel an insurmountable difficulty in taking any steps which may uselessly commit any other person as well as myself & I cannot think myself entitled to make such overtures to anyone as may produce from him concessions which he would be unwilling to make unless I could satisfy him of the propriety of such Conduct. It would be unbecoming my own Character in many respects which it is needless to state to Your Lordship, but one I cannot omit, as it ought to outweigh all the Rest & operates so strongly upon my mind that nothing would reconcile me under that impression to depart from what I submit to You as my private determination & that is the subjecting myself to the imputation of abusing the Royal Name, for under no other Sanction would I presume to make the offers which the formation of an Arrangement would require, & therefore without being authorized by His Majesty I cannot venture to make that mention of it which appears to me unavoidable under such Circumstances.

I hope it is unnecessary to assure Your Lordship that no personal consideration has mixed itself in this Opinion ; it is wholly the Result of what my duty to The King and the Publick have suggested to my thoughts. In Your Lordship I have the fullest confidence & the Delicacy, the Candour and the Liberality with which You have acted in this Negotiation which has happily procured me the honour of your acquaintance will command from me the fullest testimony of the Respect and Esteem with which I have the honour to be, My Lord, Your Lordship's most obedient & most humble servant,   PORTLAND.

Endorsed by the King.

No. 4210—*Lord Sydney to the King.*

ALBEMARLE STREET, *March* 17*th*, 1783
m. 30 *past* 12 *at night*

Lord Sydney humbly presumes to send Your Majesty a Minute of Cabinet agreed upon by those of your Servants, who met according to Your Order this evening at Lord Grantham's Office. They were sensible that the Opinion therein given must appear very limited upon so important an occasion. At the same time they wished, with all humility, to represent that the present Posture of Public Affairs, joined to the State of Your Majesty's Councils disables them from forming such a judgement as they can recommend to Your Majesty as the Formation of any permanent Plan of Measures.

Lord Sydney humbly ventures to express his sincere & hearty Wish, in which he is confident that he is joined by all those who have the honour to serve Your Majesty, that such an Administration may be speedily formed, as may have Strength & Wisdom enough to encounter the present numerous Difficultys, & whose services may be equally agreeable and satisfactory to Your Majesty, and advantageous to Your Subjects.

Endorsed by the King.

Enclosure.

MINUTE OF CABINET.

[In the handwriting of Lord Sydney.]

CLEVELAND Row, *March* 17th, 1783
m. 30 *past* 11 P.M.

Present :—Lord Chancellor, Duke of Rutland, Lord Grantham, Lord Howe, Lord Ashburton, Mr. Pitt, General Conway, Lord Sydney.

It is humbly represented to Your Majesty that the actual State of Affairs makes it necessary that the former Opinion delivered to Your Majesty by Your Cabinet of paying off & disarming the Fleet should be proceeded upon with Caution & Slowness for the Present.

No. 4211—*The King to Lord Sydney.*

QUEEN'S HOUSE, *Mar.* 18, 1783
m. 20 *past* 8 A.M.

The Minute of Cabinet is perfectly proper ; Lord Sydney will therefore give the Orders that may be necessary agreeable to it ; None of the Members of that Meeting can feel stronger than I do that pressing necessity of bringing things to a decision with the utmost expedition, for which purpose I have just wrote a letter to Ld. North in answer to one I received last night, which certainly did not advance matters, which states clearly the Negociation and which I have desired may be communicated so that in the course of this Day it is impossible, but I must receive some final answer.

Draft, written on a page of Lord Sydney's letter of 17 March. Another copy in the King's handwriting, misdated the 17th.

No. 4212—*Duke of Manchester to the King.*

Marche ye 18*th* [1783]

SIR—I beg leave to present my humble Duty to Your Majesty and to lay before You the enclosed note which I received this morning from Lord Shelburne. In obedience to Your Majesty's Commands to provide a proper Person to fill the office lately held by Colonel Egerton, it was my intent, to have laid before You tomorrow the name of Sir Henry Dashwood, whom [*sic*] I flatter'd myself might meet with Your Majesty's approbation. May I therefore presume so far, as humbly to hope that the appointment of Major Bernard may be suspended until I have had the Honor of submitting the whole of this affair for Your Majesty's final determination.

I beg leave to subscribe myself, Sir, Your Majesty's Most dutiful and devoted Subject,   MANCHESTER.

Endorsed by the King.

No. 4213—*The King to Lord North.*

QUEEN'S HOUSE. *March* 18*th*, 1783

LORD NORTH—I received your letter late the last Evening enclosing the one you had received from the D. of Portland; the clearest manner in which I can answer yours is by recalling to You what has passed; when first I sent to You, I desired to place you again at the head of the Treasury, and that You should try to form an Administration on the most extensive basis, from a conviction that no Party could alone conduct the Public Affairs and my uniform wish from the hour I first mounted the Throne, and from which I have never departed, to extinguish all odious party distinctions, and have the assistance of the best and ablest Men the Kingdom might produce. You declined from want of health accepting that situation; I then proposed you should have any other Cabinet Office that might suit You, and that You should assist Me in pointing out how an Administration could be formed on such a wide basis, the Treasury being placed in the hands of some Peer, not the Head of any large Party, whom when the other outlines were stated on paper to be laid before me for My consideration I should name ; You soon wrote that as to the Duke of Portland and his friends, they would not make part of such a[n] Extensive Plan, unless he was nominated to preside at the Treasury. After some consideration I, on Wednesday last, authorised you to continue to try to have such a plan formed for my inspection, and that if it can be effected, the D. of Portland's being at the Head of the Treasury shall not be objected to by Me. Your letter does not, nor does that from the D. of Portland to you, seem to recollect that I cannot enter into any detail till You have sent me such a Plan on Paper for my inspection ; I certainly shall not bind myself by giving any separate approbation or disapprobation to any proposal till the whole is sent to me on Paper, when I shall coolly judge whether such proposal is likely to effect my only object, the removing all dissensions and thus forming an Administration that may have weight both at home and abroad.

To prevent delays and mistakes, I authorize you to communicate this wherever You may think it necessary.

Draft, endorsed by the King.

No. 4214—*Lord North to the King.*

SIRE—Immediately upon the receipt of Your Majesty's Commands, I avail'd myself of Your Majesty's gracious permission to communicate the note to the Duke of Portland, desiring him at the same time to confine the further communication of it to as few persons as possible. His Grace promised to observe & in fact did observe the injunction but, between two & three o'clock in the afternoon He called upon me & declared that he had in no respect alter'd the sentiments which he had express'd in the letter he wrote to me yesterday, but thought it impossible for him to concur in forming the plan of any administration before he should have been admitted to the honour of an audience with Your Majesty.

Your Majesty's gracious orders to me were certainly to prepare the plan of an Administration for Your Majesty's inspection upon the most extensive basis possible. It was not in my power to attempt to form any such arrangement without the concurrence of the Duke of Portland and his friends. My most zealous endeavours, though they have been unsuccessful have not been wanting ; Your Majesty is already appriz'd of the difficulties I have met with & is now informed of the obstacle which disables me from carrying Your Majesty's Commands into execution & which I trust will appear to Your Majesty not to have arisen from any want of an earnest desire, on my part, to accomplish Your Majesty's intentions.

I humbly stated to Your Majesty on a former occasion (not only as my opinion but as the opinion of such of my friends as are best able to judge of the question) That the present state of Parties & of the House of Commons render it impossible for the Public business to be conducted in that House by a junction of my friends with the remainder of the Administration ; From hence Your Majesty will perceive to what little purpose I could attempt to prepare by myself an arrangement of a Ministry fit for Your Majesty's inspection ; Nothing can result from such an attempt useful, respectable, permanent or capable of answering in any respect Your Majesty's expectations.

I have the honour to be, with the utmost deference & the most respectful attachment, Sir, Your Majesty's most obedient and most dutiful subject & servant,   NORTH.

Tuesday Mar. 18th, 1783

Endorsed by the King.

No. 4215—*Mr. Pitt to the King.*

Mr. Pitt humbly presumes to acquaint Your Majesty that in the House of Commons today, Mr. Coke of Norfolk gave Notice that it was his Intention to move for an Address to Your Majesty on Friday next, if an Administration should not be formed before that time. Mr. Coke did not explain the Nature of his intended Motion more particularly, and Nothing was said by any other person on the subject.

Tuesday March 18th, 1783. *m.* 40 *past* 5 P.M.

Endorsed by the King.

No. 4216—*Lord Shelburne to the King.*

SIR—Lord Sydney wrote to me a note last night that he had summon'd a Cabinet at the desire of Lord Howe. I take it for granted he will lay before Your Majesty the answer which I wrote to him. I have further reasons, which I am sure will prove perfectly satisfactory to Your Majesty, for my not attending it, if those contain'd in my letter to Lord Sydney do not, when I have the honour to lay them before Your Majesty.

I have acquainted The Duke of Manchester of Your Majesty's appointment of Major Bernard, as he proposes attending Your Majesty. I have the honour to inclose to Your Majesty a Copy of the Attorney General's Opinion which the Duke says he does not recollect applies to it, as well as a List of Offices, which come under the same predicament.

I have the honour likewise to send Your Majesty the Treasury Minute respecting the Civil List. I have had that and everything regarding that subject copied into a small Book for Your Majesty's use, which will be finished today. The allowance to the Under-Secretarys of State propos'd in it will prove an increase of Salary to them of some hundred pounds a year ! I understand however they mean to apply to Your Majesty for a further increase of Two Hundred Pounds a year more ; I need not mention to Your Majesty how unreasonable, after the Secretary of the Treasury having agreed to so considerable a reduction of their Salarys, who are now going on without any sort of Provision [*sic*].

The Death of the Archbishop of Canterbury is an Event of so much consequence that it is my Duty to apprize Your Majesty of the probability or at least the possibility of it. The Bishop of St. Asaph came to acquaint me of it. Your Majesty knew, when the See of Salisbury was dispos'd of how I stand in regard to him. I can only add, that I have reason to believe him a very honest man, and capable of feeling obligation where he owes it. I need not add I hope, that passing thro' my hands, my object from every motive would be to make him feel and acknowledge his obligation to Your Majesty. At the same time I cannot presume to propose any delay on that or any other account in the Arrangements depending. I find by Mr. Pitt tonight that he attended Your Majesty yesterday to lay before Your Majesty the Importance of hastening them, and has written to Your Majesty on the subject of Mr. Coke's motion. I wish it was in my power to answer for the language, which may be held upon it, or the Vote which may take place upon it, but it's incumbent on me to apprize Your Majesty that everything is got so excessive loose, that I believe no Man can.

I have the honour to be with the highest Respect, Your Majesty's Most Dutyfull Subject, SHELBURNE.

BERKLEY SQUARE. 18th March, 1783. Tuesday Night ½ past 12

Endorsed by the King.

No. 4217—The King to Lord Shelburne.

Ld. Howe desired the Cabinet might be assembled to consider what ought to be done on the unpleasant state of the Seamen ; I am not surprised Ld Shelburne declined going to the Meeting.

I have seen the D. of Manchester ; he seems much offended and till he can understand he had no legal right to appoint to the Office vacant in the Jewel Office by the death of Lieut. Col. Egerton, He will not deliver up the Keys of the Office to Major Bernard.

The Minute of the Treasury seems on the whole very proper ; I cannot see any reason for granting more to the under Secretaries than has been settled by the Treasury.

I have seen the D. of Portland and also Ld. North this day ; whether they will form any arrangements and what, I cannot guess ; I have desired to see the whole before I decide on any part.

QUEEN'S HOUSE. Mar. 19, 1783. m. 15 past 6 P.M.

Draft, written on a page of Lord Shelburne's letter of 18 March.

No. 4218—The King to Lord North.

LORD NORTH—I desired to be here at ten this morning [sic].

QUEEN'S HOUSE, Mar. 19th, 1783. m. 10 past 8 A.M.   G. R.

No. 4219—*Lord North to the King.*

[19 *March*, 1783]

Lord North has, in obedience to His Majesty's Commands, called upon the Duke of Portland, but has not found him at home ; The Duke is riding and is expected between one & two ; he will in that case pay his Duty to His Majesty after the Levee unless His Majesty should give any orders to the contrary.

PRIVY GARDEN, WHITEHALL

Undated. Endorsed by the King, Mar. 19, 1783.

No. 4220—*Duke of Portland to the King.*

The Duke of Portland humbly requests the honour of being informed when it will please His Majesty to permit him to have the Honour of paying his duty to His Majesty.

WHITEHALL. *Thursday March 20th*, 1783

Endorsed by the King.

No. 4221—*Bishop of London to the King.*

SIR—The great and undeserved honour which Your Majesty is pleased to do me in thinking of appointing me to succeed the late excellent Archbishop of Canterbury fills me with the highest sense of obligation to Your Majesty. I should at all times have thought myself very unequal to so high and important a station ; but labouring as I do at present with many infirmities of age and ill-health I must beseech Your Majesty to excuse me from under-taking an Office of the proper discharge of which I find myself wholly incapable. I beg Your Majesty of your goodness to indulge me in this request, which will add to the many great obligations I have to Your Majesty.

I am, with the most heartfelt sense of gratitude to Your Majesty, Sir, Your Majesty's most dutiful Subject and most obliged and most devoted Servant,   R. LONDON.

LONDON HOUSE. *Mar. 20th*, 1783.

No. 4222—*Lord Sydney to the King.*

WHITEHALL, *March* 20, 1783.   9 P.M.

Lord Sydney humbly presumes to send Your Majesty in Obedience to Your Orders by Lord Grantham a Draught of an answer to the Address of the Quakers, for Your Majesty's Approbation.   He had the honour to deliver to You yesterday one conceived in nearly the same words.

The particular point concerning which Lord Sydney had desired Lord Grantham to obtain Your Majesty's Commands, was whether they were to read the Address to You at Your Levee, which Mr. Barclay told him this morning had been the usual custom.   The Address will be presented to Your Majesty by a Committee of Eight.

Endorsed by the King.

No. 4223—*The King to Lord Grantham.*

Lord Grantham did not quite comprehend Lord Sydney's question ; Mr. Barclay is to be informed that of course He or whosoever is to present the Address in the name of the Quakers is to read it at the Levee, and I shall [read] the answer, and then will pass through the Rooms as on former occasions.   G. R.

QUEEN'S HOUSE. *Mar. 20th*, 1783.   *m.* 33 *past* 9 P.M.

No. 4224—*Lord North to the King.*

Lord North has the Honour of informing His Majesty that the Duke of Portland has withdrawn the objection which in compliance with the prejudices of some of his friends, he had made to Lord Stormont, & will be ready to lay before His Majesty a plan of an Administration, whenever His Majesty shall think proper to appoint.

Friday Morng. Mar. 21 [1783]

Endorsed by the King.

No. 4225—*Duke of Portland to the King.*

The Duke of Portland has the honor of acquainting His Majesty, that the difficulty of forming the arrangement in concert with Lord North of which he thought it His Duty to apprize His Majesty last night is upon full consideration entirely removed, & that now no difference of Opinion remains between Lord North and him with respect to the formation of a Cabinet.

Friday noon. March 21, 1783

Endorsed by the King.

No. 4226—*The King to the Duke of Portland.*

I shall be ready to receive the D. of Portland as soon as He can conveniently come to Me ; if it is not inconvenient for him to call here, he may perhaps find Me before I am able to go home : if I can get away from hence He will find Me in that case at home.

ST. JAMES'S. *Mar. 21, 1783*

Draft, written on a page of the Duke of Portland's letter of same date.

No. 4227—*Lord Shelburne to the King.*

Lord Shelburne has the honour to send Your Majesty a Copy of the Attorney and Solicitor General's last Opinion in regard to the Jewel Office. The Duke of Manchester has written to Mr. Ord a Reply to it, which has been shown to the Attorney and Solicitor, who think it perfectly nugatory. There have been no Jewels kept in the Jewel Office, as Mr. Gilbert assures Lord Shelburne, but a small quantity of Plate, which has been very improperly distributed in Town and Country for the convenience of the principal Officers. Mr. Gilbert says that he gave orders some time since in the name of the Treasury to have it collected.

Lord Shelburne takes this opportunity of sending Your Majesty The Book containing the present State of the Civil List, Treasury Minute, &c.

The Gibraltar Papers some time since mention'd to Your Majesty.

A very correct Abstract of the Reports of the Commissioners of Accounts made by Mr. Pigott, so far as Lord Shelburne has been able to get him to compleat the same.

There are some other Papers for Your Majesty's use, which will be transmitted as soon as they are copied at the Treasury.

Lord Shelburne likewise has the honour to send Your Majesty a Letter, which he only received yesterday from Lord Temple.

BERKLEY SQUARE. *22nd March*, 1783. ¼ *past* 3 P.M.

Endorsed by the King.

No. 4228—*The King to Lord Shelburne.*

I return Ld Temple's letter, which is every way proper. I am at this hour still uncertain whether the Coalition can form any Arrangement : I hope before Night to have some final Answer.

QUEEN'S HOUSE. *Mar.* 22, 1783. *m.* 10 *past* 6 P.M.

Draft, written on a page of Lord Shelburne's letter of same date.

No. 4229—*Lord Grantham to the King.*

Lord Grantham has the Honour to acquaint Your Majesty, that M. del Campo arrived yesterday, and presented the Copy of his Credentials as Minister Plenipotentiary to Lord Grantham last night.

M. del Campo waits Your Majesty's Commands as to the time of receiving the Honour of his Audience ; And if Your Majesty thinks proper, Lord Grantham will introduce him on Monday after the Levee.

ST. JAMES'S. 28 *March*, 1783. 8 *o'clock* P.M.

In the King's hand, approved. *Endorsed by the King.*

No. 4230—*The King to Lord North.*

LORD NORTH—Not having heard from You since the directions I gave You yesterday, I must desire You will come instantly.

QUEEN'S HOUSE. *Mar.* 23, 1783. *m.* 30 *past* 10 A.M.   G. R.

Draft of the above. Endorsed by the King.

No. 4231—*Mr. Pitt to the King.*

Mr. Pitt humbly presumes, on reflecting on the situation which Your Majesty has graciously condescended to communicate to Him, to submit to Your Majesty's Consideration, whether it might not tend to bring the long-depending Negotiation to some speedy and decisive Issue, if Your Majesty should think fit to see both the Duke of Portland and Lord North together, in order to receive their joint Answer with respect to the Plan which Your Majesty has directed them to form, and which Mr. Pitt, the more he considers it, humbly conceives it indispensable that Your Majesty should have before the House of Commons meets tomorrow.

Sunday. March 23rd, 1783. m. 22 *past* 11 A.M.

Endorsed by the King.

No. 4232—*The King to Mr. Pitt.*

MR. PITT—I have seen Ld. North and sent him to the D. of Portland to desire the Plan of Arrangements may be instantly sent to Me, as I must coolly examine it before I can give any answer, and as I expect to have the whole finally decided before tomorrow's Debate in the House of Commons : this seems to answer the idea I have just received from Mr. Pitt.

ST. JAMES'S. *Mar.* 23, 1783. *m.* 55 *pt.* 11 A.M.

Mr. Pitt is desired to be here after the Drawing Room.

Draft, written on a page of Mr. Pitt's letter of same date.

No. 4233—*The King to Lord North.*

The Duke of Portland instead of bringing the plan of an arrangement as Ld. North had this morning intimated, and which Lord North has ever admitted to be a reasonable Measure, only offered and at last did shew a few Members of Cabinet Offices, and still persists in not bringing a list of Arrangements : I have thought it right to draw up the enclosed Message to which I desire Ld. North will write an answer at latest by Nine this Evening, having previously waited on the D. of Portland and concerted it with Him.

QUEEN'S HOUSE. *Mar. 23rd, 1783. m. 5 pt. 5 P.M.*

Draft, endorsed by the King.

Enclosure.   [In the King's handwriting.]

Whether the Duke of Portland and Lord North will not send their joint plan of Arrangements, with the exception of such Offices of small importance which cannot be immediately filled up, early this Evening : they having certainly had full time to prepare it. His Majesty having always declared He must have such a plan for consideration, and that He will give His opinion upon it without much delay.

No. 4234—*Lord North to the King.*

Lord North has the honour of His Majesty's Commands, which he will immediately communicate to the Duke of Portland.

If Lord North intimated that the Duke of Portland intended to bring a compleat plan of arrangement to His Majesty this morning, He certainly went too far, & was not authorized by anything he had heard from the Duke. His Grace had yesterday express'd the great difficulties which appear'd to him in preparing such a plan as His Majesty wish'd to have, previous to his Appointment, but intended to explain them to His Majesty either by writing, or in person, or, as he understood through the medium of the Duke of Montagu, & to endeavour to learn His Majesty's sentiments (if His Majesty should be willing to declare them) as to some points, that he might endeavour to avoid inserting in his plan what he should know beforehand to be disagreeable to His Majesty.

In saying this much Lord North begs to speak with diffidence, as he may have possibly mistaken the Duke's words, which pass'd only in general conversation, & which Lord North was not authorized to repeat.

LOWER GROSVENOR STREET. *Mar.* 23, 1783

Endorsed by the King, " No. 1."

No. 4235—*Lord North to the King.*

Lord North has the honour of informing His Majesty that, immediately upon the receipt of His Majesty's Message, He sent it to the Duke of Portland, and proposed to wait upon His Grace, according to His Majesty's directions : That the Duke, in return, acquainted Lord North that he was writing fully to His Majesty in consequence of an Audience He had had the honour of having this afternoon at St. James's, which, as Lord North apprehends, related to the matter contained in His Majesty's message. Lord North conceives That a separate answer, which is the only one that under the present circumstances, it is in the power of Lord North to give, would be contrary to His Majesty's Orders.

LOWER GROSVENOR STREET, ¾ *past* 8 P.M. *Mar.* 23, 1783

Endorsed by the King, " No. 2."

No. 4236—*The Duke of Portland to the King.*

Upon a very full and attentive consideration of the Commands which the Duke of Portland has had the honour of receiving from His Majesty, he humbly presumes to state to His Majesty that though the circumstances which would attend the formation of a new Administration to be composed of Lord North and the Duke of Portland's friends, would unavoidably occasion many Removals, the Duke of Portland ventures to apprize His Majesty that every attention would be shown to render them as little obnoxious to His Majesty as the case would possibly admit, that it would be the object of those who may be confidentially entrusted with the direction of His Majesty's business to study His Majesty's wishes & the ease of his mind in that as well as in every other particular ; that the Bedchamber would be consider'd by them as liable to no alteration while the Persons who have the honour of belonging to it conduct themselves satisfactorily to His Majesty and support his Government ; that the office of Master of the Horse is filled by a Nobleman whose character and Virtues entitle him to universal respect, but that notwithstanding this determined intention on the part of those who may be to form the arrangement, many difficulties occur to the submitting a Plan for His Majesty's Inspection until they can flatter themselves that His Majesty is graciously disposed to listen to the Recommendations which it may be their duty to offer to Him. That the Recollection of an expression of His Majesty's, is the reason of the Duke of Portland's presuming to enter into this detail, which he submits as an outline of the plan upon which the intended arrangement would be formed. Under these impressions the Duke of Portland has most seriously to lament the necessity he is under of declining the Undertaking which His Majesty was pleased to require of him, and he begs leave most humbly to apprize His Majesty that he feels the most anxious concern that in a moment of such critical Importance he should be obliged to represent to His Majesty the impossibility of his accepting a Responsible Situation without some assurance of His Majesty's confidence, which can alone enable him to discharge such a Trust, with any probability of Credit or Success, or could at any time induce him to offer himself to His Majesty's consideration for any employment.

WHITEHALL. *Sunday evening, March 23rd,* 1783

Endorsed by the King.

No. 4237—*The King to Mr. Pitt.*

Mr. Pitt is desired to come here ; the D. of Portland has wrote an answer which ends in declining to prepare a plan for my inspection, consequently the Negociation is finally ended.

QUEEN'S HOUSE. *Mar.* 23, 1783. *m.* 48 *past* 8 P.M.

Draft, endorsed by the King.

No. 4238—*The King to the Duke of Portland and Lord North.*

Printed. Donne II. 434.

The D. of Portland having uniformly declined drawing up the Plan of Arrangement and continuing to do so after my having this day at St. James's acquainted him that I would not longer delay coming to some Resolution if he did not send such a plan for my consideration this evening, I therefore take this method of acquainting him that I shall not give him any further trouble.

Ld. North must therefore see that all Negociation is at an end.

QUEEN'S HOUSE. *Mar.* 23, 1783. *m.* 35 *past* 10 P.M.

Draft, endorsed by the King, " the same to Ld North at the same time, with the addition of the last paragraph. Sunday." *Another copy, in the King's handwriting, subscribed G. R.*

No. 4239—*Lord North to the King.*

Lord North has received the honour of His Majesty's Commands, which he will immediately communicate [to] the Duke of Portland.

¼ *past* 11 P.M.

Endorsed by the King.

No. 4240—*Lord Temple to the King.*

DUBLIN CASTLE. *March 23rd.* 2 A.M.

SIRE—I have this moment received from Mr Grenville the detail of the conversation with which Your Majesty was pleased to honour him on the 16th inst. I will not attempt to state the feelings of gratitude & respect, with which I have received the testimonies of Your approbation : & the signal proof of that condescension with which Your Majesty was graciously pleased to inform me of the situation of the Kingdom at this most alarming crisis. Every feeling of duty & of inclination call upon

me to offer my situation & opinions to Your Majesty's consideration : & as I have no official means of conveying them, I trust
to your goodness to excuse what must be a long detail, but
truly interesting to me, as your good opinion must ever be the
object of my eager wishes.

When Your Majesty did me the honour to destine me to this
high office, I unaffectedly felt that diffidence which my inexperi-
ence & scale of Talents naturally suggested to me : I will not
say that I was insensible to the hopes of building my honest
fame upon the event of my administration ; but I solemnly
declare that my principal object was to contribute my small
share to the support of Your Majesty's government, abandoned
in a situation from various reasons most critical, & upon grounds
which appeared to me to be upon every principle publick and
private wholly indefensible. To the natural difficulties of my
undertaking, I had the additional misfortune of not finding
myself peculiarly in these confidential habits with Your Majesty's
Servants, to which in such a situation I should naturally look
for support : My trust under God, was in Your Majesty's goodness and protection ; & I acknowledge with pride & gratitude
that I have been honoured with the most unequivocal proofs of
that goodness. Judge then, Sire, the pain which I felt in that
moment when I thought myself called upon by every principle
of publick duty to sollicit officially Your Majesty's permission
to retire from this high station. I have not vanity enough to
conceive that my presence in Ireland is material to your service
further than as it will be always eligible to preserve (particularly
in this Kingdom) some settled system of government ; & upon
this ground I hold it my indispensable duty to lay at Your
Majesty's feet the reasons which induce me to believe that my
presence in this Kingdom can be no longer useful to that service,
to which I will beg Your permission to say that I have dedicated
every hour and every faculty since my arrival ; & as those
reasons cannot be deposited in the office with safety to the
interests of both Kingdoms, & as for many reasons it might
not be judged eligible that they should fall into the hands of
every description of gentlemen, who aspire to high office, I have
ventured upon the unusual measure of depositing them in Your
Royal breast still trusting to the indulgent goodness which I have
experienced for my excuse : And if any part of those reasons

shall appear to Your Majesty to be painted too strongly, I must apologise truly for them; though I solemnly declare that the state of facts which I am about to draw is the result of cool deliberation, & I will venture to hope that Your Majesty will believe that I will not attempt to mislead your judgement, either upon facts, character, or opinions.

From the first moment of my arrival in Ireland I have struggled with infinite difficulties; I was told in England that the situation of this Kingdom held out every hope which could be suggested by perfect confidence in English & in Irish government, & by unanimity arising from the spirit of gratitude for the liberal concessions made by Great Britain : & I was likewise told that I should find prepared to my hands such a mass of solid strength, as would effectually secure the means of conducting the ordinary purposes of government, not only with facility, but with eclat : Your Majesty will judge my mortification in finding the Kingdom engaged in a ferment on a constitutional question, more evident than that which had appeared before Lord Carlisle's departure ; & that ferment much increased by the injudicious arrangement of a measure which might have been truly useful if conducted with address ; I mean that of the Provincial Levies, which from circumstances (infinitely too long for the present detail) totally defeated the only essential object, which it ought to have accomplished ; the division of the Volunteers. To this spirit of dissatisfaction arising from these two essential objects I had not the shadow of government to oppose ; those who composed it were respectable for their parts & for their integrity & had been high in popular estimation ; but many circumstances occurred to weaken the advantages which were proposed from their support. The want of knowledge & habits of office, the thirst for popularity which pervades them all & the fetters which they had forged for themselves by popular questions during an opposition of 15 years, by making them timid and undecided, rendered them wholly unequal to the defence of government. Several characters respectable for their services, their rank, their property and connexions, had been systematically and ostentatiously depressed, except in the instance of Mr. Ponsonby, whose influence was unbounded & brought forward that spirit of discontented jealousy of which Your Majesty well remembers instances in the last weeks of the

Irish sessions. The variety of dismissals (some of which were considered as peculiarly cruel) had weakened every confidence in Government, and had spread an apprehension & distrust through every board and department ; the natural consequence of this was that the interior business of the Kingdom was much at a stand, while the general expectation was raised by professions to a pitch which it would have been found difficult to gratify, in a country where the offices are really insufficient to the purposes of government & at the same time the confidence which had been given to the volunteers by the attention paid to them at every meeting, had drawn them into the discussion of every speculative question which could embarrass the publick services.

In this situation my first object was to restore that confidence in the equity of government which I judged indispensable for quieting the alarms of the servants of the crown. Every attention was paid which could conciliate the feelings of those friends who had felt themselves proscribed, & at the same time care was taken not to alarm the very jealous feelings of those to whom the D. of Portland had trusted the administration. Your Majesty will recollect that one of my earliest objects was, that of taking the efficient government from those from whom I expected no permanent assistance, at the moment when by fighting their ground of the adequacy of simple repeal (which from the beginning I stated as very hazardous) they pledged themselves to the publick to a doctrine, which was truly unpopular & has completely ruined them in the opinions of those from whom they derived their consequence. And lastly, I have never lost sight of that first essential object, the depressing the volunteers by every caution, but with the determined purpose of endeavouring to restore the sword & the executive power to those hands in which the constitution has so wisely placed them.

Great part of these general opinions appear in my official correspondence ; other parts of this system are palpable with the smallest clue & the whole militates decisively against the opinions of the D. of Portland & of Mr. Fox, whom I particularize as they continue to keep up a constant correspondence with the popular leaders in this Kingdom. Your Majesty will therefore judge how perfectly impracticable it is for me to hope to conduct your government upon the plan which I have stated to be necessary to its existence ; & which is in the very teeth of those ideas which have been adopted by the persons, whom from the exigency of publick affairs, Your Majesty has probably been obliged to call to your councils.

To these circumstances, Sire, suffer me to add my feelings of indignation at the formation of that coalition to which your government has given way ; formed at such a time, in such a manner, having necessarily for its basis the foul abandonment of every principle, publick and private ; & holding but one principle in common & that principle avowed of forcing themselves into employments at all hazards to the Kingdom, which never was exposed to such calamities & I fear never can recover such a shock. I trust that I do not break through the bounds of that respect which I so truly feel, when I say that no consideration shall make me a friend or party to such a coalition, or to the component parts of it. These opinions I have not concealed (from a very particular circumstance) having been forced to explain them.

The whole of these considerations will I hope justify me to Your Majesty for a step which I have taken with the utmost reluctance, but which in conscience & in duty was unavoidable ; & I trust that you will not for a moment believe that I could by such a step mean to increase those difficulties, which I would relieve with my life : but that my official letter was written under the idea that the new administration was formed upon characters and principles which I could not approve, but in all contingencies this Kingdom has suffered so materially from the uncertainty of the last eight weeks, & from the necessary delay of several points which have been submitted, & which I think essential to government (so much so that I have been truly importunate respecting them) that I very much fear the general event, & my own personal credit from consequences which I foresee, but cannot now wholly prevent ; but whatever may be my fears, I will not press this consideration, till Your Majesty's arrangements shall be made, in the hopes that I may be allowed then to retire, particularly if my confidence and goodwill cannot (as is too probable) engage me to the support of the new system. I need not add that whenever Your Majesty's goodness shall relieve me from this situation, I shall quit it with the regret which is the natural result of leaving a great & essential work of government incomplete, which I had vanity enough to imagine that I might by Your Majesty's goodness be enabled to restore, & with the same vanity I will add, that I had rather that Your Majesty should collect the present state of Ireland from anyone rather than from myself.

Suffer me, then, Sire, to hope that my system and that my conduct have not been unacceptable to you : suffer me likewise to hope that Your Majesty sees the reason for this resignation, neither founded in personal motives of indolence, disinclination or inattention to that service, which is so truly flattering to me ; nor in others more disgraceful because they would be more prejudicial to your Government ; and suffer me to hope that Your Majesty sees me yielding to a necessity which I cannot avert, with a heart filled with the most lively emotions of gratitude, respect & affection. With these feelings, it is my fervent prayer that Your Majesty's wisdom and firmness may save the Kingdom from the calamities which must be the consequences of this unprincipled coalition ; unprincipled, because they can be bound by no political or moral opinions in common ; & with these feelings I shall retire with satisfaction, to that obscurity from which Your Majesty's great goodness called me, desirous however on all occasions to sacrifice every private feeling which would naturally lead me to indolence and retirement, when ever Your Majesty shall call upon me to give that assistance which every honest man owes to rescue your Government from a system which will either be disgraceful & dangerous if it comprehends the whole of this faction, or weak and inefficient if it is partial.

Once more, Sire, I entreat Your Majesty's pardon for this long detail, in which however many very important considerations which are suggested by the present situation of Ireland are necessarily omitted. My reasons for wishing to quit this Kingdom have necessarily been secret, and possibly Your Majesty will not think it for your service that they should be avowed.

To your wisdom & to your justice I submit them, & must once more urge to Your Majesty those sentiments of gratitude, affection & respect, with which it is my pride to subscribe myself, Sire, Your Majesty's Very faithful & devoted Subject & servant,

NUGENT TEMPLE.

Endorsed by the King, Recd. March 26th, 1783.

No. 4241.

PROPOSED CABINET.

[23 *March*, 1783]

[The seven persons proposed by the Duke of Portland.]

President of the Council . . V. Stormont
Privy Seal . . . . E. of Carlisle
1st Commissioner of the Treasury D. of Portland
Chancellor of the Exchequer . Ld John Cavendish
Secretaries of State . . . {Ld North
{Mr Fox
1st Commissioner of the Admiralty Vt Keppel

[In the King's handwriting.]

No. 4242—*The King to the Lord Chancellor.*

MY LORD—As I shall be extremely glad to see You this morning as early as it may suit you, I shall not detain You now by a long episode. After every sort of chicanery from the Coalition, to which I have opposed the only weapon an honest Man can employ streight dealing, I have brought it to the repeated refusal of laying a plan of Arrangements before Me for my consideration upon which with the consent of Mr. Pitt, I broke off all further Negotiation last night. He has said every thing but that He will engage to remain at the head of the Treasury which his delicacy made him wish to deferr saying till this morning when I am to expect him. I wish therefore Your Attendance here may be as early as possible.

QUEEN's HOUSE, *Mar.* 24*th*, 1783

Draft, endorsed by the King.

No. 4243—*Mr. Pitt to the King.*

Mr. Pitt humbly wishes, with Your Majesty's Permission to defer having the honor of waiting upon Your Majesty till after the Levee, conceiving that no arrangement can be announced with Propriety, before the Debate today in the House of

Commons, and thinking that He shall be better prepared to submit his thoughts to Your Majesty's consideration.

Monday, March 24th, 1783. *m.* 40 *past* 10 A.M.

Endorsed by the King.

No. 4244—*The King to Mr. Pitt.*

Mr. Pitt's idea of having nothing announced till the Debate of today meets with my thorough Approbation ; I have just seen the Ld. Chancellor, who thinks that if Mr. Pitt should say towards the close of the Debate that after such a conduct as the Coalition has held that every Man attached to this Constitution must stand forth on this occasion, and that as such he is determined to keep the Situation devolved on Him, that He will meet an applause which cannot fail to give him every encouragement.

QUEEN'S HOUSE, *Mar.* 24th, 1783. *m.* 10 *pt.* 11 A.M.

Draft, written on a page of Mr. Pitt's letter of same date.

No. 4245—*Mr. Pitt to the King.*

Mr. Pitt humbly presumes to acquaint Your Majesty that an Address was moved this day by Mr. Coke, and seconded by Lord Surrey, in substance entreating Your Majesty in consideration of the distracted State of the Country, to condescend in Compliance with the Wishes of the House to appoint an Administration which may be entitled to the Confidence of the Nation, and tend to prevent the unfortunate division in the Country. This Motion was first opposed by Mr. Buller, then assented to by Mr. Hill as conveying the very same sentiments as the Amendment He intended to have moved, after which there was no other opposition to it but from Mr. Macdonald who moved the previous Question, but which was not seconded. The other Speakers spoke on the General Situation of Affairs, and were Mr. Fox, Governor Johnstone, Mr. Jenkinson, Mr. Macdonald, Mr. Harrison, Sir C. Turner, Lord North and Lord J. Cavendish besides Mr. Pitt. The language of Lord North and

Mr. Fox conveyed that the delays which have happen'd could not proceed from any Indisposition to give Ease and Satisfaction to Your Majesty's Subjects, nor was it owing to any difference of Opinion between themselves, but threw out general Insinuations of Persons who advised Delay. Mr. Pitt thought it his duty to call upon them to declare whether they could pledge their honor, that there were no differences between them which would prevent an Arrangement, which they pretty distinctly did. The Detail of the Negotiation was not gone into, and the Debate was so desultory, that Mr. Pitt presumes to hope Your Majesty will excuse this imperfect Account; nor indeed did anything pass very strongly to mark the precise Sentiments of the House. Nothing seem'd to be collected from it, as Mr. Pitt humbly conceives, but the additional Necessity, too urgent even before, of some immediate arrangement, and unaccompanied by anything that could relieve his mind from the Embarrassments which He ventured to state to Your Majesty.

Mr. Pitt has thought it his duty to trouble Your Majesty with this Account of what passed without loss of time, hoping for a speedy opportunity of adding to it whatever more particular Information Your Majesty may be graciously pleased to command.

Downing Street, *Monday, March 24th,* 1783. 8 p.m.

Endorsed by the King.

No. 4246—*The King to Mr. Pitt.*

I am not surprised as the Debate has proved desultory that Mr. Pitt has not been able to write more fully on this occasion, after the manner I have been personally treated by both the D. of Portland and Ld. North it is impossible I can ever admit either of them into my Service; I therefore trust Mr. Pitt will exert himself tomorrow to plan his mode of filling up the Offices that will be vacant so as to be able on Wednesday morning to accept the situation his Character and Tallents fit him to hold, when I shall be in Town before twelve ready to receive him.

Windsor, *Mar.* 25, 1783. *m. 5 pt. 12 at Night.*

Draft, endorsed by the King.

No. 4247—*The King to Lord Weymouth.*

Lord Weymouth must be better apprised than I can possibly be of the Debate in the House of Commons yesterday, the short note I wrote to him must have shewn I had some suspicion of the conduct Mr. Pitt might hold ; I received the enclosed letter from Him to which I sent the following answer, as I have no copies of them I trust Ld. Weymouth after shewing both to the Chancellor will return them by my Servant who has orders to wait for Your directions. I am clear Mr. Pitt means to play false, and wants I should again negotiate with the Coalition ; but no consideration in life could bring Me to that I am decided sooner to yield the game to them and let my Son be the Puppet which Mr. Pitt's letter seems to indicate the House of Commons [is] not disinclined to see their Sovereign. I am glad I am out of Town as it gives you and the Chancellor time to think who ought to be held out in the House of Commons ; if my coming can be of the smallest utility Ld. Weymouth's answer after having consulted the Chancellor will instantly bring me ; ought the D. of Rutland not to be seen by You or the Advocate that Mr. Pitt's intentions if fathomable may be known. All I shall add is that the Chancellor can tell You my plan is not unformed if I find all combine to say that nothing but the Opposition can come forward.

WINDSOR, *Mar.* 25, 1783. *m.* 15 *pt.* 7 A.M.

Draft, endorsed by the King.

No. 4248—*Lord Sydney to the King.*

ALBEMARLE STREET, *March* 25, 1783
m. 40 *past* 11 A.M.

Lord Sydney humbly presumes to transmit to Your Majesty two Packets which he has just received from General Conway. He likewise ventures to send Your Majesty General Conway's letters accompanying them. In consequence of that part of it which mentions Your Approbation of Thanks being sent in Your Majesty's name to the Staffordshire Militia, I shall immediately write to Lord Lewisham, and shall venture to add your Approbation to the Alacrity with which he went down into

Staffordshire upon the news of the Riots which prevailed there, as Your Majesty was pleased to express yourself to me in terms, that seemed to authorise me to do so, when I mentioned it to you.

Lord Sydney thinks it necessary to observe to Your Majesty upon one part of General Conway's Letter, that he does not recollect any General Military Arrangement being come from Ireland, except a Plan, which he has already had before him, & that was rather a loose Sketch than a Plan.

Endorsed by the King.

No. 4249—*Mr. Pitt to the King.*

Mr. Pitt had the honor this Morning of receiving Your Majesty's Gracious Commands. With Infinite Pain he feels himself under the Necessity of humbly expressing to Your Majesty that with every sentiment of dutiful Attachment to Your Majesty and of zealous desire to contribute to the Public Service, It is utterly impossible for Him after the fullest consideration of the actual situation and of what passed yesterday in the House of Commons to think of undertaking, under such circumstances the Situation which Your Majesty has had the condescension and Goodness to propose to Him.

As what Mr. Pitt now presumes to write, is the final Result of his best Reflection, He should think Himself inexcusable if by delaying till tomorrow humbly to lay it before Your Majesty, he should be the cause of Your Majesty's not immediately turning your Royal Mind to such a Plan of Arrangement as the Exigency of all the present circumstances may in Your Majesty's Wisdom, seem to require.

DOWNING STREET, *March 25th*, 1783. *m. 30 pt. One P.M.*

Endorsed by the King.

No. 4250—*The King to Mr. Pitt.*

MR. PITT—I am much hurt to find you are determined to decline at an hour when those who have any regard for the

Constitution as established by Law ought to stand forth against the most daring and unprincipled faction that the Annals of this Kingdom ever produced.

WINDSOR, *Tues. Mar.* 25, 1783. *m.* 35 *pt.* 4 P.M.

Draft, written on a page of Mr. Pitt's letter of same date.

No. 4251—*The King to Lord Sydney.*

WINDSOR, *Mar.* 25, 1783
m. 50 *pt.* 6 P.M.

LD. SYDNEY—The idea proposed by G. Conway of instantly sending Transports to Guernsey to bring over the 104th Regt and when landed immediately to disband it with disgrace, is so proper that the Orders cannot be too soon expedited for that purpose ; as also my thanks to the Staffordshire Militia for its conduct during the Tumult and particularly Lord Lewisham for the alacrity and activity he has shewn on this occasion.

I quite agree with Ld. Sydney that nothing is yet come from Ld. Temple but very loose ideas which He wished might be improved by directions from hence.

Draft, written on a page of Lord Sydney's letter of same date. Duplicate in the King's handwriting.

No. 4252—*General Conway to the King.*

LITTLE WARWICK STREET, 25 *March,* 1783

SIR—I herewith enclose for Your Majesty's perusal L. Govr. Irving's letter & relation of a violent Mutiny which has happen'd in the 104th Regt. but by the proper and vigorous measures taken has been quell'd without loss.

I am humbly of opinion that transports should immediately be sent to bring that Regt. over to be broke with disgrace, Retaining the Ringleaders ; among whom, if thought consistent with the Capitulation, some proper example shou'd be made on

the spot, which I imagine from the disposition the Troops there
have shewn will have no difficulty.

I am with the greatest Respect, Your Majesty's most Dutiful
& Faithful Servant,   H. S. CONWAY.

Endorsed by the King.

No. 4253—*The King to General Conway.*

GEN. CONWAY—Transports cannot too soon be sent to
Guernsey and the 104th Regt. as soon as landed broke with
disgrace ; if the Ringleaders can be punished, it is highly proper.

WINDSOR, *Mar.* 25, 1783

Draft, written on a page of General Conway's letter of same date.

No. 4254—*Mr. Pitt to the King.*

Mr. Pitt humbly presumes to transmit to Your Majesty a copy
of the Address of the House of Commons, and to entreat Your
Majesty's permission to have the honour of waiting upon Your
Majesty either before or after the Levee, as Your Majesty may be
graciously pleased to command.

DOWNING STREET, *March 26th*, 1783. *m.* 45 *past* 11 A.M.

Endorsed by the King.

No. 4255—*Mr. Pitt to the King.*

Mr. Pitt humbly presumes to acquaint Your Majesty that
Your Majesty's answer had been reported to the House of
Commons, before Mr. Pitt could get down ; but He understands
that the only thing said in consequence, was by Lord Surrey who
after expressing his satisfaction in hearing the answer, added that
if something was not effected by Monday, he should then move
to take into consideration the causes which prevented it.

DOWNING STREET, [*Wednesday*] *March 26th*, 1783. *m.* 10 *past* 5 P.M.

No. 4256—*The King to Lord Chancellor Thurlow.*

MY LORD—I wish to see You before You go to Lincoln's Inns this day, having Ld. Weymouth's opinion that it would be right again to try Ld. Gower ; indeed My Lord I am the more pressing to attempt to catch at every thing, as I feel if some one will not assist Me, I must within a couple of days take the step I have so often hinted to you.

QUEEN'S HOUSE, *Mar.* 28, 1783. *m.* 30 *pt.* 7 P.M.

Draft, endorsed by the King.

No. 4257—*The King to Mr. Thomas Pitt.*

MR. PITT—The very handsome Message you sent to Me through Lord Gower when I desired Him to speak to You makes me desirous of seeing You here as soon as possible.

QUEEN'S HOUSE, *Mar.* 28, 1783. *m.* 20 P.M.

Draft, endorsed by the King.

No. 4258—*Mr. Pitt to the King.*

SIR—I am this moment honour'd with Your Majesties commands and shall loose no time in obeying them having the honour to subscribe myself with the utmost devotion,

Your Majesties most faithful and most obedient humble Servant,   THOS. PITT.

March 28th, 1783

Endorsed by the King.

No. 4259—*Draft of a Message from the King to the House of Commons.*

[? 28 *March,* 1783]

His Majesty acquaints the House of Commons that when He mounted the Throne now above twenty two Years, He had the pleasing hope that being born in this Kingdom, He might have proved the happy Instrument of concilliating all Parties, and thus collecting to the Service of the State, the most respectable and most able Persons this Nation produced. Of this object he has never lost sight, though sad experience now teaches Him, that selfish views are so prevalent, that they have smothered the first of Public Virtues, Attachment to the Country, which ought to warm the breast of every Individual who enjoys the Advantages of this Excellent Constitution, and the want of which Sentiment has prevented that Unanimity which must have rendered Britain invulnerable, though attacked by the most powerful Combinations.

The Inclination of His Majesty to alleviate the Distresses of his People, added to the Change of Sentiments of one Branch of the Legislature, which rendered the real object of the War impracticable, made Him undertake the arduous task of obtaining the blessings of Peace, become more difficult by the Resolution above alluded to ; He therefore rejoiced when the Preliminary Articles were concluded.

Subsequent events having made it necessary to form a new Administration, His Majesty has made repeated attempts to collect the most efficient Men of all Denominations who under His Majesty's Inspection might with Dispatch and Confidence proceed in forming the Definitive Treaties, and carry on the general business of the State to the most Advantage.

This Patriotic Endeavour has proved unsuccessful, by the Obstinacy of a Powerful Combination that has long publicly manifested a resolution of not entering into Public Service, unless the whole Executive management of affairs is thrown entirely into their hands, and from which they have not departed on the present Occasion : at the same time want of zeal prevents others from standing forth at this Critical conjuncture.

His Majesty from Obedience to the Oath He took at His Coronation will never exceed the Powers Vested in Him, nor on the other hand ever submit to be the tool of a Party. He must therefore end this conflict which certainly puts a stop to every wheel of Government, and call upon those who feel for the Spirit of the Constitution to stand forth to His Assistance.

No. 4260—*Draft of a Message from the King to Parliament.*

[? 28 *March*, 1783]

I cannot at the most serious, as well as most painful moment of My Life go out of this Great Assembly, without communicating to You My Intentions, not asking Your Advice.

The first time I appeared as Your Sovereign in this place now above twenty two years, I had the pleasing hope that being born among You, I might have proved the happy Instrument of conciliating all Parties and thus collecting to the Service of the State the most respectable and most able Persons this Kingdom produced. Of this object I have never lost sight, though sad experience now teaches Me that selfish Views are so prevalent that they have smothered the first of public Virtues, attachment to the Country, which ought to warm the breast of every Individual who enjoys the advantage of this excellent Constitution, and the want of which Sentiment has prevented that Unanimity which must have rendered Britain invulnerable, though attacked by the most Powerful Combinations.

My own Inclination to alleviate the Distresses of my People, added to the Change of Sentiments of one branch of the Legislature, which rendered the real object of the War impracticable, made Me undertake the arduous task of obtaining the Blessings of Peace, rendered indeed more difficult by the Resolution above alluded to. I cannot sufficiently acknowledge the candour with which the Courts of France and Spain have conducted themselves during the Negociation of the Preliminary Articles, which greatly accelerated that desirable Work.

Circumstances have since arisen that might make those Courts more doubtful of the stability of the Councils of this Country, *in forming the Definitive Treaties.* I have *therefore* again attempted to collect the most efficient Men of all Parties who under my Inspection might with dispatch and confidence proceed in forming the Definitive Treaties. But this Patriotic attempt has proved unsuccessful by the obstinacy of a powerful party that has long publicly manifested a resolution not to aid in the service of the Empire unless the whole Executive management of Affairs is thrown entirely into its hands, from which it has not on this occasion departed ; at the same time want of Zeal prevents others from standing forth at this critical conjuncture. My obedience to the Oath I took at my Coronation prevents my exceeding the powers vested in Me, or submitting to be a Cypher in the trammels of any self-created band.

I must therefore end a conflict which certainly puts a stop to every wheel of Government, make a final decision, and that I think myself compelled to do in this Assembly of the whole Legislature.

A long experience and a serious attention to the strange Events that have successively arisen, has gradually prepared my mind to expect the time when I should be no longer of Utility to this Empire ; that hour is now come ; I am therefore resolved to resign my Crown and all the Dominions appertaining to it to the Prince of Wales, my Eldest Son and Lawful Successor, and to retire to the care of my Electoral Dominions the Original Patrimony of my Ancestors. For which purpose I shall draw up and sign an Instrument to which I shall affix my Private Seal. I trust this Personal Sacrifice will awaken the various parties to a sense of their Duty and that they will join in the Support and Assistance of the Young Successor.

You may depend on my arduous attention to Educate My Children in the paths of Religion, Virtue and every other Good Principle that may render them if ever called in any Line to the Service of Great Britain, not unworthy of the kindness they may hereafter meet with from a People whom collective I shall ever Love.

May that All Wise Providence who can direct the inmost thoughts as well as Actions of Men give My Son and Successor not only every assistance in guiding His Conduct, but restore that sense of Religious and Moral Duties in this Kingdom to the want of which every Evil that has arisen owes its Source ; and May I to the latest hour of my Life, though now resolved for ever to quit this Island, have the Comfort of hearing that the Endeavours of My Son, though they cannot be more sincere than Mine have been, for the Prosperity of Great Britain, may be crowned with better success.

A second draft of the first two paragraphs only.

This document and No. 4259 are both of them in the King's hand.

No. 4261—*Memorandum by Thomas Pitt.*

[? 28 *March*, 1783]

When all Mankind unite in Sentiments of abhorence of the League between Ld. North and Mr. Fox for the purpose of taking possession of the King, the Parliament and the Country, it is easy to conceive what must be the feeling of His Majesty's breast, where the ingratitude of those in whom He has placed His Confidence, and upon whom He has showered all his favours must sharpen every other consideration. Yet if H.My. in his magnanimity could bring Himself to restrain those feelings (which it would be as impossible as it would be unbecoming so great a Prince to wish to *conceal* upon such an occasion) and to submit His natural resentment so far to the necessity of the times as to yield His Government and the *responsibility* of it into those hands that have had recourse to such means to acquire it ; and to be merely *passive* both in the arrangement of Offices, and in the concerting public measures, always reserving *the Royal favour* within His own breast which no man has a right to extort from Him, and which not even this united League would dare to invade as the *condition* of their Service. It appears in my poor Judgement that such a concession would be attended with many advantages to the ease and quiet of His Majesty's Government and would prevent much mischief to H.My. and the Public from a temporary and perhaps an ineffectual resistance. The present disgust against the Union, upon which alone can be founded any hopes of a Majority in the House of Commons will probably decrease both within doors and without, if they remain excluded and in possession of the popular ground of opposition, which keeps factions together by plausible topics of declamation and by the general though uncertain prospects of interest. The opinion of strength will not go to H.Mys Ministers, who will be to struggle from one difficulty to another, whilst every measure they propose will be discredited by large Minorities and the open and insiduous attacks of powerful parties. If H.My should feel the necessity at last of yielding after an unavailing struggle this step will be still more painful than at present, and the Country reduced to a more desperate situation ; If on the contrary the resolution so taken should be persisted in, at all events, the possible consequences which such a perseverance may lead to in such times as these, when there are so many ugly and alarming Symptoms of weakness and discontent, tending to a dissolution of all Government, should be well weighed in their full extent.

If on the other hand H.My. should prevail with Himself to give way in the present moment by sending at once for the D. of Portland to put his Government into his hands, the popular odium would follow them into Office with double force, their discordant principles would weaken their strength, the *interested* of their parties who were disappointed in their expectations would abandon them, those who were attached to them from principle would disclaim them for deserting their principles—the people would execrate them when they saw them united in office, reaping the fruits of their perfidy ; they would be to take upon themselves the responsibility of Loans and burthensome taxes, of projects of reform *defeated* and other cruel and almost impracticable reforms to be carried by them into execution.

Under such circumstances left to themselves and to the course of things, they would become contemptible in the eyes of the public, insignificant as leaders of party and would in a short time give way to what must be the wish of every honest Man, an administration which could at once establish itself in the confidence of H. My. and in the hearts of his People.

Copy in the King's handwriting, endorsed by him, "Mr. Thos. Pitt's first paper."

No. 4262—Lord Ashburton to the King.

Lord Ashburton has the honr. to acquaint His Majesty that he drove immediately to Ormond Street, where he found the Chancr. had dined out and had left orders for his carriage to come to him at 11 o'clock.

Ld. A. will not fail to see him in the morning before he goes to Lincoln's Inn and has left a message at his House expressing an intention to call upon him early. If any thing material should pass in their conversation requiring an earlier communication, Ld. A. will instantly convey it. If not, he will be in the way to receive his My's commands before 3.

LINCOLNS INN FIELDS, *Friday nt.* ½ *past* 9, 28 *March,* 1783

No. 4263—*Lord Sydney to the King.*

WHITEHALL, *Saturday, March* 29*th*, 1783
m. 40 *past* 1 P.M.

Lord Sydney humbly presumes to lay before Your Majesty a copy of the Address, which he has just received from the Committee of American Merchants, who have desired him to ask Your Majesty's permission for them to present the Address to you, and to receive Your Commands as to the time and place of presenting it.

The Secretary of the Commissioners of Public Accounts has acquainted Lord Sydney that they have another Report ready to present to your Majesty, whenever you are graciously pleased to receive it.

No. 4264—*The King to Lord Sydney.*

QUEEN'S HOUSE, *Mar.* 29*th*, 1783
m. 9 *pt.* 4 P.M.

Lord Sydney will acquaint the Committee of American Merchants that it will be proper for them to present their Address at my Levee on Monday, of course no answer is given.

The Commissioners of Public Accounts may also bring the fresh Report they have prepared the same day.

I desire You will send Mr. Wm. Grenville as soon as you can find him to me.   G. R.

No. 4265—*The King to Lord Sydney.*

Lord Sydney will tomorrow morning acquaint the Bishop of Bangor that He must attend at St. James's to be presented on my nomination to the Archbishop of Canterbury and at the same time order the Congé d'Elire and recommendatory letter to be prepared for my signing that day ; the Bishop of St. Davids to attend also and be presented for succeeding to Bangor.

QUEEN'S HOUSE, *Mar.* 30*th*, 1783. *m*. 38 *pt.* 10 P.M.   G. R.

No. 4266—*The Duke of Marlborough to the King.*

The Duke of Marlborough with the utmost submission has the honour to return Your Majesty his most unfeigned thanks for Your Majesty's most gracious Condescension in communicating to him Your Majesty's determination in favour of the Bishop of Bangor. He will instantly obey Your Majesty's Commands by informing the Bishop of Bangor that it is Your Royal Pleasure that he should kiss hands tomorrow.

MARLBOROUGH HOUSE, *March* 30, 1783. *m.* 20 *past* 11 P.M.

No. 4267—*Lord Dartmouth to the King.*

[1783]

SIR—Words cannot express the grateful sense I feel of Your Majesty's goodness to one, who has no other claim to so distinguished a mark of Your Majesty's favour than the most unfeigned Respect & Duty, & who must be highly unworthy of the notice Your Majesty is pleased to take of him if the whole course of his life does not uniformly manifest the attachment with which he is, Sir, Your Majesty's most dutiful & most faithful Subject,   DARTMOUTH.

No. 4268.

MEMORANDUM BY THE KING.

On Monday Feb. 24th 1783, The Earl of Shelburne in an Audience acquainted Me with his having by the advice of some of the principal Servants of the Crown in the House of Commons come to the final resolution of Resigning his situation in My service ; that though he had remained after the defeat on Monday the 17th in that House on the Address of Approbation of the Peace, the Subsequent Debate and an unpleasant Division on friday the 21st, convinced him that he could be of no further Utility.

I instantly proposed to Mr. Wm. Pitt that as by this resignation the first Seat at the Treasury Board now devolved on him, he should not think of retiring ; he begged with great propriety to have time to consider so weighty a point ; every one of the Ministers to whom I mentioned what I had said to him, applauded it.

On Thursday the 27th, Mr. Pitt declined from not seeing a certainty of obtaining a Majority in favour of Administration in the House of Commons.

I then took two or three days for consideration, during which period I sent the Lord Chancellor to Earl Gower to know whether he would decline being a Member of an Administration wherein Lord North should hold a principal situation : to which he very handsomely reply'd he should not object ; the Lord Chancellor's letter of Saturday, March 1st, shows this very clearly. I now though shocked at Lord North's having joined Mr. Fox, thought him the least objectionable part of the Coalition to which I would Address myself.

Therefore on Sunday March 2nd, I send for the Earl of Guildford whom I question on the strange Coalition his Son had made, which that worthy Peer as warmly reprobated as I could wish, and assured Me he did not believe it extended further than to the communication of Sentiments against the Articles of Peace, and the concurrence in opposing any Approbation of them.

Upon this I authorized him to go to Lord North and acquaint him that I should have that day sent for him had not his late extraordinary conduct made me doubt in what temper of mind he might be, and therefore had preferred sending him a Message through his Father ; my letter to the Lord Chancellor on that day contains the substance of it. (No. 4149.)

On Monday March 3rd, the Earl of Guildford returned with Lord North's answer stated in my letter of that day to the Lord Chancellor. (No. 4153.) I authorized the Earl of Guildford in consequence of it to appoint Lord North to attend Me in the Evening, when He confirmed the impossibility of his again feeling himself able to come to the Board of Treasury ; yet consented to be of the Cabinet without any Office, and to assist in enquiring what persons might be willing to enter into an Administration formed on the widest basis. He approved of the idea that the head of the Treasury should be a Peer, not a leader or member of a large faction.

On Tuesday the 4th He sent Me the two letters (marked No. 4156 and 4158). I saw Him in the evening and proposed to him that though Mr. Fox and his friends would not make part of such a Plan, that he, Lord North ought to try whether others would not ; this he promised to attempt, and on the 5th sent his letter of that date. (No. 4161.)

On friday March 7th I empowered Earl Gower to offer Mr. Thos. Pitt the Office of Secretary of State for the Home Department, the very able state of the Conversation (No. 4169) that past between them on this subject makes it unnecessary to add any remarks to it.

On Sunday March 9th, I sent for Earl Gower and proposed his being at the head of the Treasury, with Mr. Jenkinson and the Lord Advocate holding the efficient Ministerial Offices in the House of Commons ; He and Mr. Jenkinson declined personally, the Lord Advocate through the Lord Chancellor.

Being thus baffled in every endeavour, on Wednesday March 12th I sent for Lord North and told him provided an Administration could be formed on a broad basis, and that I could on the whole approve of the Plan of Arrangements, that then I would not object to the Duke of Portland being at the head of the Treasury, and therefore authorized him to go to that Duke with a Message to that purpose, and desiring when they had formed a joint plan that Lord North might bring it to me ; this he hoped to effect in two days.

On Friday March 14th I received Lord North's letter (No. 4188) of that date, and in consequence saw him the next Morning, when he acquainted Me that to his great surprise the Rockingham faction now objected to the Great Seal remaining in the present able hands, and to the idea he, Lord North had proposed of Lord Stormont being a Secretary of State, who on his side declined being President of the Council, which that party recommended ; as I looked on this Conversation merely as a state of the reasons which had prevented his yet bringing any Plan for my inspection, I certainly did not dissuade him from supporting two Noblemen he thought essential to any Administration in which he was to be concerned. I was consequently much surprised that Evening to receive a letter (No. 4197) from him wherein he supposes what I had said to him was a Message to the Duke of Portland.

I therefore on Sunday Evening March 16th saw Lord North and explained to him that what had past was only my private and hasty thoughts, for that I certainly would not give him any answer to any question concerning the Lord Chancellor till I had seen the whole proposed plan, nor to any other Separate part of it, that as to what regarded Lord Stormont, the whole matter was for Lord North's consideration alone.

Monday Evening, March 17th I received Lord North's letter of that date (No. 4209), enclosing the one the Duke of Portland had written to him ; the next Morning I sent Lord North my letter dated March 18th (No. 4213), and in the evening received his letter of the same date (No. 4214).

On Wednesday morning March 19th I sent for Lord North and asked him whether his not having yet prepared a Plan of Administration and Arrangements was now alone prevented by My not having seen the Duke of Portland ; this he answered in the affirmative. I thereupon desired him instantly to go for that Duke, but to explain at the same time, that I did not mean to exceed in my Conversation the bounds of the letter Lord North had received from Me the day before, which he acknowledged to be the exact State of the Negotiation.

The Duke of Portland could not therefore ever get me in conversation that day to exceed the bounds of that letter which he avowed having read, though he attempted to sound me on the propriety of Lord North being one of the two Secretarys of State ; this I replied was entering into Arrangements which I did not mean to do till a joint Plan drawn up by him and Lord North was formed and transmitted by the latter to Me, who would coolly examine it and without unnecessary delay sent either my approbation or objections to the whole or parts of the proposal.

On the next evening, March 20th, the Duke of Portland desired to see Me, when he announced that the Negociation between him and Lord North was at an end, the Duke's friends having rejected the idea of Lord Stormont being President of the Council, and Lord North having declared that in that case he could be no part of the Administration to be formed : that the Duke of Portland did not think his friends alone could form an Administration capable of carrying on the Public Affairs ; but if I insisted upon it, He would attempt to form such an Arrangement.

I told him I could not for two reasons ask him to take such

a step, first because I wanted to have an Administration on as wide a basis as if possible to exclude no party, and Secondly He not thinking his friends could alone go on, that it would be his undertaking that which could only disgrace him.

The next day Friday March 21st, during my Levee at St. James's, I received the two letters of that date, the one from the Duke of Portland (No. 4225), and the other from Lord North (No. 4224) ; as soon as I returned from St. James's I saw the Duke of Portland, who said his object in wishing to see Me was to acquaint that the cause of difference between his friends and Lord North no longer existed, they having withdrawn their objection to Lord Stormont ; that the Duke of Portland could now therefore shew me the names of the proposed Cabinet Ministers ; I declined seeing it, referring to the letter of March 18th which I had written to Lord North, and which had been communicated to Him, by which I had declared that I must see and examine the whole Plan of Arrangements before I could give any opinion on particular parts of it. He, to my astonishment said this was want of confidence in him for that the Cabinet once laid before Me, he expected that on his coming to the head of the Treasury, I should rely on his making no propositions but such as He thought necessary for my affairs and consequently that I should acquiesce in them. This unexpected idea, I fortunately did not treat with the warmth it deserved, but on finding that [the] Duke would not see the singularity of the proposition and that on discussing it he began to grow warm, said I must have time to consider of a proposition I thought so novel.

Therefore the next morning I sent for Lord North and did not disguise from him the indecency of the proposal ; but pretended to immagine it was not meant, and insisted on his going to the Duke of Portland, and on their joint plan of Arrangement being sent to Me in the course of the Evening.

Hearing nothing from Lord North, on Sunday morning, March 23rd, I sent for him to know why the Plan of Arrangement had not been transmitted to Me the night before ; He said he wondered the Duke of Portland had not either by letter or in person conveyed to Me that morning the Plan : I directed him instantly to go and acquaint the Duke that I must have it as soon as I returned from St. James's.

After the drawing Room the Duke of Portland asked an

Audience, when he said he came in consequence of the intimation through Lord North, that he had drawn up no Plan, but was ready to shew Me the list of Efficient Cabinet Ministers: I answered I was sorry to return to what past on Friday; the only alteration in his language was to press much for my looking at that list, which I desired to decline from an intention which I avowed again of not entering into parts of the Plan till he had enabled Me to examine the whole; but he pressed so much for my looking at his Paper that I so far complied, and then returned it to Him (see No. 4241). He then complained of my not saying I approved of the Names; this I told him I had before declined doing, and repeated my words. He upon that said he could not think of forming any Plan, and that he thought I might trust the Seven Persons mentioned and could not propose anything but what it would be right for me to Acquiesce in. This I replied was asking more than any Man above forty could engage to do, and insisted he should in the evening send either his Plan or a refusal of doing it.

Mr. Pitt having expressed to Me the necessity of its being known whether the Negociation was concluded or broken off previous to Mr. Coke's motion proposed for the next day, to which it had been postponed, I wrote a letter to Lord North (No. 4233), accompanied with the Message he was to carry to the Duke of Portland; in answer to this letter I immediately received one from Lord North (No. 4234), which is so unlike what he had said to Me that morning that I should be wanting to myself if I did not avow that it quite misstates what he had then said.

In the evening I received the Duke of Portland's letter (No. 4236), and the second from Lord North (No. 4235), in consequence of which I wrote the note I sent to the Duke of Portland (No. 4238), and a similar one to Lord North. Thus ended this Strange Negociation, which I have attempted to state as shortly as possible to be correct in my Narrative and not overcharge any of the Particulars.

March 30th, 1783

Some days since elapsed in attempting to again persuade Mr Pitt to continue at the head of the Treasury, but he declined much to my sorrow; since when I have attempted again to call forth Mr. Thos. Pitt to the first efficient Office in the House of Commons ; on that not succeeding I have taken the last step that could occur to Me, the sending again for Lord North and seeing whether he had no seeds of gratitude that might make him from a knowledge of my distress form a Plan, in which I have also not succeeded.

Two copies ; a first draft with many corrections, and a fair copy, both in the King's handwriting.

The documents, numbered by the King I to XXI, are here indicated by the numbers employed in this volume.

No. 4269—*Mr. Pitt to the King.*

Mr. Pitt humbly conceives it his duty to have the honor of informing Your Majesty that Lord Surry's Motion this day for an Address, thanking Your Majesty for your Gracious Message on Wednesday last, and repeating the Entreaties of the House that an administration may be form'd without delay, was after much conversation withdrawn, All Parties agreeing that it was of the last consequence that an administration should be so form'd ; but after Your Majesty's gracious Message it was more respectful to defer such a Motion for a day or two, hoping that the effect would be obtained without. This however was not done without its being understood on all sides that an Address to this Purpose would not be objected to if that hope should fail. Mr. Drake, Mr. Perceval, Sir Harry Houghton, Mr. Thomas Pitt, the Lord Advocate (who before it was understood the Motion would be withdrawn, moved the Order of the Day) and Mr. W. Pitt, spoke against the Address at present. Lord North, Mr. Fox and Mr. Burke spoke, agreeing to the Motion being withdrawn in the manner stated. Lord North and Mr. Fox repeated that they had no differences which would prevent their forming an arrangement, and used the strongest terms of respect towards Your Majesty in all they said on the Subject ; but gave no more particular Information to the House.

DOWNING STREET, *Monday, March 31st,* 1783. *m.* 50 *pt.* 7 P.M.

No. 4270—*Lord Sydney to the King.*

WHITEHALL, *March* 31, 1783
m. 40 *past* 9 P.M.

Lord Sydney humbly asks Your Majesty's forgiveness for having sent you a wrong Paper in the Room of the very valuable one with which you were graciously pleased to entrust him. Lord Sydney had put them into different Boxes and there was a mistake in delivering to the Messenger that, which was sent to Your Majesty.

Endorsed by the King.

No. 4271.

MEMORANDUM BY THE KING.

[For the " seven persons " *see* No. 4241.]

[1 *April*, 1783]

The total stagnation of Public Business by no Administration in reality subsisting at a time when the Definitive Treaties ought to be prosecuted ; the Navy and the Army reduced to a state of Peace and Taxes laid for defraying the Expenses of the State and for settling the unpaid Debt obliged Me no longer to defer submitting to the erection of an Administration whose conduct as individuals does not promise to deserve collectively my confidence.

I therefore on Tuesday evening, April 1st 1783, sent for Ld. North and enquired if the Seven Persons named by the D. of Portland and him were ready to accept the Employments proposed, on his answering in the affirmative I authorized him to acquaint them they might accept them the next day, after which the D. of Portland and He should plan the arrangements of Employments.

They accordingly were appointed the next day and that Duke and Ld. North desired to arrange the various Employments they chose to vacat ; but to my great surprise another day nearly elapsed before they would arrange the Board of Treasury and advanced no farther. The Duke proposed a

Dukedom for the E. of Hertford and a Marquisate for the E. of Fitzwilliams [*sic*], but I declined entering on that subject.

Draft, endorsed by the King, " Short Narrative of the Opening the Negociations for the formation of an Administration April 1st, 1783."

No. 4272—*The King to Lord Temple.*

QUEEN'S HOUSE, *April 1st*, 1783

MY LORD—I had the pleasure on the 26th of last month to receive from your truely amiable and right headed Brother and Secretary, your very able letter of the 23rd on the state of Ireland, couched in terms that also conveyed the warmest Attachment to my Person and Government, which makes me not deem among the least of Public Misfortunes that the want of Resolution in some and of Public Zeal in others will oblige you to quit a Station which you fill so much to the satisfaction of all honest Men as well as Mine.

Since the conversation I had with Mr. Wm. Grenville, on the 16th of last month, I have continued every possible means of forming an Administration ; an experience of now above twenty two Years convinces Me that it is impossible to erect any Stable one within the narrow bounds of any faction, for none deserve the appellation of Party and that in an Age when disobedience to Law and Authority is as prevalent as a thirst after change in the best of all Political Constitutions ; it requires that temper and sagacity which can alone be expected from a collection of the best and most calm heads and hearts the Kingdom possesses.

Judge therefore of the uneasiness of My mind at having been thwarted in every attempt to keep the Administration of Public Affairs out of the hands of the most unprincipled Coalition the Annals of this or any Nation can equal ; I have withstood it till not a single Man is willing to come to my assistance and till the House of Commons has taken every step but insisting on this faction by name being elected Ministers. To end a conflict which stops every wheel of Government and which would affect the Public Credit if it continued much longer I intend this night to acquaint that *grateful* Man Ld. North that the Seven Cabinet Counsellors the Coalition has named shall kiss hands tomorrow and then form their Arrangements as [in] the former Negociation they did not condescend to open to Me any of their intentions.

A Ministry which I have avowedly attempted to avoid by calling on every other description of Men, cannot be supposed to have either My favour or confidence and as such I shall most certainly refuse any honours that may be asked by them ; I trust the eyes of the Nation will soon be opened as my sorrow may prove fatal to my health if I remain long in this thraldom ; I trust You will be steady in Your attachment to Me and ready to join other honest Men in watching the conduct of this unnatural Combination, and I hope many months will not elapse before the Grenvilles, the Pitts and other men of abilities and character will relieve Me from a Situation that nothing but the supposition that no other means remained of preventing the public finances from being materially affected would have compelled me to submit to.

It shall be one of My first cares to acquaint those Men that you decline remaining in Ireland.

Draft, endorsed by the King.

No. 4273—*Lord North to the King.*

[1 *April*, 1783]

Lord North has in obedience to His Majesty's commands waited upon the Duke of Portland, and inform'd His Grace that His Majesty consented to appoint the seven persons recommended by His Grace for the several offices for which His Grace had recommended them. Lord North added that it was His Majesty's intention to settle the other arrangements afterwards, & that he believed His Majesty wished that the seven persons above-mentioned should be at St. James's tomorrow to receive their appointments, but as he is not quite certain as to the latter part of His Majesty's Commands, He thinks it necessary to relate to His Majesty what he has done that he may receive His Majesty's Orders time enough to prevent any mistakes.

Endorsed by the King, April 1st 1783.

No. 4274—*The King to Lord North.*

Printed. Donne II. 434.

QUEEN's HOUSE, *April 2nd*, 1783
8 *h.* A.M.

The principal Object of My sending last night to Ld. North was to acquaint Him that the seven persons named by the D. of Portland and Ld. North for several Offices might be at St. James's to kiss hands this day, by half hour past one.

Draft, written on a page of Lord North's letter of 1 *April*, 1783.

Duplicate in the King's handwriting.

No. 4275—*Lord Grantham to the King.*

Lord Grantham having received Your Majesty's Commands, cannot refrain from expressing in this manner the most submissive and dutifull Gratitude to Your Majesty, for the many and constant marks of Favour and Confidence which Your Majesty has most graciously conferred upon him.

His attachment to Your Majesty has always been inviolable, and He will ever share with the Country at large, a just sense of the Sacrifice which Your Majesty's paternal Goodness has induced you to make of your own feelings on this most trying Occasion.

WHITEHALL, *2nd April.* 10 *o'clock* A.M.

Endorsed by the King.

No. 4276—*Lord Howe to the King.*

Lord Howe has the honour to transmit for Your Majesty's information, a letter from Rear Admiral Digby received this morning by post from Glasgow. Also a note from the Master of Loyd's Coffee House respecting the arrival of Mons. Vaudrueil with the French Squadron under his direction, at Cape Francois.

ADMIRALTY OFFICE, 2 *April*, 1783. ½ *past* 3.

No. 4277—*The Duke of Portland to the King.*

The Duke of Portland has the honour of acquainting His Majesty that He last night received a letter from the Duke of Richmond signifying his intention of resigning his Office into Your Majesty's hands today, which letter the Duke of Portland will have the honour of laying before His Majesty and of submitting some other matters to His Majesty's consideration whenever it shall be His Majesty's pleasure to receive the same. The Duke of Portland humbly informs His Majesty that the Commissioners of the Treasury, Lord Surrey, Sir Grey Cooper, and Mr. Montague, that Mr. Townshend whom His Majesty was graciously pleased to approve of for the Treasurership of the Navy and Mr. Burke to whom His Majesty had condescended to give the Pay Office are sollicitous of having the honour of kissing His Majesty's hand at His Levee today, that Lord Foley would think himself highly honoured by His Majesty's permission to the same indulgence as one of the Joint Post Masters, but the Duke of Portland is very apprehensive that the arrangement of the Admiralty Board is not yet so completely settled as to enable him to lay it before His Majesty in time to obtain His Majesty's approbation so as to give notice to the Commissioners of His Majesty's gracious disposition in their favour previous to the hour of His Majesty's Levee.

DEVONSHIRE HOUSE, *Friday, 4th April,* 1783. *m. 50 past ten o'clock* A.M.

Endorsed by the King.

No. 4278—*The King to the Duke of Portland.*

QUEEN'S HOUSE, *April 4th,* 1783
m. 55 pt. 11 A.M.

If it is more convenient to the Duke of Portland to see Me before than after the Levee I shall be by the quarter after twelve at St. James's. The new Commissioners of the Treasury may be presented this day at the Levee, as also Mr. Chas. Townshend and Mr. Burke, and also Lord Foley as one of the Joint Postmaster[s] ; if the new Commissioners of the Admiralty cannot kiss hands this day it is no rule that their Seats must not be moved for in the

House of Commons.   If the Duke of Portland is ready with their names, he may appoint them to be presented this day without previously mentioning them to Me, as I do not intend to interfere with the formation of that Board.

Draft, written on a page of the Duke of Portland's letter of same date.

No. 4279—*Lord North to the King.*

Lord North has the honour of informing Your Majesty that Lord Fitzwilliam has just call'd at his Office, & acquainted him That a short time before his Lord Rockingham's death He had had the honour of kissing Your Majesty's hand upon being appointed Custos Rotulorum of the Soke of Peterborough, but that his Uncle's death, & the forgetfulness of some persons who had undertaken to mention the business to the Secretary of State had prevented the appointment from going on; upon this representation of the case Lord North has ventured to direct the necessary Letter to be made out, & has the honour of enclosing it for Your Majesty's determination.

Mr. Fox told Lord North at Court, that Lieut. General Burgoyne had a few days before Lord Sydney resign'd, applied for a Leave of Absence, but that he imagin'd that Lord Sydney had not had an opportunity of mentioning the General's request to Your Majesty before his resignation.   He desired Lord North to take Your Majesty's pleasure, but it had slipp'd his memory when he was in the Closet.

Lord North was not able to find Mr. Greville time enough to send him to St. James's today, but he has directed him to attend, & receive the Staff on Sunday.

Friday 4 P.M. [4 *April*, 1783]

Endorsed by the King.

No. 4280—*The King to Lord North.*

QUEEN'S HOUSE, *April* 4, 1783
m. 20 *pt.* 5 P.M.

I remember perfectly Ld. Fitzwilliam being appointed Custos Rotulorum of the Soke of Peterborough; Lord North will therefore send the necessary letter for having it put into execution.

Lt. G. Burgoyne has applied for leave to come from Ireland, but was told till the Peace Arrangement was put into execution his Attendance in Ireland was very material ; I am certain when Ld. North mentions this to Mr. Fox he will see it in the same light.

Mr. Greville's Attendance after the Drawing Room on Sunday will be the proper time for his receiving the Staff of Treasurer of the Household.

Ld. North must order the Warrant for the Admiralty Commission to be sent by ten this night.

Draft, written on a page of Lord North's letter of same date.

No. 4281—*General Conway to the King.*

LITTLE WARWICK STREET, 4 *April*, 1783

SIR—I am under the necessity of troubling your Majesty most humbly to entreat Your M's pardon for having by a negligence I am much ashamed of been depriv'd of the honour of paying my duty to Your Majesty at St. James's but surmising that many of Your M's Ministers were attending to have audience I had ventur'd to absent myself for a short time and on my return had the misfortune to find that Your M. had left the Palace ; which at this time particularly was the greatest mortification to me lest I might possibly seem deficient in duty and respect to Your Majesty.

I herewith send the Returns & some Memoranda of Recommendations I had propos'd to lay before Your Majesty.

I am, Sir, with the highest respect, Your Majesty's most Devoted & Dutiful Servant,   H. S. CONWAY.

Endorsed by the King.

No. 4282—*Lord North to the King.*

[4 *April*, 1783]

Lord North begs His Majesty's pardon for not having sent the Admiralty Commission at ten o'clock according to His Majesty's

order. He did not receive it from his Office till between eleven
and twelve o'clock, & a little time [? after] he had received a letter
from Lord Apsley, desiring to decline the Office ; His Lordship's
reason seems to be principally apprehension of the undertaking
and he appears to have consider'd the offer as very honourable
& deserving his best thanks ; although he seem'd diffident this
morning, yet as he had accepted the offer & came to Court
prepared to kiss His Majesty's hand, Lord North hoped that he
would not ultimately have come to this resolution, Lord North,
with His Majesty's permission, will offer it tomorrow morning
either to Mr. George Brudenell or Mr. Sloane.

LOWER GROSVENOR STREET, ½ pt. 12 o'clock P.M.

No. 4283—*The King to Lord North.*

Printed. Donne II. 435.

QUEEN'S HOUSE, *April 5th*, 1783
m. 30 *pt.* 8 A.M.

The Warrant for the new Admiralty Commission came as
directed at ten last night, when I signed it with the names only of
Ld. Keppell and Adm. Pigott, the others left blank, so that when
Ld. North has finally settled the names with the D. of Portland
they may be inserted and the Commission prepared. I certainly
do not mean to object to any part of the Arrangement of places,
and cannot have any [objection] either to Mr. Geo. Brudenell or
Mr. Sloane for a seat at that Board. G. R.

Draft, written on a page of Lord North's letter of 4 April, 1783.

Duplicate, in the King's handwriting.

No. 4284—*The King to General Conway.*

QUEEN'S HOUSE, *Ap.* 5, 1783
m. 30 *pt.* 8 P.M.

GENERAL CONWAY—I have received the Monthly Returns and
Weekly State you enclosed to Me ; as also two Papers of proposed
Successions in the Army, which I consent to, and therefore You

may give notice for the necessary Commissions being prepared agreable to them.

Draft, written on a page of General Conway's letter of 4 April 1783.

No. 4285—*Mr. Fox to the King.*

Mr. Fox has the honour of sending to Your Majesty the Project which he mentioned yesterday morning to Your Majesty. It appears to contain so little more than the preliminaries themselves, & refers to them so absolutely upon the sixteenth Article relative to the East Indies, the article of all others that seemed to require the most explanation, that Mr. Fox humbly submits to Your Majesty whether there is not much reason to fear that several explanations must take place before the definitive Treaty can be concluded.

ST. JAMES'S, *m.* 25 *past* 11 A.M.   5 *April,* 1783.

Endorsed by the King.

No. 4286—*The King to Mr. Fox.*

The project of a Definitive Treaty with France as prepared by Mr. de Rayneval is so little in detail that it must require much enlargement before it can be in a state of perfection.

QUEEN'S HOUSE, *Ap.* 5*th,* 1783.   *m.* 31 *pt.* 8 P.M.

Draft, written on a page of Mr. Fox's letter of same date.

No. 4287—*Lord Shelburne to the King.*

SIR—I deferr'd troubling Your Majesty with the enclos'd accounts of Secret Service, expecting from the Treasury the following papers for Your Majesty's use—

1. Copy of the Civil List Establishment divided into Classes, and deliver'd in to the Clerk of the House of Commons, by

Mr. Rose pursuant to the Act of the last Sessions on the 5th of April.

2. Account of the expenses of the Christmas Quarter compar'd with the Annual Estimate.

N.B. This is not an Official paper, but made out with a view of falling upon some proper mode of comparing future accounts.

3. Mr. Russell's several Reports on Crown Lands, Woods, and Exchequer Offices, particularly *Sheriffs Accounts*. This last Article deserves Your Majesty's attention.

4. Report of the American Commissioners regarding Sufferers by War. Mr. Wilmot has taken infinite pains upon this subject, and is acknowledg'd to have shewn great patience and impartiality in examining the several Claims.

5. The Attorney and Solicitor Generals Opinion on the Duke of Manchester's memorial to the Treasury about the Jewel Office.

Mr. Rose assures me, that they will be compleatly finish'd in the course of the Week, and carefully transmitted for Your Majesty's use. Mr. Ord finds likewise that it will require some little further time to compleat the Post Office Report, the Appendix to it being very long. This Enquiry has been from the beginning in his hands, and he assures me, that it shall be punctually transmitted to Your Majesty very shortly.

Your Majesty will naturally observe that the amount of the Civil List Establishment exceeds, for the moment, the disposeable Income by £6400. 19s. 0½d. This is owing to the Lord Chancellor's, Lord Grantham's and Col. Barré's as well as Sir Joseph York's Eventual Pensions being now suppos'd to commence, in consequence of the arrangement now taking place, but will still be more than compensated by the Income, which will arise from the appropriation of Fees directed by the Act to the use of the Civil List, increas'd Salarys having been given in lieu of them, and supposing the same Regulations to take place, as directed, in the other Offices, regarding Incidents and Stationary, which are actually established and conform'd to in the Treasury. It is apprehended that the Article of Fees alone will produce more than £5000 a year. They have been repeatedly call'd for, and if they can be obtain'd in time will be transmitted to Your Majesty along with the other papers by Mr. Rose. If the Paymaster and Superintendant the Inspector, the Master of the Household, and the Secretary to the Lord Chamberlain continue properly chosen, with a view to the performance of their respective Dutys, and without any political mixture, and are well supported, I am persuaded that Your Majesty's expences will come within the Estimate. I am confirm'd in thinking so by those who have been most conversant in what has pass'd concurring in the same opinion, and without taking into account Pensions and Compensations, which must fall in to a considerable amount. I take it for granted in saying so, that Your Majesty's gracious disposition continues the same and that those who hold the higher Offices of Government will be actuated by high principles of honour towards Your Majesty and the Publick. The Secret Service of the two Secretarys of State being unlimited will however always require Your Majesty's attention. Your Majesty will I hope excuse my presuming to add, that the correctness of that, which I have now the honour to inclose from the Treasury is entirely Mr. Ord's.

I should have been very happy if I could have accomplish'd before we clos'd, classing the whole Treasury Business into two books of *References* and *Payments*, with perhaps a small additional Book for miscellaneous matter, which would have shewn Your Majesty from day to day the whole state of Payments, by their being thrown into different columns, it being absurd that Your Majesty should be troubled with so many little details, and be left Ignorant of the immense Sums daily passing there, and which Your Majesty is call'd upon to sign. There has been a considerable progress made towards it, but it was impossible to finish it in time.

I dare not detain Your Majesty to express the anxious wishes I feel for Your Majesty's and the Queen's Happiness. I shall be truly happy if my future conduct merits Your Majesty's approbation, and proves the Devotion and Gratitude with which I must ever remain, Your Majesty's Dutyfull Subject and Faithfull Servant,   SHELBURNE.

BERKLEY SQUARE, 6 *April*, 1783. 5 *o'clock* P.M.

Enclosures.

No. 1.

Account of Money paid for Foreign Secret Service by the Secretary of State for the Home Department between the 13th July 1782, and the 21st March 1783.

1782.

| July 13th. | To Mr. De Wolff for Intelligence from Paris | 55 5 0 | |
| | | 22 18 6 | 78 3 6 |

13th	To Mr. Richard Oakes Do.	150 – –
August 1.	To Mr. Allaire who was brought from Flanders by Mr. Fox with a view to settle a Channel of Intelligence	100 – ··
	To Mesnard a Frenchman who was taken into Custody at Brightelmstone and brought to town upon supposition of his being a Spy	1 1 0
9	To William Clarke, for the Attendance of two of his men employed in watching motions of some Foreigners	11 1 6
15	Do. for watching Mr. Rosenhagen	{ 4 18 4 / 1 14 9
17	To Mr. Thornton One Quarter's Annuity	50 – –
	To Captain Taylor for Intelligence brought by him to Lord George Germaine Lord Shelburne and Lord Sydney from September 1781 to this day	905 15 6
	To Mr. Richard Oakes for Intelligence brought by him of the Dutch Fleet	150 0 0
20	To Thomas Green for Intelligence of practices carried on at Rye	5 5 –
29	To Paolo Rossi, the Jesuit from South America	200 – –

Carried over . . £1657 19 7

1782.	Brought over	£1657 19 7
Septr. 18	To Mr. Richard Oakes his draft from Ostend where he had accompanied Mr. Reboul Mr. De Vitre for the purpose of obtaining Intelligence	250 – –
Septr. 25	To Mr. Clarke for his trouble and expenses to Brigh[t]elmstone, from thence to Portsmouth, and back in quest of Monsr. Pelivé who was suspected of conveying Intelligence to France	47 15 4
October 1	To Thomas Green his Expences in search of persons at Rye concerned in Transmitting Intelligence to France	2 2 –
11	To Captain Ottendorp for Services performed by him	100 – –
11	To Mr. Rich. Oakes his Dft. from Ostend	250 – –
23	To Wm. Clarke for so much paid by him to Captain Killick of a smuggling cutter for his information relative to Pelivé, and as a compensation for the hire of his vessel which had been waiting for Pelivé	27 14 6
31	To Mr. Thornton One Quarter's Annuity	50 – –
	To Mr. John Green in part of his expences to Rye &c. in quest of John and Richard Turner two smugglers who had been employed in carrying Intelligence to France	11 2 10
October 31	To Captain Haddock who assisted in apprehending them for his trouble, and for a Reward to a Seaman who gave information of their sailing	10 – –
	Total expended to the 31st. Oct. 1782	£2416 14 3
November 2	To Mr. Richd. Oakes in full for his Services	250 – –
	Carried over . .	£2666 14 3

1782.		Brought over .	. £2666	14	3
Decemr. 17	To Wm. Clarke His attendance on the Motions of Monsr. La Touche, late Commander of the French Frigate L'Aigle		8	17	–
1783.					
January 18	To Mr. Thornton One Quarter's Annuity		50	–	=
Feby. 1	To Capt. Ottendorp in full for his Services		41	6	–
6	To Monsr. Rossi the Jesuit from So. America		30	–	–
Feby. 15	To Captain Taylor in full for his Services		356	14	–
March 10	To Mr. John Green the Ballance of his Expences to Rye in quest of the two men above mentioned		27	13	3½
March 21	To Richard Oakes to pay the expences of his Journey to Paris where he is sent for the purpose of gaining Intelligence of the State of the Naval force at Brest		100	–	–
		Total . . .	£3281	4	6½

The above sums have been issued according to my Order.

SYDNEY.

1782.					
August 15	By Cash received by a Treasury Warrant	2000	–	–	
October 2	By do.	1000	–	–	
December 31	By do.	1000	–	–	
		4000	–	–	
	Deduct Fee paid to Gibbons for receiving at the Exchequer at 5/– £1000	1	–	–	
			3999	–	–

Ballance remaining in the hands of Evan Nepean £717 15 5½
2nd April 1783

No. 2.

Money received for His Majesty's Secret Service by Thos. Orde Esq. between 10th July 1782 and the 5th April 1783.

		£	s	d
10 Augt. 1782	To Balance remaining in the hands of Henry Strachey Esqr.	1417	10	–
20 Novr. 1782	By Warrant dated 14th Novr. 1782	2000	–	–
1 March 1783	By Warrant dated 18th Feby. 1783	5000	–	–
	Total . . .	£8417	10	–

Account of Disbursements for His Majesty's Secret Services between 10 July 1782 and the 5th April 1783.

		£	s	d
Pensions 5th Augt. to 14 Feby.	Advanced to Sundry Persons for payment of Pensions to be re-imbursed	2550	–	–
Do.	Mr. Hay in Scotland Secret Pension	75	–	–
Do.	Mr. Principal Gordon Do.	50	–	–
Newspapers from 10 July to 5 April	To various Writers & Editors of newspapers	1084	10	9
Sundries Do.	Sundry small payments	350	–	–
7 Feby 1783	Mr. Waller	600	–	–
	Sir R. Worsley for Newtown	2200	–	–
1 April 1783	Mr. Nepean for Sundries	37	2	–
		£6946	12	9
	Recd. since of money advanced	2150	–	–
	Total disbursed	£4796	12	9

N.B. to be yet reimbursed £400

	£	s	d
Reservation to be made for Sundry Articles particularly Writers and to complete engagements with Editors of newspapers	800	–	–
For the payment of certain annual allowances to sundry Corporations	870	–	–
Donation to Col. de Pasquier	200	–	–
	£1870	–	–

Genl. Review.

Total received	8417 10	–
Total disbursed	4796 12	9

Balance in Mr. Orde's hands . . .	3620 17	3
To be added	400 –	–

Total . . .	4020 17	3

Reservation for services so that there will remain
for His Majesty's directions in Mr. Orde's hands   1870 - -

£2150 17 3

No. 3.

[The first paragraph in Lord Shelburne's handwriting.]

Col. Pasquier was recommended repeatedly by Prince Ferdinand of Brunswick for Secret Services, in case Demerary and Issequibo was attack'd and for Losses sustain'd there. He is in the utmost Distress and has promis'd with this Sum to return immediately to Brunswick through Holland.

Account of money issued for Foreign Secret Services to Lord Grantham His Majesty's Principal Secretary of State for the Foreign Department.

By warrant dated 15th Augt.

1782		£1000 –	–
Do.	3rd Octr.	2700 –	–
Do.	7th Decr.	2000 –	–
1783	3rd Jany.	1690 –	–
Do.	27th Feby.	3400 –	–
Do.	28th Feby.	3000 –	–
Do.	26th Feby.	1860 14	6
Do.	20th March	1615 –	–
Do.	24th do.	1000 –	–

£18265 14 6

Account of money expended for Foreign Secret Services by Ld. Grantham His Majesty's Principal Secretary of State for the Foreign Department.

Sundries by Mr. Sneyd . .	1000	– –
Draft of Sr. James Harris .	2700	– –
Sundries by Mr. Sneyd . .	2000	– –
Secret Payments at Post Office to 5th July 1782 . . .	1690	– –
Draft of Sr. James Harris .	3400	– –
Pension to Genl. Paoli to Michls. 1782	1500	– –
Allowance for Corsican Expences to do. . . .	1500	– –
Payments to the Post Office to Michaelmas 1782 . . .	1615	– –
Secret Services to Mr. Fitzherbert	1000	– –
To Mr. Forth for Expences .	1260 14	6
To do. for his own Allowance to Michaelmas 1782 . . .	450	– –
	£18115 14	6

```
        18265 14  6
        18115 14  6
        ──────────
              Balance  .  £150  – –
In the hands of Mr. Maddison.
```

No. 4288—*Lord North to the King.*

Lord North has the honour of transmitting to His Majesty a letter which Lord Sydney has received from the Lord Lieutenant of Ireland, and which he has received this afternoon from Lord Sydney.

LOWER GROSVENOR STREET, *April* 6, 1783.

Lord Hertford has sent to Lord North to desire him to request your Majesty's pleasure when he is to attend Your Majesty at St. James's to receive the Chamberlain's Staff.

Endorsed by the King.

No. 4289—*Lord Temple to the King.*

DUBLIN CASTLE, *April 6th,* 1783
11 *m.* 30 P.M.

SIRE—This moment has brought to me Your Majesty's letter : Every anxiety which I felt & which my letter so faintly expressed is relieved by that condescension with which you have deigned to accept the state of Ireland & of my particular situation. Permit me to express my thanks with every assurance of that attachment, which has Your Majesty's service as my only object ; & of that regret which presses upon me at the detail of the situation of your health & feelings, as well as of the kingdom. May Providence long secure to us that health & life, a resource upon which our all depends.

To yourself, Sire & to posterity you stand acquitted for every consequence, which nothing but the phrenzy of the moment could have forced upon you : The interval is truly painful, but a short time must rescue your Government from the fetters thrown round it : My respectful & (suffer me to add) cordial attachment to your person, & to that best of political constitutions which is hourly threatened, will ever lead me to sacrifice every private feeling to your service. I must however say (& truly say) that every feeling of ambition is deadened by these times & circumstances ; & that a publick situation has none of those charms for me which have brought forward this unprincipled coalition ; but I have, & ever must retain those feelings of duty & of affection which will urge me to obey Your Majesty's Commands in exerting every faculty for your satisfaction, & for the publick service.

The Scene before you is indeed unparallelled in the annals of history : May those who by timidity & weakness for some years past have driven your Kingdom to the verge of destruction, & those who by this unprincipled attack upon every part of the Constitution are now enabled to avail themselves of our distress, deeply answer it. My opinions (uninteresting as they are to Your Majesty) have never varied upon that great jewel of constitutional supremacy over all the parts of the Empire now torn from your crown ; nor upon the system of our government founded upon law & practise of ages, which draws the line between the constitution of Great Britain, & all other establishments. These principles from my earliest infancy I have imbibed & if I could reconcile a deviation from them to my political or my moral duties, I will confess that no hopes of ambition have power to tempt me.

Under these impressions I embarked on an undertaking under which nothing but Your Majesty's goodness & protection & a confidence in my own intentions could have supported me ; and with these impressions, I retire with every feeling amply satisfied by your favour & approbation.

May no circumstances delay the hour of Your Majesty's deliverance from that thraldom which bears so heavily upon you ; & may you find in those cool heads & hearts to whom Your Majesty would entrust your service, that resource to which you are so well entitled : In such an arrangement, no consideration will direct Your Majesty's thoughts for a moment towards me, except the conviction which I will beg to urge to Your Majesty, & which it will be my pride to cultivate, of the duty, gratitude, & affection, with which I have the honour to subscribe myself, Sire, Your Majesty's Ever faithful & devoted Subject & Servant,   NUGENT TEMPLE.

Endorsed by the King.

No. 4290—*The King to Lord North.*

Printed. Donne II. 436.

QUEEN'S HOUSE. *Ap.* 7*th,* 1783
m. 55 *pt.* 7 A.M.

The letter Ld. Sydney has communicated to Ld. North from the Lord Lieutenant of Ireland very clearly decides that Ld. Ely cannot have the Ensigns of the Order of St Patrick till his health enables him to go for Investiture to Ireland.

The D. of Portland intimated in the D. of Manchester's name on Friday that it would occasion some inconvenience in the payments now making in the Chamberlain's Office, if He should be removed previous to the completion of them ; but I should imagine as the Money has been issued from the Treasury for that purpose to Mr. Herbert that provided he is not removed till he has compleated that business, that no objection can arise from Ld. Hertford obtaining that Office on Wednesday ; I desire therefore Ld. North will settle this with the D. of Portland, and then write the usual letter of dismission to the D. of Manchester and acquaint him to attend for that purpose after the Levee on Wednesday.

Draft, written on a page of Lord North's letter of 6 April, 1783.

No. 4291—*Lord North to the King.*

Lord North has the honour of sending to His Majesty a Box, just arrived from India, and which Mr. James Macpherson, on the part of the Nabob of Arcot, has delivered at the Secretary's Office.

Mr. James Macpherson has likewise inform'd Lord North that the Nabob of Arcot was very desirous of knowing from him, whether a diamond of considerable value which he sent to Europe by Sir Thomas Rumbold, has been presented to Her Majesty.

Some Magistrates of Surry and Middlesex have written the inclosed letter to Lord North recommending Stephen Broadstreet to His Majesty's mercy, not so much on account of any favourable [*sic*] in his case, as on account of useful discoveries he has made since his condemnation. He was accomplice to one Cox, whose case was refer'd lately to Sr. Henry Gould who has reported unfavourably for both. Sir Henry has written a card this morning, desiring that as Cox was respited till Thursday, Broadstreet who was not more guilty than the other, should be put upon the same footing. Lord North has therefore ventured to order a respite for Broadstreet till Thursday, and has the honour of sending to His Majesty the papers that relate to this case.

WHITEHALL. *April 8th,* 1783.

Lord North has the honour of inclosing a letter from the Nabob which he received from Mr. Macpherson at the same time with the Box.

Endorsed by the King.

No. 4292—*The King to Lord North.*
Printed. Donne II. 436.

WINDSOR. *April* 8, 1783
m. 20 *past* 8 P.M.

I return the Box with the Original Letter and Copy from the Nabob of Arcot, and also the Original one to the Queen ; the copy I have delivered to Her.

In December the Queen received the Diamond Ring Sir Thos. Rumbold had been entrusted with, and had secreted till Col. Crosbie who came in the Autumn from Madrass obliged him to deliver it, since which time the Queen has wrote to the Nabob to acknowledge the receipt of it.

The application of the Surrey and Middlesex Magistrates may be a reason to spare the life of Broadstreet, but his Accomplice must, when the Respite expires, suffer Death.

I trust Ld. North has settled that the D. of Manchester is to deliver up the Ensigns of Chamberlain tomorrow and Ld Hertford attend to receive them ; the D. of Rutland means to resign on Friday ; Ld. Dartmouth should attend that day to receive that Staff.

Draft, written on a page of Lord North's letter of same date. Duplicate, in the King's handwriting.

No. 4293—*Mr. Fox to the King.*

Mr. Fox has the honour of sending inclosed to Your Majesty a Minute of Cabinet Council upon the subject of American Intercourse. It is intended to put off the Bill now depending in Parliament till some progress is made in the negociation alluded to in the Minute, and to bring in a bill immediately for the purpose of repealing the prohibitory acts made during the war, & for removing the formalities which attended the admission of Ships from the Colonies during their state of subjection. Your Majesty will immediately perceive that the line proposed is to give as much facility to the trade between the two countries as is consistent with preserving the principles of the act of Navigation. When Mr. Fox has the honour of waiting upon Your Majesty tomorrow he will

endeavour to give any further explanation which Your Majesty
may wish upon this subject, and at the same time will take Your
Majesty's Commands upon the manner of opening this negociation,
and upon the Person to be employed in it.

St. James's, 8 *April*, 1783. *m.* 10 *past* 11 P.M.

Endorsed by the King.

Enclosure.   MINUTE OF CABINET.

[In Mr. Fox's handwriting.]

St. James's, 8 *April*, 1783

Present :—Ld. President, Ld. Privy Seal, Duke of Portland,
Ld. John Cavendish, Ld. Keppel, Ld. North, Mr. Fox.

It is humbly recommended to Your Majesty to direct Mr. Fox
to enter into an immediate negociation with the American Plenipotentiaries at Paris, upon the subject of commercial intercourse
upon a footing of reciprocity with respect to intercourse & duties :
but at the same time to take care to restrain American Ships from
bringing any goods but of their own produce either to Great
Britain or to the British West Indies, and that British Ships
trading from America to Europe & vice-versâ shall touch at some
port of Great Britain.

No. 4294—*Mr. Fox to the King.*

Mr. Fox has the honour of sending Your Majesty, together
with the draught of instructions to Mr. Hartley, a paper of
a very extraordinary nature which Mr. Fox has just received
from Lord North. Mr. Fox has also the honour of transmitting to Your Majesty Lord North's letter in order to
explain to Your Majesty at once the whole of the business.
Mr. Fox conceives that there is no doubt but the Canada
Merchants have Mr. Oswald's authority for what they advance,
but at the same time he thinks that Your Majesty will be loth to
believe that terms of such important advantage can be obtained
after the signature of the provisional articles. It is equally
incredible that they could have been obtained before, for if they
could, it seems clear that the late Administration would have
made a point of obtaining them, not only on account of the solid

advantage which they would have brought to Your Majesty's Subjects, but also for the reasons alluded to in Lord North's letter. Mr. Fox will endeavour to see the Merchants as soon as possible, and after having seen them may possibly be able to explain to Your Majesty more fully this seemingly strange business. At all events, Mr. Fox humbly submits to Your Majesty that it will be proper to propose the regulations to the American Commissioners, though as Mr. Fox humbly conceives, with very little hope of success.

St. James's.   *m. 25 past* 10 p.m.   10 *April*, 1783

Endorsed by the King.

No. 4295—*The King to Mr. Fox.*

Queen's House.   *Apl.* 10, 1783
m. 5 *pt.* 11 p.m.

Mr. Fox seems so forcibly to feel the singularity of the opinion given by the Canada Merchants to Ld. North, which they say arises from the information they have received from Mr. Oswald, that it is not necessary for me to suggest anything on this subject, except that I coincide with his opinion in the propriety of proposing these Regulations to the American Commissioners, though without much expectation of success.

Draft, written on a page of Mr. Fox's letter of same date.

No. 4296—*Mr. Grenville to the King.*

Pall Mall, *Friday Ap.* 11, 1783

Sire—In obedience to the commands with which Your Majesty was graciously pleased to honour me on Wednesday last, I beg leave to acquaint You that I have received a packet from Lord Temple enclosing a letter which he has taken the liberty to address to Your Majesty : & that I humbly wait Your Majesty's Commands with respect to the delivery of it.

I have the honour to be, with the highest sense of Your Majesty's gracious condescension and goodness, Sire, Your Majesty's most dutiful and devoted Subject and Servant,

W. W. Grenville.

No. 4297—*The King to Mr. Grenville.*

QUEEN'S HOUSE. *Ap.* 11, 1783

MR. GRENVILLE—As I go this evening to the Oratorio, I desire You will bring the letters from Ld Temple at half hour after ten this night.

Draft, written on a page of Mr. Grenville's letter of same date.

No. 4298—*Lord North to the King.*

[The advertisement for a pardon would be for the benefit of deserters on rejoining their regiments.]

[11 *Ap.* 1783]

Lord North has the honour of sending for His Majesty's information a letter he received this afternoon from General Conway, and requests His Majesty's pleasure as to the proposal made by the General.

He has likewise the honour of inclosing an advertizement for a pardon, which is just come to the Office.

Friday night.

Endorsed by the King.

No. 4299—*The King to Lord North.*

Printed. Donne II. 437.

QUEEN'S HOUSE. *Ap.* 12, 1783
m. 57 *pt.* 7 A.M.

Ld. North will send the proper notice to the War Office that the Old Corps may be directed to recruit to the Peace Establishment, viz., Officers included 507, each Battalion at the usual Peace Allowance of 3½ Guineas per Man. And will direct the Advertisement and Pardon to be printed in The Gazette of this Night agreeable to the request that has been made for that purpose.

Draft, written on a page of Lord North's letter of same date.
Duplicate copy in the King's handwriting.

No. 4300—*Lord North to the King.*

12 *April*, 1783

Lord North has the honour of inclosing a letter from Mr. Justice Heath, recommending Thomas Mitchell for a free pardon, with a postscript very much in favour of Josiah Cannon, the person whose case was mention'd yesterday to His Majesty by Mr. Fox. Lord North will, with His Majesty's permission, order the proper letters to be written for these two men. Josiah Cannon is ordered to be executed on Monday next at Winchester.

WHITEHALL. 3 *o'clock*

Endorsed by the King.

No. 4301—*The King to Lord North.*
Printed. Donne II. 438.

QUEEN'S HOUSE. *Ap.* 12, 1783
m. 40 *past* 3 P.M.

The Report of Mr. Justice Heath in favour of Thos. Mitchell certainly makes a free pardon very proper ; and renders it not improper to respite Josiah Cannon, who may have further indulgence if Mr. Coxe, who interests himself for him can engage to place him in any honest way of life.

Draft, written on a page of Lord North's letter of same date. Duplicate copy in the King's handwriting, initialled G. R.

No. 4302—*The King to Lord Temple.*

QUEEN'S HOUSE. *Ap.* 13*th*, 1783

LORD TEMPLE—I cannot think of seeing Mr. Wm. Grenville set out for Ireland, without just acknowledging the receipt of Your letter of the 6th, and expressing the satisfaction I have received from finding You view the strange phrensy of the times in the same light it has struck Me ; perhaps you may be surprised how that shaddow, Popularity has already deserted those whom reason too clearly reprobated.

I shall certainly wish You may be released from Your present situation as speedily as possible : as yet no person has been proposed as Your successor, and those whose inclinations have been sounded have instantly shown a determination to avoid so difficult a charge, which I should immagine without the utmost propriety, firmness and temper will become hourly more embarassing.

Draft, written on a page of Lord Temple's letter of 6 April, 1783.

No. 4303—*Mr. Fox to the King.*

Mr. Fox has the honour of sending to Your Majesty a Minute of the opinion of Your Majesty's Confidential Servants upon the subject which Mr. Fox had the honour of mentioning to Your Majesty this morning. Expedition upon this matter seems so desirable that Mr. Fox proposes, with Your Majesty's approbation, to send off a Messenger to Mr. Fitzherbert tomorrow, although the Contre-Projet should not be ready.

St. James's. *m. 5 past eleven* P.M. 13 *April,* 1783.

Endorsed by the King.

Enclosure. Minute of Cabinet.

[In Mr. Fox's handwriting.]

St. James's. 13 *April,* 1783

Present :—Lord President, Lord Privy Seal, Duke of Portland, Lord Keppel, Lord North, Mr. Fox.

It is humbly recommended to Your Majesty to direct Mr. Fox to instruct Mr. Fitzherbert that the Requisition on the part of the Court of Versailles with respect to the immediate restitution of St. Pierre and Miquelon, and of that part of the Fishery allotted to the Subjects of his Most Christian Majesty by the Preliminaries, may be complied with, upon condition of the French Edict being so far relaxed, as to allow British and Neutral Ships to go into the Ports of the Islands intended to be restored to Great Britain, and of Tobago, for the purpose of bringing home the Produce of the said Islands. The Indulgence with respect to Tobago to be understood to last only till the period of the mutual cessions and restitutions.

No. 4304—*The King to Mr. Fox.*

QUEEN'S HOUSE. *Ap.* 14, 1783
m. 46 *pt.* 9 A.M.

Mr. Fox is quite right in dispatching as soon as possible a Messenger to Mr. Fitzherbert with directions corresponding to the Minute of Cabinet of last Night ; The Counter Project for the Definitive Treaty must require a little more time ; but it may not be improper to mention on this occasion that it will soon be sent.

Draft, written on a page of Mr. Fox's letter of 13 April.

No. 4305—*The Duke of Portland to the King.*

The Duke of Portland has the honor of inclosing to His Majesty the Key of the Box which contains an account of this day's proceeding in the House of Lords upon the Irish Bill, which he thought it his Duty to submit to His Majesty, & which he takes this method of conveying to His Majesty as the one which he has been given to understand, His Majesty most approves.

Monday night. 14 *April,* 1783

Endorsed by the King.

No. 4306—*The Duke of Portland to the King.*

The Duke of Portland has the honor of acquainting His Majesty that the Irish Judicature and Legislation Bill has been read a second time after a very long conversation opened by Lord Abingdon, who began by expressing his concurrence in the Bill, & entirely approving the concession of internal Legislation to Ireland, but doubted the propriety of its being granted externally, from an apprehension of its ultimately affecting the Maritime Power of this Kingdom, & producing the absolute Separation of the two Countries. He was followed by the Duke of Richmond, who agreed with him in approving the Bill as a necessary consequence of the Measures taken last Session with respect to Ireland, but differed from him in thinking that any distinction could be made between external and internal Legislation. The Duke of Richmond insisted further that the Resolution which the House of Lords came to in the course of last Session required other measures to be taken for fixing the connection of the two Kingdoms upon a permanent basis, and urged the Duke of Portland to declare whether any such were in contemplation, or whether the Bill before the House was to be considered as the only step intended to be taken by Your Majesty's present Servants towards the attainment of that object. I answer'd shortly that as the Bill before Us had not been objected to by either of the preceding Speakers, and had been acknowledged to be a natural consequence of the Proceedings of last Year, and of the Event that had happened in the Court of King's Bench, it was very unnecessary for me to say anything in support of it; that, as to my opinion of what was to be further done, I was in the judgement of the House whether any Explanation upon that point was necessary : that I flattered myself with the hopes of possessing so much of their Confidence as would dispose them to believe that I should attentively & faithfully discharge the duties of the Station to which Your Majesty had been graciously pleased to appoint me, & that it would be time enough to call upon me for Plans and Opinions when I appeared to have failed in the Execution of that Trust with which I had been honoured by Your Majesty. Lord Thurlow after this took the same ground, upon which the Duke of Richmond had pressed me to declare the intentions of Administration, and though he very vehemently and powerfully inforced the arguments which had been made use of by the Duke of Richmond & represented the Claim I had made to the Confidence of the House in a ludicrous as well as a serious point of view, throughout the whole of what he said, he very cautiously avoided pledging himself to support or oppose the Bill, and justified his Keeping back his Opinion entirely on the want of information respecting the future plans of Government. Lord Loughborough in reply to Lord Thurlow pointed out the fallacy of his Arguments, the unreasonableness of his expectations, & the obvious Origin of the Bill actually depending, & insisted that it carried upon the face of it very ample and sufficient reasons to enduce the House to give it Their Concurrence. This produced a reply from Lord Thurlow and much altercation between the Duke of Richmond and Lord Loughborough, after which the Duke of Chandos rose, but deviated wholly from the Question before Us, for the purpose of attacking Administration in such gross, and I should hope Your Majesty would have thought, in such unwarrantable terms as called up Lord Carlisle, who during the latter part of the Duke of Chandos's speech had impatiently submitted to the very injurious manner in which The Duke had represented Our Admission to the Honor of being employed by Your Majesty, & reprobated in very good and pointed Language the ideas which the Duke of Chandos had thrown out respecting Our Conduct, and treated them as the solitary assertions of an uninformed Individual. Lord Radnor got up to deny this last position from the coincidence of his own Opinion with that of the Duke of Chandos. Lord Carmarthen said a few words in answer to an expression he conceived to have been used by Lord Carlisle from which he apprehended some difficulty might arise in including the Definite Treaty, which being explained by Lord Carlisle, the Conversation ended, & the Bill was committed for tomorrow, but I was not able to learn, either from the Duke of Richmond or Lord Thurlow whether it is to meet with any Opposition. After this business was finished, Mr. Fox brought up the Bill for repealing the Prohibitory Acts against America, which Lord Thurlow desired to have printed, but at the recommendation of Lord Mansfield he deferred making a regular motion to that effect until tomorrow, which if he should then persist in, I humbly presume ought to be resisted, as it would effectually prevent the Bill's being ready to receive Your Majesty's Assent before the Holidays, and might thereby very materially injure the Trade & Revenue of Your Majesty's Dominions. The Duke of Portland most humbly implores Your Majesty's forgiveness if a Mistaken idea of his Duty has led him to obtrude this detail unnecessarily upon Your Majesty, but presumes to hope that Your Majesty will graciously condescend to impute it to the anxiety he feels to give Your Majesty every possible satisfaction.

Monday Night. 14 *April*, 1783

Endorsed by the King.

No. 4307—*The King to the Duke of Portland.*

The Box containing an Account of the Debate in the House of Lords on the Irish Judicature I have received : the D. of Portland has done quite right in giving himself the trouble of stating it, as it will probably occasion an Account in the Newspapers, which might have led me into error, by the fallacious Manner (not to say more) in which all events are asserted in those Vehicles of Abuse.   G. R.

WINDSOR. *Apr.* 15, 1783. *m.* 30 *past* 8 A.M.

Draft, written on a page of the Duke of Portland's letter of 14 *April.*

No. 4308—*Mr. Fox to the King.*

Mr. Fox trusts to Your Majesty's goodness and justice, that Your Majesty will give no credit to the idle report which Count Bruhl thinks fit to write to his Court.

Mr. Fox takes this opportunity of assuring Your Majesty that he never heard nor had reason to think that the removal of the Duke of Dorset was disagreeable to Your Majesty, and that he is perfectly sure that the Duke of Portland did not recommend that measure from any ill will to the Duke of Dorset, but merely from the convenience which resulted to the arrangement, from the present disposal of that Employment.

Mr. Fox hopes that Your Majesty will not think him presumptuous or improperly intruding upon Your Majesty with professions, if he begs leave most humbly to implore Your Majesty to believe that both the Duke of Portland and he have nothing so much at heart as to conduct Your Majesty's affairs, both with respect to measures and to persons, in the manner that may give Your Majesty the most satisfaction, and that, whenever Your Majesty will be graciously pleased to condescend even to hint your inclinations upon any subject, that it will be the study of Your Majesty's Ministers to show how truly sensible they are of Your Majesty's goodness.

ST. JAMES'S. *m.* 20 *past eleven.* 16 *April,* 1783

Endorsed by the King, " No answer."

No. 4309—*Viscount Keppel to the King.*

Lord Keppel has the honour to send Your Majesty Admiral Pigot's dispatches from St. Lucia ; Also Rear-Admiral Rowley's from Jamaica : and Rear Admiral Lord Hood's Correspondence with the two Admirals.

AUDLEY SQUARE. *April* 16*th*, 1783. 30 *m. past eleven* A.M.

Endorsed by the King, " No answer."

No. 4310—*Lord North to the King.*

Lord North has the honour of informing His Majesty that Mrs. Boyd, wife of Lieutenant General Boyd has desired to apply to His Majesty for his gracious permission for the Lieut-General to come to England on account of his health, which she represents as requiring that indulgence. Her representation is confirmed by the account given by the gentleman who brought the last dispatches from General Elliot.

Lord North has directed the proper instruments to be drawn for requiring on the part of His Majesty the three writings which His Majesty deliver'd to the Archbishop of Canterbury, the Lord Chancellor & the Lord President. As soon as they are drawn in due form they will be transmitted to His Majesty for his approbation. There is no precedent in the Office.

WHITEHALL. *Thursday, April* 18*th,* 1783
    [*Thursday was the* 17*th of April*]

Endorsed by the King.

No. 4311—*The King to Lord North.*

Printed. Donne II. 438.

QUEEN'S HOUSE. *Ap.* 17, 1783
m. 10 *pt.* 7 P.M.

As soon as any part of the Garrison of Gibraltar is relieved, Lieut. Gen. Boyd may have leave to come home for the recovery of his health.

Draft, written on a page of Lord North's letter of same date. Duplicate in the King's handwriting.

No. 4312—*Lord North to the King.*

[18 *April*, 1783]

Lord North did not mention to His Majesty some particulars relative to some of the papers which His Majesty has just sign'd, not knowing that they would have been sent in the same Box.

Lord North supposes that His Majesty would have the Blank in the Regency-Warrants fill'd up with Lord North's name, as the person who is to receive the three seal'd instruments, for His Majesty.

Lord North did not intend that Mr. Scott's Warrant should be sent to His Majesty, before he had had an opportunity of laying the whole of Mr. Scott's request before His Majesty. The Warrant by mistake was drawn and sent to His Majesty without Lord North's knowledge, who will, with His Majesty's permission, delay counter-signing it till he has explain'd the matter more fully to His Majesty.

Lord North has the honour of inclosing a note he received this moment from the Secretary at War.

WHITEHALL, 6 *o'clock* P.M.

Endorsed by the King.

No. 4313—*Lord North to the King.*

Lord North has the honour of informing His Majesty that the Navy Board has been alarm'd by a menace from a body of mutinous seamen, who have been at the Navy Pay Office & have demanded a Bounty, to which they are not entitled. Their number is about 110. They enter'd on board the fleet as substitutes for several persons, who were under prosecution for smuggling & were pardon'd, by virtue of His Majesty's Proclamation, upon finding two seamen each to serve on board His Majesty's Ships of War. Having received a valuable consideration from the persons in whose place they served, they have certainly no right to claim any other Bounty, but they are very turbulent and have threatened to pull down the Navy Office & the Pay Office, if their request is not complied with. Lord North, at the application of the Admiralty, has sent to the Lord Mayor & to the Secretary at War, to keep a detachment in readiness, in case the Civil Magistrates should require the assistance of the Military. After these precautions, Lord North hopes that there will be no mischief done by these rioters.

Lord North has received a message from the Lord Mayor concerning information that he had received of another large band of seamen collected in the neighbourhood of Wapping. In consequence of which he has sent for some of the County Magistrates, who, he flatters himself, may be able to prevent, by timely arrangements, any serious disturbance.

WHITEHALL. *Ap.* 18*th.* *m.* 30 *pt.* 6 P.M.

Endorsed by the King.

No. 4314—*The King to Lord North.*
Printed. Donne II. 435.

QUEEN'S HOUSE. *April* 18*th,* 1783
m. 25 *pt.* 9 P.M.

Undoubtedly the Blank in the Warrants for recalling the three Regency Instruments ought to be filled up with Lord North's name ; Lord North cannot doubt that if the Office in the Irish Court of Common Pleas is in favour of Mr. Scott the late Attorney General, I shall by no means object to any attention shewn him, provided it meets with the approbation of the present Lord Lieutenant ; if not, it should not be put into execution till a new one is named.

Lord North has done very properly in sending to the Lord Mayor and to the Surrey Justices on account of the expectation of some tumult among the Sailors ; I trust he will give similar information to Sir Sampson Wright and Mr. Addington, as also to the Tower Hamlets, for if they find the City and Waping prepared, they may remove to Westminster and the outskirts of the Town : the notice to Gen. Conway and the Secretary at War is very proper.

Draft, written on a page of Lord North's first letter of same date.

Duplicate in the King's handwriting.

No. 4315—*Mr. Fox to the King.*

Mr. Fox has the honour of sending Your Majesty the two Projects for the definitive treaties together with the minute of Cabinet. Mr. Fox will employ himself tomorrow morning in writing a dispatch to Mr. Fitzherbert, which, when it is submitted to Your Majesty, will serve to explain the alterations made from the French Project, and the Spanish Preliminaries, and the reasons for these alterations. A Blank is left for the Logwood Article, but Mr. Fox is not without hopes of being able to fill it up in the course of tomorrow.

If Your Majesty should wish for any verbal explanation upon this very great Business, Mr. Fox begs to receive Your Majesty's orders at what time he can wait upon Your Majesty tomorrow, as Mr. Fox humbly submits to Your Majesty that it will be adviseable to send off the Messenger tomorrow night if possible.

St. James's. 18 *April,* 1783. *m.* 45 *past eleven* p.m.

Endorsed by the King.

Enclosure.

MINUTE OF CABINET.

St. James's. 18 *April,* 1783

Present :—Lord President, Lord Privy Seal, Duke of Portland, Lord John Cavendish, Lord Keppel, Lord North, Mr. Fox.

It is humbly recommended to Your Majesty to direct Mr. Fox to transmit to Your Majesty's Minister at Paris the two Projects herewith submitted to Your Majesty's consideration, in order that they may be proposed to the Ministers of France and Spain, as Projects for definitive Treaties to be concluded with their respective Courts.

No. 4316—*The King to Mr. Fox.*

The Projects of the Definitive Treaties with France and Spain, and the Dispatch which is to accompany them to Mr. Fitzherbert must so fully state the reasons of the Alterations from the

Preliminary Articles, that I do not mean to call on Mr. Fox for further explanations on this subject : unnecessary discussions are not my taste, and the Cabinet having by a Minute approved of the projects, I do not propose to give myself any Additional trouble with regard to them.

QUEEN'S HOUSE. *Ap.* 19*th*, 1783. *m.* 25 *pt.* 9 A.M.

No. 4317—*Lord Hillsborough to the King.*

HANOVER SQUARE, *April* 19*th*, 1783

SIR—I presume to take the liberty in justice to myself to acquaint Your Majesty that during the several strange and unfortunate events which have happened since I was dismissed from Your Majesty's Service, I have kept myself free from all political Connections, desirous and wishing that if Your Majesty should at any time judge me fit and able to serve Your Majesty, I might receive Your Royal Commands from yourself, & determined neither to solicit nor accept any situation, thro' the power or intervention of any Minister or set of Ministers whatever. I am at present led to trespass thus far upon Your Majesty's time, from the Apprehensions I am under for Your Majesty's Service in Ireland. I am infinitely concerned to find that Lord Temple will come away & equally so to learn that the Few who might be the properest to supply his Place absolutely refuse to go. I have no reason, Sir, to suppose that any part of the Coalition, as it is called, would mention me to Your Majesty, & therefore arduous as the Undertaking will be, I humbly throw myself at Your Majesty's feet to say that if, in your Royal opinion, I should appear to be less unfitt than those who may be proposed to Your Majesty, I will with all submission obey such Commands as Your Majesty shall be pleased to honour me with.

I have the honour to be, with the most profound Respect, Sir, Your Majesty's Most Dutyfull Subject & Most Obedient & Most Humble Servant,   HILLSBOROUGH.

Endorsed by the King.

No. 4318—*Lord North to the King.*

Lord North has the honour of transmitting to His Majesty two of the Regency Appointments, which he has received this morning from Mrs Cornwallis & Lord Stormont.

Lord North call'd likewise at Lord Loughborough's but was informed that he was out of town. Lord North has, however, reason to believe, that Lord Thurlow has not yet deliver'd the instrument that was deposited in his hands to Lord Loughborough, and that Lord Thurlow is also out of Town ; Lord North having frequently perused the fifth section of the Regency Bill (5 Geo: 3rd, Cap. 27) is convinced that the Warrant ought to be directed, as it was, to the first Commissioner of the Great Seal for the time being. Lord North will write to Lord Loughborough upon the subject, & hopes to be soon able to restore the third instrument to His Majesty.

Mrs. Cornwallis, when she redeliver'd the Regency instrument put likewise into Lord North's hands, the late Archbishop's Seals, which as she has been inform'd, ought to be given up to Your Majesty, and broke in Your Majesty's presence. She did not know whether they should be sent by the Lord Chamberlain, or the Secretary of State, but hopes she has not done wrong in transmitting them by me.

From all the enquiry Lord North has been able to make, the Seamen continue perfectly quiet, & there does not seem to be any disturbance whatever either in London or Westminster.

SECRETARY OF STATE'S OFFICE. WHITEHALL
April 21, 1783. *m.* 45 *past one* P.M.

Endorsed by the King.

No. 4319—*The King to Lord North.*

Printed. Donne II. 439.

WINDSOR. *April* 21, 1783
m. 25 *pt.* 6 P.M.

I have received the two Instruments Lord North had received from Lord Stormont and Mrs. Cornwallis : the other cannot be returned till Lord Thurlow returns from Misley. The Seals of the late Archbishop of Canterbury seem to have come very properly through the Channel of Lord North, though on the former occasion through that of the Lord Chamberlain.

By what I heard Yesterday I should hope the Seamen will continue quiet, particularly if the Merchants are, as formerly, obliged again to have two thirds of the Crews on board their Ships Natives.   G. R.

No. 4320—*Lord Hertford to the King.*

Lord Hertford has the honour of inclosing herewith to His Majesty a note which he has received from Lord Northington accompanying two very long engravings, which for His Majesty's convenience he has presumed to put into the hands of his Librarian.

GROSR. STREET.   *Aprill 24th*, 1783.

Enclosure.
Lord Northington to Lord Hertford.

Lord Northington presents his Compliments to Lord Hertford, and begs His Lordship will do him the Honour of presenting with his Humble Duty to His Majesty, an Engraving done from a Drawing of Vandyke's, now in his possession.

The subject is the Procession of the Knights of the Garter, part of a great Design in four Peices for the adornment of the Banquetting House, the History of which is fully given in Mr. Walpole's Anecdotes of Painting. This Request will be delivered to Ld Hertford by Mr. Cooper, the Artist who has executed the Engraving, who will take His Lordship's Orders when and where he is to wait upon him with it.

The original design is now in London, and if His Majesty should express any Inclination to see it, Ld. Northington will have the Honor to attend His Majesty with it, whenever He shall have the Honor to receive His Majesty's Commands.

23 *April*, 1783. ST. JAMES'S PLACE

No. 4321—*Mr. Fox to the King.*

Your Majesty will undoubtedly observe that Sir Robert Keith's accounts tally exactly with Sir James Harris's confidential letter. The Emperor appears to be in a very difficult situation, but whether he will finally (if driven to the alternative) lean to France or Russia, Mr. Fox has not lights enough to submit to Your Majesty any conjecture. But Mr. Fox most humbly submits to Your Majesty that the winding up of this Business seems likely to prove very critical indeed and perhaps decisive with respect to the future System of Europe, and therefore ought to be attended to with great care.

Your Majesty must find much difficulty in reconciling the language held by Monsieur de Vergennes and Monsieur de Breteuil, with the hasty and almost unfair manner in which the former invited the Mediation of the Imperial Courts, but Mr. Fox humbly submits to Your Majesty that there is rather reason to hope that the Court of Versailles is sincere in wishing a speedy conclusion of the definitive treaty, because it is impossible to conceive what interest France can have in delaying it.

St. James's. 28 *April,* 1783. *m.* 35 P.M.

Endorsed by the King.

No. 4322—*The King to Mr. Fox.*

Windsor. *April* 28, 1783
m. 39 *past* 4 P.M.

Undoubtedly the Emperor is in a most difficult situation, and it seems impossible He should keep the friendship of Russia without a total breach with France : therefore we must wait with patience till this is unravelled, which may the easier be done as there does not appear the smallest reason for taking any immediate step.

Draft, written on a page of Mr. Fox's letter of same date.

No. 4323.

PROPOSED PEACE ESTABLISHMENT.

Admiralty Office. 28th April, 1783. { PEACE ESTABLISHMENT of the NAVAL FORCE considered as necessary, exclusive of the occasional Force that may be required by the East India Company to be employed in the East Indies.

NEWFOUNDLAND.

Rates	No.	Guns	Men	Total No. of each class
4th	1	50	320	320
5th	2	36	240	480
		38		
	2	32	200	400
Sloops	3	16	100	300
Brig	1	.	70	70
	—			——
	9			1570

The first year of the Peace will most certainly require the full force as stated for the New-foundland Fisheries; perhaps it may be found by the experience of this year that a less Force may answer when the Rights of Fishing by other Nations are in method.

HALIFAX & GULPH OF ST. LAWRENCE.

4th	1	50	320	320
5th	1	32	200	200
6th	1	28	180	180
.	1	24	140	140
Sloops	2	16	100	200
Brigs	2	.	70	140
	—			——
	8		[1180]	1280

Experience must determine the sufficiency or insufficiency of this Force.

Total . 2850

Men.

Newfoundland	1570
Lord Howe's Proposal, . .	1560
Peace Establishment 1763 took in mixed with the number employ'd on the North American Coast to the Bahama Islands	
Halifax, Quebec etc. . . .	1280
Lord Howe's Proposal, . .	1320
Plan 1772	2516
Peace 1763 includg N. America	3290
At present the two Stations included. Lord Keppel. . }	2850
Lord Howe	2880

JAMAICA.

4th	1	50	320	320
5th	1	36	240	240
.	2	32	200	400
6th	1	24	140	140
Sloop	1	16	100	100
Brig.	1	.	70	70
	—			——
	7			1270

Jamaica as proposed . . .	1270
Lord Howe's proposal . .	2020
Peace 1763	1760
Proposed 1772	3330

The reason for this Force being proposed inferior to the last Peace Establishment, is, from not having West Florida to protect.

LEEWARDS ILANDS.

Rates	No.	Guns	Men	Total No. of each class
4th	1	50	320	320
5th	1	44	250	250
		36		
.	1	32	200	200
6th	1	28	180	180
.	1	24	140	140
Sloops	2	16	100	200
Brigs.	2	.	70	140
	9			1430

The re-establishing of the possessions to the British Subjects in the Islands of Granadas, St. Vincent, Dominique, St. Christopher's, Nevis, &c. certainly will require at least for the present year's service the Force as stated, however reduced another year.

	Men.
Leewd. Islands	1430
Ld. Howe's Proposal . . .	1150
Peace 1763	1050
Plan 1772	2335

COAST OF AFRICA.

	No.	Guns	Men	Total
5th	1	44	250	250
6th	1	28	180	180
Sloop	1	16	100	100
	3			530
		Total	.	3,230

Coast of Africa	530
Lord Howe's Proposal . .	530
Peace 1763	530
Plan 1772	450

MEDITERRANEAN.

	No.	Guns	Men	Total
4th	1	50	320	320
5th	1	36	240	240
.	1	32	200	200
6th	1	23	140	140
Sloop	1	16	100	100
Brigs.	2	.	70	140
	7			1140

This Force, considering the probable loss of Credit with the Barbary States, not being in possession of Minorca, seems rather less than requisite to establish the Credit of the Flag in the Mediterranean Seas.

Proposal	1140
Lord Howe's Proposal . .	970
Peace 1763	1200
Plan 1772	1795

COAST OF GREAT BRITAIN & IRELAND.

	No.	Guns	Men	Total
5th	1	44	250	250
.	1	36	240	240
.	1	32	200	200
6th	4	24	140	560
Sloops	10	16	100	1000
Brigs & Cutters				2000
For Yachts				332
				4582
		Total	.	5,722

Proposal	4582
Lord Howe's Proposal . .	6320
Peace 1763	4122
Plan 1772	3580

GUARD SHIPS.

PORTSMOUTH.

Rates	No.	Guns	Men	Total No. of each class
2nd	2	90	450	900
3rd	6	74	400	2400
.	2	64	350	700
	10			4000

PLYMOUTH.

2nd	1	90	450	450
3rd	4	74	400	1600
.	3	64	350	1050
	8			3100

CHATHAM & SHEERNESS.

3rd	2	74	400	800
	2	64	350	700
	4			1500

Total . 8,600

	Men.
Guardships	8600
Lord Howe's Proposal . .	7550
Peace 1763	3880
Plan 1772	6830

Abstract of Lord Keppel's
Peace Establishment.

Newfoundland	1570
Halifax & River St. Lawrence .	1280
Jamaica	1270
Leeward Islands	1430
Coast of Africa	530
Mediterranean	1140
Coast of Great Britain & Ireland	4582
Guardships	8600
	20,402

Marines on Shore for the Guard
of the Dock Yards . . . 1000

21,402

At 4 per month £1102. 9. 4
Ordinary Navy.
Extra

Marines employed on shore
should be at least 200 more than
in the Plan above.

No. 4324—*Lord North to the King.*

Lord North has the honour of transmitting to His Majesty
a letter which he has received from the Recorder, on which he
begs leave to request His Majesty's pleasure.

WHITEHALL. *April 29th,* 1783

Endorsed by the King.

No. 4325—*The King to Lord North.*

QUEEN'S HOUSE. *Ap.* 30, 1738
m. 25 *pt.* 6 P.M.

The Recorder of London to have notice that He is to make his report on the Capital Convicts on Friday, a Cabinet Council to be Summoned for that business and the Attendance of Lord Mansfield Secured.

Draft.

No. 4326—*Lord North to the King.*

Lord North has the honour of informing His Majesty that the Archbishop of Canterbury is desirous of doing homage at St. James's today.

Wednesday morning [30 *April,* 1783]

Endorsed by the King.

No. 4327—*The King to Lord North.*

Printed. Donne II. 440.

The Archbishop of Canterbury may do homage after the Levee this Day.   G. R.

QUEEN'S HOUSE. *Ap.* 30*th,* 1783. *One* P.M.

No. 4328—*The Duke of Portland to the King.*

The Duke of Portland thinks it his duty most humbly to acquaint His Majesty that by the death of Dr. Stinton, which happened at five o'clock this morning, the Livings of Wrotham and All Hallows, Barking are at His Majesty's Disposal, by virtue of His Royal Prerogative, untill it may be His Majesty's Pleasure to restore the Temporalities of the See of Canterbury to the lately appointed Archbishop. That if His Majesty shall think fit to exercise his Right, and has not already destined these valuable benefices to any particular Persons, The Duke of

Portland hopes His Majesty will not think him too presumptuous in submitting to His Majesty's consideration the name of the Dean of Peterborough for the living of Wrotham and of Mr. Johns for that of All Hallows, & The Duke of Portland hopes that when His Majesty will permit him to pay His Duty to Him and state the Reasons for this Presumption that they will entitle him to His Majesty's forgiveness.

Wednesday 30 *April*, 1783. 11 *o'clock* A.M.

Endorsed by the King.

No. 4329—*Lord Rivers to the Rev.* [?]

SIR—In a short Letter, before I left town, I acknowledged the receipt of your very obliging Present, & have since read with great attention & satisfaction, both your Treatises in the Order, in which they are bound together. I admire, & most sincerely subscribe to the Doctrine they contain, but I lament, not only with the Bishop of London that the *first* was not publish'd in time to be of service to the Cause in America, but that *both* are too good & too true to serve the unfortunate times, in which they are written. A Gentleman, so well acquainted with Mankind as You seem to be, must allow that, in this Age of Depravity, the Multitude, for whose Advantage & Instruction such Works are calculated, are too abandon'd to profit from them, & that the Few, who will taste & approve them, are already safe in *the Truth*. This Consideration, however, lessens neither the Merit of the Author, nor of the Work, which highly deserves to be generally known.

In a former Letter I took the Liberty to make a hasty remark upon the first Perusal of the last of these two Treatises, & that, too, was occasion'd by the Temper of the Times. That the Demon of Republicanism should make choice of such a Reign for his Exertions must appear extraordinary to those, who do not consider that the Spirit of Liberty resembles that of Avarice ; The *latter* increases with the Increase of its Wealth, as the *former* does by the Latitude with which it is indulg'd. Whilst, therefore, the Lenity & Paternal Tenderness, so long conspicuous upon this Throne, engage the Love & Veneration of every *good* Subject, it is to be fear'd that there are too many restless spirits, with whom they operate as an Incitement to the most perverse & unnatural Resistance : Hence the disappointed Orator vomits his Sedition, & the Author publishes his Treason impunedly : and this gave Occasion to the remark above alluded to. In the untoward Temper here describ'd, the Opponents of good Order & Government are ready to seize even the Shadow of an Argument, and I hinted my fears that they would not scruple to hold you out as a Disciple of Sir Robert Filmer, & a Preacher of the exploded Doctrine of *Jus divinum.* I have not chang'd my Sentiments, upon this head, for Men of that stamp are strangers to Candour, and however evident the Distinction between the *divine Appointment of Monarchical Government*, which You have fully proved, and the *divine Right of a particular Family*, these Enemies of Law & Gospel will not hesitate to confound them. To say the truth, there are too many, & some, it is to be fear'd, of your own sacred Profession, who are ready, as well as Mr. Locke, to deny them both : and it may be fear'd also, that the fashionable popular writers on *Civil Liberty* have forc'd & stretch'd the Sentiments of that great Author, beyond his own Intention as a screen to their less upright views. It would at least be Charity to suppose that he would seriously lament the Miseries, which his Doctrine has been made to excite, since the American Revolt, were he in a situation to behold them.

My Mind, I confess, has been full of this important Subject for some Years, and this must plead my Excuse for suffering it to take up so much of my paper, without any Notice of ye Material part of Your Letter.

The just Sentiments You express (p. 44 of your first Treatise) of the extraordinary Virtues, which, in our days, fill the Throne of these Kingdoms, must excite You to lay your Thoughts, in the private Manner you intimate, at the Feet of our excellent Monarch, whose care, Qualities and Endowments appear not only to add strength to your Doctrine & Arguments, but to be calculated for better Times, and, I grieve to say, for better Subjects.

It will be some time before my Turn of waiting upon His Majesty will happen, nor do I think that Mode ye most eligible of introducing your Work, which, I am persuaded, would meet with that gracious Approbation, of which You very naturally seem so desirous. The best, & most natural Method, that offers itself, is by an application to Mr. Barnard, the Librarian, from whom you will learn the Propriety of putting your wishes in Execution, as well as the most usual & proper Mode.

I am, Sir, with great Esteem, Your Obedient humble servant,

STRATFIELDSAY. *Apr.* 30*th*, 1783　　　　　　　　　　RIVERS.

No. 4330—*Mr. Fox to the King.*

Mr. Fox has the honour of sending Your Majesty the Minute of the Cabinet, and the Project for the intended Treaty with the States General.

Mr. Fox flatters himself that he shall be able to send to Your Majesty tomorrow morning a draught of the Dispatch to the Duke of Manchester respecting the Project, as also draughts of the two Declarations alluded to in the Minute, in which case he proposes with Your Majesty's approbation, to send off a Messenger tomorrow evening.

ST. JAMES'S. 1 *May*, 1783. *m.* 45 *past* 10 P.M.

Endorsed by the King.

Enclosure.　　　　　MINUTE OF CABINET.

[In Mr. Fox's handwriting.]

ST. JAMES'S. 1 *May* 1783

Present :—Lord President, Lord Privy Seal, Duke of Portland, Lord John Cavendish, Lord Keppel, Lord North, Mr. Fox.

It is humbly recommended to Your Majesty to direct Mr. Fox to transmit to the Duke of Manchester the following Project for a Treaty with the States General.

It is further humbly recommended to Your Majesty to direct Mr. Fox to authorize the Duke of Manchester to sign two Ministerial Declarations, relative to the Fishery and St. Vincents, similar to Declarations to the same effect, agreed upon between the French Minister and Mr. Fitzherbert at the time of signing the Preliminaries.

No. 4331—*The King to Mr. Fox.*

Mr. Fox is quite right in sending if possible the Papers this Evening to the D. of Manchester, as every degree of dispatch that can be used in finishing the Definitive Treaties will abridge the period for the two Imperial Courts to cause delay.

QUEEN'S HOUSE. *May 2nd,* 1783. *m.* 31 *pt* 9 A.M.

Draft, written on a page of Mr. Fox's letter of 1 *May,* 1783.

No. 4332—*Mr. Fox to the King.*

Mr. Fox hopes that Your Majesty will not disapprove of his having sent the papers of which the draughts are inclosed without having previously submitted them to Your Majesty. Mr. Fox had ordered them to be sent to the Queen's House, where he understood Your Majesty was to be, but hearing that Your Majesty was gone out of town unexpectedly and learning with great concern that the cause of Your Majesty's going was the Indisposition of one of the Princes, Mr. Fox thought it more respectful not to trouble Your Majesty with business, especially as there was nothing in it on which he had not already spoken to Your Majesty.

ST. JAMES'S. 3 *May* 1783. *m.* 40 P.M.

Endorsed by the King.

No. 4333—*The King to Mr. Fox.*

KEW, *May 3rd* 1783
m. 15 *pt.* 2 P.M.

Mr. Fox having stated what he meant to write to the D. of Manchester was very proper in not sending the draughts last night for my inspection previous to their being dispatched to Paris ; undoubtedly the present melancholy scene that has brought Me to this place does not enable me to give up my mind to Public business.

Draft, written on a page of Mr. Fox's letter of same date.

No. 4334—*Lord North to the King.*

Lord North has received the honour of His Majesty's commands this morning, and humbly begs leave to offer his condolance to His Majesty upon the late afflicting and heavy loss in His royal family. He has communicated His Majesty's Commands to His Majesty's other Ministers.

Sunday, May 4th, 1783

Endorsed by the King.

No. 4335—*The Duke of Portland to the King.*

The Duke of Portland feels the strongest Reluctance in importuning Your Majesty at this moment with his humble request to Your Majesty to give effect to the Commission for passing The Loan and other Bills which are ready for the Royal Assent, & without which Your Majesty is apprized that no part of the money subscribed can be applied to the Public Service.

The Duke of Portland has the honour of acquainting Your Majesty that at the conclusion of a very long speech arraigning the terms of the Loan, Ld. Shelburne proposed two Resolutions, which shall be sent herewith, & which were negatived without a division.

HOUSE OF LORDS. *Monday, 5th May* 1783. *m.* 15 *past* 10 *o'clock* P.M.

Endorsed by the King.

Enclosure.

Resolutions proposed by Lord Shelburne, 5 May, 1783.

That it is the Opinion of this House, that all future Loans should be conducted in the Manner which may best conduce to the Reduction of the National Debt, or which may at least not obstruct such a Reduction, but rather manifest the Intention of Government to proceed in due time to such a Measure.

That it is the Opinion of this House, that whensoever it shall be thought expedient in negotiating a public Loan to deal with Individuals and not on the foot of an open Subscription, the whole sum to be raised shall be borrowed of or taken from such Individuals without reserve of any part for the future Disposal of any Minister.

Endorsed by the King.

No. 4336—*The King to the Duke of Portland.*

WINDSOR, *May 5th,* 1783
m. 15 *pt* 8 A.M.

The D. of Portland's reluctance at sending Me the Commission for passing the Bills, I look upon as an instance of his delicacy. I believe he has been in the Situation it has pleased the Almighty to place me now, therefore can judge of the State of my mind ; but the real trust I have in Divine Providence, and the balm I feel in Religion so far support Me, that I am fully able to sign any Papers that may be ready ; therefore I trust the D. of Portland will not let my great Misfortune prevent his sending any Warrants that may be already prepared, or that may be necessary to be made out. I trust as soon as it is decided whether the Bp. of Bangor is to be removed to Norwich that the Congé D'Élire will be prepared ; in short I hope no one thing will be delayed, and the Parks may be so settled for Ld. Sandwich that nothing unpleasant may be done to Ld. Jersey who certainly has done his Duty well.

Draft, written on a page of the Duke of Portland's letter of same date.

No. 4337—*Bishop of Worcester to the King.*

SIR—I will not pretend to express how much I feel for Your Majesty & the Queen on this trying occasion. The blow indeed, coming so suddenly, & so soon after another of the same sort, is a most severe one. But Your Majesty sees it in its proper light, &, with the Grace of God, which will not be denied when so earnestly and devoutly sought, will be enabled to bear it. Religion is the only relief in these cases, & to that Your Majesty has recourse. I shall not fail, Sir, to attend Your Majesty on

Saturday next, & to bring Mr. Fisher with me. How happy shall I be, if my performance of those sacred ministries shall contribute, as I persuade myself they will, to pour balm into My Sovereign's wounded heart, and that of his so justly beloved Consort!

I am, Sir, with the humblest duty & respect, Your Majesty's most faithful & most devoted Subject & servant,

LONDON. *May 7th,* 1783   R. WORCESTER.

Endorsed by the King.

No. 4338—*Mr. Fox to the King.*

Mr. Fox has the honour of sending to Your Majesty several Dispatches received from Mr. Fitzherbert this morning, which would naturally suggest many observations if Mr. Fox did not think it more respectful to Your Majesty at such a moment, to avoid giving Your Majesty any trouble upon public Business that is not absolutely necessary.

Mr. Fox most humbly begs leave to take this opportunity of most sincerely condoling with Your Majesty on the late melancholy event, and of assuring Your Majesty of his sensibility upon every occasion that can give concern to your Royal Mind.

Your Majesty will have heard before this time that the Duc de Chartres arrived here on Monday morning, but Mr. Fox did not think it necessary at this time to trouble Your Majesty with this intelligence; especially as from the circumstances of His Highness's being here in a private manner, Mr. Fox does not know whether he is to have the honour to receive any orders from Your Majesty respecting that Prince.

The French Ambassador is not yet arrived.

Nothing has passed in the House of Commons worthy Your Majesty's attention; it was determined Nemine Contradicente not to bring up the Petition complaining of General Conway's conduct in not ordering a Court Martial upon the Business of the Westmoreland Militia.

HERTFORD STREET, 7 *May,* 1783. *m. 50 past eleven* A.M.

Endorsed by the King.

No. 4339—*The King to Mr. Fox.*

The dispatches from Mr. Fitzherbert I return, as I did not object to the Preliminary Articles, I have no reason to complain of such Advantages as might be gained in the Definitive Treaty not being equal to the sanguine hopes of some persons.

The D. of Chartres not having given any notice of his being here, and his not being a Sovereign or Prince Apparent, I have no directions to give concerning Him.

WINDSOR. *May 7th,* 1783. *m.* 16 *past* 6 P.M.

Draft, written on a page of Mr. Fox's letter of same date.

No. 4340—*The Duke of Portland to the King.*

The Duke of Portland begs leave with all Humility to lay himself at Your Majesty's feet, to express to Your Majesty the unbounded Gratitude he feels for Your Majesty's most gracious interpretation of his Sentiments, & to offer his most devout and fervent prayers for Your Majesty's uninterrupted enjoyment of every Blessing which The Divine Providence can bestow upon Your Majesty & Your Royal House. In obedience to Your Majesty's Commands, the Duke of Portland has the honour of acquainting Your Majesty that the Bishop of St. Davids prefers the See of Bangor to that of Norwich, that as soon as an account is received of the Election at Bangor, a Congé d'Élire for Norwich will be transmitted to Your Majesty ; that Dr. Smallwell most dutifully submits to Your Majesty's destination of him to the Bishoprick of St. David's, & that Dr. Wilson has desired the Duke of Portland to represent to Your Majesty the very grateful sense he shall ever entertain of Your Majesty's great con-descension in thinking of him as a proper person to fill the See of Bristol, which he considers it his Duty to submit to, & to exert his constant endeavours to prove himself not unworthy of the Trust which Your Majesty shall be graciously pleased to commit to his Charge. The Duke of Portland will observe with the most scrupulous attention the Orders Your Majesty has given respecting Lord Jersey, but he cannot but be apprehensive that in this particular instance Lord Jersey will not demonstrate any extraordinary readiness to accommodate himself to the Arrangement which has so often had the honour of Your Majesty's Royal Sanction.

Wednesday even. 7 *May* 1783

Endorsed by the King.

No. 4341—*The King to the Duke of Portland.*

The D. of Portland's very feeling expressions for my welfare and that of my Family are not thrown away upon Me : the progress with regard to filling up the Vacant Bishopricks is very proper : I should hope as Lord Sandwich proposed if He received the larger income to withdraw any application for Ld. Hinchinbrook, that Lord Jersey will by that means be left in his present Situation.

WINDSOR, *May* 8*th*, 1783. *m.* 12 *pt* 9 A.M.

Draft, written on a page of the Duke of Portland's letter of 7 *May,* 1783.

No. 4342—*Mr. Fox to the King.*

Mr. Fox has the honour of sending to Your Majesty a Minute of what passed in the House of Commons.

HERTFORD STREET, 8 *May*, 1783. *m.* 20 *past* 3 A.M.

Endorsed by the King.

Enclosure.

Mr. W. Pitt moved three resolutions, one to prevent expence & bribery in Elections ; one to disfranchise any Borough the majority of which should be proved to have been corrupted before a Select Committee, and one to amend the representation of the People by introducing new County Members into the House of

Commons, and also some additional Members for the Metropolis. Mr. Powis moved the order of the day. The Speakers were

For the Motion.	For the order of the day.
Mr. Wm. Pitt.	Mr. Powys.
Mr. Duncombe.	Lord Mulgrave.
Mr. Thos. Pitt.	Lord North.
Sir Geo. Savile.	Mr. Ellis.
Mr. Byng.	Mr. John Luttrell.
Mr. Beaufoy.	Mr. Rigby.
Mr. Fox.	Mr. Mansfield.
Sir Chas. Turner.	Gen. Murray.
Lord Advocate of Scotland.	Mr. A. Poulett.
Lord Surry.	Mr. Dempster.
Mr. Sheridan.	Govr. Johnston.
Mr. Martin.	Sir John Delaval.
Mr. Sawbridge.	Sir Wilm. Dolben.
Sir Watkin Lewis.	Mr. Medley.
Mr. W. Pitt.	

The House divided at a quarter before two and the numbers were

For the order of the day, 293.   Agst. it, 149.

No. 4343—*The King to Mr. Fox.*

Mr. Fox's List of the Speakers in Yesterday's debate has been received.

WINDSOR. *May 8th* 1783. *m.* 12 *past* 9 A.M.

Draft, written on a page of Mr. Fox's letter of same date.

No. 4344—*The Duke of Portland to the King.*

The Duke of Portland most humbly requests Your Majesty's permission to repeat his Gratitude for Your Majesty's gracious acceptance of his dutifull & zealous attachment. In pursuance of Your Majesty's Orders he has the honor of offering to Your

Majesty's signature a Commission to pass, together with some few other Bills that for opening the intercourse with America, which having received some amendments in the House of Lords, respecting the description of the American Magistrates & the duration of the Powers to be exercised by Your Majesty, was rejected by the Commons on the point of Order, but immediately afterwards introduced as a New Bill in the precise words in which it was sent down to them, was brought up yesterday to the House of Lords where it went through all its stages with the implied consent of all Parties & now lays ready for Your Royal Assent, for which a considerable degree of anxiety is expressed, upon account of a large quantity of Goods already shipped for exportation to America, & the importation of several Commodities from thence, particularly a Lading of Tobacco which arrived in the River on Wednesday or Thursday last, neither of which can be done until Your Majesty shall be possessed of the Powers intended to be given You by this Bill.

The Duke of Portland has the honor of transmitting to Your Majesty at the same time eight Warrants, a list of which is herewith submitted to Your Majesty.

Saturday Even. 10 *May* 1783

Endorsed by the King.

No. 4345—*Lord Hertford to the King.*

Lord Hertford in order to give the King as little trouble as possible & to lose no time in forwarding any work or design which His Majesty has in view, presumes by this means to lay before Him a letter & Estimate he has received from Sr. Willm. Chambers, for which he shall venture to give directions, if he receives no orders against it from His Majesty ; he believes it will at the same time be his duty to sollicit the return of letter & estimate to the office that they may remain there as Vouchers for his conduct.

Lord H. begs leave likewise to inclose a letter he has received from St. George's hospital.

LONDON. *May* 10*th*, 1783

No. 4346—*The King to the Duke of Portland.*

WINDSOR. *May* 11*th* 1783
m. 26 *pt* 8 A.M.

The eight Warrants the D. of Portland sent for my signature, having signed them I return ; the Commission for passing the Bills ready for my Assent by some mistake did not accompany them ; I therefore give notice of it, that one may be sent time enough to be executed, that the Bills may pass tomorrow.

Draft, written on a page of the Duke of Portland's letter of 10 *May,* 1783.

No. 4347—*The Duke of Portland to the King.*

The Duke of Portland most humbly entreats Your Majesty's forgiveness for the omission of which he has been guilty, & which he has but this instant discovered by going into his Secretary's Room, where he found the Commission laying upon his writing Table ; in justice to his Secretary The Duke of Portland thinks it his duty to acquaint Your Majesty that the letter he had the honor of addressing to Your Majesty last night, was dispatched in the absence of his Secretary.

Sunday morn: 11 *May* 1783. *m.* 50 *past* 8 *o'clock*

Endorsed by the King.

No. 4348—*The King to the Duke of Portland.*

I lose no time in returning the Commission for passing the Bills, which I have signed.

WINDSOR. *May* 11*th,* 1783. *m.* 55 *past* 3 P.M.

Draft, written on a page of the Duke of Portland's letter of same date.

No. 4349—*The Duke of Portland to the King.*

The Duke of Portland has had the Honor of receiving from Your Majesty the eight Warrants & the Commission for signifying Your Royal Assent to the Bills which have passed the two Houses of Parliament. He now most humbly informs Your Majesty that Lord Jersey, actuated by the most Dutifull attachment & ardent zeal to promote Your Majesty's Service, is disposed to accept the employment of Captain of the Band of Gentlemen Pensioners, if it shall be Your Majesty's pleasure to appoint Him to that Station, & The Duke of Portland sollicits the honor of Your Majesty's Commands for the admission of Lord Jersey, Lord Sandwich & Lord Hinchinbrook to kiss Your Majesty's Hand on next Wednesday for the respective offices of the Band of Pensioners, Ranger of the Parks, & Master of the Buck Hounds, if that arrangement has the good fortune to be approved of by Your Majesty & that it should be Your Majesty's Intention to come to St. James's on that day. The Duke of Portland is also willing to hope that Your Majesty will not think him too importunate in wishing to be informed of Your Majesty's Pleasure respecting the time when Dr. Smallwell & Dr. Wilson may be permitted to have the same Honor for their intended promotion to the Bishopricks of St. Davids & Bristol. The Duke of Portland has the honor of transmitting for Your Majesty's perusal a letter he has received this afternoon from Dr. Jackson, expressing in the strongest terms that Gentleman's gratitude for the destination Your Majesty has been pleased to make of the Deanery of Christ Church in his favour & his entire Submission to Your Majesty's Will. It is with great concern that the Duke of Portland finds himself obliged to represent to Your Majesty that the Supposition of Mr. Bunbury's being induced to exchange his present employment for the honor of becoming of Your Majesty's Bedchamber is not altogether warranted ; in the course of a long conversation upon this subject with Sir Charles and Mr. Bunbury, it appeared that however desirous Mr. Bunbury might be of retiring from the Office of Comptroller of Army Accounts & however he might be ambitious of being appointed a Groom of Your Majesty's Bedchamber, an attention to his own Interest prevailed so much as to have a strong bias in his mind in favour of the larger Income & he was too well and too ably supported in this disposition by his Brother, Sir Charles, to authorize me to confirm the Report which I had had the honor of mentioning to Your Majesty upon terms less advantageous to His Income & Circumstances than those which attend the office of which by Your Majesty's favor, he is now in possession. At a Meeting yesterday of All Your Majesty's Servants upon the subject of a Memorial of the American Sufferers, it was agreed that it should be humbly recommended to Your Majesty that a Bill should be forthwith prepared to be laid before the House of Commons for the purpose of adding a certain number of Commissioners to those already appointed to investigate & settle the claims of those unfortunate Persons with powers to examine the parties interested and their Witnesses upon Oath & to make Reports of their Proceedings from time to time to the Commissioners of Your Treasury, from whom they were to receive Instructions for their Conduct in the very arduous & important business in which they were to be employed, & it was observed that the very utmost Caution would be necessary in forming the Preamble, so as not to hold out such encouragement to the unhappy Sufferers as may induce them to rely so far upon Your Majesty's well known Liberality as may dispose them to relax their endeavours to obtain from their Countrymen the fullest possible compensation for Their Losses. It was further agreed on consideration of the Demands duly received from those who held employment under Your Majesty in America for the payment of Their Salaries that Your Majesty's Pleasure should be taken by me, on the Propriety of giving notice to those who were amoveable from their Offices that their Salaries are to determine upon a certain day which Your Majesty shall please to fix, upon which I shall hope for the honor of receiving Your Majesty's Commands when Your Majesty shall have formed your Opinion upon the fitness of it. Lord Cholmondeley having desired me to present his humble Request to Your Majesty that You would be graciously pleased to permit him to resign the Lieutenancy of the County Palatine of Chester, which he thinks his disinclination to reside in that County renders him unworthy of being longer Honored with, I should presume to hope if Your Majesty should condescend to assent to Lord Cholmondeley's Petition, that Your Majesty would not be disinclined to consider Lord Stamford as a proper successor to that Employment, & I trust that my Partiality to Lord Stamford does not influence my imagination too far in supposing that the attention which he gives to the Interest of Your Majesty's Subjects in a very populous and Manufacturing part of Your Kingdom, the Punctuality with which he fulfils the Duties of his Station & his general Character have not escaped Your Majesty's Penetration, so as to render his Name unworthy to be submitted to You, in case Your Majesty shall think fit to accept Lord Cholmondeley's resignation.

Sunday Night. 11 *May* 1783

Endorsed by the King.

No. 4350—*The King to the Duke of Portland.*

WINDSOR *May* 12*th* 1783
m. 36 *pt* 9 A.M.

The D. of Portland's letter is just come. I desire He will appoint Lord Sandwich, Lord Jersey and Lord Hinchinbrook to be presented on Wednesday the first and last at the Levee, the Second as he is to receive a badge of Office in my Closet; I hope Ld. Hinchinbrook will exactly follow the steps of Lord Jersey in the management of the Hounds, as He has done them great justice. No one from Character is more proper to be Ld. Lt. of the County Palatine of Chester than Ld. Stamford. He may also be presented whenever he returns from Bath. The Bp. of Bristol Dr. Smallwill, Dr. Wilson & Dr. Jackson should also be presented on Wednesday. I am sorry Mr. Bunbury does not conduct himself so conscientiously as I think he ought, for when a Man will not or cannot fulfil the Duties of an Office he ought to quit it. The Determination on the American Sufferers seems equitable. I trust no time will be lost in putting that affair into train.

Draft, written on a page of the Duke of Portland's letter of 11 *May,* 1783.

No. 4351—*Mr. Fox to the King.*

The Comte d'Adhemar arrived Saturday night and has delivered the copies of his credentials; and M. de Moutier has also delivered copies of his letters of recall. Mr. Fox humbly begs leave to take Your Majesty's pleasure upon these two Ministers, having their audiences tomorrow.

ST. JAMES'S. *m.* 48 *past eleven* A.M. 13 *May*, 1783.

Endorsed by the King.

No. 4352—*The King to Mr. Fox.*

Mr. Fox is to give notice to Comte d'Adhemar and to M. de Moutier that they are to have their respective Audiences tomorrow.

WINDSOR. *May* 13*th* 1783. *m.* 22 *pt* 5 P.M.

Draft, written on a page of Mr. Fox's letter of same date.

No. 4353—*Lord North to the King.*

Lord North is unwilling to trouble His Majesty with this note, being convinced that with respect to all felons upon which the Recorder has made his Report, it would be inconvenient to attend to anything but new and unforeseen matter. He begs His Majesty's pardon for mentioning in any way the name of Edward Wootten, who was condemned for robbing two Ladies, and for whom Lord North had a Petition signed by the Magistrates of Newbury, & the Minister & Parishioners of Speen in Hampshire. Lord North has since had several earnest applications to save his life, & amongst other petitions, a very pressing one from the Ladies who prosecuted him. Though this circumstance does not appear to make the case quite new & different from what it was, Lord North thinks he ought to mention it, before the Law takes its course, which it will do tomorrow morning, if not prevented. The Pleas in all the petitions run upon the convict's good character before the commission of this crime, which is stated by them all to be his first offence. The ladies dwell much upon his behaviour when he committed the robbery, which was not accompanied with any rudeness or violence. Lord North fears he has done very wrong in mentioning this matter again to His Majesty, but yet he was not quite satisfied in permitting the execution to take place, without stating these circumstances, whether very important or not.

Tuesday even⁹· [13 *May*, 1783]

Endorsed by the King.

No. 4354—*The King to Lord North.*

Printed. Donne II. 440.

Lord North cannot pretend that his letter renewing the application of the two Ladies that were robbed by Edward Wootten contains any new matter; the increase of Highway Robberies has been very great even during the War, and now will naturally increase from the Number of idle persons that this Peace will occasion; therefore I cannot think myself justified on such an application in preventing the Law from taking its course : I am happy that there is no real ground for my interposing, as there is scarcely time for its having taken effect.   G. R.

WINDSOR. *May* 14*th*, 1783. *m. 42 past* 6 A.M.

Draft, written on a page of Lord North's letter of 13 *May*, 1783.

Duplicate copy in the King's handwriting.

No. 4355—*Mr. Fox to the King.*

Mr. Fox was kept so late at the House of Commons that he was not able to finish his Dispatches to Mr. Hartley as he had expected, so that it will be impossible for the Messenger to go off tomorrow morning; but he hopes to be able to send Your Majesty the draught tomorrow after the Drawing Room, and to dispatch the Messenger tomorrow evening with Your Majesty's approbation.

HERTFORD STREET, 14*th May* 1783. *m. 55 past* 11 P.M.

Endorsed by the King.

No. 4356—*Lord North to the King.*

Lord North has the honour of informing His Majesty That General Conway represented to him, that it would be extremely convenient, in forming the Military Peace Establishment of Great Britain & Ireland, if Lt. General Burgoyne could be allowed to come over to England for eight or ten days, and confer with him, & he desired Lord North to take His Majesty's pleasure upon the subject of granting that permission to Lieutenant General Burgoyne.

Friday, May 16, 1783.

Inscribed in the King's hand, " approved of."

No. 4357—*The King to Lord North.*

There seems to be great propriety in Ordering Lt. G. Burgoyne to come immediately from Ireland that He might assist in making the Plan for the Troops in Ireland correspond with that necessary for this Kingdom and its Colonies.   G. R.

QUEEN'S HOUSE, *May* 16*th* 1783.   *m.* 35 *pt.* 5 P.M.

No. 4358—*Mr. Fox to the King.*

Mr. Fox forgot to mention to Your Majesty the leave of Absence to Sir James Harris of which he has had the honour of sending a draught to Your Majesty, and which Mr. Fox is very much concerned to represent to Your Majesty that Sir James's last letter makes but too necessary.

ST. JAMES'S, 16 *May* 1783.   *m.* 16 *past three* P.M.

Endorsed by the King.

No. 4359—*The Duke of Portland to the King.*

The Duke of Portland has the honor of informing Your Majesty that he has this moment parted from Lord Northington who humbly requests Your Majesty to accept his most grateful sentiments for the condescension Your Majesty has been graciously pleased to express respecting the difficulties he shall be under of duly celebrating the Anniversary of Your Majesty's Birth, that he is so perfectly disposed to resign Himself to Your Majesty's Will that he most readily engages to be at Holyhead on Sunday, the 1st June, from whence he is willing to hope that no inconvenience can arise to Your Majesty's affairs as he shall probably arrive at Dublin in the course of the ensuing day. The Duke of Portland will immediately communicate Ld. Northington's intentions to Lord North that Lord Temple may be apprized of them without further loss of time.

DOWNING STREET, *Wednesday 16th May* 1783
m. 50 past eleven o'clock P.M.

Endorsed by the King.

No. 4360—*The King to the Duke of Portland.*

The D. of Portland is desired to express to Ld. Northington my approbation of his willingness to end all further discussion on the period of the present Administration in Ireland by fixing the first of June as the day he shall be at Holyhead ; the D. of Portland's giving Ld. North notice of this Arrangement will enable the letter to be wrote in my name to Ld. Temple pressing his continuance till the arrival of his successor.

QUEEN'S HOUSE, *May 17th* 1783. *m.* 46 *pt.* 7 A.M.

Draft, written on a page of the Duke of Portland's letter of 16 *May,* 1783.

No. 4361—*Lord Keppel to the King.*

Lord Keppel has the honour to transmit to Your Majesty Admiral Pigots dispatches from Gross Islet Bay, St. Lucia, of the 11th, 12th, & 13th, of April last, and Lord Keppel has much Satisfaction in being able to acquaint Your Majesty, that the safety of the Caton is confirmed by Accounts of her being Arrived at Antigua, tho' with the loss of her Masts and Rudder.

ADMIRALTY, *May 19th* 1783. *m.* 30 *past* 10 P.M.

No. 4362—*Mr. Fox to the King.*

Mr. Fox humbly begs leave to know whether Your Majesty has any commands for Sir John Stepney in answer to that part of his letter which relates to His Royal Highness Prince Frederic.

St. James's, 19 *May*, 1783.

Endorsed by the King.

No. 4363—*Mr. Fox to the King.*

Mr. Fox has the honour of transmitting to Your Majesty a minute of what passed in the House of Commons today.

Hertford Street, 19 *May*, 1783.   *m.* 20 *past ten* P.M.

Endorsed by the King.

Enclosure.   19 *May*, 1783

Ld. Newhaven moved to discharge the order for laying before the House the Minutes of the Treasury respecting Powell & Bembridge.   The Speakers were

For the Disharge.	*Against it.*
Ld. Newhaven.	Mr. Powys.
Mr. Burke.	Sir Cecil Wray.
Mr. Fox.	Mr. Martin.
Lord North.	Mr. K. Stewart.
Lord John Cavendish.	Mr. W. Pitt.
Mr. Mansfield.	Lord Advocate.
Gen. Conway.	Mr. Kenyon.
Mr. Sheridan.	Mr. Tho. Pitt.
Mr. Solr. General.	Mr. Charteris.
	Mr. Pulteney.
	Mr. Arden.
	Mr. Samuel Smith.
	Mr. Ricd. Hill.
	Col. Barré.

The House divided at half an hour past nine and the numbers were, *For the discharge*, 161, *against*, 137.

No. 4364—*The King to Mr. Fox.*

Mr. Fox may acquaint Sir John Stepney with my Approbation of the steps he has taken concerning my son, who will have left Berlin previous to the Arrival of Mr. Fox's letter.

WINDSOR, *May 20th*, 1783. *m. pt.* 9 A.M.

Draft, written on a page of Mr. Fox's letter of 19 *May,* 1783.

No. 4365—*The King to Lord Keppel.*

Lord Keppel's Account of the safe Arrival of the Caton at Antigua though with the loss of Her Masts and Rudder gives me infinite satisfaction.   G. R.

WINDSOR. *May 20th*, 1783. *m.* 15 *pt.* 9 A.M.

Draft, written on a page of Lord Keppel's letter of 19 *May,* 1783.

No. 4366—*Mr. Fox to the King.*

Mr. Fox humbly begs leave to take the liberty of laying before Your Majesty the inclosed note which he has received from the french Ambassador. As Mr. Fox foresees that he will be desired to trouble Your Majesty again upon this subject by the other french Ladies that are now here, he humbly begs leave to take Your Majesty's directions what answer it is Your Majesty's pleasure that he should make to applications of this kind.

HERTFORD STREET, 23 *May*, 1783. *m.* 40 *past eleven* P.M.

Endorsed by the King.

No. 4367—*Lord Hertford to the King.*

Lord Hertford has the honor of transmitting herewith to The King more Estimates from Sr. William Chambers, His Majesty knows that since the Board of Works has been thrown under the office which he has the honor of holding under the Crown that the Lord Chamberlain is the official channel through which all Estimates are to pass to His Majesty, though he is not supposed to know anything of what they contain other ways than by simple reading, nor in consequence to have a word to say upon things which he presumes to offer as an excuse for the liberty he is & shall be frequently obliged to take of this sort.

GROSR. STREET, *May 24th*, 1783

No. 4368—*The Duke of Portland to the King.*

The Duke of Portland has the honor to inform Your Majesty that the House of Lords has been considering two Motions which have been proposed by the Duke of Richmond the first of which implying a censure upon those who advised Your Majesty to put the Great Seal into Commission & being laid as the ground for the second, a copy of which is herewith submitted to Your Majesty's inspection, & which was negatived upon the previous Question, the first was with the consent of the House withdrawn, & the Duke of Richmond having taken the original Motion away with him, it is only in the Duke of Portland's power to communicate the purport of it to Your Majesty.

HOUSE OF LORDS, *Tuesday* 3 *June*, 1783. *m.* 50 *past* 7 P.M.

Endorsed by the King.

No. 4369—*Mr. Fox to the King.*

Mr. Fox is very sorry to be obliged to trouble Your Majesty with the load of Passports which accompany this, but Your Majesty is apprised that they were asked for by the Dutch Plenipotentiaries at Paris, though for what purpose at this time is not easy to be conceived.

ST. JAMES'S, 6 *June*, 1783. *m.* 10 *past* 4 P.M.

No. 4370—*Mr. Fox to the King.*

Mr. Fox takes the liberty of sending inclosed to Your Majesty two letters which Lord Mahon shewed him, and in consequence of which he took upon himself to write to the Council of Geneva. Without being able to judge upon the question Mr. Fox thought himself sure of Your Majesty's approbation in making a representation which might if Lord Mahon's intelligence is right save the life of an innocent individual, and upon which Mr. Fox does not foresee that any inconvenience can happen.

St. James's Place, 9 *June*, 1783.   48 *m. past* 11 P.M.

Endorsed by the King.

No. 4371—*The King to Mr. Fox.*

Windsor, *June* 10*th*, 1783
m. 50 *pt.* 9 A.M.

If Mr. Fox's letter to the Magistrates of Geneva can save the life of an Individual it is impossible I can object to his having taken such a Step ; but I do not see the papers delivered by Lord Mahon in the least point out more than his being confined which he certainly deserves in his Native Country, for Attempting to get Natives to expatriate ; I should doubt whether the Magistrates will look on him as an Irish Subject when he has no other Authority than his own casting off his Allegiance to his own State, and then venturing to return there ; My sentiments of Government are and ever will remain those on which States alone can subsist that obedience from Individuals is necessary, and that if every Man is at liberty to chose for himself Society must be dissolved.

No. 4372—*Mr. Fox to the King.*

Besides the two letters which were sent to Your Majesty Mr. Fox had a letter from Lord Mahon in which it was said Mr. Kelly's life was certainly in danger, which induced Mr. Fox to take the step he did without waiting for Your Majesty's Orders, Mr. Fox has the honour entirely to concur with Your Majesty in Your Majesty's just sentiments of Government so consonant to reason and so necessary for the existence of civil Society, but he must humbly submit to Your Majesty whether the peculiar circumstances under which the Government of Geneva has been lately settled by foreign Power, do not very considerably extenuate the case of those who are at present willing to emigrate, or to encourage emigration from that Country.   Mr. Fox flatters himself at all events that Your Majesty has done him the justice to observe that his letter to the Magistrates of Geneva is so worded, as not to fail in respect to that Government, or to commit in any way your Majesty's name improperly.

St. James's, 11 *June*, 1783.   *m.* 20 P.M.

Endorsed by the King.

No. 4373—*Lord Keppel to the King.*

Lord Keppel has the honour to transmit to Your Majesty Rear Admiral Rowleys dispatches from Jamaica of the 25th and 27th April, Lord Hoods having sail'd from port royal the 25th, and the packets arrival at Falmouth though sailing two days after Lord Hood, gives every reason to expect His Lordship's arrival at Spithead this day or at latest in a day or two, If the Winds continue Westerly.

Admiralty, *June 13th*, 1783.   *m.* 45 *past Eleven* A.M.

Endorsed by the King.

No. 4374—*Lord North to the King.*

His Majesty having returned a gracious answer to the Address of the Ho. of Commons respecting Scotland, Lord North humbly requests His Majesty's authority to direct the Treasury to send the Ten Thousand pounds to Scotland this evening.

As General Conway and Mr. Fitzpatrick were waiting at St. James's for audience this morning Lord North thought it would be troublesome to request one himself, but he left with Mr. Fox a letter from Governor Campbell giving an account of His Royal Highness Prince William having sail'd from Jamaica on the 29th of April.

Friday evening [13 *June*, 1783]

Endorsed by the King.

No. 4375—*The King to Lord North.*

Printed.   Donne II. 441.

Lord North has my leave to direct the Treasury to send the ten thousand pounds to Scotland, which was understood to be the purport of the Address of The House of Commons in favour of the distresses of that part of the Kingdom.

WINDSOR, 14*th June*, 1783. *m. 50 pt.* 7 A.M.

Draft, written on a page of Lord North's letter of 13 *June*, 1783.

Duplicate in the King's handwriting, with the word " authority " *instead of* " leave."

No. 4376—*Mr. Fox to the King.*

Mr. Fox takes the liberty of sending to Your Majesty a private letter from Sir James Harris on account of the very remarkable matter which is contained in the ciphered part of it.   Every thing that has come to Mr. Fox's knowledge only serves to cover the whole business in a greater degree of obscurity.

ST. JAMES'S PLACE, 14 *June*, 1783. *m. 5 past* 11 P.M.

Endorsed by the King.

No. 4377—*The King to Mr. Fox.*

WINDSOR, *June* 15*th*, 1783
m. 37 *pt.* 9 A.M.

The opinion that Sir James Harris gives in his private letter to Mr. Fox that the Empress of Russia inclines to a Treaty of Alliance in conjunction with Us with Austria not Prussia is so conformable to every idea that has come from Petersburgh for above two Years that I am convinced it is founded ; and that confirms me in the propriety of being civil to both Courts and lying by till We really see by the events which must occur in a few Months what line we ought to pursue, by being too anxious we may do wrong, and the critical situation of Russia must soon oblige Her to Court Us.

Draft, written on a page of Mr. Fox's letter of 14 June, 1783.

No. 4378—*Lord Hertford to the King.*

I flatter myself that I do not exceed the bounds of my duty in troubling Your Majesty occasionally with letters, as I do it to save Your Majesty the greater trouble of seeing me, & of being very probably interrupted from business or objects of much greater magnitude than such as occur in the Office where I am called upon to take your pleasure. Mr. Fox spoke to me a few days ago after the Levee at St. James's, & desired I would mention to Your Majesty officially what he proposed himself to take some opportunity of explaining, the case of a Dr. Smith recommended by the House of Commons which I was very unable to explain till I received the letter enclosed herewith this morning from Mr. Dempster which I presume to send to Your Majesty as an explanation of what Mr. Fox proposed by making the Gentleman in question an extraordinary Physician to Your Majesty.

My answer to Mr. Fox was that I should lay his wishes before Your Majesty, but that I was particularly delicate in any seeming interference with the medical Gentleman who had the name or the ambition of being consulted about your own health. The gentleman is unknown to me ; it becomes my duty circumstanced as the case is, to lay it before you & to return whatever Your Majesty thinks proper to command me as your answer to the Gentlemen who have applied in Dr. Smith's favour. The Master of the Horse and the Lord Steward have not sent me their lists to lay before Your Majesty in respect to the household apothecary ; my own is ready & whenever I am prepared with the whole I shall presume to submit it to your opinion ; in the mean time I am concerned to hear that there are large demands yet unsettled & unpaid upon that account from Windsor. I have the honor to be with the utmost duty & respect Sire Your Majesty's Most Faithful & most obedient humble Servt, HERTFORD.

LONDON, *June 14th,* 1783

No. 4379—*Mr. Fox to the King.*

Mr. Fox has just received the honour of Your Majesty's letter and is very happy that his opinion coincides exactly with Your Majesty's sentiments, and will write to Sir James Harris, Sir Robert Keith, and Sir John Stepney in this view. Mr. Fox however can not help suspecting that the Union between France and Austria is still the same, because if it were otherwise, it appears probable that there would be a better understanding between the Courts of Versailles and Berlin than the King of Prussia's intercepted correspondence leaves room to suppose. It appears to Mr. Fox that whatever overtures his Prussian Majesty may have made of late to France had been but coldly received and that it is to this circumstance that must be attributed the seeming desire which has lately appeared in that Monarch for a connection with Your Majesty and the Empress.

St. James's, 15 *June,* 1783. 2 *o'clock* P.M.

Endorsed by the King.

No. 4380—*The Duke of Portland to the King.*

The Duke of Portland having had the honor of humbly representing to Your Majesty on Friday last, that the reason of his not being prepared to submit to Your Majesty's consideration drafts of messages similar to those which it has been usual to send to the two Houses of Parliament in all cases which affects the interests of the Royal Family, consisted in the variety of modes which had occurred for making a provision for the Establishment of His Royal Highness The Prince of Wales, has now the honour of transmitting these to Your Majesty in obedience to Your Royal Commands.

In the two messages to the House of Commons Your Majesty will observe a difference the cause of which the Duke of Portland begs leave with all humility to state to Your Majesty on the consideration of which he presumes to hope for the signification of Your Majesty's pleasure concerning the one or the other being prepared for Your Royal Signature—Upon a very attentive consideration of the subject it was conceived that it should be submitted to Your Majesty that Parliament should enable Your Majesty to allow fifty thousand pounds part of the one hundred thousand pounds, which it is most humbly presumed may be requisite for the Prince of Wales's Establishment, by granting to Your Majesty out of the Sinking Fund an annual sum to that amount untill the Exchequer bills which have been issued for the discharge of the civil list debt are wholly paid off when the disposal of that sum would revert to Your Majesty, & that the remaining sum of fifty thousand pounds which together with the Revenues of the Dutchy of Cornwall will make in the whole the sum of one hundred thousand pounds should be advanced to Your Majesty out of the Aggregate Fund unless it should be Your Majesty's pleasure to order this sum to be paid to His Royal Highness out of the present Civil List Revenues.   But as it is obvious from the numerous Royal Family with which Providence has blessed Your Majesty that it will be impossible for Your Majesty to provide a suitable maintenance for the younger Princes and Princesses out of your present Revenues, the propriety of alluding to that happy circumstance is most dutifully submitted to Your Majesty in case Your Majesty should judge it expedient to call upon your Parliament for the whole of their assistance on the present important occasion.

Your Majesty may possibly be the rather inclined to consider this latter mode not wholly unworthy of your attention by Your Majesty's being informed of a communication which has been made to the Duke of Portland by the Prince of Wales's Order, & which His Royal Highness who has expressed in the strongest terms His determination to conceal nothing from Your Majesty has directed him to lay before Your Majesty.   It appears upon a very strict scrutiny into the state of the Prince of Wales's expenditure, that there remain due to tradesmen various sums amounting in the whole to somewhat more than twenty nine thousand pounds, for the discharge of which, there is no resource but in the great liberality of Your Majesty who may direct them to be included in the arrears of Debt which Parliament was apprized of at the opening of this Session by Your Majesty's most gracious Speech from the Throne, from which it is most reasonably to be expected that the Civil List should be exonerated, or who may order it to be paid out of such part of your Revenues as Your

Majesty has heretofore graciously condescended to appropriate to the use and maintenance of His Royal Highness. The Duke of Portland thinks he ought not to close this subject without laying before Your Majesty the assurance of His Royal Highness that He is not more or otherwise indebted than as the Duke of Portland has had the honour of representing to Your Majesty. The Duke of Portland most humbly ventures to hope that His Majesty's goodness will be so far extended to him as to forgive his having presumed to offer his poor thoughts to Your Majesty upon a subject which he most anxiously sollicits Your Majesty to believe he most devoutly wished never to have had occasion to mention to Your Majesty, or to have been otherwise employed upon but as the Instrument of carrying Your Majesty's Gracious Intentions into effect.

A sketch of an Humble address from the House of Lords is also herewith most humbly submitted.

DOWNING STREET, *Sunday*, 15 *June*, 1783

Endorsed by the King.

No. 4381—*Lord North to the King.*

Lord North hopes for His Majesty's pardon in venturing to transgress His Majesty's commands upon an occasion which appears to Lord North almost to render it unavoidable. The extremely weak state of Lord Hardwicke's health has induced His Lordship to desire Lord North to apply to His Majesty for permission to drive through the gates of the Park except the Horse Guards. Lord North believes that this indulgence is really necessary to His Lordship, & is extremely sorry to add that from what he hears of the health of this very respectable nobleman He is apprehensive that he will not long enjoy His Majesty's indulgence.

WHITEHALL, *June* 15th, 1783. 4 P.M.

Endorsed by the King.

No. 4382—*Lord Keppel to the King.*

Lord Keppel has the honour to transmit to Your Majesty two letters from Vice Admiral Sir Edward Hughs of the 20th of October 1782 and of the 15th of January 1783, giving an Account of his proceedings with the Squadron of Your Majesty's ships under his command and of the Extraordinary treatment he has met with from the Company's servants at Madrass. These dispatches were delivered this day by Captain Wolseley, who came to England from the East Indies, a passenger in the Substitute Sloop.

ADMIRALTY, *June 15th*, 1783. *m.* 10 *past* 9 *o'clock* P.M.

Endorsed by the King.

No. 4383—*Lord North to the King.*

Lord North has had the honour of receiving His Majesty's commands, which he will immediately communicate to Lord Stormont.

WHITEHALL, *June* 15 [? 16] 1783

Endorsed by the King, June 16th.

Copy in the King's handwriting.

No. 4384—*The King to the Duke of Portland.*

WINDSOR, *June 16th*, 1783
m. 59 *pt.* 10 A.M.

It is impossible for me to find words expressive enough of my utter indignation and astonishment at the letter I have just received from the D. of Portland ; these words are certainly strong and would be inexcusable if not authorised by the following facts. When the D. of Portland desired I would turn my thoughts to fixing on a sum for the Separate Establishment of the P. of Wales, when He arrives at the age of twenty one years, I desir'd he would with the rest of the efficient Ministers consider what proposal should be made to Me on that subject ; about a fortnight since He acquainted Me that it was their unanimous opinion, that a sum of one hundred thousand pounds, including the Revenue of the Dutchy of Cornwall should be obtained from Parliament ; I instantly shewed my surprise at so lavish an idea and the more so when my subjects are so much loaded with Taxes, and said I thought fifty thousand pounds in Addition to the Revenue of Cornwall which would nearly exceed Twenty seven thousand per annum of what the late King thought sufficient for Me in a similar Situation was all that could with any reason be granted ; and consequently desired that Duke to acquaint the Ministers with my opinion and of my wish that they should reconsider this business, on the 6th of this month the D. of Portland told Me they continued to think it right to propose that sum to Parliament from whom they meant the whole sum should come ; that the reasons of putting it so high arose from a knowledge that the P. of Wales had Debts which must be paid out of his Annual Income, besides the Expence of fitting himself out ; and that they meant to acquaint Him of this and that no addition could be made whenever he married : I did not deny that I still thought the Sum too large though I acknowledged if no encrease was made whenever He married that I would make no further Objection.

I therefore was surprised on the 13th to find the D. of Portland had not the Drafts of the Messages, but that they would soon be sent to me, from which time I have been in expectation of them ; but this suspence is now fully explained, for the whole proposition is changed, I am to be saddled with the whole Odium of this measure, and the expence at the same time ultimately to fall entirely on Me who am not from my numerous progeny in a Situation to bear it ; though I had been assured no part was to be paid by Me, and in addition I am pressed to take twenty nine thousand pounds of debts on myself which I have not incurred, that the Public May blame me and the P. of Wales with so unreasonable an income not be subject to this sum which can alone have arisen from shameful extravagance.

I therefore must declare that unless the proposal is brought back to the mode in which the D. of Portland first stated it to Me and that all expences are thrown on the P. of Wales, I cannot proceed in this business, and shall think myself obliged to let the

Public know the cause of the delay and my opinion of the whole transaction. I cannot conclude without saying that when the D. of Portland came into Office I had at least hoped he would have thought himself obliged to have my interest and that of the Public at heart, and not have neglected both to gratify the passions of an ill advised Young Man.

Draft, endorsed by the King.

No. 4385—*The Duke of Portland to the King.*

The Duke of Portland should feel himself too much oppressed by the signification of Your Majesty's Displeasure if he could not acquit his own conscience of every idea of having intentionally incurred it. He therefore with the utmost sincerity implores Your Majesty to be graciously pleased to reconsider the Propositions which he had the honor of submitting to Your Majesty not with a view to the adoption of either of them, but in the humble hope of its being possible that Your Majesty may be so indulgent as to allow that such Ideas might not have appeared to him totally inconsistent with the Plan first proposed to Your Majesty's consideration. But as Your Majesty seems to prefer a direct application to Parliament for such a sum as together with the Revenues of the Dutchy of Cornwall will amount to one hundred thousand pounds per annum, it only remains for Your Majesty's Servants to give effect to that Preference, & the Duke of Portland most readily recurs to it as the mode distinguished by Your Majesty's Approbation. Your Majesty will forgive the Duke of Portland presuming to take the liberty of representing to Your Majesty that the Proposition respecting the Prince of Wales's debt rested entirely upon the idea of the Civil Lists being exonerated from the allowance Your Majesty has heretofore made to His Royal Highness, or by Parliaments taking the payment of it upon themselves, but in this he concludes himself mistaken, & is ready to acknowledge his error, at the same time he can not but request Your Majesty's permission to disavow every idea of escaping from the Odium which any measure may be subject to, which he may feel it his duty to recommend to Your Majesty. It has always been his Opinion that such Blame should fall

entirely upon those who have the honor of being advised with by
Your Majesty, & from those sentiments Your Majesty will never
find him deviate in the least degree, he also must beg leave to
declare that however he may have been mistaken in the Propositions he had the honor of laying before Your Majesty for Your
Majesty's choice of the mode in which your Liberality was to be
extended to the Prince of Wales, & not as a substitute for the Plan
first submitted to Your Majesty, he never had any other motive
but His regard to Your Majesty's honor and the Interests of Your
People which he knows it so essential to attend to entitle himself
to any share of Your Majesty's approbation.

The Duke of Portland takes the liberty of offering to Your
Majesty's consideration the messages he. had the honor of transmitting to Your Majesty this morning, & of again availing himself
of the opportunity of repeating his declaration that it never was
his intention or that of Your Majesty's Servants to attempt to
influence Your Majesty to deviate from the Plan originally prepared, & that what was suggested to Your Majesty was implicitly
submitted to Your Majesty's Option which was to be considered
by them as the Rule of their Conduct.

DOWNING STREET, *Monday*, 16 *June*, 1783. *Half past five* P.M.

Endorsed by the King.

No. 4386—*The King to Lord North.*

WINDSOR, *June 16th*, 1783
m. 35 *pt.* 11 A.M.

LORD NORTH—The treatment I have received from the D. of
Portland, if the other Ministers are not equally privy to the
transactions concerning the Establishment of the P. of Wales is
such that I have thought it necessary to send an immediate
answer to the letter I have received from the D. of Portland, of
which the enclosed is a copy ; I can scarcely suppose you and Ld.
Stormont can have known the whole and acquiessed in it ; I
therefore send this for the perusal of both and that You may
exculpate Yourselves ; though it may not be necessary to assure
You of the truth of every sillable of my letter, yet as it is so

strong it may not be wrong to add that I could take an Oath with regard to every circumstance.

Draft, endorsed by the King.
Duplicate copy in the King's handwriting.

No. 4387—*The King to Lord North.*
Printed.   Donne II. 441.

WINDSOR, *June* 16*th*, 1783
m. 52 *pt.* 8 P.M.

LORD NORTH—l am sorry the E. of Hardwicke has so solid a plea for the indulgence of driving through the Park which I certainly will grant as desired by him for leave to pass through except at the Horse Guards.   I am sorry so respectable a Nobleman is not likely to last long.

Draft, written on a page of Lord North's letter of 15 *June*, 1783.
Duplicate in the King's handwriting.

No. 4388—*The King to the Duke of Portland.*

WINDSOR, *June* 16*th*, 1783
m. 22 *pt.* 10 P.M.

The letter I have this instant received from the D. of Portland does not in the least alter my opinion with regard to the one I have received this morning and to which I wrote the feelings of my heart ; if the P. of Wales's Establishment is to fall on Me it is a weight I am unable to bear, if on the Public I cannot in conscience give my acquiescence to what I deem a shameful squandering of Public Money, besides an encouragement of extravagance and likely to prevent the P. of Wales at a proper time wishing to marry, as it would be lessening his expenditure ; to shew that my ideas do not arise from any other motive than Duty towards the Public, I make the Proposal on the adjoining Sheet.

Draft, endorsed by the King.
Fair copy in the King's handwriting.

Enclosure.

Not thinking it advisable to apply to Parliament for an Establishment for the P. of Wales till He choses to Marry, my Subjects being so much loaded with Taxes ; I have examined the Civil List and having put every expence upon the lowest possible Establishment, only fifty thousand pounds remain, which I am willing to allow the P. of Wales in addition to the Revenue of the Duchy of Cornwall which will make his income twenty seven thousand pounds more than the late King thought expedient to grant me in a similar situation ; but then I do not mean any encrease should be made of his Attendants but those of an Inferior kind ; which the having a separate house and Table will require ; and if He will promise to avoid running again in Debt, I will apply to Parliament for a sum to pay his present ones and for furnishing His House and other Expences, which Articles together shall amount to fifty thousand pounds.

Therefore all that is required is a Message to both Houses of Parliament for a Sum to pay the Debts of the P. of Wales and to fit him out on the present Occasion ; the sum to be moved for will be fifty thousand pounds ; thus, he will be comfortably but not extravagantly settled.

Draft, endorsed by the King.
Fair copy in his handwriting.

No. 4389—*Lord North to the King.*

Lord North has the honour of informing Your Majesty that Lord Stormont was at Wandsworth Hill, when he sent Your Majesty's letters to him, & did not arrive in town till late in the evening ; upon recollecting what had pass'd upon the subject of the proposed establishment for his Royal Highness the Prince of Wales, They have set down, to the best of their remembrance, the exact state of the Fact, Many reasons might occur after the Cabinet sufficient to induce the Duke of Portland to think it his duty to submit the alterations in question to Your Majesty's consideration.

Monday night, June 16, 1783

Endorsed by the King.
A copy in the King's handwriting.

No. 4390—*Lord North to the King.*

Your Majesty having done Lord Stormont, & Lord North the honour of communicating to them Your Majesty's letter to the Duke of Portland, & having been pleased to command them to acquaint Your Majesty, whether they were inform'd of the alterations made in the first plan proposed for the Prince of Wales's Establishment, beg leave, in obedience to these, Your Majesty's Commands, to submit to Your Majesty, That the said alterations were made since the last meeting of the Cabinet, & consequently without their knowledge, but they imagine that the Duke of Portland finding a difference of opinion among those he had conversed with, thought it right to state the matter to Your Majesty in all its different views.

Monday night, June 16, 1783.

Endorsed by the King.

A copy in the King's handwriting.

No. 4391—*The King to Lord North.*

WINDSOR, *June 17th,* 1783
m. 30 pt. 7 A.M.

I have just received Ld. North's letter stating what He and Ld. Stormont remember concerning the transactions on the proposal of a Separate Establishment for the P. of Wales ; and it is so much less explicit than I should have expected from to a degree their joint production, that it convinces Me they have not been thoroughly apprized of the whole, and rather than avow that, evade the question ; for it is impossible they can seriously think that if persons objected to the largeness of the Provision, [they] made it right to increase it by paying his Debts.   I have received a second letter from the D. of Portland which certainly does not set his conduct in a more favourable light in my eyes, to which I have wrote an answer a copy of which I herewith enclose, as well as my proposal.   This whole business shews who has the interest of the Public at heart, and who has virtue enough to cast aside all private feelings where that interest is intended to be sacrificed ;

I desire all these Papers may also be communicated to Ld. Stormont ; believe me no consideration can ever make me either forget or forgive what has past, and the public shall know how well founded the principles of Œconomy are in those who have so loudly preached it up, who have so shamefully on that supposed principle diminished the Peace Establishment, yet when they think it will answer their own wicked purposes, are ready to be most barefacedly lavish.

Draft, endorsed by the King.

A fair copy in the King's handwriting.

No. 4392—*The Duke of Portland to the King.*

The Duke of Portland is extremely concerned to find by the Commands he has had the honor of receiving from Your Majesty that Your Majesty's opinion remains unaltered by the Representation he humbly submitted yesterday to Your Majesty's consideration.   It is impossible for him to presume to trespass upon Your Majesty's Patience at this moment, & he has only most humbly to request Your Majesty's permission to have the honour of attending Your Majesty as soon as Your Majesty may think proper to order him.

DOWNING STREET, *Tuesday,* 17 *June,* 1783.   1 *o'clock* P.M.

Endorsed by the King.

A copy in the King's handwriting.

No. 4393—*The King to the Duke of Portland.*

WINDSOR, *June* 17*th,* 1783
m. 17 *pt.* 4 P.M.

I have this instant received a letter from the D. of Portland but to my great surprise no answer on the proposal I sent him last night for such an Establishment as on the maturest reflection I can think fit for the P. of Wales on the present Occasion ; and He may depend on my not agreeing to one of farther Extent.   I shall be in town by half hour past twelve tomorrow when I shall be ready to hear the Duke's ideas on the mode which the circumstances of the time makes me think fully adequate and the only one I can with justice to my People propose.

Draft, endorsed by the King.

Fair copy in the King's handwriting.

No. 4394—*Mr. Fox to the King.*

Mr. Fox can not help congratulating Your Majesty on the fair prospect which is opened in Sir James Harris's dispatch of forming such a system as may make a counterpoise to the power of the House of Bourbon, and may under Your Majesty's Auspices preserve the Peace of Europe. Mr. Fox is aware that the levity of the Court of Petersburgh makes every thing uncertain that is to come from that quarter, but so many circumstances now concur to shew her Imperial Majesty the necessity of some Plan of this sort that Mr. Fox can not help being more sanguine than ever he was before.

St. James's, 22 *June*, 1783. *m.* 15 p.m.

Endorsed by the King.

No. 4395—*The King to Mr. Fox.*

My opinion entirely coincides with that of Mr. Fox that appearances favour the idea of Russia beginning to wish a closer intercourse with this Country ; but circumstanced as the Political Atmosphere is at present with Clouds, it is quite right to wait for Events when We shall be better able to judge what may be proper to be done.

Windsor, *June 22nd*, 1783. *m.* 59 [*past*] 5 p.m.

Draft, written on a sheet of Mr. Fox's letter of same date.

No. 4396—*The Duke of Portland to the King.*

The Duke of Portland has the honor of transmitting to Your Majesty the Address of the House of Lords in answer to Your Majesty's most Gracious Message which in obedience to Your Majesty's Commands the Duke of Portland had the honor of delivering to the House. Although the Address as Your Majesty will observe, passed unanimously, it gave rise to a short conversation begun by Lord Abingdon and supported by Lord Temple and the Duke of Chandos, in which Your Majesty's Servants were urged to declare what were the measures in contemplation by which they hoped to fulfill Your Majesty's Design of forming an Establishment for His Royal Highness The Prince of Wales, and when it was found that every attempt of the kind would be fruitless, Lord Temple expressed an inclination to take the sense of the House, but without forcing a Division, upon the Propriety of fixing a day for taking Your Majesty's Gracious Message into consideration, but no encouragement being given from any part of the House, the idea was dropped, and there seems little probability of its being revived, as it is by no means reconcileable to Parliamentary Usage. Your Majesty will receive in another Box, the Key of which the Duke of Portland has the honor of sending herewith, the Commission for signifying your Royal Assent to the Bills which have passed the two Houses of Parliament.

DOWNING STREET, *Monday Even: 23rd June,* 1783

Endorsed by the King.

No. 4397—*The King to the Duke of Portland.*

I return the Key of the Box which contains the Commission for passing the Bills now waiting for my Assent, as also the Green Box, just come from the D. of Portland.

WINDSOR, *June 24th,* 1783. *m. 46 pt.* 7 A.M.

Draft, written on a page of the Duke of Portland's letter of 23 *June,* 1783.

No. 4398—*Lord North to the King.*

Lord North has the honour of transmitting to His Majesty the inclosed letter from the Recorder of London, & to request His Majesty's pleasure with respect to the day when he would chose to receive the Recorder's Report. He has reason to believe that, if it should be equally agreable to His Majesty, the Recorder would be glad to have the report received on Friday next.

Tuesday, June 24, 1783

Endorsed by the King.

No. 4399—*The King to Lord North.*

WINDSOR, *June 24th*, 1783
m. 37 *pt.* 8 P.M.

The receiving the Recorder's Report on Friday is perfectly agreable to Me ; Ld. North will therefore appoint him and give notice of it to Ld. Mansfield.   G. R.

No. 4400—*The Duke of Portland to the King.*

The Duke of Portland has the honour of transmitting to Your Majesty the Messages which he is informed by Lord John Cavendish Your Majesty had been pleased to approve and to order to be sent to Windsor to receive Your Royal Signature ; he also humbly presumes to offer to Your Majesty for the same purpose copies thereof with the necessary alterations, to be delivered to the House of Lords. It is the Duke of Portland's Duty to acknowledge with great shame and confusion that he was so ignorant as to suppose that it was only in Cases in which Your Majesty extended Your Liberality to Your Majesty's Immediate Descendants & the Branches of Your Royal House that Your Majesty's Intentions were signified to the House of Lords as well as to the Commons, or he should have done himself the honor of submitting to Your Majesty's Approbation drafts thereof when he had last the honor of paying his Duty to Your

Majesty. But as he has since learned that Your Majesty has always heretofore thought fit to make communications of this sort to the two Houses of Parliament, & that there is no other alteration in the Messages, but what the Respective Circumstances of those Houses seem particularly to require he most humbly ventures to hope that Your Majesty will be most graciously pleased to condescend to pardon his want of Information, & to honor the Messages to the House of Lords as well as those to the House of Commons with the sanction of your Royal Name.

DOWNING STREET, *Saturday night,* 28 *June,* 1783

Endorsed by the King.

No. 4401—*The King to the Duke of Portland.*

Having signed the Message in favour of Ld. Rodney and Sir Geo. Elliott, I return them to the D. of Portland ; though all Money grants take their rise in the House of Commons, yet as the House of Lords must give its consent before it can be conclusion [*sic*] ; the Crown always thinks it right to communicate to that House by Message every Application to the House of Commons for any Extraordinary Grants.

WINDSOR, *June 29th,* 1783. *m.* 5 *pt.* 10 A.M.

Draft, written on a page of the Duke of Portland's letter of 28 *June,* 1783.

No. 4402—*The Duke of Portland to the King.*

The Duke of Portland most dutifully transmits to Your Majesty Copies of the Addresses unanimously voted to the House of Lords in answer to the Messages he was commanded by Your Majesty to deliver to them respecting the Annuities Your Majesty has been graciously pleased to bestow on Lord Rodney and Sir George Augustus Eliott ; he also hereby begs leave to inform Your Majesty of the Rejection of the Bill " for preventing Abuses & establishing certain Regulations in the several Public Offices therein mentioned " by a Majority of 21 & 14 Proxies, against

20 & 4 Proxies, and that previous to the second Reading of the abovementioned Bill a motion was made by Lord Temple for all the papers which had been laid before the House of Commons in the course of its progress through that House which was resisted upon the grounds of the inadequacy of the Bill to the purpose it professed to aim at, the sufficiency of the Powers of Government to effect any necessary Reform, the unavoidable delay and expence that would be incurred by adopting the mode proposed by the Bill, & the apparent inutility of the Papers in the other House which was inferred from the Preambles not containing any one positive assertion to warrant such a measure ; After taking the sense of the House upon this Question it was negatived by 32 against 22.

DOWNING STREET, *Monday,* 30 *June,* 1783. *m.* 20 *pt. ten o'clock* P.M.

Endorsed by the King.

No. 4403—*The King to the Duke of Portland.*

No one more sincerely wishes that Public Œconomy may be introduced into all the Public Offices, and more strongly feels that in many cases the perquisites are enormous ; but I believe the Bill which the House of Lords has rejected would have prevented the Commissioners of Accounts from continuing their present very useful enquiries, and that if the Heads of each Department will with zeal undertake the reform, that it may be better done without any interference of Men quite Strangers to the business of the Various Offices, and consequently not aware of the Evils some Changes may Occasion.

WINDSOR, *July* 1*st,* 1783. *m.* 46 *pt.* 8 A.M.

Draft, written on a page of the Duke of Portland's letter of 30 *June,* 1783.

No. 4404—*Lord North to the King.*

Lord North has the honour of inclosing for Your Majesty's perusal a letter he received last night from the Lord Lieutenant of Ireland, & of submitting his Excellency's request, that Lord

Charlemont, Mr. Grattan, & Mr. Tottenham Loftus may be nominated to the Privy Council in Ireland.

As His Excellency seems to think it of great consequence to Your Majesty's affairs that These gentlemen should take their seats at the Council before the dissolution of Parliament, in case His Excellency's recommendation should meet with Your Majesty's approbation, Lord North directed Warrants to be made out, which he has the honour humbly to submit to Your Majesty's consideration.

WHITEHALL. *July* 1, 1783

Endorsed by the King.

No. 4405—*The King to Lord North.*
Printed. Donne II. 442.

WINDSOR, *July* 1st, 1783
m. 40 *pt.* 6 P.M.

The recommendation made by the Lord Lieutenant of Ireland of Ld. Charlemont, Mr. Grattan and Mr. Tottenham Loftus to be nominated of the Irish Privy Council is so very pressing that Ld. North has judged very properly in accompanying his letter with Warrants for that purpose for my consideration : I have signed them, therefore they may be sent immediately to Ireland.

Draft, written on a page of Lord North's letter of same date. Another copy in the King's handwriting.

No. 4406—*Lord North to the King.*

Lord North has the honour of inclosing a letter from Higginson, a convict, to Mr. Akerman, the Gaoler of Newgate, which was sent him last night after he was in bed by Mr. Nepean, but which he did not see till this morning. Lord North has added Mr. Nepean's note to him, which will explain the letter, & which contains the whole of the affair, so far as it has come to the knowledge of Lord North. As the letter was brought to Mr Nepean by the Sheriff of London with the advice of the Recorder, & as the discovery made by Higginson appears to be *new matter*, Lord North thought that it was right to lay the fact before His Majesty & hopes that, in so doing, he has [not] transgressed his Majesty's former orders, or acted in a manner that His Majesty will disapprove.

Wednesday morning. July 2nd [1783]

Endorsed by the King.

No. 4407—*Mr. Fox to the King.*

Mr. Fox takes the liberty of sending to Your Majesty the Minute of Cabinet and the draughts written in conseqûence of it in a separate box ; in order that if it so pleases Your Majesty they may be returned soon, and the Messenger set out for Paris early this afternoon.

St. James's Place. 2 *July*, 1783. *m.* 1 p.m.

Endorsed by the King.

No. 4408—*Mr. Fox to the King.*

Mr. Fox has the honour of informing Your Majesty that upon the report of the Exchequer Place Bill, Lord Thurlow's business came again into discussion when Mr. Byng and several other Members opposed Mr. Rigby's clause.   The debate lasted till nine o'clock and was supported chiefly by Mr. Rigby, Mr. Pitt, Mr. Arden, Lord North, Mr. Dempster and Lord Graham on one side, and by Mr. Byng, Mr. Courtenay, Mr. Sheridan, Mr. Pulteney and Mr. Fox on the other.   Upon a division there was a majority of fifty-seven to forty-nine against Mr. Rigby's clause.

Mr. Fox humbly presumes to hope that Your Majesty will not think it too great a liberty in him if his solicitude for Your Majesty's good opinion makes him entreat Your Majesty to believe that, if the words of the Patent had not been so strong as to make the claim utterly inadmissible, he would have been happy in an opportunity of showing how incapable he is of acting from motives of personal ill-will to Lord Thurlow.

St. James's.   8 *July*, 1783

Endorsed by the King.

No. 4409—*Lord North to the King.*

Lord North had omitted the name of Mrs. Hutchinson in his List of Lord Nottingham's recommendations for Irish Peerages, but, as His Majesty seem'd graciously pleased to approve of Lord Nottingham's recommendations in general, Lord North thinks it probable that His Majesty approves of the creating Mrs. Hutchinson a Baroness, but has the honour of taking this method of requesting His Majesty's pleasure.

m. 10 *past* 9 P.M. *Wednesday*

Endorsed by the King.

No. 4410—*The Duke of Portland to the King.*

The Duke of Portland most humbly submits to Your Majesty the Commission for signifying Your Royal Assent to the Bills which have passed the two Houses of Parliament.

DOWNING STREET. *Thursday even.* 10 *July,* 1783

Endorsed by the King.

No. 4411—*Lord North to the King.*

Lord North has the honour of sending to His Majesty, a recommendation of Lord Surrey, in his capacity of Lord Lieutenant, of a Militia Officer & an application of Lord Bulkeley, as Lord Lieutenant of Carnarvonshire, for His Majesty's permission to remove the Adjutant of his Regiment for very dishonourable behaviour, & a letter of Lieutenant Colonel Thompson soliciting for Colonel's rank in America, & accompanying his letter with several papers calculated to support his petition.

Lord North has the honour to add a letter from Mr. Mainwaring, Chairman of the Quarter Sessions for Middlesex, desiring, in the name of all the Justices, that the remainder of the Imprisonment of the Keepers of the E.O. Tables should be remitted. Mr. Alderman Townshend mention'd to Lord North that he thought it would not be admissable to grant this request, but as it comes from the same Court who first condemn'd these persons, Lord North thought it right to transmit it to His Majesty.

WHITEHALL, 10 *July.* 40 *m. pt.* 2 P.M.

Endorsed by the King.

No. 4412—*The King to Lord North.*

The peerage in favour of Mrs. Hutchinson being one of those in the List transmitted by the Lord Lieutenant of Ireland to be recommended on the present Occasion, He having been so moderate in his requests on that head, I certainly mean no exclusion to it on this present occasion.

Lord North will give the customary approbation to the recommendation of Ld. Surrey for an Ensign in the First Regt. of the West Riding Militia ; as also for the removal of the Adjutant of the Carnarvonshire Militia, agreeable to the proposal of that Ld. Lieutenant. I can see no real right in Mr. Thompson to obtaining the rank of Colonel, which ought to be granted with a most sparing hand ; considering the few Years he has served that of Lieut. Colonel seems very sufficient.

The keeping E.O. tables is so growing an evil that I cannot see the smallest pretence for shortening the imprisonment of those Harpies that have in defiance of Law established them.

WINDSOR, *July* 10*th*, 1783. *m.* 20 *past* 7 A.M.

Draft, written on a page of Lord North's letter of same date.

No. 4413—*Lord North to the King.*

[11 *July,* 1783]

Lord North has the honour to send to Your Majesty a Minute which [was] made yesterday at a Cabinet at Mr. Fox's Office.

Lord North has since heard from Mr. Moore that he is willing to take immediately on board his ships 150 healthy & able-bodied convicts for Virginia & Maryland at no other expense but the fees to the Clerks of Assize & Keepers of Gaols. Mr. Moore has not room in his ships for more than 150 convicts at present, but it is probable that he will not be unwilling to make a further agreement.

Mr. Heneage Legge having last night applied to Lord North to solicit Your Majesty for leave for Mrs. Legge, who is still in a most infirm state of health to pass through the Park on her way to Tunbridge & back again, & Lord North having found in his office that this permission has been granted her for four years past, ventured to give directions, in Your Majesty's absence, that the same indulgence should be now granted to her, which has been granted on the former occasions. Mrs. Legge has pass'd through the Parks this morning. Lord North hopes that, as the case was pressing, his conduct will not be disapproved by Your Majesty.

Endorsed by the King, July 11, 1783.

No. 4414—*The King to Lord North.*
Printed. Donne II. 442.

WINDSOR, *July* 12*th*, 1783
m. 46 *pt.* 7 A.M.

Undoubtedly the Americans cannot expect nor ever will receive any favour from Me, but the permitting them to obtain Men unworthy to remain in this Island I shall certainly consent to.

Lord North acted very properly in the case of Mrs. Hen. Legge. Lt. Gen. Burgoyne's plan for saving the 17th & 18th Regt. of Drg. meets with my Approbation.

Draft, written on a page of Lord North's letter of 11 *July,* 1783. *Another copy in the King's handwriting.*

No. 4415—*Mr. Fox to the King.*

Mr. Fox humbly begs leave to observe to Your Majesty that the Duke of Manchester's last dispatch gives but too much countenance to what Mr. Fox humbly submitted to Your Majesty as his opinion that no consideration would induce the Spaniards to consent to any Article which should not exclude Your Majesty's subjects from the Mosquito Shore and every other part of that Continent.

ST. JAMES'S PLACE. 12 *July,* 1783

Endorsed by the King.

No. 4416—*The Duke of Portland to the King.*

The Duke of Portland most dutifully acquaints Your Majesty that All the Bills which were depending in Parliament passed The House of Lords this day, & most humbly offers for Your Royal Signature a Commission, in consequence of which three Bills only will remain to receive Your Royal Assent when Your Majesty shall please to put an end to the present Session. In pursuance of the Approbation Your Majesty was graciously pleased to signify of the Speech which it was The Duke of Portland's Duty to submit to Your Majesty, The Duke of Portland has presumed to have a Copy transcribed, & to transmit it herewith, & at the particular instance of Lord Mansfield, he begs leave, with all humility to request Your Majesty's Commands respecting the hour on next Wednesday at which Your Majesty will be pleased to be attended in the House of Lords.

DOWNING STREET. *Monday Even.* 14 *July*, 1783

Endorsed by the King.

No. 4417—*The King to the Duke of Portland.*

WINDSOR, *July* 15th, 1783
m. 2 *pt.* 9 A.M.

Having signed the Commission for passing the Bills ready for my Assent which will leave only three for me tomorrow to pass in Person ; I return it to the D. of Portland, and desire he will give notice to Ld. Mansfield that I shall be at the House of Lords a little before three tomorrow as the Hour that will probably best suit the convenience of both Houses of Parliament.

Draft, written on a page of the Duke of Portland's letter of 14 *July*, 1783.

No. 4418—*Viscount Keppel to the King.*

Lord Keppel is honoured with Your Majesty's Commands of this day, upon the subject of the Augusta Yacht's readiness for the reception of Your Majesties' third son on board of her at Greenwich. Lord Keppel begs to assure Your Majesty that he took the most necessary steps for her preparation, before he left London, & will be equally carefull that there is no delay in her compleat equipment, taking at the same time care that Your Majesties' Commands are punctually obey'd by Mr. Stephens, & that he Acquaints Your Majesty, as soon as it can be judg'd Captain Vandeput finds himself able to fix the date the Yacht may be ready for His Royal Highness's reception. Lord Keppel has the honour to observe to Your Majesty that he will be in London at any moment Your Majesty may be pleased to wish it, & will please signify it.

BRIGHTHELMSTON, 16th July, 1783
m. 55 past 10 P.M.

Endorsed by the King.

No. 4419—*Lord North to the King.*

[18 *July*, 1783]

Lord North was summon'd this morning to attend Mr. Bembridge's trial in Westminster Hall, which lasted till Three o'clock, & prevented Lord North from paying his duty at St. James's. If Lord North had been there, He would have requested Their Majesty's pleasure respecting the presents & the other requisites of the Emperor of Morocco, contain'd in Sr. Roger Curtis's letter ; & would have stated to Your Majesty that the Man who was to have carried the convicts to Maryland, has learned that Congress has come to a Resolution not to receive any. He will, however, set out upon his voyage, and if the convicts cannot be landed in any part of the United States, he will land them in Nova Scotia, but in this latter case He will expect 3 guineas a head, which is very considerably below the offer made by Hamilton.

Lord North has the honour of inclosing two Common Militia applications from Lord Poulett and Lord Bulkeley.

Friday ½ past 4 P.M.

Endorsed by the King, July 18, 1783.

No. 4420—*The King to Lord North.*
Printed. Donne II. 442.

WINDSOR, *July* 18*th*, 1783
m. 13 *pt.* 11 P.M.

The presents requested by the Emperor of Morocco seems so reasonable that Ld North ought to order them. As Moore's offer of conveying the Convicts to Nova Scotia if they are not admitted in the Rebel Provinces is so much more moderate than the proposal of Hamilton, it ought to be accepted.

The usual answer ought to be made to the Militia recommendations of Ld. Poulett and Ld. Bulkeley.

Draft, written on a page of Lord North's letter of same date.
Another copy in the King's handwriting.

No. 4421—*Mr. Fox to the King.*

Mr. Fox has the honour of transmitting to Your Majesty a minute of Cabinet upon the important point of the sixth Article of the Spanish Treaty. There has been a great deal of discussion upon this matter, but it appearing to be still in our power to put our own interpretation upon the words *Continent Espagnol,* and to determine upon prudential considerations whether the Mosquito Shore comes under that description or not, it was ultimately the opinion of all Your Majesty's Confidential Servants present except Lord Stormont, that the desirableness of getting the Definitive Treaties signed as soon as possible ought to prevail : and Mr. Fox will accordingly, if it should meet with Your Majesty's approbation write immediately to this effect to the Duke of Manchester. The Duke of Portland delivered Lord Keppel's opinion that, after the expressions of Lord Grantham's private letter, and other circumstances of the same tendency which appear to have passed during the negociation, it would not be adviseable to refuse signing the definitive Treaty upon the ground of the Mosquito Shore.

ST. JAMES'S. 19 *July*, 1783
m. 10 *past one* A.M.

Endorsed by the King.

No. 4422—*The King to Mr. Fox.*

WINDSOR, *July* 19*th*, 1783
m. 40 *past* 7 A.M.

It is a very untoward circumstance that a Definitive Treaty cannot be concluded without leaving clear ground for fresh Disputes ; but I do not mean by this reflection to object to the Opinion of the Cabinet that the Spanish Treaty should be longer delayed on Account of the Sixth Article ; [for] every difficulty in concluding Peace this Country has alone to blame itself ; after the extraordinary and never to be forgot Vote of Feb. 1782, and the hurry for Negociation that ensued, it is no wonder our Enemies seeing our Spirit so fallen, have taken advantage of it.

Draft, written on a page of Mr. Fox's letter of same date.

No. 4423—*Lord North to the King.*

Lord North has the honour of sending to Your Majesty two Instruments for authorizing the holding a new Parliament in Ireland, which require to be immediately executed.   Lord North is sorry that he was not acquainted with the Irish Act of Parliament which enacts that Your Majesty's License for holding a New Parliament should be under the Great Seal of Great Britain.   If the principal Counsellers of the Lord Lieutenant, who must have been acquainted with it, had apprized His Excellency of this necessity & sent over the proper Draughts, time & trouble might have been saved.   Lord North believes that it is now of great importance that the proper instrument should be return'd, & to prevent all further delay He has inclosed to Your Majesty two different instruments, one for Letters Patent, the other for a simple License to be pass'd under the Great Seal, & humbly requests Your Majesty's signature to both.   The Commissioners will determine which is the proper instrument, & then the other may be cancell'd.   Lord North hopes and believes that the Simple License is sufficient & Letters Patent are unnecessary.

BUSHY PARK.   *Saturday evening, July* 19 [1783]

Endorsed by the King.

No. 4424—*Mr. Fox to the King.*

Mr. Fox has the honour of transmitting to Your Majesty the draughts prepared in consequence of the Minute of last night. Mr. Fox entirely agrees with Your Majesty in regretting that there should remain any seeds of dispute in the definitive treaty, but most humbly submits to Your Majesty that, after all that had passed, there was no choice but either to leave the point undecided, or to consent to it's being decided against us, which latter way, if it should be found necessary in order to prevent disputes (and Mr. Fox is far from thinking it impossible but it may) it will always be time enough to take.

The Messenger with Your Majesty's approbation, will set out tomorrow, and Mr. Fox can not help flattering himself that the Definitive Treaties will now be signed without any further trouble or delay.

ST. JAMES'S. 19 *July*, 1783

Endorsed by the King.

No. 4425—*Lord North to the King.*

Lord North has the honour of transmitting for Your Majesty's signature a Bill of the Attorney General preparatory to Letters Patent for a License to call a new Parliament in Ireland. A License for that purpose in another form is already gone over, & Your Majesty's Lawyers on this side of the water think it sufficient, but lest the Irish Lawyers should deem Letters Patent necessary, Mr. Windham wished that Letters Patent might be prepar'd. If the License already sent is satisfactory, the Letters Patent may be cancell'd. This being the first summons of a Parliament under the new Act of Parliament, the proper manner of carrying the Act into execution is a little uncertain.

Lord North has the honour of inclosing for Your Majesty's signature the permission for Sergeant Walker to go the Oxford Circuit. Lord Loughborough would have prevented it, as usual, but his health will not permit him to go to Court. He desired Lord North to lay him at His Majesty's feet with his most grateful acknowledgements of His Majesty's great goodness in granting him this indulgence.

Lord North has had some conversation today with the Arch Bp of Canterbury upon the subject of the Divinity Professorship at Oxford, who seems to be of opinion that the University would be very glad to see the Professorship given to Doctor Townson, who received, a few years ago, a degree by Diploma from the Convocation, in acknowledgement of his merit & service to Religion by a much esteemed publication. Lord North knew Dr. Townson when he was at Oxford, & remembers that he was then much respected, & thinks it very likely that the University would be pleased to see the Divinity Chair confer'd upon a gentleman whom they themselves have lately honour'd by a distinguish'd mark of their good opinion on the score of his Theological merit. Lord North will endeavour to learn more concerning him, before he has the honour of seeing His Majesty tomorrow.

Lord Loughborough not being able to attend tomorrow at Court, Lord North has sent to Lord Mansfield, to know if he will be able to be present at the Recorder's Report. If His Lordship should not, Lord North will, with Your Majesty's permission, defer the Report till Wednesday next.

Lord North has just received Lord Mansfield's answer, & will postpone the Report till Wednesday, unless he receives Your Majesty's Commands to the contrary. He has the honour of inclosing Lord Mansfield's letter.

Thursday, July 24th [1783]

Endorsed by the King.

No. 4426—*The King to Lord North.*
Printed. Donne II. 443.

WINDSOR. *July 24th*, 1783
m. 8 *pt.* 9 P.M.

Undoubtedly there is less regularity in the modes of conducting business in this Kingdom than in any other European, or the mode of calling a new Parliament in Ireland ought to have been so clearly stated in the change of that Constitution that no room ought to have been left for doubt as to the proper method of effecting it; but I fear folly, not reason, dictated the measure, and therefore it is not surprising every step has not been well weighed.

By Ld North's account, Dr. Townson seems to answer the idea of a proper person to fill the Chair of Divinity Professor.

The Council for receiving the Recorder's Report must be postponed to Wednesday.

Draft, written on a page of Lord North's letter of same date.

Another copy in the King's handwriting.

No. 4427—*Viscount Keppel to the King.*

Lord Keppel has the honour to transmit to Your Majesty Sir Roger Curtis's dispatches of the 9th instant from Leghorn respecting the Algerine Business.

ADMIRALTY, *July 28th*, 1783
    10 *minutes past three* P.M.

Endorsed by the King.

No. 4428—*Viscount Keppel to the King.*

Lord Keppel has the Honour to send Your Majesty The Marine Commission made out conformable to the Establishment for that Corps, as before presented to Your Majesty. If Your Majesty is pleased to approve of them, The Messenger will either remain at Windsor, or return to Windsor, to receive the Boxes, at the hour Your Majesty may judge proper to order.

ADMIRALTY, *July 28th*, 1783
    20 *m. past three* P.M.

Endorsed by the King.

No. 4429—*Lord North to the King.*

Lord North has the honour of informing Your Majesty That Lord Loughborough continues so ill as to render it impossible for him to attend the Recorder's Report tomorrow, & that Lord North, having directed Mr. Nepean to wait upon Lord Mansfield and desire his attendance, has just received the inclosed Note, by which Your Majesty will see that his Lordship is not able to assist tomorrow.

Lord North is confined by a slight fit of the gout, & will, if the Report takes place tomorrow, be obliged to request Your Majesty's permission to desire Mr. Fox to attend in his place. Lord North has little doubt of being recovered in a few days time sufficiently to perform that part of his duty.

Lord North has received this afternoon a letter from the Recorder, which he has the honour of inclosing, in which The Recorder desires that His Majesty will permit the Deputy Recorder to make the next Report to Your Majesty.

Lord North humbly requests His Majesty's pleasure, whether the Report should be fix'd for Wednesday next. He apprehends that Lord Loughborough will certainly not be well enough to attend on Friday.

BUSHY PARK. *Tuesday, July* 29 [1783]

Endorsed by the King.

No. 4430—*The King to Lord North.*

Neither Ld Mansfield nor Ld. Loughborough being able to attend the Report of the Capital Convicts, Lord North will give notice for postponing it till the next Wednesday when I presume both Ld Loughborough and Ld. North will be able to attend ; The Deputy Recorder must have notice to appear.

WINDSOR. *July* 29*th,* 1783
    m. 47 *past* 10 P.M.

Draft, written on a page of Lord North's letter of same date.

Another copy in the King's handwriting.

No. 4431—*Mr. Fox to the King.*

Mr. Fox takes the liberty of sending to Your Majesty a private letter from Sir John Stepney giving an account of Mr. Elliott's affair with M. de Kniphausen.

ST. JAMES'S. 29 *July,* 1783

Endorsed by the King.

No. 4432—*General Conway to the King.*

Gen. Conway presents his most Humble duty & begs permission to lay before His Majesty for his information an account just received & brought by Major Mulcatter from Jersey, of a melancholy & unfortunate accident lately happened there, by which His Majesty's Sixth Regiment in Garrison there have suffer'd greatly, but all the reports concurr in declaring that no conjecture can be found of the cause ; that no care was wanting in the Officers who had the charge of the Stores & Ammunition ; & that the utmost exertions were us'd both by the Officers & men of the Corps to prevent the spreading of the calamity.

A Report is just come in of the arrival of the 72nd Regt. from Gibraltar to Plymouth in good health.

LITTLE WARWICK STREET. *30th July,* 1783

No. 4433—*General Conway to the King.*

LITTLE WARWICK STREET
1 *Augt.* 1783

SIR—Having troubled Your Majesty the two last days, I humbly beg permission in this manner to lay before Your M. in order to incroach no further on Your time, the inclos'd Memoranda for Promotions which cou'd not be ready yesterday, tho' for some time agreed upon, being for Purchases.

Col. Hill is a very Old & meritorious Officer, but worn out, & Major Campbell propos'd to come into the 9th Regiment by Lord Saye & Sele's recommendation, a very active & attentive Young Officer, who has been distinguish'd on Service, having been severely wounded in America, where he behav'd with great bravoury ; he is also a Young Man of Family & Fortune much recommended & was disappointed in the 96th by the advancement of Lt. Col. Legge, his junior Major in the same Corps.

Ld. Caithness has desir'd Your Majesty's leave to go to Spa for a few months. And Col. R. Whyte of the late 96th to go on a tour to Germany.

I beg leave also to transmit for Your M.'s approbation some recommendations and appointments from Sir Eyre Coote. Only

I humbly submit whether as it is not usual for those Commanders who have the power of Appointing to Commissions to give Brevets in the Army, whether Capt. Grattan's Rank as Major shou'd not be confin'd to India only, as that of Major Cathcart is propos'd to be.

I should have mention'd to Your Majesty that Col. Fancourt is a very Old Officer who has serv'd above 28 years was at the Siege of the Havannah in the late War, & now during all the Blockade & Siege of Gibraltar & also purchas'd his present Commission.

I am, Sir, also to mention to Your M. that some doubt has been rais'd in regard to the Adjutant & Quarter Master Gen. in India on account of the Pay till it is known whether the Company will grant it.

I am, Sir, with the greatest submission, Your Majesty's most Dutiful servant,   H. S. CONWAY.

To HIS MAJESTY.

No. 4434—Lord North to the King.

Lord North has the honour of informing Your Majesty, That Sir John Delaval requests to have the honour of kissing Your Majesty's hand at the Levee tomorrow. He is soon going out of town to the North of England, & it would be very inconvenient to him to remain longer in London. He would not otherwise have troubled Your Majesty with this request, after Your Majesty's gracious condescension to his late application.

BUSHY PARK. *Monday, Aug.* 4 [1783]

Endorsed by the King.

No. 4435—Lord North to the King.

Lord North having received to-day at two o'clock an account that Lord Loughborough continued so ill that he could not possibly attend the Report tomorrow, wrote immediately to Lord Mansfield, from whom he has just received the letter which he has the honour of transmitting to Your Majesty, & of intreating at the same time Your Majesty's pleasure, whether the Report should be again postponed, or if Your Majesty, according to Lord Mansfield's advice will have the Report tomorrow, &, if there is any case of difficulty or doubt, postpone it for a fortnight, when he promises to attend.

LOWER GROSVENOR STREET
Tuesday night, Aug. 5 [1783]

Endorsed by the King.

No. 4436—*The King to Lord North.*
Printed. Donne II. 443.

WINDSOR, *Augt.* 6th, 1783
m. 2 past 8 A.M.

LORD NORTH—The Queen, finding Herself not quite well, has desired Me to stay with Her, and Dr. Ford having told Me that probably it will prove a Labour, You will give notice to the other Ministers that I shall not come to town till Friday. As soon as the Queen is delivered, You shall certainly receive an Account from Me, who till then cannot be but in a state of great anxiety.

As no Law Lord could attend this day, and as my absence prevents holding the Council, I think it is best to appoint the Deputy Recorder for next Wednesday, which will give a chance of having Ld. Loughborough's attendance ; but should I again be disappointed, I will do my best without them and postpone any difficult case that may occur till the return of Lord Mansfield.

No. 4437—*Lord North to the King.*

Lord North is sorry to be obliged to trouble Your Majesty with letters upon matters of inferior consequence, but, as he will not have the honour of paying his duty personally to Your Majesty till Friday, He thinks it necessary to send over to Your Majesty a letter which he has received this afternoon from the Lord Lieutenant of Ireland.

LOWER GROSVENOR STREET
Aug. 6th, 1783

Endorsed by the King.

No. 4438—*The King to Lord North.*
Printed.   Donne II. 444.

WINDSOR, *August 7th,* 1783
[*sic*] *m. pt.* A.M.

Undoubtedly the Lord Lieutenant of Ireland is the proper person to represent Me at the Baptism of the Marquis of Kildare. The usual approbation to be given to the Ld. Lieutenant's recommendation of Mr. Stanley for Colonel of the Lancashire Regt. of Militia.

Draft, written on a page of Lord North's letter of 6 *August,* 1783. *Another copy in the King's handwriting.*

No. 4439—*Lord Howe to the King.*

Lord Howe has the honor to transmit to Your Majesty, the Dispatches from Vice Admiral Sir Edward Hughes, brought by Captain Carpenter ; who came a Passenger in the East India Company's Packet the Rodney, which arrived at Limerick the 31st of last Month.

GRAFTON STREET.   6 *August,* 1783.   30 *m. past* 7 P.M.

No. 4440—*Mr. Fox to the King.*

Monsieur de Kazeneck was with Mr. Fox this morning in order to say to him what he had intended to have had the honour of saying to Your Majesty at the Levee ; that he had acquainted the Emperor with Your Majesty's intentions with respect to His Royal Highness Prince William, and that his Imperial Majesty had ordered him to testify to Your Majesty how agreeable it would be to him that His Royal Highness should be present at his Camps which are now forming, & how much satisfaction it would give him upon this occasion and all others to shew any marks of attention to Your Majesty's Royal Family. Monsieur de Kazeneck further wished Mr. Fox to mention to Your Majesty that the Camps will begin in Austria on the fifteenth of this month and continue in Moravia and Bohemia till the fifth of September.

The French Ambassadour pressed Mr. Fox again yesterday upon the subject of Turkish Affairs and acquainted him that the Court of France would go so far as to prevail upon the Porte to allow the Empress to annex the Kuban entirely to her dominions, and to put Crim Tartary upon such a footing as would give Her there everything of Sovereignty except the name. Mr. Fox meant humbly to have submitted to Your Majesty this day whether it might not be proper to send off a Messenger immediately to Sir James Harris with an account of this conversation, and for this purpose has drawn the draught which attends Your Majesty with this, and will send the Messenger tomorrow with Your Majesty's approbation.

Mr. Laurens was yesterday with Mr. Fox to desire him to take Your Majesty's Pleasure whether it would be agreeable to Your Majesty to receive a Minister from the United States. Mr. Fox, knowing Your Majesty's opinion upon this subject from what Your Majesty did him the honour to say to him some time since, and feeling that it cannot be an agreeable subject to dwell upon, would have taken upon himself to have answered in the affirmative if it had not been rather pointedly put to him to take Your Majesty's Royal Pleasure.

Mr. Fox most humbly begs Your Majesty's pardon for troubling Your Majesty with so much business especially at this time, and would certainly avoid it if everything in this letter did not require dispatch.

St. James's. 6 *August,* 1783

Endorsed by the King.

No. 4441—*The King to Mr. Fox.*

Windsor, *Aug 7th,* 1783

Monsr. de Kazeneck's attention in acquainting Me when the Camps are to be in Austria is not lost on Me : my intention was not to have sent my third but my second son there ; but as they are so much sooner than was expected it would be impossible for Him to be there this Year. I trust He will be more fortunate another ; besides the business of taking possession of the Bishoprick of Osnabruck will exactly fall on the time that if He had gone his presence was most necessary ; that I therefore trust Mr. de Kazeneck will in the properest manner convey how glad I should have been if my son could have been at Vienna this Year ; but that I flatter myself the Emperor will not object to his availing himself of it another Year.

Mr. Fox is very right in keeping Sir James Harris apprized of everything the French Ambassador mentions on the present Turkish Affairs.

As to the question whether l wish to have a Minister accredited from America, I certainly can never say that it will be agreeable to Me, and I should think it wisest for both parties if only Agents were appointed ; but so far I cannot help adding that I shall have a very bad opinion of any Englishman that can accept being sent as a Minister for a Revolted State, and which certainly for many Years cannot have any stable Government.   G. R.

No. 4442—*Mr. Fox to the King.*

Mr. Fox humbly begs leave to congratulate Your Majesty upon the safe arrival of his Royal Highness Prince William which is announced in Mr. Mathias's and Mr. Hanbury's dispatches.

WIMBLEDON. 10 *August*, 1783.

Endorsed by the King.

No. 4443—*Lord Hillsborough to the King.*

Lord Hillsborough presumes to mention to Your Majesty that two small American Boxes are with Your Majesty, & are wanted at the Office if Your Majesty has done with them. Some fine Maps are lately arrived from Mr. Holland, & Lord Hillsborough wishes to receive Your Majesty's Commands whether Your Majesty would be pleased to have them sent to You. The several Surveys of the Mississippi laid some time since before Your Majesty have, pursuant to Your Majesty's Command been reduced into one Map, & Mr. Pownall informs me that he shall soon be able to send them to Your Majesty.

HANOVER SQUARE. *Thursday, 13th August.* ½ *past* 10 A.M. [1783]

No. 4444—*Viscount Keppel to the King.*

Lord Keppel has the honour to send Your Majesty Captain Farnham's dispatches, of the Winchelsea, of the 28th of July, from the Island of St. Piers.

ADMIRALTY. *August 14th. m. 15 past twelve* P.M. [1783]

Endorsed by the King.

No. 4445—*Lord North to the King.*

Lord North has the honour of transmitting to Your Majesty a letter which he received from the Deputy Recorder after he had left the Closet, & of informing Your Majesty that Lord Loughborough is gone to Buxton, so that he will not be able to attend the next Report. Lord North will, with Your Majesty's permission, endeavour to learn from Lord Mansfield when he will be able to give his attendance.

ST. JAMES'S. *Friday* [15 *August,* 1783]

Endorsed by the King.

No. 4446—*The King to Lord North.*

WINDSOR, *Aug. 16th,* 1783
m. 20 *past* 7 A.M.

Lord North must suit the convening the Council for the Report of the Deputy Recorder to such time as may be convenient to Ld. Mansfield.

Draft, written at the foot of Lord North's letter of 15 *August,* 1783.

No. 4447—*Mr. Fox to the King.*

Mr. Fox has the honour of sending to Your Majesty Mr. Hastings's letters to the Mogul which he mentioned to Your Majesty, and Sir John Cumming's account of the transaction, though without a name, as Lord Loughborough wished it might be so, knowing that the papers must be shewn to all your Majesty's Confidential Servants. Mr. Fox has likewise taken the liberty of sending Your Majesty a copy of the letter he writes to M. de Potemkin, with the Portrait which he has had the honour of mentioning to Your Majesty.

Mr. Fox makes no doubt but Your Majesty will be much surprised to hear that there is nothing yet arrived from Paris.

WIMBLEDON. 16 *August,* 1783

Endorsed by the King.

No. 4448—*The King to Mr. Fox.*

I cannot say the supposed letter of Mr. Hastings gives great lustre to his prudential as well as Moral Character, though it does not destroy the idea of his Activity.

I cannot say I am surprised at France not putting the last strokes to the Definitive Treaty as soon as we may wish, as our having totally disarmed in addition to the extreme anxiety shewn for Peace during the whole conduct that has ensued [since] the end of February 1782, certainly makes Her feel that She can have no reason to apprehend any Evil from so shifting a proceeding.

WINDSOR. *Aug.* 16*th,* 1783. *m.* 48 *pt.* 9 A.M.

Draft, written on a page of Mr. Fox's letter of same date.

No. 4449—*Lord Cowper to the King.*

SIRE—I take the liberty of enclosing to Your Majesty a copy of a letter I have received from his Serene Highness the Elector Palatine, Duke of Bavaria, by which Your Majesty will see his Electoral Highness's intention of conferring upon me his Order of St. Hubert, a very distinguished one in Germany, and which is reserved for the Princes of the Empire only. I have written a temporary answer to his Electoral Highness, until I receive Your Majesty's Royal approbation for my accepting it ; the gracious manner with which it has been offered me, inducing me to hope that Your Majesty will permit me to accept it. The Garter would certainly flatter my ambition more than anything I could desire, but Your Majesty must undoubtedly have many Candidates for so respectable an honour, and of far more merit than myself, so permit me, Sire, to intreat you, if ever Your Majesty creates any Dukes, to be so gracious as to include me in the number, which would be putting me in England upon an equality with Princes of the Empire. Nothing could have prevented me from returning to England, but Lady Cowper's ill state of health. She is however better though not yet able to undertake so long a journey ; but I flatter myself it will not be long before I shall have the happiness of paying my most humble duty to Your Majesty, and of assuring you, Sire, that nobody can be with greater submission and veneration, Sire, Your Majesty's most dutifull Servant and Subject,

FLORENCE. 18 *August*, 1783   NASSAU CLAVERING COWPER.

No. 4450—*Description of a Meteor observed from Windsor.*

August the 18th 1783. Being upon the castle terrace at Windsor in company with my friend Dr. Js. Lind, Dr. Lockman, Mr. T. Sandby, and a few other persons, we observed a very extraordinary meteor in the sky, such as none of us remembered to have seen before. We stood upon the north-east corner of the terrace, where we had a perfect view of the whole phenomenon, and as every one of the company remarked some particular circumstance, the collection of all which furnished the materials for this account, it may be presumed, that this description is as true as the nature of the subject can admit of.

The weather was calm, agreeably warm, and the sky was serene excepting very near the horizon, where an haziness just prevented the appearance of the stars. A narrow, ragged and oblong cloud stood on the north-west side of the heavens, reaching from the extremity of the horizon, which rose as high as 18 to 20 degrees, and stretching itself for several degrees towards the east, in a direction nearly parallel to the horizon. It was a little below this cloud, and consequently in the hazy part of the atmosphere and about the N by W ½ W point of the compass, that this luminous meteor was first perceived. Some flashes of lambent light, much like the *aurora borealis* were first observed on the northern part of the heavens, which were soon perceived to proceed from a roundish luminous body, nearly as big as the semidiameter of the moon, and almost stationary in the above mentioned point of the heavens. (See A in the annexed drawing.) It was then about 25 minutes after nine o'clock in the evening. This ball at the beginning appeared of a faint bluish light perhaps from its being just kindled, or from its appearing through the haziness ; but it gradually increased its light, and soon began to move at first ascending above the horizon in an oblique direction towards the east. Its course in this direction was very short, perhaps of five or six degrees, after which it turned itself towards the east, and moving in a direction nearly parallel to the horizon reached as far as S E by E, where it finally disappeared. The whole duration of the meteor was half a minute or rather less, and the altitude of its track seemed to be about 25 degrees above the horizon. A short time after the beginning of its motion, the luminous body passed behind the above mentioned small cloud, so that during this passage we observed only the light that was cast in the sky behind the cloud, without actually seen [seeing] the body from which it proceeded, for about the sixth, or at most, the fifth part of its track ; but as soon as the meteor emerged from behind the cloud, its light was prodigious. Every object appeared very distinct, the whole face of the country in that beautiful prospect before the terrace, being instantly illuminated. At this moment the body of the meteor appeared of an oblong form, like that represented at B in the drawing ; but it presently acquired a tail, and soon after it parted into several small bodies, each having a tail, and all moving in the same direction, at a small distance from each other, and very little behind the principal body, the size of which was gradually reduced after the division (see D). In this form the whole meteor moved as far as S E by E, where the light decreasing rather abruptly, the whole disappeared.

During the phenomenon no noise was heard by any of our company, excepting one person, who imagined to have perceived a crackling noise, something like that which is occasioned by small wood when burning. But about ten minutes after the disappearance of the meteor, and when we were just going to retire from the terrace, we heard a rumbling noise, as if it were of a thunder at a great distance, which to all probability was the report of the meteor's explosion ; and it may be supposed that this explosion happened when the meteor parted into small bodies, which happened at about the middle of its course.

Now if that noise was really the report of the explosion happened in the above mentioned place, the distance, altitude, course and other particulars relating to this meteor, must be very nearly as expressed in the following list ; they being calculated with mathematical accuracy, upon the preceding particulars, and upon the supposition that sound travels 1150 yards per second. But if the noise we heard was not that of the meteor's explosion, then the following calculation must be considered as quite useless and erroneous.

Distance of the meteor from Windsor Castle   130 miles
Length of the path it described in the heavens 550 miles
Diameter of the luminous body when it came
first out of the cloud   ..   ..   ..   1070 yards
It's height above the surface of the earth   56½ miles

The explosion seems to have happened perpendicularly over Lincolnshire.   T. CAVELLO.

WINDSOR, *August the 20th*, 1783

No. 4451—*Lord North to the King.*

Lord North has the honour of informing His Majesty that Lord Mansfield will be able to attend the Recorder's Report on Friday, & that he has accordingly order'd the Cabinet to be summon'd for that day.

Lord North has the honour of inclosing a private letter he has just received from the Lord Lieutenant of Ireland.

August 18th, 1783

Endorsed by the King.

No. 4452—*The King to Lord North.*

WINDSOR.   *Aug.* 19th, 1783
m.   pt   P.M. [*sic*]

As Ld. Mansfield has arranged to attend the Dep. Recorder's Report on friday, Ld. North has done right in ordering the Summonses to be issued for holding the Cabinet that day.

Ld. North should write to Ld. Brudenel for the usual fee given at Christenings of Duke's Children, and must transmit it to the Lord Lieut. to be distributed as in common cases.

Draft, written on a page of Lord North's letter of 18 *August*, 1783.

No. 4453—*The Duke of Portland to the King.*

The Duke of Portland most humbly acquaints Your Majesty that he has received an answer from The Lord Lieutenant of Ireland expressive of the satisfaction he feels in Mr. Pelham's disposition to accept the employment of Chief Secretary, & humbly hoping that Your Majesty will graciously condescend to approve the appointment of Mr. Pelham. The Duke of Portland begs leave with all humility to inform Your Majesty that Mr. Randolph has desired to be laid at Your Majesty's Feet, & to offer to Your Majesty his most gratefull acknowledgements for the very distinguished honor Your Majesty has been pleased to confer upon him by appointing him Professor of Divinity in the University of Oxford, & the Duke of Portland requests to be honored with Your Majesty's Commands respecting the time when Your Majesty may be pleased to admit Mr. Randolph to the honor of Kissing Your Majesty's Hand. As the business of the Treasury requires the attendance of three Commissioners, The Duke of Portland most humbly hopes that Your Majesty will not think him too presumptuous in submitting to Your Majesty's superior Wisdom, the advantage with which the Official Business might be dispatched if Your Majesty would be pleased to permit him to receive Your Majesty's commands tomorrow before Your Levee.

CHISWICK. *Tuesday even.* 19 *August,* 1783

Endorsed by the King.

No. 4454—*The King to the Duke of Portland.*

The D. of Portland having received the answer of Ld. Northington on the proposal of recommending to Him Mr. Pelham as his Secretary, may direct that Gentleman to take leave at St. James's either this day or Friday.

Mr. Randolph ought to be presented on Friday as Divinity Professor. I shall be at St. James's by twelve this day, that the D. of Portland may if it suits him come to me before the Levee and then go to the Treasury.

WINDSOR. *August 20th*, 1783. *m. 15 past* 7 A.M.

Draft, written on a page of the Duke of Portland's letter of 19 *August*, 1783.

No. 4455—*Lord Hertford to the King.*

Lord Hertford presumes to acquaint the King that Mr. Edwards, recommended by Lord Mountstuart, whom His Majesty has graciously accepted for one of his Chaplains, declines having that honor, saying that he is now in retirement & does not intend to appear again in publick life.

Amongst the Candidates to succeed, Mr. Butt, a Gentleman & a Scholar, educated at a church in Oxford, seems to be the properest person.

Lord H. has ventured to inclose herewith two letters in his favor from the Bishops of Winchester & Norwich. He has been in company with the Gentleman himself, & his manners, behaviour and conversation correspond perfectly with the character given by their Lordships.

If His Majesty has any choice, or person in view, Mr. Butt is out of the question. If His Majesty expresses none, nor any dis-approbation of Mr. Butt, Lord H. will presume to appoint him in order to save His Majesty any further trouble upon the occasion.

GROSR. STREET. *August 20th*, 1783

No. 4456—*Mr. Fox to the King.*

Mr. Fox takes the liberty of transmitting to Your Majesty, together with the Duke of Manchester's and Mr. Hartley's dispatches, a private letter from the former, as it contains some accounts of the general ideas at Paris with respect to their Administration.

Your Majesty may have observed from Sir James Harris's accounts of the interview at Frederickshaven compared with the letter in the German Interceptions that Monsieur de Creutz keeps up entirely to the character which Your Majesty mentioned to be that of the Swedish Nation.

WIMBLEDON. 24 *August*, 1783. *m*. 30 *past* 11 A.M.

Endorsed by the King.

No. 4457—*The King to Mr. Fox.*

The private letter of the D. of Manchester gives an unexpected reason for Ct. de Vergennes' delay in signing the Definitive Treaties, though I ever looked upon the introduction of so intriguing a Man as Mr. de Breteuil in the Council as a dangerous measure for Ct. de Vergennes unless they understand one another ; yet I did not think a change in the Ministry so near ; perhaps Breteuil being unfriendly to the Court of Vienna may be rather with Vergennes than Castries.

WINDSOR. *Aug.* 24*th*, 1783. *m*. 26 *past* 2 P.M.

Draft, written on a page of Mr. Fox's letter of same date.

No. 4458—*Earl of Clarendon to the King.*

THE GROVE. 26*th Aug*, 1783

SIR—Convinced, & the conviction raised comfort & gratitude, that Your Majesty did not wish my removal from my last office, I venture humbly to apply, on the present vacancy, for restoration, which from Your Majesty's known goodness, may be supposed an intended reversion in your royal breast.

I will not be importunate with arguments of long, acknowledged services, of steadiness to the crown & of consequential constitutional principles, being most ambitious to owe any favor, I may ever receive, to Your Majesty's bounty. What a consolation such a patronage would be to a Veteran, who has survived all his Ministerial Friends ?

The liberty of stating my request by letter I should not assume but from thinking that it will be less troublesome, than granting an audience.

I can, Sir, have no greater glory in publick life, nor act more consistently with my principles than by appearing, as I am, Your Majesty's most dutyful, faithful, devoted subject,   CLARENDON.

Endorsed by the King.

No. 4459—*The King to the Earl of Clarendon.*

WINDSOR. *Aug.* 26*th*, 1783

The Earl of Clarendon does but justice to what I think is owing to His long services, in thinking I should with pleasure see Him reinstated in the Office from which He was removed last year, by one of those convulsions which if not unprecedented in a mixed Government, does it no great honour.   But this last Spring a fresh change with very extraordinary Circumstances not less against my Will, which I have and ever shall avow, renders it impossible for Me to add more than that I shall be ready to consent to His reinstatement, if the Ministers shall propose it.   G. R.

Draft, written on a page of Lord Clarendon's letter of same date.

No. 4460—*Mr. Fox to the King.*

Mr. Fox takes the liberty of sending to Your Majesty a private letter which he has just received from the Duke of Manchester, giving an account of poor Mr. Maddison.

Mr. Fox humbly submits to Your Majesty that the Duke of Manchester's slight mention of the intended signature on Wednesday seems to confirm the idea that there can be no longer delay.

HARROW. 1 *Sept*, 1783. *m.* 5 *past one* A.M.

Endorsed by the King.

No. 4461—*The King to Mr. Fox.*

WINDSOR. *Sept.* 1*st*, 1783
m. 25 *past* 9 A.M.

I am sorry to find by the private letter of the D. of Manchester to Mr. Fox that Mr Maddison is dead ; and the more so as it appears to have been occasioned by Poison, which I should rather suppose, if so, was accidental, as I cannot conceive that anyone would be interested in putting an end to his existence.

Draft, written on a page of Mr. Fox's letter of same date.

No. 4462—*Mr. Nepean to the King.*

WHITEHALL, 2d *September*, 1783
5 P.M.

Mr. Nepean most humbly presumes to transmit to His Majesty, a Letter from the Master of the Ship, on board of which 152 Convicts were embarked for Nova Scotia, giving an account of their having taken possession of the Ship, and that 48 of them had escaped in her Boats, and landed on the Coast of Sussex.

In consequence of information received last night by Sir Sampson Wright, from the Magistrates of Rye, a diligent search was made at 3 o'clock this morning, in different parts of London and Westminster ; but, only four of the Convicts have as yet been taken into custody. The Sheriffs' Officers, Constables and Patrols are now posted in all the avenues leading to this Metropolis, with a view to apprehend the rest, in case they should come this way, and information of this unlucky event has been sent to the Magistrates of the several Towns upon the Coasts.

Endorsed by the King.

No. 4463—*The King to Mr. Nepean.*

WINDSOR, *Sept. 2nd*, 1783
m. 31 *past* 8 P.M.

The Account Mr. Nepean has very properly transmitted of the strange escape 48 Convicts have made from on board the Vessel that was conveying them to Nova Scotia, is so flagrant a breach of the favour shewn them, that as soon as taken very strict justice must be inflicted on them. As to the two Reports of Mr. Justice Nares, Ann Price seems to deserve a free Pardon : but as to Scudamore, the law must take its course.

Draft, written on a page of Mr. Nepean's letter of same date.

No. 4464—*The Duke of Portland to the King.*

The Duke of Portland has this moment the pain and mortification of receiving the signification which Your Majesty has graciously condescended to make him of the unhappy causes which prevent Your Majesty's being this day in Town. He most humbly begs to offer his most earnest prayers for the speedy removal of them, & that Your Majesty may experience no interruption in the enjoyment of Your Health, & every other Blessing.

BURLINGTON HOUSE. *Wednesday, 3rd September,* 1783
m. 11 *past one* P.M.

Endorsed by the King.

No. 4465—*The Bishop of Worcester to the King.*

WORCESTER, *Sept 5th,* 1783

SIR—Being here for some days upon business, I have but this morning received, from Hartlebury, the Letter, which Your Majesty was pleased to honour me with from Windsor Aug. 31st. Your Majesty will see from the enclosed letter of Mr. Bridges, the Acting Trustee for Dr. Arnold, that he perfectly agrees to the proposal made to him, & has written to the Dean of Windsor to that purpose. I hope by this time his letter has been received. But to prevent further delay, if by any accident it has not, I have myself assured The Dean by this post that the Trustees fully authorize him to make his option of Dr. Majendie's house for Dr. Arnold & to let it to Her Majesty. This measure is clearly for the interest of the poor man, & if he was capable of judging for himself, he would be very happy in directing it.

Tho' I write this letter immediately, I foresee it will not reach Windsor till Monday next, as no post sets out on friday for London.

I thank God for the continuance of the Queen's good health, & for the further satisfaction Your Majesty receives in the favourable accounts of Prince Frederick.

I am, with the most perfect duty & respect, Sir, Your Majesty's most obliged & most humble subject & servant,

R. WORCESTER.

No. 4466—*Mr. Fox to the King.*

Mr. Fox has detained the inclosed papers till this hour in hopes of being able to send to Your Majesty some news from Paris, but none is yet arrived.

Mr. Fox humbly submits to Your Majesty how very just Your Majesty's bad opinion of the Court of Portugal was, if the contents of this Lisbon Mail are really true. M. Pinto in his last conversation with Mr. Fox assured him there was nothing of this sort to be apprehended, and he appeared to be so sincere in the whole of his discourse, that Mr. Fox is satisfied either that the fact is not as it is represented, or that Mr Pinto was ignorant of it. If it be true, Mr. Fox humbly submits to Your Majesty that Portugal can no longer be considered as an Ally of this country, and that the probability is that She will fall a sacrifice to the first fit of Ambition that may seize her powerful Neighbour.

HARROW. 6 *September*, 1783. *m.* 55 *past* 11 P.M.

Endorsed by the King.

No. 4467—*Mr. Fox to the King.*

Mr. Fox has the honour of transmitting to Your Majesty the dispatches which are just arrived from the Duke of Manchester, and has at the same time the honour of informing Your Majesty that Captain Warner is arrived with an account of the Definitive Treaties having been signed on Wednesday.

HARROW. 7 *September*, 1783. *m.* 30 *past two* A.M.

Endorsed by the King.

No. 4468—*The King to Mr. Fox.*

WINDSOR, *Sept. 7th,* 1783
m. 30 *pt.* 7 A.M.

It seems extraordinary that France should have so long delayed signing the Definitive Treaty ; the Arrival of it must remove any doubts persons might otherwise have harboured on that Account.

I cannot agree in opinion with the D. of Manchester, that it is desirable to give ease to the Dutch in the Definitive Treaty, to regain their affection ; whilst the French Party are the Directors, and M. de Linden is the person fixed on by Ct. Welderen for Minister at this Court, any concessions will only encourage them in their Gallican System from less feeling the inconvenience of the rupture ; whilst if the Treaty is less favourable, those who drew them into the War will become the cause of Public hatred and by subsequent kindnesses they may be perhaps regained ; though in States as well as in Men, where dislike has once arose, I never expect to see cordiality.

Nothing can be more avowed than the desertion of the Court of Lisbon ; but after Britain has so much lowered Herself, can one be surprised that Courts treat her accordingly.

No. 4469—*Lord North to the King.*

Lord North has the honour of inclosing for His Majesty's signature a Warrant to the Deputy Earl Marshal for the attendance of the Heralds & Pursuivants at the Proclamation of the Peace. Lord North has left the day in Blank, but he believes it will be very convenient to fix Tuesday next the 7th for that ceremony, as there will be sufficient time before that day to give notice to all the persons who ought to attend. If His Majesty approves of Tuesday next, Lord North will direct the Blank to be so filled up, when it returns from His Majesty.

BUSHY PARK. *Septr.* 7, 1783. *m.* 15 *pt.* 3 P.M.

Endorsed by the King.

No. 4470—*The King to Lord North.*

WINDSOR. *Sept.* 7*th*, 1783
m. 44 *past* 5 P.M.

I have signed the Warrant for the Attendance of the Heralds for the Proclamation of Peace ; I have no objection to that Ceremony being performed on Tuesday ; indeed I am glad it is on a day I am not in Town, as I think this compleats the Downfall of the lustre of this Empire : but when Religion and Public Spirit are quite absorbed by Vice and Dissipation, what has now occurred is but the natural consequence ; one comfort I have, that I have alone tried to support the Dignity of my Crown and feel I am innocent of the Evils that have occurred, though deeply wounded that it should have happened during my Reign.

Draft, written on a page of Lord North's letter of same date.

No. 4471—*Lord North to the King.*

Lord North has the honour of inclosing to His Majesty a letter he has received from Mr. Nepean, by which His Majesty will perceive that the Proclamation for the Peace cannot be issued as yet. Mr. Nepean brought down to Bushy yesterday from London the Warrt. which Lord North had the honour of sending to His Majesty. When Lord North returned it, He desired Mr. Nepean to consult the Heralds before he issued it, which order he is glad that he gave, as the Heralds have stated an obstacle with which Mr. Nepean was unacquainted when Lord North saw him yesterday.

Lord North has also the honour of inclosing some dispatches received from General Haldimand & General Riedesel. Lord North supposes that he may give the latter leave to come to Town from Portsmouth.

BUSHY PARK. *Monday, Sept. 8th. m.* 40 *pt.* 5 P.M.

No. 4472—*The King to Lord North.*

WINDSOR, *Sept 8th,* 1783
m. 22 *past* 8 P.M.

Undoubtedly from every man brought forward into Offices of business being either Declamers or owing their situation to such Persons instead of being regularly bred as in other Countries in the Offices in which [they] become Secretaries, occasions the endless mistakes in matters of form.

Gen. Riedesel must have instant leave to come to Town, as the taking in Water will naturally delay the sailing of the Foreign Troops for Germany for some days.

Draft, written on a page of Lord North's letter of same date.

No. 4473—*Lord North to the King.*

Lord North has the honour of sending Your Majesty the Address which the City of London intends to present tomorrow, together with two plans of answers, between which the difference is not very material ; Lord North thinks, however, that it is better to send them both to Your Majesty.

Mr. Fawcett has told Mr Nepean this morning that he believes that the Commander-in-Chief in Ireland expects no more than 8 £ per diem ; 6 £ when absent, & 2 £ additional when present.

BUSHY PARK. 10 *Septr. m.* 27 *pt.* 7 P.M.

Endorsed by the King.

No. 4474—*The King to Lord North.*

WINDSOR. *Sept. 9th* [*sic 10th*] 1783
m. 37 *past* 9 P.M.

I prefer the Draft of an answer to the City which I have marked No. 1, but would propose to leave out the words underlined, as they run bald, both in the address and in the answer, and contain nothing, for the Pe. of Wales being twenty-one of course is called to the Great Council of the Nation.

I think it will certainly be better liked in Ireland that the Commander in Chief there when present should have 8 £ per diem than ten, and the more so as the one here, though of superior Rank has but 10 £ ; therefore I desire it may be so fixed with the Ld. Lieut. of Ireland.

Draft, written on a page of Lord North's letter of 10 *September,* 1783.

No. 4475—*Mr. Fox to the King.*

Mr. Fox humbly begs leave to inform Your Majesty that Mr. Hartley arrived last night with the definitive Treaty with the United States.

Mr. Fox humbly begs leave to point out to Your Majesty's attention the interceptions from M. Mapardi to Prince Caramanico which correspond entirely with all the other accounts which Mr. Fox has had from Holland.

WIMBLEDON. 13 *Septr.* 1783

Endorsed by the King.

No. 4476—*Lord North to the King.*

Lord North has the honour of transmitting to His Majesty a note from Baron Kutzleben, who apprehends that the Landgrave, his Master, will be better pleased if General Kospoth waits in the Downs till he is join'd by the Troops which were put under his Command at New York, in order to accompany them to Germany. Lord North humbly intreats Your Majesty's pleasure whether he may give to the Hessian General the directions which Baron Kutzleben desires.

BUSHY PARK. *Sept.* 14

Endorsed by the King.

Enclosure.

Baron Kutzleben presents his Respectfull Compts. to Lord North, takes the liberty of reminding His Lordship of His kind promiss (of yesterday) that He would be pleased to give such Directions, that General Kospoth who is arrived in the Downs at Deal *on board the Vesel Hind* (which has been separated from the rest of the fleet) might remain there till the rest of the fleet arrives, of which troops the General is the Commanding Officer.

SACKVILLE STREET. *Sunday morning. Septr. 14th.*

No. 4477—*The King to Lord North.*

I very willingly authorize Ld. North to send orders to General Kospoth at Deal, agreeable to the suggestion of Bn. Kutzleben ; the sooner they are dispatched the better, otherwise He may apply for leave to come to London, which had better be avoided.

WINDSOR. *Sept.* 14*th*, 1783. *m.* 21 *past* 2 P.M.   G. R.

Draft, written on a page of Lord North's letter of same date.

No. 4478—*Mr. Fox to the King.*

Mr. Fox humbly begs leave to know Your Majesty's pleasure whether he shall acquaint M. Simolin that he may have the honour of an audience of Your Majesty Wednesday or any other day.

WIMBLEDON. 15 *September,* 1783

Endorsed by the King.

No. 4479—*Lord North to the King.*

Lord North has the honour of sending His Majesty some papers which he has just received from London. Among them is a letter from the Sheriff of London, which has been already sent to His Majesty, but returned without any remark. Lord North imagines that His Majesty by his silence approved of the proposal made by Sir Robert Taylor, in concurrence with the Judges, but Mr. Nepean thought it right to lay the letter once more before His Majesty, & has sent it accordingly. Lord North trusts in His Majesty to excuse any trouble which may arise from the great precaution of Mr. Nepean.

BUSHY PARK. *m.* 20 *pt.* 3 P.M. *Septr.* 15, 1783.

Endorsed by the King.

No. 4480—*The King to Lord North.*

WINDSOR. *Sept.* 15*th,* 1783
m. 17 *past* 7 P.M.

As the list for the Irish Peerage is agreeable to what was approved of, Ld. North will have the Warrants prepared in the order proposed by the Ld. Lieut. of Ireland ; as Sir John Delaval is the Superior in rank He should come next to the Irish Gentlemen, then Mr. Pennington, He being a prior promise to Mr. Pennant. I cannot in the least consent to an assurance that no English Men will be made Irish Peers ; the granting Honours is a sole right to the Crown, who alone is the Judge of the propriety of that measure ; the utmost that can be said is that it will not be lavishly granted. Negatives ought to be given to the two Memorials of the Earl of Antrim, and the Son of Lord Westmeath. The proposal of Sir Robt. Taylor in concurrence with the Judges I approve of.

Draft, written on a page of Lord North's letter of same date.

No. 4481—*Mr. Fox to the King.*

Mr. Fox humbly begs leave to take Your Majesty's pleasure with respect to the Spanish Minister's Audience. He supposes tomorrow will be as agreeable to Your Majesty as any other day.

WIMBLEDON. 16 *September,* 1783

Endorsed by the King.

No. 4482—*Lord North to the King.*

Lord North has just received a letter from Mr. Frazer, in which he desires him to apply to His Majesty for his pleasure, as to the paragraph respecting the Christening of the young Princess, which Mr. Frazer thinks he ought to insert in the Gazette tonight, but waits for Your Majesty's commands. He informs Lord North that he used to receive Your Majesty's Commands in Your Majesty's handwriting on similar occasions. In consequence of Mr. Frazer's desire, Lord North has the honour of forwarding a Messenger to Your Majesty with all possible expedition.

Saturday, Septr. 20th

Endorsed by the King.

No. 4483—*Lord North to the King.*

Lord North has the honour of informing His Majesty That in consequence of the inclosed precedent, orders were given this morning to fire the Tower & Park Guns. This was done with the advice of Mr. Frazer, & Lord North hopes that it was not improper.

BUSHY PARK. *m.* 40 *pt.* 3 P.M.

Endorsed by the King.

No. 4484—*The King to Lord North.*

WINDSOR. *Sept.* 23*rd*, 1783
m. 44 *pt.* 5 P.M.

As precedents authorized the firing the Park and Tower Guns this morning, Lord North is justified in giving Orders for that purpose.

Draft, written on a page of Lord North's letter of same date.

No. 4485—*Mr. Fox to the King.*

Mr. Fox takes the liberty of sending Your Majesty a private letter from the Duke of Manchester, by which Your Majesty will see that nothing has been left unattempted with respect to the prevention of the appointment of M. Lynden.

ST. JAMES'S. 24 *Septr.* 1783. 5 *m. past* 4 P.M.

Endorsed by the King.

No. 4486—*The King to Mr. Fox.*

If there is the least remains of Decency in the Dutch after the Strong representations against Mr. Lynden's nomination, this cannot take place ; but should passion prevail, I quite agree with Mr. Boerse that from hence He must be refused.

QUEEN'S HOUSE. *Septr.* 24*th*, 1783. *m.* 46 *pt.* 6 P.M.

Draft, written on a page of Mr. Fox's letter of same date.

No. 4487—*The King to Mr. Fox.*

I enclose the letter I have written to the P. of Orange, as also one to P. Lewis, who would be hurt if on such an Occasion I did not call for his opinion also : General O'Hara had best go to the Greffier and open himself fully, but explaining to Him that it is as to a friend of the Stadtholder, not in his Official capacity, and get his opinion as to the least public method of conveying my two letters. I owne I am gloomy on the subject from an opinion of the Prince's want of natural Vigour which I fear will make him at least lose the efficiency of his Station, and the name without the reality can neither be creditable to himself nor of utility to the Republic.

WINDSOR. *Sept.* 27, 1783. *m.* 58 *pt.* 8 A.M.

Draft.

Enclosure.

The King to the Prince Lewis of Brûnswick-Luneburg.

MÒN COUSIN—La situation du Prince d'Orange me paroit si critique que j'ai envoyé le General O'Hara secrettement à La Haye. Tous les avis s'accordent que le parti dominant veut nommer M. de Linden de la part de la République à ma Cour ; sa conduite envers le Prince et même envers Vous Mon Cousin a été si notoire que j'incline à refuser tel Ministre ; mais je souhaite de savoir si ce pas peu nuire aux interets du Prince ; je me flatte que vous ne perdrez de Vue les projets des Ennemis, en verité si les Amis du Prince ne s'unissent pour les contre currer les suits peuvent être très facheuses ; au reste je Vous prie d'être convaincu que je serai toujours, Mon Cousin, Votre bon Cousin.

WINDSOR. *le 27me Sept.* 1783.

Draft.

No. 4488—*Mr. Fox to the King.*

Mr. Fox humbly begs leave to acknowledge the honour of Your Majesty's commands of yesterday. He has taken the liberty of sending to Your Majesty a copy of his private letter to General O'Hara as well as of the paper inclosed in it, and of his letter to the Greffier Fagel, in order that Your Majesty may be the better able to judge whether what was intended by Your Majesty has been carried into execution conformably to Your Majesty's ideas. Mr. Storer is setting out and is strictly charged to deliver the packet for General O'Hara with his own hands.

ST. JAMES'S. 28 *Septr.* 1783. *m.* 15 P.M.

Endorsed by the King.

No. 4489—*The King to Mr. Fox.*

The letter to General O'hara, the paper inclosed in it, and the one to the Greffier contain all that occurs to Me as necessary to be wrote on the present occasion.

WINDSOR. *Sept. 28th*, 1783. *m.* 35 *past* 5 P.M.

Draft, written on a page of Mr. Fox's letter of same date.

No. 4490—*Mr. Fox to the King.*

Mr. Fox is happy to have the honour of acquainting Your Majesty that the Packet for General O'hara is now come back from Mr Storer by the hands of a Gentleman who has brought also a dispatch from the Duke of Manchester.

Mr. Fox will see General O'hara as soon as possible and has no doubt but he will be able to set out for the Hague tomorrow.

ST. JAMES'S. 10 *October*, 1783. *m.* 40 *past* 2 P.M.

Endorsed by the King.

No. 4491—*Mr. Fox to the King.*

Mr. Fox has the honour of informing Your Majesty that General O'hara set out this Evening for the Hague.

ST. JAMES'S PLACE. 11 *Octr.* 1783. *m.* 30 *past* 11 P.M.

Endorsed by the King.

No. 4492—*The Duke of Portland to the King.*

The Duke of Portland begs leave with all humility to lay before Your Majesty the substance of The Duke of Manchester's answer to the inquiry Your Majesty commanded him to make respecting the value of the Presents given by His Most Christian Majesty to the Embassadors & Ministers of The High Contracting & Mediating Powers on occasion of the signature of the Definitive Treaty of Peace.

His Most Christian Majesty's Picture ornamented with a

Crown and Cercle of Diamonds has been given to all the Embassadors & Ministers who have been employed in negotiating The Peace, & the only difference in the Presents consists in the size & value of the Diamonds with which they are ornamented ; that given to the Imperial Embassador is estimated at fifty five thousand Livres, those which have been received by the Russian Ministers are only valued at twenty four thousand Livres each, & Monsr. de Vergennes observed to Your Majesty's Embassador that the present he delivered to him had cost The King His Master the sum of thirty five thousand Livres, but according to the opinion of experienced Jewellers, whom the Duke of Manchester has consulted, the Diamonds are not thought to be worth more than between nine hundred and a thousand pounds. A very costly present of French Porcelaine has been made to the Duchess of Manchester, & His Most Christian Majesty's Picture set round with Diamonds in a Snuff Box has been given to Mr. Warner, in consideration, as the Duke of Manchester supposes, of his having acted as Secretary of the Embassy & not in the capacity of the Duke's private Secretary. The expence of this box is valued at between ten and twelve thousand livres ; it is supposed that one of equal value will be given to the Secretary of the Spanish Embassy & that Monsr. de Rayneval will receive the same Compliment from the Court of Spain.

BULSTRODE. *Sunday, 12th November,* 1783. *m.* 15 *past* 3 *o'clock* P.M.

Endorsed by the King.

No. 4493—*The King to the Duke of Portland.*

The answer from the D. of Manchester will enable the D. of Portland to give the order to Duvals for setting the Pictures ; that for C. de Vergennes, the Austrian Ambassador and the Spaniard to cost each £1,000 ; that for the Russian Envoys should be of less value, and a box must be prepared for the Spanish Secretary of a similar kind to the one Ld. Grantham fabricated for Mr. Rayneval, but of less value.

WINDSOR. *Oct.* 12th, 1783. *m.* 16 *past* 5 P.M.

Draft, written on a page of the Duke of Portland's letter of same date.

No. 4494—*Lord North to the King.*

Lord North has the honour of transmitting to Your Majesty a letter he received a few days ago from the Commander in Chief respecting the Officers of Colonel Erskine's Regiment, with a list of the said Officers, & two Extracts from the Votes of the House of Commons upon that business, by which Lord North apprehends that Your Majesty is impower'd to grant them half pay if Your Majesty should think proper. Lord North humbly requests to know Your Majesty's pleasure upon the premises, but thinks it his duty to suggest at the same time, That if Your Majesty adopts the proposal of the Commander in Chief respecting Mr. Erskine's Officers, The Corsicans who have not received near so great an allowance will be aggrieved, if they are not put upon the same footing; especially, as they served very meritoriously at Port Mahon & Gibraltar, and were much commended by the Commanders of both those fortresses for their good behaviour.

WHITEHALL. *Oct.* 21, 1783. 4 *o'clock* P.M.

Endorsed by the King.

No. 4495—*The King to Lord North.*

Printed. Donne II. 444.

By every enquiry I have made of Ld Amherst, He ever denied Government being in the smallest degree concerned in the transaction of the East India Company with Col. Erskine. I therefore certainly look on the granting half pay as a wanton expenditure of public money, and think the Officers ought to be at best treated as the Corsican ones were, who served at Minorca ; but if Ministry wish to grant Erskine's Corps what certainly they have not deserved, I agree with Ld North the Corsican Officers must have as good terms : I therefore hope Ld North will consult the Treasury before He takes any step agreeable to General Conway's letter.

WINDSOR. *Oct.* 24*th*, 1783. *m.* 25 *past* 8 P.M.

Draft, written on a page of Lord North's letter of same date.

Another copy in the King's hand, initialled G. R.

No. 4496—*Mr. Fox to the King.*

Mr. Fox has the honour to acquaint Your Majesty that General O'hara arrived in town this morning from the Hague, where upon consulting the Greffier Fagel, he judged it most prudent not to deliver Your Majesty's letter. The Greffier told him that he knew the weak state of mind of the Prince of Orange so well that if Your Majesty's letter should be delivered, he apprehended the worst consequences and had no doubt but the Prince through timidity & confusion would shew the letter to M. Blyswick or to some other of his Enemies. It is with true concern that Mr. Fox informs Your Majesty that the Greffier throughout talked the most desponding language with respect to the Stadholder's situation, and at the same time represented the Inveteracy of his Countrymen against the English Nation in the strongest colours, inasmuch that he had no doubt but that the Stadholder's receiving a letter from Your Majesty, notwithstanding the signature & ratification of the Preliminaries, would by these infatuated People be termed a correspondence with an Enemy. Upon the whole it was clearly his opinion that either the rejection of M. Lynden or any other step taken by this Country with a view to be serviceable to the Stadholder would be infinitely prejudicial to him. In all his conversation this Minister spoke as a cordial friend to Great Britain, and with respect to the other points mentioned in the paper given to General O'hara expressed himself with great frankness. He recommended the sending an authorized Minister to the Hague as soon as possible, whose conduct he said ought to be firm and even proud, but ought not to appear to have any reference whatever to the Prince of Orange's interests. He thought it should by all means be insisted upon that the definitive Treaty should be signed either at the Hague or at London, not at Paris, and that no disposition should be shown at present to any concession from the terms of the Preliminaries. He likewise thought it might be useful that your Majesty's Minister should have the character of Ambassadour in order to have more weight. He described the Prince of Orange's affairs to be at present *absolutely* desperate, nor had he any hopes from the King of Prussia ; but he made no doubt but if Great Britain could recover the respect in which She was formerly held by the Republic, the Stadholder's consequence would immediately rise in proportion. These are the principal points in his conversation, as related by General O'haia, which Mr Fox recollects sufficiently to put down upon paper, but Mr. Fox will see General O'hara again before he pays his duty to Your Majesty, and will endeavour to give Your Majesty a more accurate account. General O'hara conversed also with Colonel Bentinck, whose ideas of the state of Holland corresponded entirely with the Greffier's.

St. James's Palace. *25th October*, 1783

Endorsed by the King.

No. 4497—*The King to Mr. Fox.*

Windsor, *Oct. 26th*, 1783
m. 15 *past* 9 A.M.

The Account Stated by Mr. Fox of the results of M. Gen O'hara's interview with the Greffier Fagel gives but a melancholy prospect of the P. of Orange's situation ; but where energy is wanting on one side and daring injustice is the Character of the other, the solution is natural ; a Public Minister being immediately named might perhaps be right, though I do not think much is to be expected ; if an Ambassador is the proper Character the only one that can occur would be Sir Joseph Yorke ; He certainly would not wish to stay many months, which would fill up the time till Sir James Harris can be ready to go there, and Sir Joseph would certainly carry his head high enough, which at the present hour seems absolutely incumbent on whoever goes from hence.

Draft written on a page of Mr. Fox's letter of 25 *October*, 1783.

No. 4498—*Lord North to the King.*

Lord North is very unwilling to trouble Your Majesty with the inclosed Letters and Petitions, but as they were sent to the Secretary's Office by the Sheriff He is afraid that He might be liable to blame, if he did not send them to Your Majesty, but he has sent with them the letter he has received from Mr. Nepean, which will serve to explain them, and, particularly to show that the proof brought by Thomas Daxton of his innocence though seemingly of great weight does not deserve all that attention to which, at first sight, it may seem entitled.

BUSHY PARK. *Oct. 26th*, 1783. *m. 25 past* 7 P.M.

Endorsed by the King.

No. 4499—*The King to Lord North.*

WINDSOR, *Oct. 26th*, 1783
m. 8 *past* 10 P.M.

Lord North's note very clearly shews He does not think the Petition in favour of Pilkington contains much and that it's being forwarded by Mr. Sheriff Turner is the cause of his laying it before Me, which perfectly agrees with my sentiments, as I cannot see any reason to prevent the Law taking it's course. As to the stale trick again used in favour of Daxton, it shall certainly avail nothing, therefore both convicts must suffer agreeable to the Sentence that has been pronounced.

Draft, written on a page of Lord North's letter of same date.

No. 4500—*Lord North to the King.*

Lord North is very uneasy at finding himself under the necessity of troubling His Majesty again, & is extremely unwilling to do it. In his justification, He begs leave to enclose a letter he has this moment received from Mr. Nepean, which will explain the whole matter to His Majesty : If His Majesty should be graciously pleased to grant a respite, Lord North, upon the signification of His Majesty's pleasure, [will] send an order immediately to Town and hopes it may arrive time enough.

He makes it his general rule never to send any Application to His Majesty after the report, but in his present dilemma, press'd as he is, & without any opportunity of talking with the persons who sollicit for the Convict, He is afraid that he should be thought blamable if he withheld the letter of Mr. Nepean from His Majesty's knowledge.

Tuesday morning, 1 *o'clock* A.M. *October* 28*th*

If any respite can be granted, perhaps it should be granted for a short time, till the prisoner mentioned by Sr. Robert Taylor has been tried, which he will soon be as the Sessions begin tomorrow. If that man should acknowledge himself to be the Accomplice as it is expected, Daxton may then be saved.   Otherwise, he will not be flatter'd with the hopes of finally escaping, and the Law will take its course in a very short time.

Below, in the King's handwriting,

Substance of Ans. to be respited till friday sevennight if on the trial of the Prisoner it does not come out that Daxton was not present the Law then to take its course.

WINDSOR.   *Oct.* 27, 1783.   *m.* 50 *past* 6 A.M.

Endorsed by the King.

No. 4501—*Lord Carmarthen to the King.*

Lord Carmarthen with all humility begs leave to assure Your Majesty how much he is concerned that any mistake should have arisen respecting the message with which Your Majesty honoured him to Prince Reuss.

Lord Carmarthen on leaving Your Majesty on Fryday last, went home and immediately wrote to the Prince to inform him that Your Majesty & the Queen desired to see the Prince & Princess at Windsor at twelve o'clock on Monday, this letter was directed to Prince Reuss & delivered by Lord Carmarthen's servant to Mr. Hamilton's Porter with orders to forward it to the Prince if in the Country.

Prince Reuss has been with Lord Carmarthen this morning and is extremely concerned at not having received the letter ; the Prince & Princess will not fail to wait upon Your Majesty & The Queen on Thursday next at Twelve.

WHITEHALL.   *Oct.* 30, 1 P.M.

No. 4502—*Lord North to the King.*

Lord North has been much solicited to apply to Your Majesty for a reference to Lord Gardenstone in behalf of Hugh Chisholm convicted of Receiving stolen goods at the last Council at Inverness, but the representations of Mr. Frazer on the part of the Magistrates of Inverness, prevented him for some days, but the repeated representations of Sr James Cockburn, & the character given him by the Officers of the 40th Regiment where he served with great credit, and was wounded in action, make me think it right to lay the matter before Your Majesty.

The Friends of Chisholm state that there is great prejudice of the Frazer's residing at Inverness against Chisholm ; that one of the Lads whose life was saved by being admitted as evidence against him is a near relation of the Provost of Inverness, by which circumstance the judgment of that Magistrate was biass'd ; That if he bought the goods cheap he sold them equally cheap, so as to receive only a common profit ; that he exposed the goods in an open shop, & never made the least concealment of his transactions, or endeavour'd to escape ; that the youngest of these Lads whom he is supposed to have seduced is above 21 years of age, that they sold goods to other persons, one of whom is now in prison on a charge of receiving goods from them, & that Chisholm was convicted solely upon the evidence of two accomplices whose lives were saved in consequence of the evidence they gave, & that no other evidence of any kind appear'd against him. On all these accounts, Sir James Cockburn most earnestly solicits that the case of Chisholm may be refer'd to Lord Gardenstone, notwithstanding the representations that He was so well satisfied with the verdict. If upon a review of the matter His Lordship still thinks Chisholm deserving of death, Sir James & his other friends will acquiesce, & admit that no further justice can be required on the part of the convict.

Lord North did not think it right to send this reference without laying the case at length before Your Majesty, & submitting it to Your Majesty's consideration.

Lord North was detained by this & other businesses yesterday till he was afraid that he should have kept Your Majesty too long in town, if he had requested an Audience, which prevented him from paying his duty at St. James's.

LOWER GROSVENOR STREET. *Oct. 30th*, 1783. *m. 5 past* 11 A.M.

Endorsed by the King.

No. 4503—*The King to Lord North.*

I will not object to Ld. North's sending the Papers relating to Hugh Chisholm to Ld. Gardenstone, and if necessary to his granting a respite till his report can be received ; the case I should imagine will not turn out favourable ; and Sir James Cockburne chusing to defame the conduct of the Provost of Inverness rather appears as if prejudice was as strong in the friends of the convict as in the family of Frazers. I look upon strict justice as the only line I can hold as an honest Man ; therefore on the Report of the Judge I shall act, and if He is clear against Chisholm, Sir James shall know his aspersions of Men of Character is highly blameable.

WINDSOR. *Oct. 30th*, 1783. *m. 30 pt.* 3 P.M.

Draft, written at the foot of Lord North's letter of same date.

No. 4504—*The Duke of Portland to the King.*

The Duke of Portland most humbly begs leave to lay before Your Majesty the draft of Your Majesty's Speech proposed for the opening of the Session, and most Dutifully to submit it to Your Majesty's Royal Consideration.

DOWNING STREET. *Tuesday, 4th November*, 1783. 4 *o'clock* P.M.

Below, in the King's handwriting :

I have just received the Draft of the Speech which the D. of Portland has sent & to which I make no objection.

WINDSOR. *Nov.* 4, 1783. *m. 30 pt.* 7 P.M.

Endorsed by the King.

No. 4505—*Lord North to the King.*

Lord North has the honor of transmitting to Your Majesty Copies of the Licenses granted to Lord Dillon to continue in the French, & to Mr. Fitzgerald to enter into the Spanish service. He has accompanied them with a License for Mr. James Eyre, drawn upon the model of the others, & containing, as well as the others, a restriction with respect to the enemies of Great Britain.

Lord North had the honour of applying to Your Majesty a few years ago in behalf of this Mr. James Eyre in order to obtain Your Majesty's Royal License for him to serve in the Imperial Army, but that project by some means or other, appears to have failed. Lord North had the honour of mentioning on the former occasion that he was acquainted with Mr. and Lady Mary Eyre, the Parents of Mr. James Eyre, & knew them to be very deserving & respectable.

Lord North has the honour of inclosing a letter which the Duke of Portland has received from Mr. Justice Heath, and which seems substantially to amount to a Report in favour of a young Irishman who was condemn'd at Exeter for forging a Frank.

WHITEHALL. *Nov. 5th. m. 35 past 4*

Endorsed by the King.

No. 4506—*The King to Lord North.*

[5 *November*, 1783.]

Signed the License and pardoned the Convict on condition of his transporting himself for life out of the Island.

Draft, written at the foot of Lord North's letter of same date.

No. 4507—*Mr. Fox to the King.*

Mr. Fox avoided troubling Your Majesty with an Audience today on account of the lateness of the hour, lest it might have incommoded Your Majesty ; but he humbly recommends to Your

Majesty to attend to the two Interceptions from Potzdam & Berlin in which his Prussian Majesty's sentiments with regard to the Prince of Orange's affairs seem to deserve notice. Mr. Fox having by some mistake missed seeing M. de Simolin yesterday, did not till this morning receive the very important papers delivered to him by that Minister.

St. James's.   5 *November*, 1783

Endorsed by the King.

No. 4508—*The Duke of Portland to the King.*

The Duke of Portland most humbly begs leave to acquaint Your Majesty that exception having been taken by All the Gentlemen who met this evening at Mr. Fox's, to that sentence of the Speech which states, that, " alarming outrages in defiance of all law have been committed " as not being distinctly enough pointed to the practice of smuggling, as being liable to misconstruction, & possibly applicable to the supposed State of Ireland, it has been thought adviseable to make the alteration inserted in the margin of the Speech herewith transmitted to Your Majesty, wherein the words proposed to be left out are underlined, which is most Dutifully submitted to Your Majesty's consideration.

Downing Street.   *Sunday night, 9th November,* 1783

Endorsed by the King.

No. 4509—*Lord Hertford to the King.*

Sire—I returned to town last night after a long indulgence which Your Majesty has been pleased to give me, & should have taken the first moment of making my acknowledgements in person if Your Majesty's residence had made it proper.

In these circumstances Your Majesty will permit me to lay before You by this means (as I may have no other opportunity before the occasion occurs) some entries which Lord Southampton has just put into my hands respecting the Prince of Wales's introduction into the House of Peers, forwarded him by Mr. Hiatt in pursuance of Your Majesty's Commands.

By the ceremonial prescribed therein, I perceive that His Royal Highness is to be seated previously to Your Majesty going to the House & that Your Lord Chamberlain is one of the great officers included in the Ceremony.

It will therefore require Your Majesty's Commands for my conduct, as I shall by my attendance on this service necessarily neglect that upon Your Majesty's own person at St. James's.

I shall likewise be very happy to learn from Your Majesty's judgment, as it is not specified in the entry to whom the Crown which the Prince of Wales is to have laid before him is to be delivered ; I presume to some Officer of his own Household but I am fearful of giving any opinion which is not dictated by Your Majesty.

I have the honor to be with all possible duty and respect, Sire, Your Majesty's most faithful & most obedient humble servt,

LONDON. *Nov. 9th,* 1783   HERTFORD.

No. 4510—*The King to the Duke of Portland.*

The objection to the Sentence in the Speech seems very material and the Amendment certainly rectifies it ; perhaps if smuggling were still clearer specified it would not be improper.

WINDSOR. *Nov. 10th,* 1783. *m.* 35 *pt.* 7 A.M.

Draft, written on a page of the Duke of Portland's letter of 9 *November,* 1783.

No. 4511—*The Duke of Portland to the King.*

The Duke of Portland most dutifully offers to Your Majesty a copy of the Speech altered in the manner by which Your Majesty is pleased to think the objection suggested at Mr. Fox's will be rectified, & begs leave to assure Your Majesty that he has not been wanting in his endeavours to specify more clearly that the Outrages have been committed in the Practice of Smuggling, but has not been fortunate enough to devise any form of words, with which he is sufficiently satisfied, to submit to Your Majesty's consideration, & therefore humbly presumes to rest upon the Opinion Your Majesty has graciously condescended to express of the proposed amendment to the Paragraph, as it will now stand. The Duke of Portland most humbly presents to Your Majesty a copy of the intended Address of the House of Lords to Your Majesty, & of the Message to The Queen, the former of which the Earl of Scarborough has under taken to move for, & will be seconded by Lord Hampden, & the latter will be moved by the Earl of Powis. The Duke of Portland begs leave with all humility to acquaint Your Majesty that by a private Letter from Ireland of the 3rd inst., which he has just received, he is informed that Mr. Flood intended on that day to go at large into the State of that Nation, & that it was understood that he intended to attack the Military Establishment in point of economy that Government was fully prepared to meet it in all respects.

DOWNING STREET. *Monday, 10th November, 1783.* 3 *o'clock* P.M.

Endorsed by the King.

No. 4512—*The King to the Duke of Portland.*

I have received a Copy of the Speech as corrected at the Meeting last night, as also of the proposed Address of the House of Lords and Message from that House to the Queen.

I am not sufficiently Master of the subject of the Post Office Regulations proposed from Ireland to give a decided opinion, though it appears as if from thence as usual some unfair advantage is sought for.

WINDSOR. *Nov. 10th, 1783. m. 23 pt. 6* P.M.

Draft, written on a page of the Duke of Portland's letter of same date.

No. 4513—*The Duke of Portland to the King.*

The Duke of Portland conceiving it his Duty to submit to Your Majesty any alterations which may have been thought necessary in the Address of the House of Lords as well as in the Speech, most humbly requests Your Majesty's permission to lay before Your

Majesty another Copy of the Address which has undergone a very material correction which will appear by a Line drawn under the words newly inserted ; the propriety of which was suggested by an apprehension of umbrage being taken by The Courts of France & Spain at the manner in which that Paragraph was originally worded.

DOWNING STREET. *Monday night.* 10 *November,* 1783.

Endorsed by the King.

No. 4514—*The King to the Duke of Portland.*

I have received this Morning a Copy of the intended Address of the House of Lords with the proposed omission in the Paragraph which relates to the Definitive Treaties and Preliminary Articles.

WINDSOR. *Nov.* 11*th,* 1783. *m.* 30 *pt.* 7 A.M.

Draft, written on a page of the Duke of Portland's letter of 10 *November,* 1783.

No. 4515—*The Duke of Portland to the King.*

The Duke of Portland most humbly begs leave to acquaint Your Majesty, that excepting a short speech from Ld. Temple arraigning the affected mysteriousness of the Speech, and stating the Topicks on which it ought to have been more explicitly detailed, No opposition or observation was made to or upon the Address, which as Ld. Temple had not objected to the purport of it passed, Nemine Dissentiente.

As Lord North informed the Duke of Portland that he had not received any dispatches from Ireland, he presumes with all humility to inform Your Majesty that by a private Letter from thence, written at the rising of the House of Commons on Monday the 3rd at midnight, Mr. Flood's motion for a reduction of the Military Establishment had been rejected by a Majority of 138 to 54.

DOWNING STREET. *Tuesday,* 11 *Novr* 1783. *m.* 20 *past* 5 P.M.

Endorsed by the King.

No. 4516—*The King to the Duke of Portland.*

I have this instant received the Duke of Portland's intimation of the Address having been Assented to without any dissent ; as also that Mr. Flood's motion for a reduction of the Military Establishment had been rejected by a Majority of 138 to 54.

Nov. 11th, 1783. *m.* 12 past 6 P.M.

Draft, written on a page of the Duke of Portland's letter of same date.

No. 4517—*The Duke of Portland to the King.*

The Duke of Portland begs leave with all humility to submit to Your Majesty the draft of an answer to the Address of the House of Lords.

DOWNING STREET. *Wednesday,* 12 *Nov.* 1783. 11 *o'clock* A.M.

Endorsed by the King.

No. 4518—*The King to the Duke of Portland.*

I do not mean to object to the Answer to the Address, therefore desire the D. of Portland will order the fair Copy to be prepared ; the House of Lords are as usual appointed at two this Day.

QUEEN'S HOUSE. *Nov. 12th,* 1783. *m.* 35 P.M.

Draft, written on a page of the Duke of Portland's letter of same date.

No. 4519—*Lord Dartmouth to the King.*

Lord Dartmouth must not presume to express the sense he entertains of Yr. Majesty's goodness otherwise than by assuring Your Majesty that the Bust will ever be dear to him on many accounts, & that it is the very sincere & earnest wish of his heart that he could make himself worthy of so distinguished a mark of Your Majesty's favor, & regard, the sense of which will ever be one of the comforts of his life.

ST. JAMES'S SQUARE. 14 *Novr.* 1783.

No. 4520—*Lord Temple to the King.*

PALL MALL, *Nov.* 15*th*, 1783

SIRE—In consequence of the gracious communications with which Your Majesty was pleased to honour me on Friday the 7th inst., Mr. Pitt and I think it our duty to submit in this mode which we imagine may be most agreeable to Your Majesty, and for Your Majesty's private information, that on Thursday last an opening was made to Mr Pitt on the part of Mr. Fox, inviting him to discuss the measure of acceding to the present coalition, which without waiting for explanation was immediately negatived by Mr. Pitt. As various circumstances seemed then to point out the possibility of this ineffectual attempt being followed by more distinct propositions, we have delayed till this moment troubling Your Majesty with the communication of it.

I have the honour to be, with the most inviolable duty and attachment, Sire, Your Majesty's most dutiful & devoted subject & servant, NUGENT TEMPLE.

Endorsed by the King.

No. 4521—*Lord North to the King.*

Lord Sydney having thought it right last year to forbid the Directors of the E. India Company transmitting to India the resolutions of the Court of Proprietors respecting Mr. Hastings, & having, upon laying the matter before the House of Commons, met with their approbation, Lord North, as that business continues in the same state, has thought it his duty to prevent in the same manner the transmission of the Resolutions of the Court of Proprietors of the 7th of this month, & has the honour of sending to his Majesty the letter he has directed on this occasion, accompanied by the Draught of the Directors' Orders & by Lord Sydney's letter.

Nov. 16. 1783. 40 *minutes past three* P.M.

Lord North has the honour of transmitting to His Majesty a letter he has just received from Sir Francis Buller containing a request to ride through the Park.

Endorsed by the King.

No. 4522—*The King to Lord North.*

Printed. Donne II. 445.

Lord Sydney's having prevented the Directors of the East India Company the last Year transmitting to India the Resolutions of the Court of Proprietors respecting Mr. Hastings, and the business being in the same situation now, Lord North seems warranted in giving a similar prohibition.

Mr. Justice Buller may have liberty to ride through the Park.

WINDSOR. *Nov. 16th*, 1783. *m. 47 past* 7 P.M.

Draft, written on a page of Lord North's letter of same date. Another copy in the King's handwriting.

No. 4523—*The Duke of Portland to the King.*

The Duke of Portland most humbly begs leave to acquaint Your Majesty that Mr. Lee & Mr. Mansfield are most anxious to acknowledge the sentiments of Duty & Gratitude in which they are bound by Your Majesty's most Gracious Favour, & to show the most implicit Obedience to the Commands Your Majesty was pleased to direct the Duke of Portland to convey to them respecting their succession to the Offices of Your Majesty's Attorney and Solicitor General, & Mr. Mansfield having intimated to the Duke of Portland that many difficulties might probably be prevented by his being enabled to proceed speedily to his re-election, the Duke of Portland ventures to hope that Your Majesty will not disapprove the intention of moving tomorrow for new Writs for the Borough of Clitheroe & for the University of Cambridge.

DOWNING STREET. *Sunday night,* 16 *Novr.* 1783

Endorsed by the King.

No. 4524—*The King to the Duke of Portland.*

The Duke of Portland has done very properly in directing new Writs to be moved this day for the University of Cambridge and the Borough of Clitheroe, on the Successions in the Law Departments occasioned by the death of the late worthy Attorney General.

WINDSOR. *Nov. 17th*, 1783. *m. 50 past* 8 A.M.

Draft, written on a page of the Duke of Portland's letter of 16 *November, 1783.*

No. 4525—*Lord North to the King.*

Lord North has the honour of transmitting to His Majesty a letter he has just received from Mr. Mathias, Lord Guildford's Deputy. He is very sorry to hear of the misfortune that has happen'd, but he has learnt from Mr. Mathias that Her Majesty's loss does not exceed fifteen guineas. Lord North has the honour of submitting Mr. Mathias's request to His Majesty's consideration.

Nov. 19th

Endorsed by the King.

No. 4526—*The King to Lord North.*

Lord North should apprize the Field Officer in Waiting of the Foot Guards with the application for a Centinel to be placed at the Queen's Treasury and desire Him when I give the Parole tomorrow to mention it to Me.

QUEEN'S HOUSE. *Nov. 19th*, 1783. *m. 37 pt.* 5 P.M.

Draft, written on a page of Lord North's letter of same date.

No. 4527—*Lord North to the King.*

Lord North has the honour of informing His Majesty that Governor Johnston made a motion at the India House today for referring to the standing council of the Company the resignation of Mr. Hastings and consequent appointment of Mr. Wheler, but a previous question was put upon it, and a majority of 107 votes against 38 decided against putting Governor Johnston's question.

DOWNING STREET, *Wednesday night*, 12 *o'clock, Novr.* 20th

No. 4528—*Major General Haldimand to Lord Amherst.*

Copy. Quebec *le* 20*e Nobe.* 1783.

My Lord—Un Paquet arrivé depuis deux jours par la Voye d'Halifax, ma enfin apporté des Lettres du 8me Aoust qui m'anoncent la reduction, et le nouvel Etablissement qui est fixé pour cette Province, et quoy qu'on aye reduit les appointements du Genl. en Chef de la Moitié, Sa Majesté souhaittant que je continue icy sur ce pied la ; Je n'ay pas hesitté un Moment dans la persuasion que je puis étre Utille a son Service, seul Mottif qui puisse M'engagér à rester icy ; Je souhaitterais Seulement d'avoir l'assistance de Personnes actives et qui coñoissent le Pays, et Je ne connois personne qui puisse Mieux remplir ces Vues que le Genl. Christie ; Mais puisquon à reduit ce comendement à un Lt. General et un Brigadier : Je ne sais par quele Moyen Il pouroit étre employé, Mais au cas Mi Lord que vous y puissiés contribuer, ce seroit Un Nouveau Service que Vous rendriés a ce Pays.

Le Vaisseau devant Mettre à la Voille Je n'ay que le temps d'offrir Mes humbles respects a Mi Lady Amherst, et de Vous asseurer Mi Lord de la Vraye Estime et du parfait Devouement avec les quels J'ay l'honneur d'etre Mi Lord, Votre tres humble et tres obeissant Serviteur, Fred. Haldimand.

No. 4529—*Lord North to the King.*

Lord North has the honour of transmitting to His Majesty, with Lord Northington's publick letters, two private ones, one concerning the calling Mr. Prime Serjeant Kelly & Mr. Fitzgibbon to the Privy Council, and the other for appointing Mr. Yelverton, Chief Baron.

Lord North understands that Mr. Kelly will be made a Puisne Judge & Mr. Scott appointed Prime Serjeant in his room. These nominations of Mr. Scott & Mr. Fitzgibbon show that the Lord Lieutenant is obliged to have recourse to the old servants of the Castle, & the affairs of the Government will probably go on the better for it.

The other letter respects a renewal of Lord Antrim's petition for a remainder of his honours to his daughters, in case of failure of male issue.   If Lord North was not apprized of the favour His Majesty granted to Lord Sheffield, it was owing to Mr. Windham's illness, & continuance at Oxford, as Lord North had desired him to mention it to the Lord Lieutenant.

Lord North adds a letter from the Recorder concerning his report.   Lord North intended to have taken His Majesty's pleasure upon it this morning, but the House of Commons yesterday had so increased the swelling of his leg this morning that he found it difficult to walk.

Friday Night [28 *November*, 1783]

Endorsed by the King.

No. 4530—*The King to Lord North.*

Printed.   Donne II. 445.

The Appointment of Mr. Yelverton to be Chief Baron, and of Mr. Kelly and Mr. Fitzgibbons to be Privy Counsellors in Ireland may be prepared agreeable to the Lord Lieutenant's recommendations.   I am glad to hear Mr. Scott is proposed to be Prime Serjeant ;   He certainly was a very faithful Servant of the Crown when Attorney General.   Ireland is in fact disunited from this Kingdom, whether He can be of the use he was previous to the sad Measures that have been adopted, I am totally ignorant.   Lord Antrim should have the answer that his request will be at a proper time considered ;   but accompanied with the declaration that it is a favour that will be rarely granted, that other Suitors may not be brought forward.   The Recorder may make his Report on Wednesday.

WINDSOR.   *Nov. 29th*, 1783.   *m.* 46 *past* 7 A.M.

Draft, written on a page of Lord North's letter of 28 *November,* 1783.

Another copy in the King's handwriting.

No. 4531—*Lord North to the King.*

Lord North has the honour of informing His Majesty that he has heard from his Office that Mr. Thompson call'd there today and press'd very much to have the necessary instruments sign'd for his investment tomorrow, which Lord North has done, & hopes that Mr. Thompson will have prepared everything else, but is afraid everything will hardly be ready at so short a notice.

Monday evening, Decr. 2 [1783]. *Nine* P.M.

Endorsed by the King.

No. 4532—*The King to Lord North.*

I very clearly told the D. of Portland on Friday that till I received the Ensigns of the Order of the Bath I should not think of filling up the Vacancy ; therefore as Lord North has Summoned a Chapter this day without my knowledge I must insist on his forbidding it till He has further orders from Me.

WINDSOR. *Dec. 4th,* 1783. *m.* 30 *past* 7 A.M.

Draft, written on a page of Lord North's letter of 2 December, 1783.

No. 4533—*Lord North to the King.*

Lord North has the honour of transmitting to Your Majesty a letter he has just received from the Recorder, with an inclosure from Mr. Justice Nares, recommending to Your Majesty's mercy one of the Convicts, whose case was reported yesterday to Your Majesty, but the Recorder, though he mention'd the recommendation of the Prosecutor, forgot to mention the recommendation of the Judge.

Thursday, Decr. 4, 1783

Endorsed by the King.

No. 4534—*The King to Lord North.*

John Smith to be sent to the Hulks for three Years as Transportation at the present moment is impracticable.

ST. JAMES'S. *Dec. 4th,* 1783. *m.* 37 *pt. one* P.M.

Draft, written on a page of Lord North's letter of same date.

No. 4535—*The Duke of Portland to the King.*

The Duke of Portland unwilling to delay for a moment the intelligence contained in Mr. Pelham's letter, humbly offers it to Your Majesty's perusal & anxiously hopes it will confirm the Satisfaction Your Majesty was graciously pleased to express at the prospect of this event.

DOWNING STREET. *Thursday,* 4 *Decr.* 1783. *m.* 45 *past* 4 P.M.

Endorsed by the King.

No. 4536—*The King to the Duke of Portland.*

I am highly pleased at the House of Commons as stated by Mr. Pelham having with Spirit withstood the motion for introducing a Reform Bill, and lose no time in returning it to the Duke of Portland.

QUEEN'S HOUSE. *Decr.* 4*th,* 1783. *m.* 3 *past* 6 P.M.

Draft, written on a page of the Duke of Portland's letter of same date.

No. 4537—*The King to Lord North.*

Lord North's idea that Mr. Sheriff Skinner is not very eager for the case He is employed to solicit seems on the face of his letter well founded ; but were it otherwise nothing appears that can justify altering the Sentence.   G. R.

WINDSOR. *Dec.* 7*th,* 1783. *m.* 15 *pt.* 4 P.M.

No. 4538—*Lord North to the King.*

Lord North has the honour of informing His Majesty that Mr. Flood is now in the House of Commons, & has, probably, in his pocket the address from the National Convention to which Mr. Pelham alludes in his letter to Mr. North.

HO. OF COMMONS, 9 *o'clock* [8 *December,* 1783]

Endorsed by the King.

No. 4539—*The King to Lord North.*

Printed. Donne II. 446.

I entirely coincide in the opinion given by Mr. Pelham that the Address of the Volunteers should if possible not be received ; but as Mr. Flood may without saying anything present it at the Levee, it ought to be considered whether in that case it should be by the Lord of the Bedchamber returned to Him ; the case is new and therefore ought to be thought on.   G. R.

WINDSOR. *Decr. 9th,* 1783. *m.* 55 *pt.* 7 A.M.

Draft, written on a page of Lord North's letter of 8 December, 1783.

Another copy in the King's handwriting.

No. 4540—*The Duke of Portland to the King.*

The Duke of Portland begs leave with all humility to inform Your Majesty that the Bill for regulating the affairs of the East India Company was brought this day from the House of Commons & read a first time & ordered to be read a second time on next Monday without a word of objection or obstruction from either side of The House—that after that Business was closed, a question was put by Lord Temple respecting the extent of the Evidence intended to be laid before the House, which being answered by the Duke of Portland, who thought the Papers already upon the Table contained sufficient matter to shew the necessity of the Bill which had been just introduced, though he at the same time declared it not to be his intention to object to such further evidence as might be thought necessary, or even to preclude himself from asking for more information if any other should occur to him to be requisite, a very desultory Conversation arose in which it was insisted that the House could not proceed with propriety upon this Bill unless every particle of evidence which had been laid before the House and Committees of the Commons was brought upon the Table, the whole merits of the Bill were very fully discussed, & the conduct of those who recorded their objections to the East India Regulating Bill in 1773 was most severely arraigned. This conversation was supported on one side by the Dukes of Richmond & Chandos & the Lords Thurlow, Temple, Sydney & Abingdon, & on the other by the Lords Lough-borough, Townshend, Derby, Carlisle & The Duke of Portland, and was not put an end to till near nine o'clock, when a Petition from the East India Company praying to be heard by their Counsel against the second reading of the Bill was presented by Lord Temple : & agreed to by the House which then adjourned to tomorrow.

DOWNING STREET. *Tuesday even. 9 Decr. 1783. m. 40 past nine o'clock.*

Endorsed by the King.

No. 4541—*The Duke of Portland to the King.*

The Duke of Portland humbly begs leave to acquaint Your Majesty that when the Council had proceeded some way in examining Witnesses & reading written Evidence against the East India Bill, it was moved to adjourn, which being opposed, was carried after some debate, the numbers were Contents 69 ; Proxies 18 ; Not Contents 57, Proxies 22.

DOWNING STREET. *Tuesday morn. 16 December, 1783. half past one o'clock*

Endorsed by the King.

The division lists are enclosed, but are not printed.

No. 4542—*The King to the Duke of Portland.*

I have just received the Duke of Portland's note acquainting me with the Division on a question of Adjournment on the East India Bill.

WINDSOR. *Dec. 16th, 1783. m. 30 past 9 A.M.*

Draft, written on a page of the Duke of Portland's letter of same date.

No. 4543—*The Duke of Portland to the King.*

The Duke of Portland most humbly begs permission to acquaint Your Majesty that the Commitment of the East India Bill has been negatived by a Majority, Proxies included, of 19. The Contents were 57, Proxies 19 ; The Not Contents 75, Proxies 20 & the Bill was afterwards rejected without a Division.

DOWNING STREET. *Wednesday,* 17 *Decr.* 1783. *at midnight.*

No. 4544—*A list of certain members of the House of Lords.*

[In the King's handwriting.]

[? *December,* 1783]

H.R.H. D. of Gloucester.		E. of Graham.
H.R.H. D. of Cumberland.		E. Ker.
D. of Norfolk	.. Papist.	E. of Ashburnham
D. of Somerset.		E. of Oxford.
D. of Grafton.		E. of Portsmouth.
D. of Beaufort.		Vt. Montague.
D. of St. Albans.		Vt. Falmouth.
D. of Bedford ..	.. Minor.	Vt. Torrington.
D. of Newcastle.		Vt. Dudley.
D. of Montagu.		Vt. Mount Edgcumbe.
E. of Shrewsbury	.. Papist.	Ld. Clifford of Appleby Minor.
E. of Northampton.		Ld. Dacre.
E. of Thanet		Ld. Stourton .. Papist.
E. of Shaftesbury	.. Minor.	Ld. Petre .. .. do.
E. Berkley.		Ld. Arundel of Wardour do.
E. of Gainsborough.		Ld. Clifton .. Minor.
E. of Rochford.		Ld. Dormer .. Papist.
E. of Albemarle	.. Minor.	Ld. Leigh.
E. Poulett.		Ld. Byron.
E. of Strafford.		Ld. Clifford of Chudley Papist.
E. of Bristol.		Ld. Godolphin
E. Cowper.		Ld. Hay
E. of Pomfret.		Ld Ravensworth

Ld. Wycombe		Ld. Porchester.	
Ld. Stawel		Ld. Ashburton .. Minor.	
Ld. Holland .. Minor.			
Ld. Lovel.		E. Dalhousie.	
Ld. Milton.		Bp. of Hereford.	
Ld. Ducie.		Bp. of Chichester.	
Ld. Sundridge.		Bp. of Bath & Wells.	
Ld. Mount Stuart.		Bp of Ely	
Ld. Southampton.		Bp. of Landaff.	

No. 4545—*Lord North to the King.*

Lord North has the honour of transmitting to His Majesty a copy of the Address from the Delegates of the Volunteers in Ireland, which was put into Lord North's hands yesterday by Mr. Flood, who will present the address at the Levee tomorrow. As the Address is, in itself, respectful, & exceptionable only as coming from such a body as the Convention of Volunteers, Lord North imagines that it would be liable to objection if His Majesty were to refuse to receive the address. It may be question'd whether it ought to be printed in the Gazette. His Majesty has already declined to treat it with any peculiar marks of favour, & His Majesty's receiving the Address can never be construed into an acknowledgement of the legality of the National Convention.

Dec. 18*th,* 1783

Endorsed by the King.

No. 4546—*The King to Lord North.*

Lord North Is by this required to send Me the Seals of His Department, and to acquaint Mr. Fox to send those of the Foreign Department. Mr. Frazer or Mr. Nepean will be the proper Channel of delivering them to Me this Night; I choose this method as Audiences on such occasions must be unpleasant.

QUEEN'S HOUSE. *Dec.* 18*th,* 1783. *m.* 43 *past* 10 P.M.

Draft, endorsed by the King.

No. 4547—*Lord North to the King.*

Lord North has, in obedience to His Majesty's commands, sent Mr. Nepean with the Seals of the Home department, and has communicated His Majesty's pleasure to Mr. Fox.

December 18, 1783

Endorsed by the King.

No. 4548—*The King to Lord Stormont.*

Things are so situated that I cannot but change the present Administration : I can easily conceive that Lord Stormont cannot immediately take a share in a new one ; but after His handsome conduct before He accepted the Presidency of the Council, I should not do justice to my feelings if I did not thus express to Him my sorrow at His being out of my Service.

QUEEN'S HOUSE. *Dec.* 19*th*, 1783. *m.* 48 *pt.* 9 A.M.

Draft, endorsed by the King.

No. 4549—*Lord Temple to the King.*

PALL MALL. *Friday morn.* 20 *m. p.* 10
[19 *December*, 1783]

SIRE—The extreme lateness of the hour at which I left Your Majesty last night delayed my notes so much that most of the Lords to whom I conveyed Your Majesty's Commands to attend You at ten o'clock did not receive them till this morning. Under these circumstances I fear that we may not be so punctual as we could wish, but we hope for Your Majesty's excuse.

I have the honour to be, with the highest duty & respect, Sire, Your Majesty's most devoted & obedient Subject & servt.

NUGENT TEMPLE.

Endorsed by the King.

No. 4550—*Viscount Stormont to the King.*

Lord Stormont has this moment received Your Majesty's most gracious Note and is penetrated with the deepest and most grateful sense of the Goodness Your Majesty has shewn him upon this as upon every other occasion.

Decr. 19, 1783. 25 *m. p.* 10 A.M.

Endorsed by the King.

No. 4551—*Lord Temple to the King.*

Lord Temple humbly presumes to acquaint Your Majesty that a debate has been started upon the question of adjournment which Dr. Dundas has moved for tomorrow, & which is proposed to be amended for Monday next with the professed view of delaying the supplies. L. Thurlow had desired that the letters to the Lord Commissioners of the great seal might be delayed in the contingency of such an event, till the complexion of things were more clearly ascertained, which measure we hope will meet Your Majesty's approbation.

PALL MALL. *Friday, Dec.* 18*th* [19*th*, 1783]. *m.* 40 *p.* 6.

Endorsed by the King.

No. 4552—*The King to Lord Temple.*

I am so fully persuaded that both the Earl Temple and Lord Thurlow must feel that it is impossible for Me to retract ; and that consequently the delay proposed as to the time of receiving the Great Seal from the Commissioners can be only matter of decorum : I do not object to their settling it in the mode most agreeable to their own judgement ; I trust I shall hear farther on the event of the House of Commons, though the Coalition is so strong there that the event must depend on their own temper, not the propriety of the question.

QUEEN'S HOUSE. *Dec.* 19*th*, 1783. *m.* 48 *pt.* 7 P.M.

Draft, written on a page of Lord Temple's letter of same date.

No. 4553—*Lord Temple to the King.*

Lord Temple humbly presumes to inform Your Majesty that he has just seen Mr. Dundass who reports the Opposition made to the Motion to have been couched in eager terms, but at the same time very ambiguous as to the ultimate intention respecting the supplies. Lord Thurlow will be here in the course of a short time & Your Majesty's note shall be communicated to him ; but in all events, little can be conclusively argued from the resolution to adjourn till Monday.

PALL MALL. *Decr.* 18*th* [19*th*], 1783. 45 *m. p.* 8 P.M.

Endorsed by the King.

INDEX

Abingdon, Lord, see Bertie, Willoughby
Accra, capture of, 3849
Act 6, George I., repeal of, 3789
Adam, Mr., 4124
Addington, Mr., 4314
Advocate, The Lord, see Dundas, Henry
Affleck, Commodore, 3761, 3762, 3958
Akerman, Mr., gaoler of Newgate, 4406
Albemarle, Lord, see Keppel, William
Alfred, Prince, death of, 3886
Allaire, Mr., p. 339
Almodovar, Mons., 4179, 4180
Amelia, Princess, birth of, 4436
American Colonies—
    America and the negotiations for peace, see Peace
    address from merchants of, 4263, 4264
    debts to British merchants, 3979
    address from loyalists, p. 383
    proposal to send convicts to, 4413, 4414, 4419, 4420
Amherst, Jeffery, Lord, letter to, 4528
Antrim, Lord, see McDonnell, Randal
Apsley, Lord, see Bathurst
Arcot, Nabob of, 4291, 4292
Arden, Pepper (Solicitor - General), 3949, 3950, 4363, 4408
Army, The British—
    mutiny of the 68th and 77th Regiments, 4089-92, 4095-8, 4113, 4137
    mutiny of the 104th, 4251, 4252
Arnald, Dr., 3852, 3884, 4463
Arran, Earl of, see Gore, Arthur
Ashburton, Lord, see Dunning, John
Austria, see Peace negotiations and Keith, Sir R. Murray-

Bagott, Lord, 4150
Bahama Islands, 4001, 4007, 4019

Bailey, Major, 4089
Baker, Mr., 3723
Balguy, Dr., 3718, 3726
Ball, Capt., 3748
Balster, Mary, 3799, 3800
Bangor, Bishop of, 4265, 4266
Barclay, Mr., 4222, 4223
Baring, Mr., 3941, 3942, 3959
Barnard, Frederick Augustus, p. 372
Barré, Col., 3729, p. 78, 3841, 3886, p. 337, 4363
Barrington, Vice-Admiral, 3782, 3886, 4053
Basset, Sir Francis, 4124
Bates, Mr., 3715
Bathurst, Henry, Earl of, 3779, 4185
    Letter from, 4136
Bathurst, Henry, Lord Apsley, 4282
Bavaria, Duke of, 4449
Beauchamp, Lord, see Seymour, Francis
Beaufoy, Mr., 4342
Belgioioso, Count (Austrian Ambassador), see Belgioso
Belgioso, Count de, 3794, 3815, 3816
Bellamont, Earl of, see Coote
Bentinck, Col., 4496
Bernard, Major, 4212, 4216, 4217
Bertie, Capt., 3858
Bertie, Willoughby, Earl of Abingdon, 4306, 4396, 4540
Bickerton, Commodore Sir Richard, 3860
Blyswick, Mons., 4496
Boerse, Mr., 4486
Bootle, Mr. W., 4124
Boyd, Lieut.-Gen., 4310, 4311
Boyd, Mrs., 4310
Bridges, Mr., 4463
British merchants, American debts to, 3979
Broadstreet, Stephen, 4291, 4292
Bromedge, Capt., 3898

481

486 PAPERS OF GEORGE III

George III., King (contd.)—
Letters from (contd.)—
4115, 4122, 4123, 4125, 4127,
4129, 4131, 4133, 4139, 4140,
4142, 4143, 4145, 4150, 4152,
4153, 4155, 4157, 4160, 4166,
4168, 4170, 4171, 4173, 4176,
4178, 4180, 4181, 4184, 4187,
4189, 4191, 4193, 4196, 4199,
4200, 4202, 4203, 4205, 4208,
4211, 4213, 4217, 4218, 4223,
4226, 4228, 4230, 4232, 4233,
4237, 4238, 4242, 4244, 4246,
4247, 4250, 4251, 4256, 4257,
4259, 4260, 4264, 4265, 4268,
4271, 4272, 4274, 4278, 4280,
4283, 4284, 4286, 4290, 4292,
4295, 4297, 4299, 4301, 4302,
4304, 4307, 4311, 4314, 4316,
4319, 4322, 4325, 4327, 4331,
4333, 4336, 4339, 4341, 4343,
4346, 4348, 4350, 4352, 4354,
4357, 4360, 4364, 4365, 4371,
4375, 4377, 4384, 4386-8, 4391,
4393, 4395, 4397, 4399, 4401,
4403, 4405, 4412, 4414, 4417,
4420, 4422, 4426, 4430, 4436,
4438, 4441, 4446, 4448, 4452,
4454, 4457, 4459, 4461, 4463,
4468, 4470, 4472, 4474, 4477,
4480, 4484, 4486, 4487, 4489,
4493, 4495, 4497, 4499, 4503,
4510, 4512, 4514, 4516, 4518,
4522, 4524, 4530, 4532, 4534,
4536, 4537, 4539, 4542, 4546,
4548, 4552
Letters to
1782 : 3704, 3706, 3707, 3709,
3710, 3712, 3716, 3717, 3720,
3723-7, 3729-32, 3735, 3736,
3738, 3739, 3742, 3743, 3745,
3746, 3748, 3749, 3751, 3753-5,
3757, 3758, 3761, 3763, 3765,
3766, 3769, 3771, 3773, 3775-7,
3779, 3780, 3782, 3784, 3785,
3787-90, 3792, 3794, 3796, 3798,
3799, 3801, 3802, 3804, 3807,
3809, 3810, 3813, 3815, 3817,
3818, 3822, 3824, 3826, 3828,
3831-3, 3835, 3837, 3839, 3840,
3842, 3844, 3846, 3848, 3850,
3852, 3853, 3856, 3858, 3860-2,
3864, 3866, 3868, 3870, 3873-5,
3877, 3879, 3880, 3882, 3884,
3886, 3888, 3890, 3891, 3893,
3895, 3897, 3898, 3901-3, 3905,

George III., King (contd.)—
Letters to (contd.—
3907, 3908, 3911, 3912, 3914,
3916, 3918, 3920, 3922, 3924,
3926, 3929, 3930, 3932, 3933,
3936, 3938, 3939, 3941, 3943-5,
3948, 3949, 3951, 3953, 3954,
3958, 3959, 3961, 3963-5, 3967,
3969, 3970, 3972, 3974, 3977,
3980-3, 3985, 3986, 3989, 3991,
3993, 3996, 3998, 3999, 4001,
4003, 4005, 4008, 4010, 4011,
4013, 4014, 4017, 4018, 4024,
4025, 4027, 4030, 4032, 4033,
4035, 4036, 4038, 4040, 4042,
4046, 4048
1783 : 4052, 4054, 4056, 4058-60,
4063, 4065, 4066, 4068, 4070,
4072, 4073, 4076, 4078, 4080,
4083, 4084, 4087, 4089, 4091,
4093, 4095, 4097, 4099, 4100,
4103-6, 4108, 4109, 4111, 4112,
4114, 4117-21, 4124, 4126, 4128,
4130, 4132, 4134-8, 4141, 4144,
4146-9, 4151, 4154, 4156, 4158,
4159, 4161-5, 4172, 4174, 4175,
4177, 4179, 4182, 4183, 4186,
4188, 4190, 4192, 4194, 4195,
4197, 4198, 4201, 4204, 4206,
4207, 4209, 4210, 4212, 4214-16,
4219-22, 4224, 4225, 4227, 4229,
4231, 4234-6, 4239, 4240, 4243,
4245, 4248, 4249, 4252, 4254,
4255, 4258, 4262, 4263, 4266,
4267, 4269, 4270, 4273, 4275-
4277, 4279, 4281, 4282, 4285,
4287-9, 4291, 4293, 4294, 4296,
4298, 4300, 4303, 4305, 4306,
4308-10, 4312, 4313, 4315, 4317,
4318, 4320, 4321, 4326, 4328,
4330, 4332, 4334, 4335, 4337,
4338, 4340, 4344, 4345, 4349,
4351, 4353, 4355, 4358, 4359,
4361-3, 4366-70, 4373, 4374,
4376, 4378-83, 4385, 4389, 4390,
4392, 4394, 4396, 4398, 4400,
4402, 4404, 4406-11, 4413, 4415,
4416, 4418, 4419, 4421, 4423-5,
4427-9, 4431-5, 4437, 4439,
4440, 4442-5, 4447, 4449, 4451,
4453, 4455, 4456, 4458, 4460,
4462, 4464-7, 4469, 4471, 4473,
4475, 4476, 4478, 4479, 4481-3,
4485, 4488, 4490, 4494, 4496,
4498, 4500, 4502, 4504-9, 4511,
4513, 4515, 4517, 4519-21, 4523,